The History of Civilization

The Rise of the Celts

PLATE I

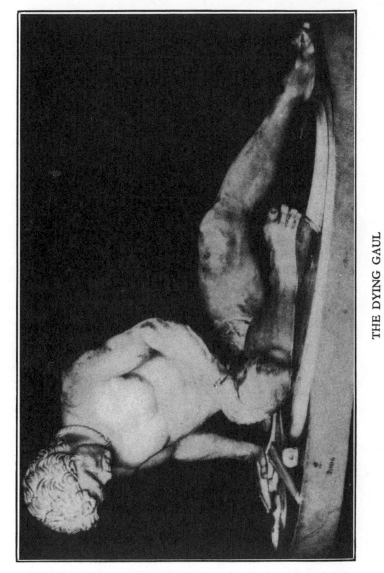

THE DYING GAUL
Capitoline Museum, Rome

The Rise
of the
Celts

By
HENRI HUBERT

DORSET PRESS
New York

This edition published by Dorset Press,
a division of Marboro Books Corporation.
1988 Dorset Press

ISBN 0-88029-283-0

Edited and brought up to date in 1934 by
Marcel Mauss, Raymond Lantier and Jean Marx

Translated from the French by
M. R. Dobie

New Introduction for this edition by
Professor Gearoid Mac Eoin, University of Ireland

The paper used in this book meets
the minimum requirements of the
American National. Standard for
Permanence of Paper for Printed
Library Materials Z39.48-1948.

Printed in the United States of America

M 9 8 7 6 5 4 3 2

CONTENTS

CONTENTS

PART TWO

PLATES

ILLUSTRATIONS IN THE TEXT

PLATES

MAPS

INTRODUCTION

The early years of the twentieth century, when Henri Hubert planned this book, must have seemed to him an opportune time to undertake a synoptic history of the Celtic peoples. During the previous 150 years the Celts had come to be known to the literate public in a way that was completely new. This was due, in the first instance, to the popularity of the writings of James MacPherson which, whatever one may say about their legitimacy or merit as literature, succeeded in drawing Europe's attention to the existence of a people and a tradition which was neither Germanic nor Latin but which represented an early phase in the growth of European civilization. Ernest Renan's *Essai sur la poésie des races celtiques* (1854) and Matthew Arnold's lectures *On the Study of Celtic Literature* (1867) served in some measure to correct the exaggerated impression of wild romanticism given by MacPherson's poems and pointed to the existence of a literature in the Celtic languages which bore little resemblance to MacPherson's compositions. The work of German and French philologists in elucidating the descent and history of the Celtic languages within the Indo-European family gave a scientific basis and an international linguistic dimension to the work being done on medieval texts, contemporary languages and folk traditions in Britain and Ireland by native writers who traced their scholastic ancestry to seventeenth-century scholars like Archbishop Ussher, Sir James Ware, and Edward Lhuyd, and even beyond them to the last remnants of the schools of native learning which survived the collapse of the indigenous social institutions in the Celtic regions of Britain and Ireland in the sixteenth and seventeenth centuries. Celtic literature began for the first time to appear in reliable translations in English, French, and German. Publications like Lady Guest's *Mabinogion*, de la Villemarqué's *Barzaz Breiz*, and Windisch's *Táin Bó Cuailnge* made original documents available to modern Europeans, and allowed a glimpse

ix

of the true form of that literature which proved in many respects more exciting than the romancings of James MacPherson. In the second half of the nineteenth century archaeologists laid bare in the soil of Europe the material evidence for the early Celtic culture which Greek and Roman authors had tantalizingly alluded to and even partly described, and which medieval Celtic literature described in an imaginative and fictional form. The intellectual climate of France in the Second Empire was particularly receptive to a sympathetic view of the Gauls whose martial qualities the French always liked to imagine as foreshadowing their own. So we find Hubert repeatedly claiming that the French are the heirs and descendants of the Celtic Gauls and that 'the civilization of the Celts lies at the bottom of French civilization' (I. 14).

By background and experience Hubert was perhaps not the most likely likely author of a history of the Celts. His education at the École Normale led to an *agrégé* in History in 1895, and his subsequent interest was in the history of religions, particularly those of the Near East. But he found employment in the Musée de Saint Germain in Paris, where he came under the influence of the great archaeologist and art-historian, Salomon Reinach, and at the École des Hautes Études, where he became acquainted with Joseph Vendryes, the greatest of French Celtic linguists, so that Hubert's interests turned to Celtic archaeology and history. However he had not yet published anything on Celtic matters when Henri Berr invited him to write the Celtic volume for his series 'L'Évolution de l'Humanité'. That was some time before the First World War, and Hubert accepted. In 1927 Hubert died at the age of fifty-five without having quite finished his task. The work was brought to a conclusion and seen through the press by a group of friends who included an archaeologist (Lantier), a linguist (Vendryes), and a social historian (Marx).

In the sixty years since the death of Hubert our knowledge of the Celts, their language, and their civilization has increased considerably and become more discriminating. The picture of wandering hordes of richly caparisoned warriors which Hubert gives us, while it has not been altogether abandoned, is now seen to be only part of the reality of Celtic civilization in the 500 or so years in which it flourished on the continent of Europe. Today one would probably say that the Celts were first and foremost farmers tilling their fields and raising their stock on the good lands of Germany and France. Their wealth derived in the first instance from food-production, and the proclivity of its owners to flaunt it by acquiring prestige goods led to the manufacture of high-quality, artistically decorated weapons, horse-trappings, household goods, and particularly ornaments for personal wear. The second source of their wealth was in mining the natural resources of the land, gold, silver, tin, lead, iron, and, by no means the least important, salt. These products provided the purchasing-power which enabled the Celts to buy the luxury goods, above all wine, which the Mediterranean climate of Greece and Italy produced more easily than the cooler air of the North European plains. The valleys of the great rivers running on a north-south axis, the Rhône/Saône, the Loire, the Seine, and the Rhine/Mosel, provided the routes along which trade developed in the sixth century BC between the Mediterranean coasts and Europe north and west of the Alps. Round the eastern flanks of the Alps another trade-route linked the valley of the Danube to the plain of the Po. This trade had the effect of making the rich Celts richer and the less rich avaricious. Thereby began the first expansion of Celts outside their own traditional territories in the first years of the fourth century. Hubert's (II. 10, n. 8) idea of connecting the 300,000-strong mob which then descended into Italy with the inheritance-customs of the Celts as exemplified in Early Irish Law seems to be a particularly valid insight. Similar mobs of fighting men, camp-followers, and cattle are known from Ireland in the later Middle Ages (in contemporary English called *creaght* from Irish *caoraigheacht*) and it has been suggested that the nucleus of these bands was formed by landless men who were forced to move about, driving their cattle before them, in search of unoccupied or unguarded land where they could let their stock out to pasture. They were men of low legal status and tended to become outlaws and the scourge of the countryside. Similar economic and social pressures may have been the reason why so many Celtic warriors left their homes at the turn of the fourth century BC and set in motion one of the great migrations of European history.

In the swirl of peoples which resulted from this movement we try to identify the Celts in the dim twilight between historical linguistics and archaeology. The definition of 'Celt' varies with the background and terms of reference of the definer. The Celts never called themselves 'Celts' in any source known to us before modern times. The name is first found in Greek sources and may be a variant of the name given to the Anatolian branch of the family, Galatae, which must itself be a variant of Galli, the name by which the Romans knew the Celts who occupied Gaul and Northern Italy. Medieval British and Irish sources, though they sometimes recognized the relationship between their languages, never expressed that relationship in ethnic terms and were probably unaware that their languages were any closer to one another than they were to Latin or Scandinavian. The concept of a Celtic race originated among the Greeks and Romans who applied it only to the nations known to them on the continent of Europe. The extension of the definition to the natives of Britain and Ireland is due to modern historians, linguists and archaeologists, beginning with the Scottish historian, George Buchanan, in the sixteenth century. In our own time the linguists would define 'Celt' historically as a person who spoke a Celtic language, but the weakness of this definition for any period becomes clear when one considers that many of today's native Irish speakers are shown by their surnames to be of Scandinavian or English descent. Archaeologists, on the other hand, would define 'Celt' as a person belonging to a particular culture, namely that which they label 'Hallstatt' and 'La Tène', though they might differ among themselves as to where they would draw the line in a chronological or geographical sense. In the case of most Celts known to us in prehistory or protohistory, their language and material culture would qualify them under either definition. But the two definitions are not co-extensive. There were speakers of Celtic languages whose material culture was not in the Hallstatt-La Tène tradition – the Irish are perhaps the best example of this. There were people whose culture was of the Hallstatt-La Tène type but whose language was not Celtic, like the Belgae or the Suevi. We have no means of discovering the limits of the area in which Celtic was spoken before the emergence of these material cultures which define the Celtic world in early historic times. But it has to be accepted that the language existed somewhere in Central Europe between its formation as an Indo-European dialect and our earliest written testimony on North Italian inscriptions.

The emergence of the Celts is seen by Hubert in terms of an incursion from an area such as the Indo-European homeland or from some intermediate staging-point. Modern writers tend rather to see the Celts as an indigenous population who, under some impetus from outside, developed a particular culture in the area which they had inhabited for many generations. The impetus came mainly through trade with the Mediterranean countries but also through contacts with other barbarian peoples who were their neighbours in northern and central Europe, the Scythians, the Thracians, and the Germans. One is tempted to think that the Celtic language may have come into being in a similar process of merging and separation among the closely related languages or dialects spoken by a number of neighbouring peoples somewhere in Central Europe in the second or early first millennium BC. However, the good Indo-European ancestry of so much of Celtic grammar and vocabulary would seem to indicate a direct descent from the ancestral language.

In his account of the spread of the Celts throughout Europe, Hubert, in company with many older writers, exaggerates the importance of the dialect divisions perceptible among them, and turns dialect groups into nations and tribes. Thus he speaks of 'Brythons' and 'Goidels' traversing the Continent and settling in Britain and Ireland respectively. Contrast this with the axiom enunciated by the late David Greene at the Sixth International Congress of Celtic Studies in 1979, that 'the only useful meaning of the terms "Brythonic" and "Goidelic" is as labels for the forms of Celtic attested from the islands of Britain and Ireland respectively'. No scholar would today write of Brythons and Goidels on the Continent or see in the allophonic variants of their dialects the distinguishing marks of rival nations. Today these terms are applied only to the languages of Britain and Ireland and, by extension, to the speakers of these languages. The fact that some of the typical differences between the Celtic languages of the two islands are also found between some of the Celtic languages of the Continent does not entitle us to assign the names of the insular peoples to any on the Continent.

Since Hubert's day our knowledge of the continental Celtic languages has increased considerably, though not to the extent that it is possible to construct anything like a complete grammar for any of them. The fragmentary state of the languages means that research must proceed by piecing the fragments painstakingly together before attempting an interpretation of the result through comparison with other languages. The state of the art has been described authoritatively by D. Ellis Evans: *The Labyrinth of Continental Celtic* (Rhys Memorial Lecture, British Academy, 1977) and by Karl Horst Schmidt: 'The Celtic Languages of Continental Europe', *Bulletin of the Board of Celtic Studies*, xxviii, Pt. ii, May 1979. On the early history of the insular Celtic languages Kenneth Jackson's *Language and History in Early Britain* (Edinburgh 1956) is unsurpassed.

In archaeology progress has been no less impressive than in linguistics. In all the countries of continental Europe which were at one time inhabited by Celtic peoples, noteworthy excavations and finds have brought the material culture of the Celts to light and established immediate contact with the reality of Celtic civilization. The most spectacular excavations have been those of the 'princely' graves of Germany and France; the most informative possibly that of the Dürrnberg near Salzburg in Austria, where for the last twenty years the excavation has been going on of a prehistoric salt-mining settlement consisting of a village, a cemetery containing 2,000 graves, and a salt-mine which is still in use. To bridge the gap between Hubert and the present time the reader may find the following books in English useful: Jan Filip, *Celtic Civilization and its Heritage* (2nd ed., Prague 1977); Jean-Jacques Hatt, *Celts and Gallo-Romans* (London 1970); J. V. S. Megaw, *The Art of the European Iron Age* (Bath 1970); Anne Ross, *The Pagan Celts* (2nd ed., London 1986); and in French the magnificent volume of Paul-Marie Duval, *Les Celtes* (Paris 1977).

On the religion and mythology of the Celts the main works of this century have been: Jan de Vries, *Keltische Religion* (Stuttgart 1961, also in French translation); Thomas F. O'Rahilly, *Early Irish History and Mythology* (Dublin 1946); Marie-Louise Sjoestedt, *Gods and Heroes of the Celts* (London 1949); Proinsias Mac Cana, *Celtic Mythology* (London 1970); and Alwyn Rees and Brinley Rees, *Celtic Heritage* (London 1961).

Since no documentary evidence survives which relates immediately to the social insitutions of the Celts on the continent of Europe, our sources of information about them are references in the writings of Greek and Roman authors, deduction from archaeological evidence, and comparison with the relatively well documented social structures of early medieval Ireland and Wales. The greatest achievement in this field has been D. A. Binchy's *Corpus Juris Hibernici* (6 vols., Dublin 1979) which provides an authoritative text for the early Irish laws. It contains no translation and very little commentary. This work is being done for individual texts in periodical publications and in monographs. No general account of Celtic law and institutions yet exists but Eoin Mac Neill's *Early Irish Laws and Institutions* (Dublin 1935) and D. A. Binchy's 'Irish History and Irish Law' in *Studia Hibernica* 15 (1975) 7–36, 16 (1976) 7–45, go some way towards filling that gap. On Welsh law there have been many important publications during this century but it may be sufficient to mention Dafydd Jenkins's *Hywel Dda and the Law of Medieval Wales* (Cardiff 1985).

The time which has elapsed since the first publication of Hubert's book, in French in 1932 and in English in 1934, provides us with the distance from which to judge it. As a summary statement of what was known about Celtic history in the early years of this century it is excellent. Inevitably it champions some ideas and attitudes which have since fallen out of favour, such as the theory of Italo-Celtic unity (I. 57–62). The progress which has been made in Celtic scholarship during the past half-century requires that a new summary of current knowledge and thought should be compiled. But increased specialization has brought about the fragmentation of the discipline, so that it would be difficult today to find an author with the competence in archaeology, history, and linguistics, not to speak of the familiarity with Latin and Greek, which Hubert possessed. The future history of the Celts will probably be the cooperative effort of many scholars and will clearly be the work of many years. Until such a book appears Hubert's two volumes may stand us in good stead, as they have done in the past.

Gearóid Mac Eoin
Department of Old and Middle Irish and Celtic Philology,
University College,
Galway

FOREWORD

THE EXPANSION OF THE CELTS

*W*ITH *the Celts a very important factor enters into the history of civilization, and a much-expected work appears in this series—expected for the subject's sake and for the author's.*

About this racial group, and the capital part which it played in European history, it was known that the best-informed scholar, whose knowledge was both widest and most profoundly thought out, was Henri Hubert. Now Hubert died four years ago, and many despaired of ever seeing the work announced under his name.

It appears, with a long and grievous story behind it. "The main part of the work," in Hubert's own words, was done in 1914 (his letter of the 15th June, 1915). After the unavoidable interruption of the war—during which he did valued work chiefly with the Ministry of Armament—he hastened to pick up the threads, and on the 5th January, 1923, he wrote to me: "To-day I wrote the last line of my last chapter." He added: "Now I have to take up the whole thing again, to cut, patch together, and check." Various circumstances—a cruel loss, family concerns, and ill-health which gradually grew worse— delayed this work of revision, which he was carrying on at the same time as he was preparing his book on the Germans. In July, August, and October, 1925, he sent me news which was at once reassuring and saddening. "I am at work. I progress slowly but surely. I was kept in bed all May. I am gradually climbing up the hill . . . My work progresses steadily, but in very adverse circumstances. I have got rid of all my lectures. You can therefore count on me to the full extent of my will. But it seems that an evil fortune dogs me, and I do not know what it still has in store for me." On the 9th October, 1926, he again reassured me. "All intensive work upsets me, whatever it is. But I have done a little work, all the same, and I shall be able to do more. I cannot tell you when I shall have finished. It would be absurd. But it cannot be long now."

On Wednesday, the 18th May, 1927, he was once again telling me how his task had progressed, and concluded, " It is obviously not easy to write the history of the Celts to-day. But that is done. It is chiefly mechanical work which remains." On Thursday, the 26th, a note from our common friend, Marcel Mauss, told me that he had just died of a heart attack. And Mauss added a detail which was very affecting for me : " The manuscript of the Celts was on his table ; he had been working at it on Tuesday."

Three devoted friends undertook to prepare the manuscript for publication. For four years they have in turn given up to this duty all the time which they could afford. One of them, in pages which you will read later, tells the exact share of each. That this work should appear, representing Hubert's scientific testament and giving an idea of his knowledge and his talents to a large public which was not reached by his learned treatises, is a great satisfaction to all his friends. But that it should appear after his death, and that he should not reap the harvest of success and esteem which he may not have sought, but had at least slowly earned, is a great grief to those who had grown attached both to the scholar and thinker and to the man—the man of heart, the man of taste, the rare and most attractive personality.

From his youth onwards Hubert had won many strong friendships. One of the close intimates of his years at the École Normale has told how far his ability rose above the lessons which he was doing at that time, how much more mature he was than his fellows, being already " sure of his vocation and his methods ". Another chosen brother has related his life— too short, but so full of work and thought.[1] The beginnings, the achievement of ancient or primitive peoples, both of an intellectual and of a material kind—languages, categories of thought, religions, arts, tools—were what gradually came to compel his interest, which was at once very wide and very penetrating. Much travel, including a voyage round the world which enabled him to see various types of man and to become acquainted with the chief institutes and museums of ethnography, prehistory, and archæology, brought him and kept him in touch with the realities of mankind, past and present. His mind was thereby enriched and stimulated. Work on the Semitic religions,

---

[1] *Marcel Drouin,* in Annuaire de l'Association amicale des anciens élèves de l'École normale supérieure, 1929, *pp.* 45–51.

a class in the history of the primitive religions of Europe at the École des Hautes-Études, a class in national archæology at the École du Louvre, Celtic research connected with his post as Keeper at the Saint-Germain Museum, active collaboration on the Année sociologique, were the expression of his keenness to know and to understand. Hubert was a historian in the strongest sense of the word. His whole career was inspired by the spirit of synthesis. He was a born collaborator for this series, and he was one of the first to promise me his whole-hearted assistance.

When I published Marcel Granet's Chinese Civilization and announced a second volume, Chinese Thought, I justified the division into two volumes and declared that there was no intention of making it a precedent. On the whole, it is better, in conducting a series on a very large scale, to avoid definite statements and over-absolute principles. The manuscript handed to me by Hubert's friend amounted, with the illustrations and the usual additional matter, to seven or eight hundred pages of type. It would have been inconvenient to offer such a compact volume and one so unlike the others in size. On the other hand, it was impossible, after all the reductions which Hubert had either made himself or allowed for,[1] to cut any more out of a work which is so valuable in every respect.

What Hubert conceived, and has been the first to carry out, is a history of all the Celts, a picture of every part of the Celtic world. From the most distant origins to which we can in the present state of our knowledge go back, to the last submergences or survivals, he embraces the whole of Celticism, with incomparable knowledge and a sympathy which does not blind him, but rather gives him vision. This wealth of material, fortunately, was of a nature to be divided without difficulty into two volumes of about the same size.[2]

The present volume tells of the Celtic world down to the La Tène period, that is to the second Iron Age. The second will treat of the three phases of that period, and, after a picture of

---

[1] See the Note by Marcel Mauss.

[2] The second part of the work, on the movements of the Celtic peoples, which contained twelve long chapters, fairly logically falls into three divisions—Celtic expansion to the La Tène period (second part of the first volume), Celtic expansion in the La Tène period, and the end of the Celtic world (first and second parts of the second volume).

*the decline of the Celts, it will describe the essential features of
their civilization. There we shall see them more and more
appearing as a factor in the history of the world, and more
particularly in Roman history, until at last they are incorporated
in the Empire.*[1]

*In accordance with the principle which we have adopted
of placing human groups in our general scheme at the moment
when their activities visibly enter into the great stream of
historical evolution, we have placed the* Celts *in the Roman
section, before the formation of the Empire* [2] *; but it was desirable
at this point to look backwards, to show what the Celts were,
whence they came, and what they did in the obscure times of
their life as barbarians. These questions are exactly what this
present volume covers, so far as it is possible to answer them at
all. It links up with the works of J. de Morgan on* Prehistoric
Man *and Eugène Pittard on* Race and History, *and, in general,
it comes as a completion to all those which, in this first section,
have dealt with the great movements of mankind and the peopling
of the earth.*

*In this volume, then, we have to do with barbarians, not
in the ancient sense of* βάρβαρος, barbarus *" foreign to Greece
or Rome " (for we do not regard the Egyptians and Persians
as barbarians), but in the sense of peoples incompletely stabilized
and civilized, of masses in process of moving and changing.*[3]
*We are dealing with barbarians whom the Greeks and Romans
doubtless knew, but knew very little at first, and about whom the
ancients, in their writings, give us information which at first
is very vague or disputable.*[4] *There are human groups which,
as we know, came only very late into the ken of " civilized men ".
How, then, are we at this day to come to know that protohistoric
Europe, which lay on the borders of a Mediterranean Europe
already rich in history? How, in particular, are we to know
those Celts and Germans, who were to play such a great part one
day in the Roman Empire, the former strengthening it and the
latter overthrowing it? How are we to know them, save from*

---

[1] *See V. Chapot,* The Roman Empire, *in this series, pp. 293 ff.*

[2] *We had a glimpse of them in* Homo, *Primitive Italy, in this series,
pp. 165 ff.*

[3] *See* Lot, The End of the Ancient World, *Foreword, p. xiii, n. 3.*

[4] *" A great part of ancient ethnology has come down to us in the form of
fables and myths through the epic or lyric poets and the polygraphers " (p. 299).*

*what they themselves tell us, gathering up the only evidence
which survives of their racial personality and their doings—
linguistic facts and archæological facts?*

*Hubert in the first part of this volume has laid stress on the
methods which he uses to determine, to isolate, the Celtic element,
to know " what the Celts were ".*

*Without excluding anthropology,[1] he carefully limits its
rôle. " One must not resort to that inexhaustible source of error
and contradictions, save with great moderation and in a very
critical spirit ; it must not be forgotten that peoples and races,
being different things, do not necessarily coincide, and, in fact,
never coincide exactly."[2] The Celts " are not a race " ; it is
the name of a people or of a group of peoples, and that group is
an aggregate of anthropological types.*

*It is, then, the ethnography of the Celts that Hubert endeavours
to constitute, by studying the surviving traces of their civilization.
If the history of civilization as a whole is something quite other
than ethnography, and, as I believe, requires to be clearly
differentiated from it,[3] we must recognize that the various
civilizations, when their special characteristics are studied,
" represent and distinguish peoples."   And, for civilizations
which have " left their remnants in the ground ", it is largely
archæology that, finding in them " legitimate indications of
vanished peoples ", " brings together the scattered data of their
ethnography " (p. 80). There is, in Hubert's words, an*
archæological ethnography *(p. 129). Once again we note, as
J. de Morgan, Pittard, Moret, and yet others have given us
occasion to do, the marvellous range of that militant history
which burrows in the ground and reconstructs the past with
documents of stone and metal, or recreates life from fossil
skeletons.[4]   And we must lay weight on Hubert's appeal when*

---

[1] " *Every group of men living together forms a physical, social, and moral
unit* " (*p. 21*). *Anthropological study is at the foundation.*

[2] *p. 31 ; cf. pp. 28, 32, and Pittard,* Race and History, *passim.
Cf. M. Boule,* Les Hommes fossiles, *p. 320 : the word " Celtic " means to
some a language, to others a special civilization ; it is often used as a synonym
for Gallic ; in the mind of some writers, it represents the fair, tall, long-headed
type of the North ; others say that it should be applied to a dark, short, round-
headed type from the Central Plateau or the Alps. " The best thing for
anthropologists to do is to leave the word to archæologists and historians."*

[3] *See, among the publications of the Centre International de Synthèse,*
Civilisation : le mot et l'idée, 1930 ; *and, in the* Revue de Synthèse, *June,
1931, p. 195, " Ethnographie et ethnologie," a draft of an article for the*
Vocabulaire historique.

[4] *On this subject, see* Revue de Synthèse, *Dec., 1931.*

he asks for more intense activity (for exploration is still singularly incomplete), and wishes that, instead of the chance which usually directs archæological discoveries, there may be more and more methodical and certain exploitation of these material records.[1]

Secondly there is a linguistic ethnography *(p. 33). If the study of speech belongs to the history of civilization, languages are facts of civilization which count among " the most typical or most apparent " of such facts, among " the clearest and truest " characteristics of peoples (p. 33). Perhaps the greatest achievement of Hubert, that complete historian, has been to make such extensive and original use of European philology of which he had a vast knowledge. " Nothing else could take the place of this kind of information. That is why," he says, " we must spend some time in examining the Celtic languages and their affinities " (p. 34). And he shows that one of the most valuable achievements of philology has been to compare the remains of Celtic supplied by names of places and people and a few inscriptions with the Celtic languages which are still spoken. " The unity of the Celtic languages is plain. There were very close similarities between them, such as did not exist between any of them and any other language " (p. 42). In general, the study of the island Celts, which is almost always left to the philologists, seems to Hubert to be indispensable to a knowledge of " Celticness " ; for there are deep strata of the past which can be reached through their literature.*

Hubert's effort to utilize both kinds of evidence and to make the combination of them fruitful is truly admirable. It is conducted with exemplary caution, with " the sternest and most austere method " (p. 17). " It is, of course, true," he says, " that phonetic facts, like archæological, have no absolute racial significance." Often delicate interpretation is called for (pp. 132, 144). " I am inclined to think, without being quite sure " (p. 31)—phrases of the kind constantly fall from that ingenious but prudent pen.

There are, however, objects, forms of tombs, manners of speech, which allow us to classify the Celts as Indo-Europeans, to place them among the Europeans, to distinguish them from the Græco-Latins, Germans, and Balto-Slavs, to contrast them with the Iberians and Ligurians, to determine the Celtic world

---

[1] *p. 81 and the following volume, pt. i, chaps. i, v.*

and its boundaries. Hubert clearly brings out the racial unity of the Celts ; it may not be anthropological, but " common life produced a kind of unification of physical types in a sort of habitus common to all " (p. 32). He perceives diversity within the unity, but reduces that diversity to a division into four groups—Goidels, Picts, Brythons (including the Gauls), and Belgæ.

There are in this preliminary essay in Celtic ethnography two points on which especial weight should be laid : Hubert's indications on the Goidels and those on the relations of the Celts and the Germans, in which he touches on the subject of the volume which he has devoted to this last people.

Neither archæologists nor historians distinguish, at any rate clearly enough, between the two groups of Celts, the Brythons of the Continent and Britain and the Goidels of Ireland and Scotland, "who had advanced furthest west of the Cells " (p. 137). By an extremely ingenious demonstration Hubert establishes an important fact—that the Goidelic group broke off at a very early date (pp. 138-9, 169). By an equally convincing demonstration he reveals the close contact which subsisted between Germans and Celts, and the influence exerted by Celtic culture on Germanic, extending, indeed, beyond the Germans to the Balto-Slavs and Finns (p. 68). This influence is manifest in linguistic and material borrowings. " The Celts seem to have been for long ages the schoolmasters of the Germanic peoples." The facts adduced by Hubert and the conclusions which he draws from them conflict curiously with the theories of the rôle of Germanentum which have inspired so many modern German books. If, as seems to have been the case, there were intimate relations, phenomena of " reception " and even of inter-mingling, and if the Celts appeared as the preponderant people, we must, at the least, regard this as one of those cases of contamination and racial fusion which have been for the good of mankind.[1]

The same archæological and linguistic facts which first enable Hubert, by collecting them all together, to describe Celticism as a whole, afterwards enable him, by setting them in their proper place and time, " to find out whence the Celts came,

---

[1] pp. 67-8, 224 ; cf. pp. 64 ff., 156, 182, and second volume, pt. i, ch. iv, and pt. iii, ch. i.

*where they went, how they expanded, and where they stopped—
in short, to trace their history* " (p. 131).[1]

So, taking as his starting-point the Indo-European unity
of which he sees signs in the East (pp. 75–6), he follows the
group as it breaks off into what will long be its habitat, the
centre of Europe, the future Germany—for the Rhine is Celtic
and the Danube, too (pp. 148–152). Before the first millennium
before Christ, he sees the Goidels breaking off, and the Italici,
and then the Picts. Beginning in the Bronze Age, this expansion
goes on in the first Iron Age, in what is known as the Hallstatt
period, and a homogeneous civilization extends, down to the
fifth century, over Western Germany, Upper Austria, Switzerland, Lorraine, Franche-Comté, and Burgundy. And beyond
that domain the Celtic drive will reach to the British Isles
and Italy and Spain, to go on, as we shall see in the next volume,
through the La Tène period; so, by the absorption of borrowed
elements into the culture of Hallstatt, it will help to make the
civilization of the new period.

This history of Celtic expansion, the migrations, the settlements, the daring advances of smaller bodies in every direction,
the contacts and conflicts with various peoples, need not be
repeated here in its complex detail; what I wish to do, rather,
is to emphasize the marvellously vivid and picturesque manner
in which Hubert has described it.

Imagination is a dangerous thing when it lets itself go on
insufficient evidence; but, as I have often said, it plays
a legitimate part when it comes in to crown a long piece of
analysis, when it is inspired by a wealth of learning, when it
completes and vivifies a synthesis by a sort of spontaneous
generation of images which have arisen to the inward eye. Here,
precisely, is the great historian's gift of recreating; he is, as
he has been called, " the seer of the past."

Now a man who for many years has handled the weapons,
helmets, shields, brooches, and torques of his Celts, who has
looked into their tumuli and seen, not only objects, but skulls
and skeletons (grandiaque effossis mirabitur ossa sepulcris—
Hubert himself quotes Virgil's line somewhere), although
historical discipline and critical sense restrain and govern his
imagination, cannot help picturing all that past in which he has
lived in spirit.

---

[1] *See p. 139 for certain hypotheses on which this work is based.*

" One may try to imagine "—*" We can form a fairly true picture "*—*" I imagine "*—*such are the phrases which continually express that effort, or, rather, that achievement of the imagination. As a result of following, on the ground or on the map,[1] the migrations of archæological and linguistic forms, and of observing all those human footprints, he comes to see the groups themselves migrating, settling, advancing, and receding. In this volume, and in the second, in which he follows the Gauls and the Galatians on their epic inroads, you will find pictures of great power. Hubert sees, and he makes you see.*

Between the North Sea and Switzerland, the Meuse and the Oder, there was a population, not very dense, very mobile, partly pastoral and partly agricultural (and therefore attracted and held for some time by good land), intermingled with warlike tribes, hunters, fishers, and brigands, who were attracted by forests and hills or rivers (pp. 180–1). " We must not imagine these prehistoric peoples as keeping strictly within neat frontiers " (p. 186), and we must not imagine them as being always unmixed, " divided racially into clearly defined watertight compartments." It was amid diffusion and interspersion in the " racial hotchpotch " of Western Germany that " those Celtic societies came into being, round which the whole population finally crystallized " and a " single civilization of their own " was built up (pp. 157, 182, 241). But it was not until the Bronze Age that the Celts were numerous and homogeneous enough to go and found huge settlements at a distance. For we must distinguish migrations in mass, the movements of " the great hordes which periodically descended on the good lands of Europe ; sometimes shy, sometimes raging, laden with baggage and loot . . . sometimes led by chiefs of astonishing clearness of mind, sometimes seeming to be guided by chance and instinct "[2] from the forays of daring bands of adventurers and fortune-seekers (p. 217) ; the sea is a " great road " (p. 200) favourable to this latter kind of incursion. So the " vagabondage " of the Celts took many forms ; and small bands often went before or after the great masses, social units and more or less composite groups of social units.

Once the great Celtic migrations had started they continued

---

[1] *He is always cautious : " When one starts pricking out routes on a map, one is too easily led into imagining movements and directions " (p. 143).*
[2] *Next volume, pt. i, chap. iv. Cf. Homo, loc. cit.*

in successive waves. It seems that each wave, " exactly following its predecessors and tending to spread on the top of them, went as far as it could, until it was forced to stop " (p. 229) *; and as each left a deposit, each altered the racial structure and the domain of the Celtic world. Hubert sees Goidels, Picts, Brythons, and Belgæ spreading out in turn ; he traces the routes by which they went ; he pictures, in the Hallstatt period, " the warriors, with shaven faces (they took their razors with them into their graves), long, broad iron swords with heavy conical pommels and wooden sheaths, seldom wearing helmets . . . seldom having breastplates, and carrying round shields " (p.* 256).

When Hubert comes to the invasions of the second and first centuries, for which we have literary evidence, he finds in the contemporary accounts details and features which seem to him to have a retrospective interest outside the period with which they deal. Thus Cæsar's story of the last migration of the Continental Celts—the Helvetii and Boii—gives, he says, " a very vivid picture, and certainly an idea of the very typical fashion in which the great migrations were prepared and took place, of the conditions, the objects, the collective phantoms which rose up, the pow-wows in which the programme was settled, and the start organized." [1] *All through his work, to give strength and precision to the picture called up by the vestiges of the past, he takes inspiration from the " model " offered by the last invasions ; they have supplied him with a* transposable image.[2]

But outside the movements of the Celtic peoples, the image which Hubert gives of them is equally transposable. We are indebted to him for a better idea, in general, of all those phenomena of migration which are one of the most characteristic and most interesting aspects of the early history of mankind. At the beginning of the Bronze Age and at the beginning of the Iron Age there were movements on a huge scale, which went beyond the confines of the Celtic world. And in prehistory as in protohistory there were periods of unrest, in which " demographic laws ", " general facts in the history of civilization," produced great movements of the masses of mankind (pp. 138, 263).

The expressions which I have just quoted would be sufficient to show that Hubert does not give merely the transposable image. *The very intensity of his vision makes his understanding of the*

---

[1] *Next volume, pt. i, chap. i.*   [2] *Ibid.*

*phenomenon more natural and surer.   So he makes one under-
stand at the same time as he makes one see ; in his work one can
glean sober but suggestive remarks on the general causes of
migrations.   Their causes, like the ways in which they were
carried out, vary greatly.*

*There are physical causes.   Changes in climate create
vacancies and new attractions ; cold and abundant rain drive
the population to a more favoured region.   Sudden cataclysms
produce the same effect ; the Celts soon found that it was useless
to advance, arms in hand, against high tides or floods.*[1]

*There are social causes, economic or political.   Increase of
the population leads to a search for better soil or a wider field
of activity.   And the progress of political institutions may have
a similar result.*[2]

*There are moral causes.   Here the love of adventure, the
" desire for room ", play an obvious part, and the charm of
the unknown is only surpassed by the attraction of the lands of
civilization.*

*There are technical causes.   It is plain that inventions in
the matter of navigation, the possession of bronze tools, and then
of iron, and progress in wagon-building and armament helped
in various ways to make peoples more mobile and more
enterprising.*[3] *M. Boule has observed that from Neolithic times
onwards, " thanks to the development of his crafts, man freed
himself much more easily from physical circumstances " ;
" his migrations in mass," he adds, " now depended almost
entirely on his own will or on that of his leaders "*[4]—*let us say,
on social and logical causes.*

*But we must not omit, among the contingent and persistent
causes of migrations, the effect which an initial movement has
on the neighbouring peoples, or those met on the way by direct
attack, or by rubbing shoulders, and, in general, by " setting
free to move or encouraging to follow ".*[5] *That, too, contributes
to the " tremendous commotion " of the times of great migrations.*

*So in Hubert's work, while the study of primitive man on
the move is continued, what was suggested by other volumes in*

---

[1] *See pp.* 141, 188, 260–1, 263, *and the next volume, pt. i, chap. iv.*
[2] *Ibid.*
[3] *See pp.* 188, 263.
[4] Les Hommes fossiles, *p.* 321.
[5] *pp.* 262–3 ; *next volume, pt. i, chap. iv.*

this section about the essence of the phenomenon of migration is confirmed or completed.[1]

The degree of social organization reached by the Celts, and the culture which they spread over the top of that of the megaliths and the pile-villages, will be shown expressly in the next volume. There I shall lay stress on their character and on the part which they have played in the making of France. Here I shall make only one more remark, or, rather, I shall repeat what has already been said elsewhere.[2] We sometimes hear of a Celtic Empire and also of a Ligurian Empire and an Indo-European Empire.[3] In all three cases, like Hubert, I consider the term improper.[4] There can be no empire without political unity, central power, domination intended and carried into effect. Unity of racial character and unity of civilization do not necessarily imply the existence of an empire. And it was because they could not create one by themselves that the Celts rallied, without much resistance, to the imperial idea which animated Rome in her conquests.[5]

HENRI BERR.

(*Owing to the death of M. Hubert before the publication of this work, the French text contained a certain number of errors. Many of these have been corrected in this English edition, but in the circumstances it has not been possible to check all references.—Trs.*)

---

[1] *Cf.* F. Hertz, " Die Wanderungen : ihre Typen und ihre geschichtliche Bedeutung," in Kölner Vierteljahrshefte für Soziologie, 1929, i, p. 36. *I have previously distinguished* migration *and* invasion. *Migration is when the mass moves on to free ground or among non-sedentary populations ; invasion is when it comes among settled populations* (Race and History, Foreword, p. xiii). *On* conquest, colonization, emigration, *and* nomadism, *see* Forewords *to* Prehistoric Man, A Geographical Introduction to History, From Tribe to Empire, Israël, *and* The End of the Ancient World.

[2] *See* Homo, Primitive Italy, Foreword, p. ix.

[3] *See e.g.* A Grenier, *in an excellent little book*, Les Gaulois, *pp.* 27, 29, 35–6, 38, 49, 83.

[4] " *Nothing in the prehistoric archæology of the Celtic world or the Ligurian world gives the least suggestion of an empire, even in the nature of the Aztec Empire* " (p. 145).

[5] *See next volume, pt. iii, chap. ii.*

NOTE

By Marcel Mauss

THIS work is the last which Henri Hubert expressly prepared for printing. He had promised it to M. Berr long before the War.[1]

He had worked long at it. He had lectured on the subject twice in his class of Celtic Archæology at the École du Louvre. He did so a third time in two years, in 1923–4 and 1924–5. We have the complete draft of these courses.

All that remained to be done was to give it the form of a book. Two-thirds of this task was done when Hubert died. The manuscript was in almost perfect condition, notes included, down to the end of the second part (the chapter on the Celts of the Danube).[2] Beyond that point the executors of Hubert's wishes had only his course of lectures, which, it is true, was in an admirable state. The illustrations were almost entirely arranged.

It was our duty to make good the promise which he had made to our friend M. Berr. With the lectures, we have finished the book. For that there were three of us co-operating.

It was only right that M. P. Lantier, Hubert's successor at Saint-Germain and one of the men whom he had trained in archæology, should draw up the text of what was lacking in the second part of the book.[3] Here the lectures are in excellent condition. I myself have dealt with one chapter (second volume, Part II, Chapter I).

The third part of the book, that which treats of the social life and civilization of the Celts,[4] has a different history. It had formed the subject of a very long course, lasting a year. But the present work, although published in two volumes, would have been too long for this series if Hubert had published without alteration the admirable matter which he had prepared with this intention. To come into line with the instructions of the director

[1] *Together with another on the Germans, which, we hope, will appear shortly, with the aid of M. Janse.*
[2] *Second volume, pt. i, chap. ii.*
[3] *Second volume, pts. i and ii.*
[4] *Second volume, pt. iii.*

and editors of the series, he had promised to summarize it in two chapters. In his place we have ventured, as we were bound to do, to fulfil this undertaking. For that purpose we have attempted the barbarous task of condensing into a few pages the matter of a large book. But, using only sentences taken from Hubert's own text, and being authorized to abridge sometimes by his own notes, we are sure that we have never been untrue to his ideas, to his manner of expressing himself and proving his case. In this work M. Jean Marx, another pupil, historian and Celticist, has taken on most of the chapters. M. Lantier has written the summary of the lectures condensed in the paragraphs concerning the crafts and arts of the Celts.

The chapter of Conclusions alone is rather patchy, since we had several versions to choose from.

We hope elsewhere to publish in full in another volume in Hubert's name, this Course in the Descriptive Sociology of the Celts of which we here give only the fundamental idea.

M. Vendryès, who was a friend of Hubert, and from whom Hubert took lessons in Celtic, has revised the text and the proof-sheets of the chapters on language. His great authority guarantees the value of this part of the work.

In over thirty years of friendly collaboration Henri Hubert had satisfied himself that I was a faithful depositary of his ideas, and that I knew the secrets of his style well enough to be a conscientious editor of those parts of his work which had not been published and could be published. I have therefore assumed the responsibility for this book.

But it is fair to say that my part has chiefly consisted in associating myself with the work of Hubert's two posthumous collaborators. Both, in addition to the labour of bringing the book out, have seen to it that it included all information received down to 1930. Moreover, M. Lantier has checked all Hubert's references, added his own, and adapted them to the bibliographical methods of the series. He has also perfected and completed the illustrative material for which Hubert had provided.

The good things, then, which will be found here are Hubert's and theirs ; any mistakes which I have left in are mine. They are certainly not the doing of Henri Hubert. I sincerely believe that they will not be many, compared with the size and the learning of a work like this. If we have been so daring as to expose ourselves to the risk of making them, it was to save the rest from oblivion.

Pie factum est.

To this note, which I owed to the reader, I may be allowed to add some scientific considerations regarding facts and method.

First as to method. Hubert would, no doubt, have explained somewhere the methods of archæology and ethnographic history which he followed and perfected from year to year in the immense work which he did as Keeper at the Museum of National Antiquities at Saint-Germain. Being no lover of adjectives, he would not have expatiated on their excellence, but he would certainly have explained their principles. I merely ask the reader to pay attention to them. I must tell him that this work, like the forthcoming book on the Germans, and all Hubert's courses in prehistory, formed part of an ethnographic history of Europe and mankind which he had in view. And I may permit myself, being myself a sociologist and ethnologist, as Hubert was, to emphasize the agreement of history, so understood in this book, with the other branches of learning on which Hubert left his mark—sociology and prehistoric archæology. There is no opposition between these branches of knowledge, in Hubert's mind, or in the facts, or in logic, neither for us nor for anyone, in the case of a complete account of human events such as is attempted here.

There is another consideration, of facts this time. One must feel how completely some of Hubert's fundamental ideas, historical ideas regarding the origins of the Celts, have been justified. Our friend was not a man to glory when the facts confirmed hypotheses which he had put forward. For one thing, as you will see, he offers very few hypotheses. It was not that he was not capable of inventing many, and those very just. But he made it a strict rule never to formulate one prematurely. In this matter he showed a delicate and scrupulous modesty. In the expression of his personal beliefs in history, he always came far short of his conviction of their truth. Those who are experts in these matters will see clearly that he accepted very few of the orthodox assumptions which, often without foundation, make the texture of almost all our current knowledge of the Celtic world. He recognized none as valid and reasonable until he had tested it himself; he used his criticism on himself, and never offered anything as certain except facts.

Yet this strict method led him to the most distant truths. I may justifiably extol the excellence of his reasoning, and call attention to the brilliant confirmation which some of his leading ideas on the early homes of the Celts and their contacts with other civilizations have received from recent discoveries. I am speaking of the great number of works which have revived the question, since the discoveries of Winckler and the decipherment of inscriptions by Hrozny, Forrer, and others threw new light on the languages of Asia Minor and Hither Asia, commonly classed together as Hittite, and since we obtained a clear notion of the archæology of the civilizations—very mixed in origin, but fairly uniform—of the whole area in which those languages were spoken for nearly a thousand years. This new knowledge led M. Meillet [1] and others to conceive in a new fashion, no longer only linguistic, but historical, clear, probable, and proved (by the best of all proofs, that of the document, written or otherwise, found in situ), something which they had not previously been able to conceive with the same definiteness— the antiquity, the kinship, and even the certain contacts of the two groups of languages, Italo-Celtic and Indo-Iranian, and their relations with this Hittite group. So, to-day, we no longer suppose; we are beginning to know when and where things happened, if nothing more.

At the end of his life Henri Hubert was fully acquainted with all this new material in history, archæology, and historical philology, which was beginning to accumulate, even if order and clarity were not brought into it until after his death. In any case, he knew that it agreed with what he had written here of the very early breaking-off of the first Goidelic branch and the contact, direct and indirect, which the Celts had had and maintained with the East, the Near East and even further countries. [2] And he knew that he himself contributed to these researches by remarking on the almost Celtic character of the torques and bracelets of Byblos and the tombs of Kutaïs. [3] He only suggested

---

[1] " *Essai de chronologie des langues indo-européennes,*" *in* Bull. de la Soc. de Linguistique, 1931, *xxxii, pp.* 1 *ff.*

[2] " *La Numeration sexagésimale en Europe à l'âge du Bronze,*" *in* l'Anthropologie, *xxx,* 1920, *pp.* 578–580 ; L'Origine des Aryens (*with reference to the American excavations in Turkestan*), *ibid., xxi,* 1910, *pp.* 519–528.

[3] " *De quelques objets de bronze trouvés à Byblos,*" *in* Syria, *i,* 1925, *pp.* 16–29.

these connections, without any emphasis. Let me say outright that he always believed in them, and that they lay at the bottom of his oral teaching.

The recent discoveries would have led him on to further discoveries yet. On this point he had unique knowledge. He had the double competence of a Celticist and an Assyriologist. And what an archæologist he was ! He stood at a point where history and archæology met, and he could survey the whole question.

It was worth while to note here the historical value of his general theories. And I shall be forgiven the melancholy pleasure which I take in saying here what a discoverer we have lost.

M. M.

INTRODUCTION

I

THE BARBARIANS

THE European borders of the Græco-Roman world were inhabited by barbarians, some of whom have earned a place in history. There were the Scythians in the east, the Iberians and Ligurians in the west, and the Thracians, Illyrians, Germans, and Celts in the centre. Classical authors took the trouble to write down their names, and some inquired with curiosity into their life and manners. Mediterranean merchants visited them, and may have penetrated among the very remotest, in search of amber, tin, furs, and slaves. Barbarians appeared in Greek and Italian cities as slaves or travellers. There were certainly some among them who were prophets of civilization, and some were cited as models of wisdom.

As Greece and Italy expanded, the nearest of these barbarians were absorbed by them. Others, later, appearing on the horizon like a hurricane, waged furious war on Greece and Rome. In any case, they entered into various kinds of relations with classical civilization and with the Roman Empire, which became its base, and thereby were to some extent incorporated in that civilization and with it helped to make the civilization of the future.

We shall attempt to draw a historical outline for the best-known of these peoples, the Celts and the Germans. Some of the others will come into the story incidentally. Those not mentioned in this history of the Celts, nor in that of the Germans, nor in previous volumes of this series dealing with Greece and Rome, belong to the domain of prehistoric archæology.

II

THE CELTS AND THE GREEKS

This is what the Greek writers tell us of their advance. We are given two dates which enable us to judge from the

Greek point of view: one by the Hesiodic poems, and the other by the historian Ephoros who lived in the second half of the fourth century before Christ. The former suppose that there is in the north-west of the " world " a great Ligurian region ; the latter imagines a great Celtic region.

At the time when the Hesiodic poems were written the Ligurians were one of the three great peoples which dwelt at the ends of the world known to the Greeks :—

Αἰθίοπάς τε Λίγυς τε ἰδὲ Σκύθας ἱππημολγούς.

This line in the *Catalogues* (fr. 132) [1] must date from the beginning of the sixth century. A hundred years later the first Greek historian, Hecatæos of Miletos, in his *Europe* talks of a Celtic part of this Liguria ; the lexicographer Stephanos of Byzantion quotes the *Europe* when speaking of Marseilles, which, like Hecatæos, he describes as " a city in the Ligystic country, near the Celtic country ". Hecatæos also mentioned a Celtic city named Nyrax, which cannot be identified.[2] Marseilles had been founded by Phocæan settlers about 600, a century before.

What exactly was the extent of this Ligystic country ? There is an old *periplus*, or account of a voyage, perhaps written by a Marseilles man and probably at the end of the sixth century, which, after being refashioned several times, has come down to us in a Latin verse translation from the pen of one Rufus Festus Avienus,[3] a person of consular rank who fancied himself as a man of letters. According to this account, the Ligurians had once extended as far as the North Sea, but had been driven back to the Alps by the Celts.[4] But the peoples mentioned in the *Ora Maritima* of Avienus as dwelling near the Lake of Geneva bear names which have disappeared from geographical literature,[5] and when, later than the original *periplus*, Aristotle speaks in his *Meteorologica* [6] of the Perte du Rhône at Bellegarde, he still places it in Liguria, περὶ τὴν Λιγυστικήν. Was this information out of date ?

---

[1] In Strabo, vii, 3, 7. "Ethiopians and Ligyans and mare-milking Scythians." Cf. d'Arbois de Jubainville, **CCXLVIII**, xii, *passim*.

[2] Stephanos, s.v. ; for Narbonne, see Dottin, **CCCXXII**, p. 298. E. Philipon, in **DXVI**, p. 121, rejects the other passages from Hecatæos, in allegiance to his theory regarding the relative positions of the Ligurians and the Iberians, whom he places in the Marseilles district.

[3] 130–145.   [4] 637–640.   [5] 674–6.   [6] i, 13.

There was a time when the southern limits of the Celts lay there. Apollonios of Rhodes, who used the earlier geographers conscientiously, describes, in his Book IV, the Argonauts going up the Rhone, which they reached by way of the Po, and being tossed by storms on the Swiss lakes, under the Hercynian Mountains, which extend into the midst of the country of the Celts.[1] In the time of Herodotos, whose information was far more up-to-date, the Celts were separated from the Mediterranean not only by the Ligurians but by the Sigynnes. These latter occupied the country inland from the Veneti on the Adriatic side.[2] But their name was also to be found near Marseilles. " The Ligyes," says Herodotos, " dwelling in the heights above Marseilles, call small traders ' Sigynnes '." There was not one people, but a whole succession of peoples, between the Celts and the inhabitants of the Mediterranean coast, and these peoples practised a prosperous trade, as excavations bear witness. As late as about 350 that valuable geographical document, the *Periplus* attributed to Scylax of Caryanda, makes no mention of Celts on the coasts of the Western Mediterranean, and yet they were already very near.

Long before, they had come into contact on the Atlantic coast with mariners of Tartessus, who had eventually spoken of them to the people of Marseilles. The old *periplus* which Avienus translated mentioned them as being on the shores of the North Sea, from which they had driven the Ligurians.[3] It designated Brittany, and also Spain, by the name of Œstrymnis,[4] in which we may perhaps see the name of the Osismii or the Ostiæi, who still occupied Finistère in Cæsar's day. At the beginning of the fifth century Herodotos mentions them as being south of the Pyrenees, and probably on the Ocean. " The Danube," he says, " starts from the country of the Celts and the city of Pyrene, and flows all through Europe, which it divides in two. Now the Celts are outside the Pillars of Heracles, and march with the Cynesii, who are the westernmost people of Europe "[5]; and, indeed, Cape St. Vincent was in their territory.

[1] *Argon.*, 627–647. The (probably late) author of the *Orphic Argonautica* likewise takes the Argonauts through the country of the Celts, and even to Ireland (1. 161). [2] v, 9. [3] Avien., 130–145. [4] Avien., 91 ff., 152–5. [5] ii, 33 ; iv, 49. Aristotle, in *Meteorologica*, i, 13, 19, repeats Herodotos's mistake about the sources of the Danube.

The first Greek who was in a position to give more definite and circumstantial information about the Celts of the Ocean was a traveller of Marseilles named Pytheas.[1] Unfortunately his account of his voyage, *Of the Ocean*, was severely mishandled by erudite persons, like Polybios and Strabo, for whose critical spirit it was too much. He was a strange individual, no doubt, but he knew as much of mathematics and astronomy as anyone of his time, and he had the spirit of the explorer. He embarked twice with a few companions in Phœnician vessels, and sailed from Spain to Britain, to distant Thule, and eastwards to Denmark, perhaps further. He saw the sea icebound, and days which lasted twenty-four hours. He came across the Osismii at the end of Finistère. He knew the Celtic name of the Isle of Ushant, " Uxisama," [2] that of Kent, " Cantion," [3] and also the name by which Britain was to be henceforth always called, " the Prettanic Isles," which superseded its Ligurian or Iberian name of Albion.[4] Pytheas lived in the fourth century. Some decades after his time the Sicilian historian Timæos stated that the rivers which flow into the Atlantic went through the Celtic country.[5]

So the Greeks knew that the Celts had arrived on the coasts of the western seas before 600 B.C. and on the Atlantic seaboard of Spain before 500, and that those of them whom we now call the Brythons had reached Britain and Brittany and occupied the whole of the Gallic coast of the Ocean before 300. By that time they had at last come down on to the Mediterranean, but only within the last few decades. On the whole, it was on the Atlantic side that the Celts first came into direct contact with the Mediterranean mariner. Behind Pytheas lay a long past of seafaring—Ægean, Mycenæan, and Tartessian—in the course of which Northern Europe had received much of Mediterranean civilization. The navigators of the West knew the Celts, the names of their countries and of their peoples ; things on the Celtic coast were familiar to them and, so far as the Greeks were concerned,

[1] D'Arbois, **CCXLVIII**, xii, pp. 63 ff. ; Müllenhoff, **CCCLXII**, i, pp. 327 ff. ; Jullian, **CCCXLVII**, i, pp. 415 ff. ; A. Blazquez, in **XXXVI**, Jan.–Mar., 1913.
[2] Loth in **CXL**, x, p. 352.
[3] Strabo, i, 4, 3 ; Rhys, **CCXXX**, p. 22 ; Irish *céte*, market.
[4] E. Philipon, **CCCLXI**, pp. 294 ff.
[5] Fr. 36, in Plutarch, *De Plac. Phil.*, iii, 17, 2.

could be brought into the domain of Greek legend,[1] whereas, hidden behind misty mountains, the Celts of the Continent were still something mysterious and remote. No doubt the mariners of that time could keep their discoveries secret. There were, too, catastrophes in the Mediterranean world in which local traditions were lost. Nevertheless, a writer who about 150 B.C. could say that the discovery of the countries on the Great Ocean was quite recent [2] was displaying lamentable ignorance. But the great majority of the Greeks were no wiser. Meanwhile, the whole interior of the Celtic region and the movements of the Celts remained quite unknown to the mass of Greeks and Romans until Cæsar conquered Gaul.[3]

In the Mediterranean region, on the other hand, the Celts advanced rapidly from the fourth century onwards. One fine day the Greeks, or rather the Macedonians, found themselves face to face with their military organization to the north of the Balkans. This was in the time of Alexander, in 335 B.C. Alexander, in the course of an expedition against the Getæ, was receiving the representatives of the Danubian peoples. " Some, too, came," says Arrian,[4] " from the Celts established on the Ionic Gulf." Alexander received them amicably. This was the occasion on which he asked them, at a feast, what they feared most in the world. " That the sky should fall on our heads," is their alleged reply. The scene was described, so Strabo assures us,[5] by Ptolemy, son of Lagos, who added that the Celts of the Adriatic coast (τοὺς περὶ τὴν 'Αδρίαν) had entered into bonds of friendship and hospitality with him.

If these Celts who came to Alexander really lived on the Adriatic, they came from the Italian coast of that sea.[6] The story of the events which had brought them thither had already reached Greece. In his *Life of Camillus* Plutarch quotes a curious passage from Heracleides Ponticos,

---

[1] e.g., the legend of Geryon. Cf. Reinach, **CCCLXXII**, pp. 121, 177 ; **CCCLXXIV**, i, p. 244.

[2] Polybios, iii, 37–8. For Greek ignorance of geography, see Bertrand and Reinach, **DXLII**, p. 4. Cf. Xenophon, *Cyr.*, 2.

[3] Cicero, Ep. clxi.

[4] *Anab.*, i, 4, 6.

[5] vii, 3, 8.

[6] The *Periplus* of Scylax (18–19) speaks of Celts on the Adriatic as early as 350.

a philosopher of the fourth century. " Heracleides," he says, " relates in his *Treatise on the Soul* that news came to Pontus, simultaneously with the event, that an army from the land of the Hyperboreians had taken a Greek city named Rome, situated near the Great Sea." [1] He was astonished at the speed with which the news had travelled, and it seems to have created some excitement. It was a kind of cataclysm, and one could not foretell how far-reaching it might be ; and it is plain that the world of the Greek cities of Italy, no longer at their best in military power, was alarmed.

The events which followed the fall of Rome brought the Celts into more direct contact with the Greeks, but lacked the sensational effect of the capture of Rome and the legendary glamour of the meeting with Alexander. After Rome was delivered, the Celts had returned and gone past it. In 367 they were in Apulia. In the previous year Dionysios I of Syracuse, having treated with them, took a band of them into his service and sent them to the aid of the Macedonians against the Thebans.[2] This was really the first occasion on which the Greeks as a whole came into contact with the Celts.

Just about this time the historian Ephoros substituted the Celts for the Ligurians among the three great peoples on the circumference of the world, and assigned to them the whole north-west of Europe as far as the borders of the Scythians.[3]

Some years after the appearance of the Celts at the camp of Alexander, in 310, a sudden disaster fell on the Antariatae, a great Illyrian people living north of the Veneti. They started fleeing *en masse*. There was talk of plagues, of lands ravaged by invasive mice.[4] It was a great Celtic incursion, led by a chief named Molistomos. The flying Antariatae came up against the Macedonians, who defeated them and then settled them down. But the collapse of the Antariatae was like the breaking of a dike. Celtic bands invaded Greece and looted Delphi. They did not stop until they reached Asia Minor, where they founded Galatia. Others went on along the coast of the Black Sea to the Sea of Azov. There the ancient geographers place the extreme limit of their advance.

[1] xxii, 2–3.
[2] Justin, xx, 4, 9 ; Xen., *Hell.*, vii, 1, 20, 31 ; Diod., xv, 70.
[3] Fr. 38 ; Strabo, iv, 46 ; Diod., v, 25, 4 ; 32, 1.
[4] Appian, *Illyrica*, 4.

At the same time others were at last coming, through the midst of Iberians and Ligurians, to the shores of the Gulf of Lions, where Hannibal found them established in 218.[1] Later the conquest of the Province, followed by that of Gaul, brought them into the orbit of a Mediterranean empire. Then they found someone to write about them in Poseidonios, who visited them as Pytheas had done their ancestors, but was happy in inspiring more confidence than his predecessor.

From this survey we see that the rise of the Celts, from their first appearance on the Greek horizon, was extremely rapid. For in three hundred years they attained the height of their power. Also we see that it occurred at the same time as that of the Latins and shortly after that of the Greeks, for the Celts entered into Greek history after that history had begun.

III

CELTIC MIGRATIONS AND THEIR DIRECTION

But we see something else : that the Celts whom the amber-traders encountered on their journeys up the Rhone and Danube, and the coasting vessels found again on the low shores of the North Sea, must have belonged to a people which came originally from Central Europe, gaining ground westwards at the expense of the Ligurians and Iberians, and had its first centre of gravity towards the east of the region which it occupied when it attained its greatest extension. A map of their present location gives quite a different picture.[2] It is in the very west of Europe, in the islands and peninsulas, in the Finistères and Land's Ends in fact (Map 1), that the Celtic languages are still spoken—in Ireland, in the Isle of Man, in Wales, in the north of Scotland and the neighbouring isles, and in the tip of Brittany west of a line drawn from Morbihan to Saint-Brieuc. Cornish was spoken in Cornwall down into the eighteenth century.

Which is the truer picture ? Did Celticism survive in

---

[1] Schulten, **DXIX**, i, p. 96. The Celts are said to have been reported on the shore of Provence in the time of Timæos, who wrote about 260, for the following passage in Polybios (xii, 28a) is ascribed to him : πολυπραγμονῆσαι τὰ Λιγύων ἔθη καὶ Κελτῶν, ἅμα δὲ τούτοις Ἰβήρων.

[2] Ripley, **CCCLXXVIII**, p. 23.

the western end of its domain because it was most firmly established there, or because it was driven there ? Is it not in these parts that we should look for the main mass of the Celts, their origin, and their purest type ? Is it not an abuse and a faulty interpretation of a collection of historical texts

NORWEGIAN

DANISH

SAXON

CELTIC

MAP 1. The Movement of the Celts and their Present Habitat. (W. Z. Ripley, *The Races of Europe*, p. 313.)

to look elsewhere ? Here, at the beginning of a story bristling with contradictions, is a first conflict.

The impression given by the map of to-day could be confirmed by traditions and facts. Livy regarded Gaul as the centre of the Celts and the starting-point of their migrations. Cæsar asserts that the institution of the Druids originated in Britain. When the Roman Empire declined bands of Irishmen came as adventurers to Gaul and as settlers to Britain ; the kingdom of Scotland was their most lasting foundation. The Celts of Britain were not behindhand ; they colonized Armorica, which they made into what we call Brittany.

But these are untrue traditions or mere individual facts. In the main the Celts, after advancing to the west of Europe, retreated in the same direction. If we look carefully at the map we shall see that the districts where they are found are refuges. The Celts came to a stop there at the sea, clinging to the rocks. Beyond the sea was their next world. They stayed on the shore, waiting for the ferry, like the dead in Procopios. One of the nicest stories in the collection of epic and mythical tales which forms the Welsh Mabinogion [1] relates the adventures of a Roman emperor, Macsen Wledig, who, having fallen asleep while hunting and dreamed of a wonderful princess, set out to seek her, and found her in Britain. She was called Elen Lluyddawg, " Leader of Hosts." The emperor married her, and with her he raised Britain to its greatest power and glory. But Rome had forgotten him, and he had to reconquer it. Britain sent forth hosts which never came back, and the army of Elen Lluyddawg dwells in Llydaw, or Litavia, the country of the dead. Apart from the few facts of purely local significance mentioned above, none but phantom armies or armies of romance— like that of Arthur, who likewise conquered Gaul and Italy and Rome—ever went out from the British Isles to occupy the lands to which the Celtic name is attached. What now remains of the Celts, in the west of their ancient dominion, was driven there and confined there by other peoples arriving or growing up behind them. This general movement of

[1] Loth, **CCLXX**, i, pp. 210 ff., " Le Songe de Maxen Wledig." Macsen is simply the usurper Maximus, who commanded in Britain under Gratian, was proclaimed Augustus in A.D. 383, and was defeated and slain by Theodosius in August, 388.

expansion and contraction taking the Celts to the west and confining them there may be called the law of Celticism. It must be studied as a capital fact of European history.

IV

WHAT REMAINS OF THE CELTS AND THEIR PART IN HISTORY

The greatness of the Celts has gone, but what has it left behind ? A remnant of Celtic tongues, of which only one, Irish, is endeavouring to-day to become once more the speech of a nation ; a fringe, of varying depth, in which Celtic died out only recently and its long survival is attested by place-names and folk-lore ; and, lastly, in regions where the Celts were subdued, assimilated, or wiped out in ancient times, recognizable descendants, traces of their social structure, the spirit of their civilization, or, at least, the dead records of history and archæology. The Celts, who have almost disappeared from Western Europe, are one of the chief elements of which it is composed. In one place this element reveals itself in individual characteristics ; in another in collective characteristics. This is particularly the case in France, where the Celtic inheritance seems to be greatest and least diffused.

The Celts were preceded in Gaul by Iberians and Ligurians, who left indelible traces of their occupation in the names of rivers and mountains [1] and perhaps of a few towns.[2] They have bequeathed to the French much of their blood, but apparently nothing of their social structure. They were clearly not mere hordes, but organized societies. Records of that pre-Celtic past, such as the megalithic monuments, bear witness to common effort and a social life. But all that has survived of that is preserved only within the structure of Gaulish society and under Gaulish names. While the physical geography of France is dotted with Ibero-Ligurian names, the oldest features of her political geography are Gaulish, and these are the fundamental features.

---

[1] For the Ligurians, see d'Arboís, **CCCI,** ii, pp. 87 ff. ; Dottin, **CCCXXI,** pp. 180 ff. ; for the Iberians, Philipon, **CCCLXIX,** pp. 161 ff.
[2] For the Ligurians, see Philipon, op. cit., pp. 129 ff. ; **DXVI,** p. 180.

The large towns of modern France, save for some exceptions which are easily explained, were the capitals of Gallic peoples or of sub-groups which formed those peoples. Their boundaries are almost exactly followed by modern administrative divisions. Arras was the town of the Atrebates ; Amiens, of the Ambiani ; Rheims, of the Remi ; Soissons, of the Suessiones ; Senlis, of the Silvanectes ; Paris, of the Parisii (the Silvanectes and Parisii were sub-groups of the Suessiones) ; Troyes, of the Tricasses ; Langres, of the Lingones ; Chartres, of the Carnutes. At the time of the Roman Conquest the peoples were in process of becoming cities. Their meeting-places or strongholds were developing into towns. That is why most French towns are called after the names of peoples. The old names of Rheims (Diviocortorum), Paris (Lutetia), and Soissons (Noviodunum, now Pommiers, near that city) have vanished. The territories of the Gallic peoples became those of the Roman *civitates* and *pagi*, the centres of Roman Gaul, and these became bishoprics and bailliwicks (the latter word being perhaps Celtic).[1]

Of these Gallic peoples some may have previously been Iberian or Ligurian. But even in the south, in Aquitaine, where the foreign character of the communities was manifest to outsiders like Cæsar and his men, the political stamp of the Gauls was deeply impressed.[2] But it must not be thought that Gaul was mainly an Iberian or Ligurian society, politically assimilated by its conquerors and supplied by them with names with Celtic inflexions. It was not. In the greater part of Gaul the Celts chose their places of residence for themselves. Where they established themselves on the site of earlier settlements, these latter seem as a rule to have already disappeared when the Celts took possession. There were in Gaul cities or fortified villages of the Neolithic and Bronze Ages. The Celts did not settle in them at once, or if they did they abandoned them and did not return till long afterwards. In short, they did not take over from the first inhabitants. They built their own houses and cities ; they arranged the country to suit themselves, and as they arranged it so it still remains, for wherever the Celts

---

[1] Irish, *baile*, district, estate of a great family.
[2] See the following volume in this Series.

established themselves permanently, without exception the French have remained. They were the founders of the towns and villages of modern France. Doubtless, the Celts had neither the same needs nor the same methods of making use of the soil as their forerunners. That is why they settled in other places. They have bequeathed to France habits which have outlived the reasons for them. For example, they have left their system of land-measurement. The Gaul which Cæsar conquered was so well surveyed that the officials of the Roman *fiscus* had only to enrol the Gallic surveyors, from whom they took over some technical terms, and in any case their measures ; the *arpent* and the *lieue* are Celtic.[1] The face of France is still very much what the Celts made it.

In short, from the coming of the Celts to France, and from then only, the groups of men established there adopted a structure which is still to be seen in French society. The origins of the French nation go back to the Celts. Behind them there is a formless past, without a history or even a name.

Our societies—nations, as they now are—are complex things, composed of elements of different kinds, some physical and some moral. They are not formed by the mere adding on of features. Their growth may be compared to that of a crystal. In French society the first element to cause the mixture to crystallize was the Celtic element, and the process of crystallization has been so well defined that the crystal has preserved its bold edges and its clear facets.

It is more correct to say that Gaul first began to look like France when the main body of the Celtic peoples was settled west of the Rhine. At that time there were still Celts in Spain, in Italy, and in Asia Minor, but after that, as one section after another was conquered by alien races, they disappeared or lost their identity. These were not driven into Gaul. Those on the right bank of the Rhine were driven to the river after long wars. In Gaul they formed a more concentrated mass, and were able to assimilate everyone else. A fairly loose political organization was formed ; a national consciousness, cloudy but capable of occasional flashes, came into being. The nation was in process of formation when the Romans conquered it. It did not sink

---

[1] *Arpent = arepennis*, Irish *airchenn* ; *lieue* (league) = *leuca*.

in the wreck of the Roman Empire.[1] Like Poland, it survived conquest.

Thus I am inclined to think, without being quite sure, that the conflicts which ended with the Celtic peoples finding themselves west of the Rhine contributed to the making of the nation. I say that I am not sure because, among the information which has come down to us from the ancient writers, there is no sign that the Belgæ, who were the last to have to maintain these conflicts, were conscious of any opposition, racial or national, between themselves and the Germans. On the other hand, it is my belief that the invasion of the Cimbri had quite certain effects. We see from reading Cæsar that that of Ariovistus threatened to be followed by others.

But if a nation already existed it was because that which makes the deep-seated unity of a nation existed—a common ideal, the same ways of thinking and feeling, in short, everything that nations express by symbols and all the most intimate part of their civilization. For the Celts, like the Greeks, were more united, more consciously united, by their common ways of thinking and feeling than by their sense of nationality. In speaking of them one may, without paradox, use the word " civilization " in its widest sense. The Greeks and Romans regarded them as barbarians, but as barbarians of a superior kind. They held that the Druids preserved the Pythagorean tradition. Cicero makes the Druid Diviciacus (an Æduan who really existed, a combination of churchman and warrior) a speaker in one of his dialogues.[2]

The ancients credited the Druids with metaphysical speculations of which all trace has vanished. I should say, rather, that the Druids—judges, physicians, directors of consciences, and poets as they were—were moral observers and psychologists. It is true that they studied the metaphysics of death, but that borders on psychology. The Celts thought much about death ; it was a familiar companion whose alarming character they liked to disguise. All that has come down to us from the Druids themselves is one of the tripartite maxims of which the Celts are known to have been fond. This is the form in which Diogenes Laertios gives it in the

---

[1] Jullian, **CCCXLVI**, pp. 154 ff.　　[2] *De Div.*

preface to his *Lives of the Philosophers* : Σέβειν θεοὺς καὶ μηδὲν κακὸν δρᾶν καὶ ἀνδρείαν ἀσκεῖν—" To worship the gods, to do nothing base, and to practise manhood." [1] It is a moral maxim of a fairly noble and manly kind.

But we catch a glimpse of the spirit of their doctrine and the soul of Celticism in the literatures of Ireland and Wales. These literatures, especially the Irish, are to a great extent sententious, or gnomic. Even in the narrative parts the gnomic spirit appears frequently. But these narratives are surprisingly successful in the creation of characters, especially for a literature which has left no trace of drama. In the epic of Ulster the hero Cuchulainn, King Conchobar, the Druid Cathbad, and Queen Medb are types whose individuality is all the more remarkable since the works in which they appear are not altogether works of art. The Celts of Gaul deliberately jettisoned the whole of their epic tradition for the sake of the more sophisticated culture which the Romans brought. But they must have kept its spirit ; it is to that that I should attribute the dramatic character which the history of France spontaneously assumes in the writings of its chroniclers. For in what other history are social standpoints so happily expressed in the typical figures of heroes ?

The archæology of Roman Gaul is deceptive as to the kinship of the French people. The Gallo-Romans mostly continued to be disguised Celts. So much was this the case that after the Germanic invasions we find modes and tastes which had been those of the Celts reappearing in Gaul. They survived the impress of Rome. Romanesque art often recalls Gallic art, or that of the Gallic stone-masons working in the Roman manner, so that one is sometimes misled.[2] But that is only one sign. Language is another. The Romans slowly imposed their speech on Gaul. But French is Latin pronounced by Celts and applied to the needs of Celtic minds. The analytical character of the verb, the use of demonstratives and demonstrative particles, the turn of the spoken sentence, are common to French and the Celtic languages.[3]

In short, the civilization of the Celts lies at the bottom of

[1] 6.
[2] e.g. the monument at Virecourt, sometimes regarded as Romanesque, sometimes as Gallic.
[3] Dottin, **CXCVI**, pp. 77–9.

French civilization, just as the nation into which the Celts of Gaul were beginning to form is at the bottom of the French nation. It is a commonplace to tell the French how Gallic they are. Much of the Celts, then, remains where the Celtic name is lost.

But so far as Celtic social organization is concerned, all the upper parts have gone. The state in France is not Celtic ; it is Germanic or Roman. No Celtic state has survived ; Scotland is the ghost of one, and Ireland is a new creation. Celticism has left only possibilities of nations. It survives only in the foundations of our Western Europe and has made hardly any contribution to its superstructures. It failed through defects of organization which we shall have to examine.

The part played by the Celts in history was not political, for their political formations were unsound. But it was the part of civilizers. One especially characteristic thing happened when they absorbed Roman civilization—the wonderful development of Roman schools, which succeeded the Celtic schools of the Druids.[1] Gaul got her classical culture from Gallic teachers, trained by the Druids, and, what is more, some of them were fit to teach in Rome. Naturally they could interpret Mediterranean civilization— science, art, philosophy, and moral culture—to the Gauls better than foreigners could have done. But it is an interesting fact that they did so act as interpreters. Later, in the Middle Ages, Irish monks brought Europe back to the cultivation of letters and Greek and Latin philosophy. Earlier the Celts had been the middlemen who brought Greek civilization to Central Europe, where they had not failed to propagate their own culture.

The Celts were torch-bearers in the ancient world, and the French have succeeded them. With their love of beauty and general ideas the French have acted in Europe as the middlemen through whom it has received the lofty, mellow civilizations of antiquity which they have helped to make into the civilization of the world. The Celts contributed certain forms of sensibility and humanity which are still the possession of Western Europeans and of the French.

---

[1] e.g. the school of Autun (Tac., *Ann.*, iii, 43).

V

CELTS OF THE CONTINENT AND CELTS OF THE ISLES

When ancient historians speak of the Celts, they usually confine themselves to those of the Continent ; in other words, to the Celts of Gaul, the Gauls, whose progress can be followed with the aid of those writers and whose antecedents have been indicated above. The Celts of the British Isles are left to the Celtic student, and we have to turn to the philologist and other specialists. In this work we shall deal both with the Celts of the Continent and with those of the islands, and we shall most certainly find that we cannot possibly understand the history of the former if we ignore the latter.

The Celts of the islands have a literature which, except for a few Gallic inscriptions, constitutes the whole written tradition of the race. It is true that that literature all belongs to a time later than our period, and that the oldest of the manuscripts in which it is preserved is not earlier than the twelfth century.[1] The languages in which it is presented are already a long way from the stage at which Gaulish stopped. At first sight, it seems rash to connect data which appear so far removed from each other and so unrelated in time or place.

Nevertheless, the very difference between the dialects, Irish on the one hand and Welsh or British on the other, brings us face to face with a really fundamental fact in the history of the Celts—with a kind of prehistoric cleavage of the Celtic body, parallel to a similar cleavage of the Italic peoples, to which I call attention at this early stage of my work, because archæologists who study the Celts [2] do not take it into account, or not sufficiently.

As for their literature, it is already generally accepted that it represents a tradition much older than the earliest date at which the surviving works were set down in writing. In the descriptions of objects of which the ancient literature of Ireland is so full, attempts have been made to identify weapons and jewels of the Hallstatt period,[3] but this is,

---

[1] Dottin, *Les Littératures celtiques*, pp. 17 ff.
[2] Déchelette, ii, 2, pp. 572 ff.
[3] MacNeill, **CCCCXLI**, chap. ii.

in my opinion, a mistake. In any case, it contains traces of things belonging to a time three or four hundred years before Christ, of which we shall have to take note in our survey. I believe that its origins are still older and that it contains large remnants of a Pan-Celtic tradition, going back beyond the time when the Celts reached the British Isles. By analysis and comparison one may distinguish the different strata of this literary tradition. Even if its antiquity were less likely it would be unscientific to ignore it and deny its existence.

For the history of Celtic civilization, be it that of technical processes, trades, and domestic life, or that of social organization, clans, tribes, kingdoms, confederations, and the way in which they changed the face of the land, or, again, that of art and religion, the actual materials will be supplied chiefly by the literature and the law of the island Celts. But whether we consider institutions or characters—for it is very tempting to look to the Celtic epics and tales for psychological illustrations to a rather dry history—we must never forget that the Gauls whom Cæsar conquered had already advanced far beyond the type of civilization represented by the laws and epics of Ireland.

Lastly the island Celts are of interest to us in their development of the Celtic tradition, which, on the Continent, was diverted from its original course by the Roman conquest.

There are, moreover, several ways of utilizing literary or linguistic data to reconstruct the history of the Celts. Some very dubious methods have been employed—with some good result, to tell the truth, for it was the wild imaginings of the Celtic Academy that opened the way to prehistory. I shall try to adopt the sternest and most austere method.

VI

PLAN OF THIS WORK

First of all, we must try to define what we mean by " Celts ". There is no real obscurity about the matter, but obscurities have arisen from the differences of the various groups of students which have dealt with the Celts, each from its own point of view. The elements from which we have to make up our picture do not agree exactly. We must interpret, select, and give each element its true and proportionate value. That which is least subject to controversy is the linguistic element. Celtic speech is the chief sign of Celticness, if one may use the word. Anyone who spoke Celtic was a Celt, wherever he came from. Those who ceased to speak it disappeared among the peoples who absorbed them, and ceased to be Celts. But the smallest trace of Celtic speech, in names of men or places, in inscriptions or in later languages, proves beyond doubt the presence of the Celts at a certain place and at a certain date. We may accept it that the boundaries of the Celtic tongues correspond roughly to those of the Celtic communities and civilizations.

Secondly, we have to determine their changing boundaries, and for that purpose to discover the facts which make up the internal and external history of their communities, which have no history properly so called, so that we may see how they grew, how their tribes were grouped and how subdivided, and follow their wanderings, their colonizations, the concentric waves of their successive advances, their new settlements, the states which were created, and the nations which accumulated at the end of their journey to their Chosen Land.

Our evidence will be names—place-names, personal names, names of peoples attached to places. On the way, we shall come upon archæological facts. These will take their place among the other evidence, and we shall see how fruitful that assemblage of different kinds of evidence can be.

In the course of this inquiry it will be necessary to venture outside our limits and to attempt a systematic account of Celtic civilization. We shall have to anticipate, and to define the civilization of La Tène, that is to describe the series of characteristic objects which the term covers, because those characteristic objects are just what we have to use as indications of race. For the same reason we shall have to note their chronological classification and the different forms which objects have in different periods.

The last part of this work will be a study of Celtic civilization. Here some of the archæological facts will come in again to bear witness to the industrial capacity of the Celts, their wealth, their trade, their way of life, and their dress. But we shall above all consider the structure of Celtic communities, the units of various sizes—family, tribe, nation—and the social activities—religion, art, etc.—which developed in those communities.

The Rise of the Celts

PART ONE

WHAT THE CELTS WERE

CHAPTER I

The Name and the Race

W HAT, then, were the Celts ?   We must first have some
idea of what they were if we are to find out where
they were.   Every group of men living together forms
a physical, social, and moral unit.   Its members know one
another and are known to others by their physical type, and,
still more, by their manner of life, their language, certain
sides of their civilization, their name, if they have a common
name implying that they belong to the group, or some other
symbol.   Let us see how these various indications will help
us in our study of the Celts.

I

THE NAME OF THE CELTS

The ancient Greek writers who have left information
about the Celts used the name Κελτοί, Latin *Celtæ*, as
a general racial designation applying to large peoples living
a long way off.   At the beginning of the third century before
Christ, a new name, that of Galatians, Γαλάται, appears
for the first time in the historian Hieronymos of Cardia,[1]
who wrote of their invasion of Macedonia and Greece and
their settlement in Asia Minor.   It appeared in the epitaph
of young Cydias, who was killed at Delphi in 279.[2]   It is
probable that the name of *Galli* came into use among the
Italians, as a rival to the old name of Celts, about the same
time or a little before.   The words Galatians and Galli were
likewise used as general terms, and were not the names of
small groups which became generalized.

---

[1] *F.H.G.*, ii, 450–461.   [2] Paus., x, 21, 5.

These various designations were used concurrently. The ancients tried to give them special application,[1] and modern historians have attempted to assign them to different groups of Celtic tribes.[2] The tribes did, indeed, form groups of different kinds, but we must give up any attempt to divide them into Celts and Galatians.[3]

These names came from the Celts themselves. The proper name Celtillos, the name of the Celtici (a Celtic people), and the personal names found in Spain—Celtigum, Celtus, Celticus [4]—lead one to think that the root-word was, indeed, Celtic. As for the word *Galli* its equivalent is found in the Irish texts. There were in Ireland tribes of Gaileoin or Galians. In the *Táin Bó Chuailgné* (the Cattle-lifting of Cooley), in which a contingent of them forms part of the army of Connacht, they are distinguished from the other Irish by their military habits and strict discipline ; they have the air of foreigners—almost of foreign mercenaries.[5] They were Gauls settled in Ireland. At the beginning of a poem describing the marriage of Cuchulainn, the *Tochmarc Emire* (the wooing of Emer), the hero, Forgall Monach, Emer's father, comes to the court of Conchobar, King of Ulster, disguised as an ambassador of the King of the Gauls, with gifts, which are objects of gold and wine of Gaul (*fin Gall*).[6] In these two cases we have, not tribal names, but general names, although they do not apply to born Irishmen or to the whole of the Celtic countries.

We need not, therefore, make too much of Cæsar's definition at the beginning of the Commentaries : *Qui ipsorum lingua Celtæ, nostra Galli appellantur*—" Who are called Celts in their own language, and Gauls in ours." [7] At the very most, the passage might mean that Cæsar considered that there were two different pronunciations of the same word.

---

[1] Diod., v, 32 ; Strabo, iv, 77. On the use of the two names in Polybios, see Bertrand, **CCCIII**, p. 433.

[2] Bertrand, ibid., pp. 249 ff. ; Bertrand and Reinach, **DXLII**, pp. 28, 36 ; Jullian, **CCCXLVII**, i, p. 316 ; Read, **CCCLXXXIV**, p. 47.

[3] Rhys, **CCXXX** ; Ripley, **CCCLXXVIII**, p. 127.

[4] Schulten, **DXIX**, i, pp. 26, 107.

[5] Windisch, **CCXCVI**.

[6] *Tochmarc Emire*, in **CXL**, xi, p. 442. The later copyist did not understand *Gall* to mean Gaul ; for him, *Gall* meant Norwegian, and he combined the two words.

[7] *Bell. Gall.*, i, 1.

The number and the doubtfulness of the etymologies suggested leads us in the same direction.[1] It is not surprising that these names are hard to explain and that their etymological meaning has gone. All that matters from this point of view is that they are not too alien to the Celtic languages in appearance. Probably we are dealing with three forms of one same name, heard at different times and in different places by different ears, and written down by people with different ways of spelling. The initial guttural was transcribed by a surd in the Western Mediterranean area, and (perhaps under the influence of the Tartessians, who sailed to the Celtic countries before the Greeks) by a sonant in Greece. It is equally probable that the same word had two forms, one with a dental at the end and one without.

The fact that there was something that could be called by a name, whether the name was Celts or Gauls, was forced upon the ancients, no doubt by the bearers of the name themselves. But did these general names apply to the Celtic peoples as a whole, or only to some of them ? Did they apply to the Celts of Ireland ? When the ancient

---

[1] The following are the usual conjectures : *Celta* is supposed to come from a root *quel*, implying the notion of raising. It is the root of *celsus*, and of Lithuanian *kéltas* " elevated ". It has been compared to an Old Irish word, a dictionary word, *cléthe* (Stokes, **CCXXXVI**, pp. 70–1, gloss of O'Davoren) " great, noble, elevated ". In composition, the root is found in Old Irish *ar-celim*, Middle Irish *ar-chell-ain*, " I carry off," and the substantive *tochell* " victory, gain ". D'Arbois supposes that the Germanic *-childis* (Brunichildis), O. Nor. *hildr*, O. Sax. *hild*, is derived from it through a word *Celtis* (the word *Held*, O. Sax. *helid*, A.-S. *hœleþ*, O. Nor. *holdr* and *halr*, O.H.G. *helid*, is derived from the Celtic : Irish *calath*, Breton *calet* " hard ").

There was another root *quel* which meant " strike ". It occurs in the Latin *-cello* (*percello*), *calamitas*, *incolumis*, *cladus*, and *clava*, and in the Lithuanian *kalti* " strike ".

The word *Celta* may also be connected with the root of Sanskrit *cárati* " it goes round ", in Greek τέλομαι " I go round, I flow ", and in Latin *cultura*, *cola*, *incola*, *inquilinus*, *exquiliœ*. In Old Irish, the verb *imm-e-chella*, 3rd person, means " goes all round, starting from the sun and moon " ; *timchell* " the act of going round " ; *tóichell*, " journey ". If *Celta* was connected with this root, it would mean something like " the inhabitants ".

When we think of the association of the name of the Belgæ with their dress, we may be inclined to refer to the Scottish kilt. Cf. Joyce, ii, p. 203 ; Cormac, s.v. " Celt vesta ". Welsh *celu* ; Indo-Eur. *quel*.

Galli has been connected with the Old Irish and British word *gal*, which means " worth ", " war ", " power ", " heat ", etc.—i.e. something strong and unpleasant. In Middle Irish there is a word *gall*, meaning " foreigner ", which was used by the English of the Scandinavians. Possibly it comes from *Gallus* (Zimmer), and is a memory of the inroads of the Gauls into Ireland. It has also been ascribed to the root which gives Latin *hostis* (*ghas*, *ghaslo*) (Stokes). The root of the Latin *garrulus* has also been suggested. But what has not ?

writers, in describing the races of the West, started to speak
of the Celts instead of the Ligurians, they imagined, in the
place of the great Ligurian region (*Ligystike*), a great Celtic
region (*Keltike*), which covered the whole West, including
the islands. The islands disappeared into the region as a whole.
The Celts were the great people of the West. Did the islanders
really call themselves Celts ? That is another question,
and one that was probably not asked. It is extremely
doubtful whether the inhabitants of Ireland ever gave
themselves a name of the kind.[1] Moreover, the Irish seem to
have exhausted the resources of their ethnographical sense
when they described themselves in reference to themselves
and distinguished the elements of which they were composed.
The Celts of Britain behaved differently ; indeed, it is just
possible that the Galians of Ireland were recruited among
them.[2]

The names of Celt and Gaul are properly the names of the
Celtic peoples of the Continent.

It is, too, on the eastern limit of the Celts that the evidence
found regarding the use of these racial names and the resulting
distinctions are of value and usefully supplement linguistic
and other indications. In the East there were isolated peoples,
thrown out in advance of the main body, which were called
Celtic—the Cotini and Osi in Silesia, the Scordisci, the
Iapodes. On the other hand, a certain number of Belgic
peoples styled themselves Germanic ; yet the Belgæ were
called Gauls and Galatians, just like the Gauls of Lugdunensis
and Cisalpine Gaul.

We can, to a great extent, trust the ancient authors in
their use of the name of Celts, although it is not always
ultimately based on native evidence. Such terms as Celto-
Ligurian, Celtiberian, Gallo-Greek, Celto-Scythian, reveal
an appreciation of shades of difference, a fairly conscientious
interest in the racial distinctions expressed by names. They
are not, indeed, all of equal value ; Celto-Scythian,[3] for

---

[1] On the names of the Goidels and Brythons, see below, pp. 197 ff.
On the ethnology of Ireland, see below, pp. 207 ff.

[2] The name of Wales, given to that country by the Saxon conquerors,
does not come into the question here. It is the name of a particular Celtic
people, the Volcæ, which was first extended by the Germans to all their
Celto-Romanic neighbours (*welsch*) and then appropriated, as often happened.

[3] Strabo, xi, 6, 2 ; cf. i, 2, 27 ; Plut., *Mar.*, 11 ; Heracl. Pont., in Plut.,
Cam., 22, 2. D'Arbois, CCCI, i, pp. 233–4.

example, merely designates an unknown man who was
neither a Celt nor a Scythian.   But the use of a racial
designation covering more than the group which obviously
forms one community is always vitiated by the same causes
of error, whether the term be used by a geographer or by an
explorer or by a native. Artificial, preconceived classifications
are among the most dangerous.

As to the area covered by the name of the Celts, the
evidence of the ancients is based on their notion of the racial
arrangement of the world, according to which there were
great barbarian peoples spread equally all round the
circumference.

Unfortunately the Greek writers somehow came to
combine their idea of the Celts with that of the Hyperboreians.
Many use the two words as synonyms.[1]   From this confusion
the Greek geographers got the idea that there was a Celtic
belt covering all Northern Europe as far as Scythia, and thus
were led into mistakes about the relations of the Celts and
the Germans,[2] and the true extent of the Celtic region.

Another confusion, that of the Cimmerians and the
Cimbri, which was started by Poseidonios,[3] has raged like
a pestilence among modern historians,[4] and has recently
been given a new lease of life by the latest work dealing with
the Celts and Celtic archæology.[5]   This theory enlarges their
domain considerably towards Eastern Europe, with very
little trouble.   It is accepted that the Welsh call themselves
Cymry.   By connecting this name with that of the Cimbri
it was natural to hang it on to the Belgæ.   But " Cymry "
has nothing to do with " Cimbri ".   At the time of the
Cimbrian invasion the word Cymry must have had the form
Combroges [6] (people of the same country, brog).   The word
still had this form when it was taken over by the Irish

---

[1] Dottin, **CCCXXII**, p. 22. Hecatæos of Abdera said that, opposite the
Celtic country, there was a large island inhabited by the Hyperboreians,
which was the British Isles (*F.H.G.*, ii, 286, fr. 2).

[2] In the time of Augustus, Dionysios of Halicarnassos (fragments of
Bks. xiv and xv, 1) made Germany part of the Celtic region. Cf. Plut., *Mar.*,
11, 6. D'Arbois, **CCCI**, ii, p. 303.

[3] In Strabo, vii, 2, 2.   He was speaking of the Cimmerians of the *Odyssey*,
whom he confused with those of Scythia and Asia Minor, the Gimicai of the
Assyrian inscriptions.   His opinion was adopted by Diodoros (v, 32, 4) and
Plutarch (*Mar.*, ii, 9).   Cf. Dottin, **CCCXXII**, p. 20.

[4] On this confusion cf. Dottin, op. cit., p. 23.

[5] Peake, **CCCCXLVII**, p. 162.

[6] Or *Combrogi*. Loth, in **CXL**, xxx, p. 384.

(*combreic*, dative of the adjective, " Cymric ").[1] Who were the Cimbri? Probably Germans, doubtless very much Celticized. But if there can still be any doubt about their race there is none at all about that of the Cimmerians. They were Thracians, or a kindred people.[2]

The efforts of the myth-writers to bring the Celts into mythological tradition, by giving them a place in the two cycles which are divided into compartments—that of Heracles and that of Troy [3]—has led to trouble of another kind. They encouraged the Celtic peoples to forge Mediterranean pedigrees for themselves at the expense of their Celtic inheritance. In Gaul, the Ædui and the Arverni connected themselves with the Trojan stock, by lines unknown to us, and thereby justified themselves in maintaining or adopting a pro-Roman policy.

> *Arvernique ausi Latio se fingere fratres,*
> *Sanguine ab Iliaco populi—*

" And the Arvernian peoples, who dared imagine themselves brothers of the Latin, from their Trojan blood." [4] The Irish did likewise, and this was the beginning of their history writing.[5] They took bits from the Bible and the Latin historians and geographers. They placed themselves among the great peoples of the world. The only connection they did not boast was the Celtic. They claimed kinship with the Iberians because they called themselves *Hiberni*, and with the Scythians because they called themselves *Scotti*. They

---

[1] D'Arbois, **CCCI**, i, pp. 257–8 ; Müllenhoff, ii, pp. 116–121.

[2] D'Arbois, op. cit., p. 251 ; Dottin, **CCCXXII**, pp. 169–172. But quite lately they have been turned into Tokharians (Charpentier, **CLXVI**, 1917, p. 347). According to this theory, the Cimmerians of the shores of the Black Sea were divided by the Scythians into two sections, one of which moved south towards the Danube and so into Asia Minor, where it came into conflict with the army of Gyges, while the other was driven eastwards and settled in Turkestan. Some of them remained in the delta of the Danube and formed the nucleus of the Celtic settlements which we shall find in that region later. The whole construction is highly fanciful.

[3] They gave the Galatians an eponymous hero—Galates, whom some made a son of Heracles and a Celtic woman (Diod., v, 24) and others a son of Polyphemos and Galateia (Γαλατία, in Timæos). Jullian, **CCCXLVII**, ii, p. 417. On the possible identification of the Celts with the Læstrygons, see Dottin, **CCCXXII**, p. 26.

[4] Lucan, *Pharsalia*, i, 427–8, and scholia. Amm. Marc., xv, 9, 5 ; Propertius, ii, 13, 48 ; Tac., *Germ.*, 3 ; Hirschfeld, **CXLVIII**, 1897, pp. 1105 ff. ; T. Dirt, in **CXLIV**, 1896, pp. 506 ff. ; Weerth, **XXXVII**, lxix, 1880, p. 69 ; Castra Trajana, (near Xanten) = *Trojana* ; Sieburg, **CLX**, 1904, p. 312.

[5] E. MacNeill, **CCCCXLI**, pp. 11 ff., 93 ff.

credited their forbears with the wildest of wanderings, but they did not make them come from the lands which really were the Celtic cradle. So the Celts assumed an illustrious classical pedigree, which they could share with the great civilized peoples, but disowned themselves and their own forefathers. A whole movement of ideas, partly scientific and partly political, the effects of which are still in operation, had to take place before the intellectuals of the Celtic countries, the scholars of Ireland, Scotland, Wales, and Brittany, recovered the consciousness of their racial kinship.

There was a time when the Celts were sufficiently aware of that kinship to impress foreigners with the notion of their unity and to give themselves a name which, if not common to all, was at least very general. But their racial consciousness was too incomplete, and was too often destroyed. They have left us evidence that distant or different groups considered themselves as being of one race, and we shall consider that evidence carefully. The existence of an institution like that of the Druids must have helped to keep the feeling alive. Nevertheless, it weakened, becoming limited to such groups or political relationships as could keep it up, and declining even there. So the Celts are not good witnesses to the use of the name of Celt. When the ancients used it, they generally had very good reasons. Moreover, we are not compelled to accept their evidence without being able to criticize it.

II

THE ANTHROPOLOGICAL EVIDENCE

A wind of confusion has blown among the anthropologists whenever they have come to deal with the Celts, and they have dealt with them far too much. For a long time their great aspiration was to attach racial proper names to pure races. It was with the Celts as with the Aryans. Attempts were made to give their name to one or another of the physical types prevailing in Europe. Not all students, luckily, have fallen into this quagmire, and in the works of Messrs. Boule, Deniker, Ripley, and Fleure [1] the most reasonable discussions

---

[1] Boule, *Les Hommes fossiles*, p. 320 ; Deniker, **CCCXX** ; Ripley, **CCCLXXVIII**, pp. 124–5 ; Fleure, **CCCXXVIII**, *passim*.

will be found. But errors of simplification, which are the most natural of all, continue to create trouble in the language of science long after they have been exploded. An anthropologist who speaks of the Celts must always make a moral effort in order to restrain himself from applying the name as a label to a series of similar skulls. It would be better never to use it at all.

The Greek and Latin writers who speak of the Celts regarded them as a tall people, with lymphatic bodies, white skins, and fair hair.[1] They alarmed the Italians by their resemblance to large, though magnificent, beasts.

> *Aurea cæsaries ollis atque aurea vestis :*
> *virgatis lucent sagulis : tum lactea colla*
> *auro innectantur* [2]—

" Golden is their hair, and golden their garb. They are resplendent in their striped cloaks, and their milk-white necks are circled with gold." Since the ancients return over and over again to their fair hair and their milk-white skin, modern writers have supposed that the bands which invaded Italy and Greece were recruited among the tall, fair longheads of Northern Europe.

Others of the ancients knew that there were Celts who were less fair than the rest, particularly the Britons [3] ; that the Celts were not so fair as the Germans ; and that to produce a parade of tall, fair Celts it was necessary to pick out suitable specimens and dye their hair. Suetonius, for instance, tells us that Caligula, wishing, after an alleged campaign against the Germans, to increase the number of prisoners who were to follow his chariot in his triumph, picked out the tallest Gauls that could be found and made them let their hair grow and dye it red.[4] The Greek and Roman writers knew plenty of Celts, if it was only as slaves, Gallic and British, for these must have been very numerous ; but, being used to the dark-skinned, black-haired people of the South, they especially noticed foreigners who had fair or red hair. There were doubtless many dark Gauls.

---

[1] Diod., v, 28 ; Amm. Marc., xv, 12, 1 ; both passages come from Timagenes. Livy, v, 48 ; xx, 55 ; xxviii, 17, 21 ; Silius Ital., iv, 201–3 ; Martial, xi, 53 ; Pliny Eld., iv, 31. Claud., *Stil.*, ii, 651. Cf. Boule, op. cit., pp. 348–350.
[2] Virg., *Æn.*, viii, 658–660.   [3] Tac., *Agr.*, xi.   [4] *Cal.*, 62.

Since Broca wrote, the name of Celts has been attached to the type of dark round-heads of Western Europe and the Alpine regions.[1] This, too, is done in virtue of an ancient authority, namely the first words of Cæsar's *Commentaries: Gallia est omnis divisa in partes tres, quarum unam incolunt Belgæ, aliam Aquitani, tertiam qui ipsorum lingua Celtæ, nostra Galli appellantur*—" Gaul is divided into three parts, one of which is inhabited by the Belgæ, another by the Aquitani, and the third by men who are called Celts in their own language and Galli in ours." [2] The dark type, which is widespread in Central France, has been attributed to the Celts. Broca assigned the fair type to the Belgæ.

Still keeping the Celts round-headed, other anthropologists have identified them with the tall brachycephals or mesaticephals of the north and north-west of Europe, often designated as the Borreby type,[3] who are distinguished from the other European round-heads by the height of the face, the accentuation of the supraciliary ridge, the pentagonal shape of the skull as seen from above, and the stature. The very strange term of " Celto-Slavs " which has been applied to all brachycephals as a whole is due to the diffusion of this special type all over Northern Europe, from east to west.[4] The descendants of this type who are found from England to Russia lead one to think that we have to do with fair brachycephals, perhaps the result of crossing between Nordic long-heads and Alpine round-heads. Herr Schliz, of Heilbronn, an anthropologist whose work deserves to be followed very closely, since he makes an interesting attempt to establish a concordance between forms of civilization and physical types in the centre and north-west of Europe in prehistoric times, has selected this very type to assign to the Celts.[5] For, he says, this is the type found in the graves of the La Tène period in Bavaria, and it is beyond dispute

---

[1] P. Broca, **LXXXVIII**, 1860, pp. 1–56 ; **XLI**, 1860, pp. 457–464, 557–562, 569, 573 ; 1873, pp. 247–252, 317–320 ; 1874, pp. 658–663. Beddoe, **XCVIII**, 1864, pp. 348–357 ; **XLI**, 1877, p. 483. Virchow, **LXXXII**, 1895, pp. 130–3 ; Ranke, **CCCLXX**, ii, pp. 261–8 ; F. W. Rudler, **CXXVII**, 1880, pp. 609–619 ; Ripley, **CCCLXXVIII**, pp. 125 ff.

[2] *Bell. Gall.*, i, 1.

[3] Ebert, **CCCXXIV**, ii, p. 121 ; Ripley, **CCCLXXVIII**, p. 212 ; F. G. Parsons, **LXXVI**, 1913, p. 550.

[4] Ripley, op. cit., pp. 355 ff. (following Topinard) ; Sergi, **DXL**, chap. vi.

[5] Schliz, **XXIII**, 1909, pp. 239 ff. ; 1910, pp. 202 ff., 355 ff. ; id., **LXXXV**, 1911, p. 313.

that the country was at that time occupied by Gauls. If Herr Schliz is in error, he is only partly so, for there certainly were Celts of this type. It is the type represented by the great figures of Galatians which are supposed to have adorned some Pergamene trophy, such as the Dying Gaul of the Capitol and the Ludovisi Gaul. These round heads, the high faces, the straight foreheads with strongly marked brow-ridges, the noses set back at the base, and the stiff hair with rebellious locks, are evidently copied from nature, and the copy is true, for the type is familiar to the modern Frenchman ; he finds it all round him. But it is also the typical Gaul as described by the ancients, tall, fair-haired, and white-skinned, and he is not a dolichocephal.

It is certain that the three types described above existed among the Celts, both on the Continent and in the islands. Here the Irish texts bear their witness. In the *Táin* there are fair heroes (*find-buide*) and also a few dark ones (*dond-temin*).[1] One is called Fiacha Cinn Fionnann, or Fairhead.[2] But no one has any objection to admitting the fact. For even the extremist can save the situation by talking of non-Aryan peoples which have been Aryanized and non-Celtic peoples which have been Celticized. It has, moreover, been almost universally admitted since the time of Roget de Belloguet [3] that the Celts were never more than an aristocracy in the lands which they occupied.

But the difficulty comes just when one passes from determining the anthropological composition of the groups which are known to have been designated as Celtic to giving a name to something formed by those groups. It is in this respect that the attribution of names to one type rather than to another is apt to produce contradictions between the ethnographical conclusions of the anthropologists and those of the archæologists, philologists, or historians. Are the Celts Nordic heroes, who conquer and rule majorities of brunets, Alpine or Mediterranean ? Or are they the brunets of Western or Central Europe, absorbing minorities of Nordic heroes [4] ? The whole meaning of history alters according

---

[1] **CCXCVI**, ll. 5173, 5186, 5245.
[2] Cf. Kuno Meyer, **CCLXXIII**, i, for fair hair.
[3] **CCCLXXIX**, iii, pp. 370 ff. ; Ripley, **CCCCXXVII**, p. 127.
[4] Peake, **CCCCXLVII**, pp. 81 ff.

to the answer, and the question cannot be settled by anthropological prejudices.

Herr Schliz, who is very dogmatic, gives the following account of the succession of human types in Southern Germany, which is the field of his studies, during the Hallstatt and La Tène periods.[1] At the beginning of the Hallstatt age there were in that region short, dolichocephalic men, of Mediterranean appearance, who had apparently come from the South-west. At the height of the same period their place was taken by tall men, also dolichocephalic, who, he says, came from the Balkans. The tall brachycephals appear only in the La Tène period. Herr Schliz makes them come from the West or North-west, and he makes them Celts, so presenting yet another view of the history of that people. This substitution of one unmixed anthropological type for another in succession, which Herr Schliz holds to have taken place in Germany, whenever civilization took a new turn, needs to be considered. Herr Schliz restores to favour the idea of peoples of pure race which has lost ground considerably.[2] To compel acceptance of it is another affair.

One must not resort to that inexhaustible source of errors and contradictions, save with great moderation and in a very critical spirit ; it must not be forgotten that peoples and races, being different things, do not necessarily coincide, and, in fact, never coincide exactly. We do not know of any human group in Europe, from the Quaternary Period and the age of chipped stone downwards, which is not composed of different anthropological elements. The physical characteristics of these groups vary, and they can do so without their variations having the least connection with their history. They may change automatically, as it were, without any new element coming in, through variation of the proportion of the elements of which they are already composed ; or they may change with the introduction of new

---

[1] Schliz, pp. 237 ff.

[2] If we examine Herr Schliz's writings carefully, we notice that he is working on very few facts. He is one of those men who never have the luck to find exceptions on their path ; but they may lie at one side. So far as the Iron Age in Germany is concerned, archæology furnishes nothing to correspond to the racial revolutions which he supposes. Where he sees discontinuity, I see continuity, and continuity in the Celts. Moreover, the tall, long-headed type existed in Germany before the La Tène period ; it has been reported, in particular, in the zoned-vase graves of the beginning of the Bronze Age.

elements, such as slaves or resident aliens, which do not shift
the political axis of their composition. Races and peoples
have their variations. These do not necessarily take place
in the same direction ; they may possibly run counter to
each other.

In any case, it is very rash to identify the Celts with one
of the elements found in one of their groups. We shall see
that the composition of the groups is different from the very
beginning.[1] It is particularly rash to identify the Celts with
the dominant elements in their Western groups which were
not autochthonous and were altered from their original
type by the large proportion of alien elements which they
must have absorbed. It is unscientific to label a group of men,
ancient or modern, by physical characteristics defined in that
way. It is equally unscientific to go on from that to searching
in the anthropology of Europe for Proto-Celts.[2]

It is, however, true that the Celts formed a racial unit,
or several kindred racial units, in which common life produced
a kind of unification of physical types in a sort of *habitus*
common to all. So an ideal type was created, to which all
strove to approach. The Gauls dyed or bleached their hair,
and with that object had invented the prototype of soap,
sapo.[3] They painted their bodies.[4] Just as, in our time,
the individuals of any nation have the family likeness by
which they are recognized as French, English, Italian, or
German, so the ancients could recognize a Celt.

In short, while anthropology has nothing to tell us about
the Celts, and, in spite of many efforts, has never told us
anything, the anthropological materials which it collects and
studies should be taken into account with our other evidence
when we try to describe their groupings and look for their
ethical relationships.

---

[1] **CCCCLXXXIV**, p. 82 ; Ripley, **CCCLXXVIII**, p. 298 ; F. Dumas, **CXLIII**,
1908, p. 338 ; cf. Hamy, **XV**, 1906, p. 1.
[2] Kossinna, **LXXXV**, 1909, pp. 26 ff. ;   225 ff. ;   1910, pp. 59 ff.
[3] Pliny Eld., xxviii, 191 ; cf. Dottin, **CCCXXII**, p. 283.
[4] In **XXIII** (1913), Hoefler published an excellent article entitled
" Somatologie der Gallo-Kelten " (pp. 54 ff.), in which he examines the
little that we know of this artificial aspect of the Celts. From our point
of view, this manner of studying the anthropology of a human society is
the safest. Unfortunately, it does not help us to find out and bring together
the relics of the Celts.

CHAPTER II

LANGUAGE

I

LANGUAGE AS THE MARK OF A SOCIETY

THE Celts were not a race, but a group of peoples, or, to speak more accurately, a group of societies. Language is one of the clearest and truest characteristics of societies. Among the cultural facts which are bounded by the boundaries of a community, it is one of the most typical or the most apparent. There are exceptions to this rule. France is, perhaps, the best example of the rule and of the exceptions. In that country there are spoken, in addition to French, dialects of the *Langue d'oc*, Basque, Breton, Flemish, German, and Italian. Except the *Langue d'oc* dialects, which are fairly widespread, these tongues are spoken by comparatively small groups on the fringes of the nation. For all these groups, French is the language of civilization. The French-speaking countries beyond her frontiers have the closest social and moral relations with France. Such is France and such are the French-speaking countries. National states which speak two or three languages, like Belgium and Switzerland, are really societies divided by language, whose moral and political unity is maintained by veritable social contracts. The great states (which, in any case, were short-lived), such as those of Asia, in which many languages were spoken, were never anything but empires, and never had any unity but that of the sovereign. On the whole, to speak roughly, the language coincides with the society.

We may, therefore, say that the Celts are the group of the peoples which spoke or still speak dialects of a certain family, which are called the Celtic languages. Wherever the Celts have lived they have left place-names, inscriptions with personal names, and in history the memory of other names, which can be recognized as different from all others and, in general, are the same everywhere. The faintest traces of Celtic speech are certain evidence of the presence of the Celts at a certain place at a certain time. They enable us to stake out the domain of the Celts and its changing boundaries with a maximum of confidence.

But for the history of ancient peoples, especially when it is transmitted only by scanty and uncertain evidence, the consideration of their language, or of what remains of it, is equally useful from another point of view. Languages, in their constitution, show how different societies have been related to one another by blood or neighbourhood. The Celtic languages are not something quite apart among the European tongues. It is, therefore, possible, by comparing them and the other families of languages to obtain information as to where they stand in the genealogical tree of the Indo-European languages, which are, for the greater part, the languages of Europe, what neighbours the Celts had at different moments in their past, and, consequently, where they lived. Nothing else could take the place of this kind of information. That is why we must spend some time in examining the Celtic languages and their affinities.

II

THE CELTIC LANGUAGES [1]

We know of almost as many Celtic languages as separate groups of Celts.

The modern languages are, on the one hand, Irish,[2] comprising three groups of dialects,[3] the Gaelic of Scotland,[4] and the Manx of the Isle of Man [5]; and, on the other hand, Welsh,[6] including two groups of dialects,[7] Cornish, which

---

[1] Vendryès, in Meillet and Cohen, **CCXVIII**; Pedersen, **CCXXVII**; L. Weisgerber, "Die Sprache der Festlandkelten," in **XXIX**, xx, 1930, pp. 147–226.

[2] O'Donovan, **CCXXV**; Molloy, **CCXIX**; O'Nolan, **CCXXVI**.

[3] The southern dialect of Munster (Henebry, **CCV**; J. Loth, **CXXXIII**, iii, p. 317); the western dialect of Connacht (Finck, **CXCIX**; G. Dottin, **CXL**, xiv, p. 97; xvi, p. 421; xx, p. 306); and the northern dialect of Donegal (Quiggin, **CCXXVIII**; Sommerfelt, **CCXXXIX**).

[4] Gillies, **CCIII**, 1902; Reid, **CCXXIX**.

[5] H. Jenner, "The Manx Language," in **CLIV**, 1875.

[6] Rhys, **CCCCLIII**, ch. xii; Morris Jones, **CCVIII**, with the additions and corrections of J. Loth, **CXL**, xxxvi (1915), pp. 108 ff., 391 ff.; xxxvii (1917–19), pp. 26 ff.

[7] The dialects of the north (Anglesey, Carnarvon, and Merioneth) and south (Cardigan, Carmarthen, and Glamorgan) (Fynes Clinton, **CXCII**; Morris, **CCXX**).

died out in Cornwall at the end of the eighteenth century,[1] and Breton, with its four dialects, Trégorois, Léonard, Cornouaillais, and Vannetais.[2] The former are called Goidelic, from the name Goidel, that is Irish ; the latter are called Brythonic, from the name of the Brythons, the ancient inhabitants of Britain.[3] There are great differences between the two groups.

The many ancient Celtic languages are represented by what is called Gaulish or Gallic,[4] which covers the remnants of several dialects, if not of several languages,[5] spoken on the Continent and in Britain. These remnants include about sixty inscriptions,[6] some of which, written in Etruscan or Greek characters, range from the descent of the Gauls into Italy to the conquest of Gaul, while others are in Latin characters, epigraphic or cursive,[7] the latest belonging to a time shortly after the Roman conquest. The remainder consists of proper names, some inscribed on coins and others preserved by Græco-Roman tradition, and a few common nouns.[8]

Old Irish is known from inscriptions written in what is known as the ogham alphabet, the oldest of which date from the fifth century,[9] from a few inscriptions in Latin characters, and from copious glosses of the eighth and ninth centuries.[10] Ancient British is known from much briefer glosses of the same period [11] and from proper names preserved in Christian inscriptions of Britain and in Breton tradition.[12]

Between these somewhat incomplete records of the ancient state of those languages which still survive and the Gallic inscriptions or other contemporary documents, we may place

[1] J. Loth, **CXL,** xvii–xxiv, xxxii–xxxvii ; H. Jenner, *Handbook of the Cornish Language,* London, 1904.
[2] Loth, **CXL,** xxiv, p. 295, and **CCXIII** ; Vallée, **CCXLI** ; Ernault, **CXCVIII.**
[3] Macbain, **CLXXXIX.**
[4] G. Dottin, **CXCVI.**
[5] e.g. the Coligny Calendar has been regarded by Sir John Rhys as representing a language similar to Irish (Rhys, **VIII** ; cf. Nicholson, **CCXXIV** ; Macbain, **CLXXXIX,** iii ; cf. below, pp. 233 ff.
[6] Dottin, **CXCVI,** pp. 136–212.
[7] Abbé Hermet, **CCVI** ; J. Loth, **CXL,** xli, 1.
[8] Dottin, op. cit., pp. 223–302 (glossary) ; 133 (history of the Gaulish glossary) ; Roget de Belloguet, **CCCLXXIX,** i.
[9] Macalister, **CCXV.**
[10] Stokes and Strachan, **CCXXXV.**
[11] J. Loth, **CCXIV.**
[12] Loth, **CCXIII.**

a certain number of Latin glosses,[1] and also the Gaulish
formulæ [2] given in the *De Medicamentis* of Marcellus of
Bordeaux, who wrote about A.D. 400,[3] and a small Gaulish
vocabulary which is preserved in a manuscript of the eighth
century in Vienna,[4] but must date from the fifth century.[5]
It is called Endlicher's Glossary, after the philologist who
discovered it.

This, then, is our chain of evidence on the Celtic languages.
It looks fairly loose and exiguous. The Celtic dialects of the
islands seem to be à long way from ancient Gaulish, which
itself is but little known. It is not surprising that it took a long
time to discover their kinship, once the tradition was broken,
and that, down to the nineteenth century, historians and
antiquaries looked for equivalents of Gaulish words anywhere
but in the living Celtic dialects.

With the *Grammatica Celtica* of Zeuss, published in 1853,
the scientific comparative study of the Celtic languages
began. It is an old book, which has been superseded but
not forgotten. In the very first edition Zeuss instituted
a methodical comparison between Goidelic, Brythonic, and
the remains of ancient Gaulish, and since then the fact of their
relationship has been accepted. Zeuss belongs to the same
generation as Bopp ; and one of the great scientific achievements of that generation was to disentangle the science of
language and to put it together again.

III

AGREEMENTS BETWEEN THE CELTIC LANGUAGES

The kinship of the Celtic languages appears, first, in the
agreement of their vocabularies, two or three of which will
express the same idea by the same word. Sometimes these
words are lacking in other languages, such as *magos*, plain
(Gaulish Noviomagus, Noyon, New Plain ; Irish *magh* ;

---

[1] For old Celtic in general, the most complete collection is Alfred Holder's
Altceltischer Sprachschatz, 3 vols.
[2] Pliny, xxvii, 101 : *limeum = cervarium* ; cf. Jullian, **CXXXIV**, 1911,
p. 344.
[3] Dottin, **CXCVI**, p. 214.
[4] Ibid., p. 212. We have six other manuscripts of this text, less complete
and later than that mentioned.
[5] H. Zimmer, **CLXXIV**, xxxii, pp. 230–240.

Welsh *ma*; Breton *maes*),[1] or they may be found in other forms, for example, the Gaulish adjective *nŏvios* (as in Noviodunum), formed by adding the suffix *-io-* [2] to the root, as contrasted with the Germanic *nĕvios*, of which we have evidence in the Gothic *niujis*, modern German *neu*, etc., and with the Latin *nŏvus*, a simple stem in *o*, and the Greek νέος = *nĕvos*. One has only to glance through the comparative lexicons to see how general this is.[3] Out of the thousand Gaulish words or parts of words contained in M. Dottin's glossary [4] there are very few for which there is no corresponding word in Welsh or Irish, or both. For these last two languages, philologists have endeavoured, by using the comparative method, to draw up an ancestral vocabulary,[5] representing a common Celtic, from which the Gaulish dialects themselves were derived in ancient times.

Moreover, the Celtic vocabularies resemble one another not only in their simple words, but in their compounds. Many are of the same type,[6] and some are actually alike, in Irish, Welsh, and Gaulish. For the Gallic Vernomagus we have the Irish Fernmag, Alder Field; for the Welsh Trineint, Three Valleys, we have the Gaulish Trinanto. A name like Senomagus (Senan, in Loiret) at once strikes us; it is the Irish Sen Mag, the Old Plain, not just any plain, but a mythical plain, the earthly equivalent of which lay in the centre of Ireland, just as the country of the Carnutes, of which Loiret was part, lay in the centre of Gaul.

The few words which we know of the Celtic dialects of the Continent outside Gaul have equivalents in the Gaulish of Gaul and the languages of the islands. Celtiberian *viriæ* corresponds to Gaulish *viriolæ*,[7] from which French *virole* (" ferrule ") comes, and to Irish *ferenn* " belt ". For Spanish *gurdus* " heavy " [8] there is the Gallo-Roman derivative *gurdunicus*,[9] *gwrdd* in Welsh, and *gourd* (" numb ") in French.

---

[1] D'Arbois, **CCCI**, ii, p. 268. The root may be the Indo-European *magh-*, from which words meaning " great " are derived—Skt. *mahas*, Lat. *magnus*.
[2] Ibid., p. 256. O. Irish *nue*, *nuide*; Mod. Irish, *nuadh*; Welsh *newydd* (the regular termination of stems in *-io*); Breton *nevez*.
[3] Stokes, **CCXXXVII**.
[4] Dottin, **CXCVI**, pp. 217–302.
[5] Ibid., p. 80.
[6] Ibid., pp. 85–6, 105 ff.
[7] Pliny, xxxiii, 40.
[8] Quintilian, i, 5, 57.
[9] Sulp. Sev., *Dial.*, i, 27, 2.

Spanish *acnuna* [1] is explained by the Gaulish *acina*, a land-measure. Many Spanish proper names are like Gaulish or British proper names (Boudica, cf. Boudicca, the correct form of Boadicea), or are explained by common nouns belonging to the other Celtic tongues (Broccus : Irish *broc*, Welsh *broch*, a brock or badger), or are formed like Gallic names (Medugenus).[2] The same is true of the Cisalpine and Galatian dialects. For Cisalpine Gaulish μανιάκης, a collar, we have Irish *muince* and Old Welsh *minci*. *Rumpus*,[3] a vine which grows attached to trees, and *rumpotinus*, the tree which supports it, recall, less directly, Old Welsh *rump* (?), an auger. *Sasiam* (acc.),[4] the name for rye among the Taurini, a Ligurian people which had taken much of its civilization from its Celtic neighbours, is the same as the Brythonic word for barley (Welsh *haidd*, Breton *heiz*). In Galatian μάρκαν (acc.) is exactly like Irish *marc* and Welsh *march* [5]; ἄλκη is like Gallic *alce* " dash " ; ἀδάρκης,[6] a medicinal plant, is like Irish *adarc* " horn ". Here, too, the evidence of the common nouns is confirmed by that of the proper names which are our only witnesses for the language of the Celts of the Upper and Lower Danube.

This agreement extends to peculiarities in the declension of nouns [7] and conjugation of verbs.[8] One example taken from conjugation will be sufficient to show it. There are traces in Irish and Welsh of an ancient conjugation in which the first person singular of the indicative ended in *u* (Old Celtic *-ō*) : Irish *biu*, *tau* " I am ", *tiagu* " I go ", *tongu* " I swear ". In Welsh the *u* became *i* : *carais* = *cărāsī* " I have loved ". There is an example of this conjugation in the bilingual Latin and Gaulish inscription found at Todi in 1839,[9] which

---

[1] I, ii, 430.
[2] Dottin, **CXCVI**, p. 22.
[3] Varro, *De Re Rust.*, i, 8, 4.
[4] Pliny, xviii, 141. It is not surprising that in these two instances the resemblance is only approximate. In each case the civilization is borrowed, and the Celtic words are modified.
[5] Paus., x, 19, 11 ; Dottin, **CXCVI**, p. 24. It is probable that the words recorded by Pausanias belong to the dialect of the Celts who invaded Greece and Thrace, i.e. the Galatians.
[6] Dioscorides, v, 136 ; *adarca*, Pliny, xx, 241.
[7] Dottin, **CXCVI**, pp. 81, 112 ff., esp. pp. 117–19, on stems in *o* with genitive in *i*, stems in *a* with genitive in *as*, stems in *i* or a consonant with genitive in *os*.
[8] Ibid., pp. 122 ff.
[9] Ibid., p. 153. The inscription has two faces, which partly complement

contains the word *karnitu*. The two texts differ slightly, for the Latin sentence is in the third person, as is usual in inscriptions (*locavit* and *statuit*), whereas the Gaulish sentence must be in the first person (the use of the first person in dedicatory inscriptions is attested by Latin inscriptions found in Gaul). In *karnitu*, which corresponds to *locavit* and *statuit*, we find the root of the Gaelic *cairn*; it means " I heaped up ".[1]

So the grammar of Gaulish coincides to a remarkable extent with that of the living Celtic languages. Unfortunately we have not much information about it, and all the resources of the comparative grammar of the Celtic tongues which have been applied to the subject have not succeeded in making it easy for us to read the Gallic inscriptions. The reason may be that the surviving remnants of Gaulish contain elements which cannot be fitted together by the methods of reconstruction employed by Celticists, or, more probably, that they are so fragmentary that they are doomed to remain an insoluble mystery.

M. Dottin suggests that it was probably very different from the Celtic spoken in the islands, Goidelic or even Brythonic. The two following facts, however, studied by M. Loth [2] show that phonetic development took place along the same lines in the islands and on the Continent; this means that the languages were fairly alike, and that the people who spoke them had the same tricks of pronunciation, which they had inherited from their ancestors who all spoke the same speech and which they kept up by their intercourse.

First, the group of letters *ct* became *cht* in Irish and *ith* in Old Welsh; that is, in both families of languages the guttural tended to become a sort of spirant. It was the same in Gaulish. There is evidence of this in the oldest Gaulish

---

one another. Face B, restored, runs : *Ategnato Drutei urnum Coisis Drutei f. frater eius minimus locavit et statuit. Ateknati Trutikni karnitu artuass Koisi Trutiknos.* The termination *-knos* is the patronymic suffix. In *artuas* we see the Irish *art*. The monument in question is of stone, and that, doubtless, is the meaning of the unknown Italic word *urnum*. The inscription means : " To Ategnatos, son of Druteos, I, Coisis, son of Druteos, his youngest brother, raised this monument." It should be noted that this bilingual inscription was found in Italy, on the border of the Celtic and Italic domains.

[1] See also d'Arbois, **CLXXXVIII**, pp. 122-4. Pedersen holds that there is a third person singular deponent (**CCXXVII**, i, p. 245 ; ii, p. 406) ; Dottin, op. cit., p. 122.

[2] J. Loth, **CXXXIX**, xiii (1922), pp. 108–119.

inscriptions in which the uniformity of the Latin alphabet has not yet prevailed. We find the name of the man whom Cæsar calls Lucterius written as $\Lambda v\chi\tau\epsilon\rho\iota os$, with a χ. In Irish it is *luchtaire*, glossed as *lanista*, master of gladiators (Old Irish *lucht* " portion ", " troop " ; Welsh *llwyth*). Gaulish wavered between the two sounds.

The second fact is the variety of ways in which the sounds usually written *ss* and *s* are written. The spelling hesitates between *s, ss, ds, d, sd, st, θ, đ,* and *đđ*. For example, the name of the goddess Sirona is written as Dirona and Đirona.[1] On coins we find Veliocassi and Veliocaθi. One name is variously spelt Assedomarus and Addedomarus, the first element of which is found in the form Adeda in Carinthia.[2] So, too, the Fair Iseult appears in Welsh as Etthilt, Ethylt, and Essylt. The sound in question was probably a cerebral, that is a dental pronounced with the tongue pressed very high above the alveoli.

The starting-point is the same, there is the same initial impulse or the same environment—that is the reason of these resemblances. These languages were the same or similar at the beginning, and they were still so to a great extent at the time of the facts which we are discussing, because the reasons for their identity or similarity still existed. Of British and Gaulish Tacitus says in his *Agricola* that they are very little different, and we have no reason to doubt his evidence. As for Goidelic, I have been struck by the fact that in all the stories of Irishmen travelling to Britain and Welshmen travelling to Ireland there is never a word of interpreters. Indeed, there were British colonies in Ireland and Irish colonies in Britain. There is no suggestion that their languages were different. I am inclined to believe that, in the time of the Roman Empire, even the most different of the Celtic languages were not so different that their speakers did not understand one another. In the absence of other evidence, the great number of Irish words which can be shown to have been borrowed from Welsh and vice versa before the literary period of the history of those languages may serve as a proof. The learned Danish scholar, Holger Pedersen,[3] has made

---

[1] Loth, **CXL,** 1911, p. 416. Two etymologies are possible : (i) Welsh *seren*, Breton *sterenn*, " star " (Dottin, **CXCVI,** p. 287) ; (ii) Irish *sir*, Welsh *hir* " long ", i.e. the Longlived One.

[2] Dottin, **CXCVI,** p. 52.   [3] **CCXXVII,** p. 23.

out a long list of these reciprocal borrowings, which prove that the speakers of the two languages understood one another and that the two languages were spoken together.

St. Jerome, a great traveller, says in his commentary on the *Epistle to the Galatians*,[1] that the Galatians of Asia Minor spoke a Celtic dialect which was much the same as that of the people of Treves, among whom he had stayed. The Galatians were Belgæ, and the language of the Belgæ was a Brythonic dialect. St. Jerome lived at the end of the fourth century after Christ, and the Celts had settled in Galatia in the third century B.C. After seven hundred years, cut off from their main stock and living in a country where the common tongue was Greek, the Galatians had kept their language such that it could be recognized and understood by their linguistic kinsfolk. Doubts have been cast on St. Jerome's authority, quite undeservedly; it has been supposed that he copied an earlier author. This criticism is absurd, for two or three centuries more or less do not affect the value of the fact in the least.

The Goidels and the Brythons had been separated, in my opinion, for a much longer time, yet not so long that they had become incapable of recognizing and understanding each other. The Celtic languages which bear their names have very marked and significant characteristics which I shall discuss in their place. But at the time of the ogham inscriptions the laws by which they became differentiated had left in each tongue many words which were similar to words in the other or could be understood by speakers of the other.[2] It is certainly true, on the other hand, that what remains of Gaulish is very different from the living Celtic languages, and that it lacks some of the characteristics of the modern Celtic group.[3] But it would be a marvel if Gaulish, like those languages, had accomplished a phonetic evolution which is parallel to that which has produced the Romance tongues; syntax and conjugation are just that side of Gaulish of which we know least, and it is at any rate very remarkable that one of the inscriptions of Alise contains an example of relative conjugation similar to that of Irish.[4]

[1] In Migne, *Patrologie latine*, xxvi, 382.
[2] Cf. Gaulish *enigeno-*, ogham *inigena*, Irish *ingen* "girl"; Gaulish *magalo-maglo*, ogham *maglus*, Irish *mál* "prince". Dottin, **CXCVI**, glossary, s.v.
[3] Ibid., p. 125.　　　　[4] **CXCVI**, p. 160; cf. p. 122, *dugiiontiio*.

So the unity of the Celtic languages is plain. There were very close similarities between them, such as did not exist between any of them and any other language. They were homogeneous, they had attained a certain degree of stability, and they were still fairly far, at the time when we shall have to bid the Celts farewell, from the differentiation which they present to-day.

IV

THE CELTIC LANGUAGES AND THE INDO-EUROPEAN LANGUAGES

Some years before the publication of Zeuss's *Grammar* Bopp caused the Celtic languages to be finally received into the family of Indo-European tongues by a treatise which for a long time was regarded as authoritative.[1] It is, then, generally admitted that the Celtic languages are Indo-European languages, and have a certain place in the whole body of those languages. That is how they are defined. A definition is a classification. Classification results from comparison ; it is based on the recording of resemblances and differences. We must, therefore, survey the work which has been done in this matter by philologists ; we must try to see on what branch of the family tree of the Indo-European languages the Celtic languages grew, whether any other elements went to their make-up, and what these were.

The data for this study are, on the one hand, grammar and phonetics, and on the other vocabulary. Philologists have established a whole system of equations between the consonants and vowels of the various Indo-European tongues.[2] They have done the same for the grammatical forms of conjugation and declension, for the elements which are added to a word to make noun-stems and verb-stems of it, or to give it different meanings, and, lastly, for the roots themselves.

One of the objects of this study is the reconstruction of theoretical prototypes for each series of words and elements. When all the supposed prototypes for all the Indo-European

---

[1] **IX**, 1838, pp. 187–292.   [2] Meillet, **CCXVII**.

languages are collected together we have the hypothetical
" Indo-European ".   Another object is the establishment
of the genealogical order of the languages.   This gives us
groups of languages which are especially closely related,
and an order of derivation between groups and individual
languages.   Modern philologists no longer believe that
" Indo-European " is even the shadow of a spoken language.
But whether it was spoken or not does not much affect our
power to draw conclusions of all kinds from its composition
and its relationship with languages which really have been
spoken.   It is a system of linguistic facts.

From the composition of the vocabulary, conclusions
have been reached regarding the date when the Indo-
Europeans split.   They already knew of copper at the time.
Conclusions have likewise been reached regarding their first
habitat, which is supposed to have been bounded by the
southern limit of the beech, their manner of life, their social
organization, their crafts, and their ideas about this world
and the next.   The same has been done for the various groups
of Indo-Europeans as for the Indo-Europeans in their
undivided state, but with less strictness and regard for detail.

These conclusions have been corrected.   It has been
pointed out that the historical interpretation of the data of
the Indo-European problem was open to serious criticism.
Nevertheless, the same method has in quite recent years
produced some admirable and instructive works,[1] even if,
like those which preceded them, they sometimes exaggerate
the importance of the similarities and differences of languages.

The kinship of the Celtic and the Indo-European languages
is attested by their grammars and confirmed by a comparison
of these with the grammars of languages which are not Indo-
European.   Take, for example, Semitic grammar ; it is
impossible to mistake a Semitic verb, with its many voices,
for an Indo-European verb, which is richer in tenses.   But the
comparison of the vocabularies furnishes plainer arguments.

The word for " mother ", for example (Old Irish *máthir*,
gen. *máthar* ; Gaulish *matres, matrebo*), is the same in all
the families of Indo-European languages (Old Icelandic
mader ;   modern German *Mutter* ;   Latin *mater* ;   Doric
Greek μάτηρ ; Sanskrit *mātár* ; Armenian *mayr* ; Tokharian

---

[1] Hirt, **CCCXXXVIII** ; Schrader, **CCCLXXXI** ; Feist, **CCCLXXVI**.

A *mācar*; Tokharian B *mādhar*). The word has hardly changed at all.

Old Irish *fert*, modern Irish *feart*, meaning " tomb, tumulus ", but also " ditch, enclosure ",[1] has an exact equivalent in Indo-Iranian : Sanskrit *vṛtiḥ* " hedge, enclosure " ; Zend *varetiš*.[2] The root of these words has supplied words to the whole Indo-European family—Greek ἔρυσθαι (*Ϝερυσθαι*) " protect ", " repel " ; Gothic *warjan* " protect " ; modern German *wehren* " defend ". From the sense of enclosure, one passes easily to that of territory, boundary of territory. Irish has *ferann* (*fearann*). The word corresponds, letter for letter, with the Sanskrit *varaṇḍh* " entrenchment ", " dike ", and the Zend *uarɜnā* " envelope ", " cover ". The same extension of the meaning occurred with other words, for example Greek ὅρος (that is *ϜορϜο*) ; Corcyræan ὅρβος, *hορϜος* ; Ionic οὖρος ; Cretan ὦρος ; Old Latin *uruus*. The word is translated in a gloss by *circuitus civitatis*. *Amburuare* means to surround with a furrow as a boundary ; *ueruactum* " fallow land ". In Umbrian *uruvú* is frontier.[3]

The Celtic languages are distinguished from all the other Indo-European languages by very clearly marked and quite constant features. These are of a phonetic nature.[4]

(i) The most striking of these phonetic changes is the dropping of the Indo-European *p* at the beginning or in the middle of a word.[5] In the name Aremorici *are* comes from an old **pare*, equivalent to Greek παρά, Latin *prae*, and modern German *vor*. They were the people who lived by the sea, *mor*.[6] In " Vercingetorix " we have *ver*, which is *for* in

---

[1] Cf. *Grab* and *graben*, *fert-i-cladh*.

[2] Walde, **CCXLIII.** Cf. Skt. *api-vṛṇoti* " he closes " ; *apa-vṛṇoti* " he uncovers ". Sanskrit employs the same prefixes, *api* = ἐπί = ob and *apa* = ἀπό = *ab*. This concordance shows that the root keeps throughout its length the meaning of an action the direction of which is undetermined. Cf. Lithuanian *užveriu* " I close " ; *atveriu* " I open ".

[3] Ibid. From the same root, which I have chosen in order to give an example of the luxuriant growths which sprang from Indo-European roots, several Indo-European languages have derived the word for " door "—Oscan *ueru* " door " ; Umbrian *uerofe* " to the door ", and *uerisco* " door, little door " ; Latin *uesti-bulum* ; Lithuanian *vartai* (plur.). With the Greek θυραῖος, " public, outside the door ", we may compare the Czech adjective *veřejný* and the Oscan substantive *uerehia* " the public as a whole ".

[4] D'Arbois, **CCCI**, p. 270.

[5] Ibid., p. 275 ; **CCXCIX**, p. 17.

[6] D'Arbois, **CCCI**, ii, pp. 175–7.

Irish and *guor* in Old Welsh, corresponding to Greek ὑπέρ. The name means " Chief King of those who march against the foe ". For Latin *pater* and Sanskrit *pitár* we have Old Irish *athir*, and for Latin *plenus*, Sanskrit *prâṇas*, we have Old Irish *lán*, Welsh *llawn*, and Breton *leun*.[1]

The *p* is perhaps preserved in the group *pt*, as in Neptacus, Mœnicaptus.[2] It is certainly preserved in the group *ps* and in the group *sp* between vowels, but only to become a guttural afterwards—Ucsello, Latinized as Uxello ; cf. Welsh *uchel*, Old Irish *uasal*, from *upsello (cf. Greek ὑψηλός) ; Crixos, Welsh *crych* ; cf. Latin *crispus* " curly ".[3]

(ii) Indo-European had vowel-consonants, which are called sonants—m̥, n̥, r̥, l̥. The r̥ is regularly represented by *rĭ* before a consonant in Celtic.[4]

(iii) The Indo-European diphthong *ei*, which was at first partially preserved,[5] became *ē* in Celtic.[6] *Dēvos*[7] was the Gaulish pronunciation of a word, the Indo-European root-word of which contained the diphthong *ei*.[8] In Irish *dēvos* is represented by *dia* ; when the inflexion was dropped *dé* was left, and this *ē* in a syllable not followed by an *i* split up into *i-a* in Irish.

[1] Ibid., p. 277.

[2] The form Neptacus is not certain, the *P* being possibly an incomplete *R* (Holder, CCVII, s.v.). Nor is Moenicaptus. Irish *cacht* " servant " (Welsh *cacth*, Breton *caez*), may be derived from the Latin. On Old Irish *secht*, Welsh *seith*, see Dottin, CXCVI, p. 286 ; Philipon, CCCLXIX, p. 198. For the passing from labial *p* to gutturals and vice versa, see below, p. 52.

[3] Philipon, CCCLXIX, pp. 198 ff. Cf. Old Breton *guohi*, Cornish *guhienn* " wasp ", from *uops*, Latin *vespa* ; also Welsh *ucher* " evening ", Latin *vesper*, Old Irish *fescor*.

[4] Ibid., p. 196. In a certain number of cases, r̥ is rendered by *ar*, even before a consonant : *artos*, from r̥kto, Greek ἄρκτος ; *carros*, Old Irish and Welsh *carr*, from kr̥sos, Latin *cursus*.

There was a Gaulish word *rĭtu-*, meaning " ford ", which appears in place-names—Novioritum (Niort), Ritumagos (Radepont). The word is *rhŷd* in Welsh, *rit* in Old Breton, *rid* in Cornish, *rith* in Irish. It is formed by the addition of a noun-suffix to the root *per*, pr̥ : pr̥-tu. Latin gives *portus*, and Germanic *furt*, both with the sense of " passage ". Zend has *pertu*.

The l̥ has the same vocalization. Old Welsh *litan* and Breton *ledan* reproduce an adjective *litanos*, which is attested by place-names : Litanobriga, the forest Litana (in Cisalpine Gaul). It comes from a word pl̥tanos, to which the Greek πλάτανος, from πλατύς " broad ", corresponds. Before a vowel, r̥ and l̥ were vocalized as *ar* and *al* : Gaulish *carnu-* " corn ", Welsh *carn* ; Gaulish *talo-s* " brow ", Breton *tal*.

[5] CCCLXIX, p. 194. Deiviciacos, on a coin from Soissons ; Deivaru, in a Latin inscription from Brescia (CXLIX, v, 4164).

[6] D'Arbois, CCCI, ii, p. 270.

[7] I, xii, 140. Cf. Deva and Devana, the names of British rivers. In France, Devona was Latinized as Divona.

[8] Old Prussian *deiws*, Lithuanian *deive* " ghost ", Oscan *deivai*.

(iv) The Indo-European $\bar{e}$ became $\bar{\imath}$ in Celtic.[1] Typical examples are supplied by the contrast between Latin *rēx* and Celtic *rix*, and by that between Latin *uĕrus* and Irish *fír*, or Old Breton *guir*. In the fifth century the Celts gave *i* a sound intermediate between *i* and *e*, and in the Romanic language they confused Latin *i* and *e*.[2]

These four facts clearly mark off Celtic from the other Indo-European languages. If we compare the grammars and fragments of grammars of the Celtic tongues [3] we shall find other indications of a less general and a less certain nature—the change of Indo-European $\bar{o}$ to $\bar{a}$,[4] wavering between the diphthongs *eu* and *ou*, *ou* and *au*,[5] the assimilation of *ns* into *ss* and *rs* into *rr*,[6] the dropping of *v* in initial groups of a dental $+ v$,[7] uncertainty in the pronunciation of occlusives between vowels.[8]

Some of the characteristics of modern Celtic languages [9] had not yet appeared in Gaulish, or we have no evidence for them; in particular the extreme variability of their initial phonemes and the extreme irregularity of their verb-inflexions. But Gaulish changed,[10] and changed quickly, and it was developing in the same direction as the languages of the islands. We have indications of this, and, in particular, of the weakness which was already appearing in the two sounds *s* and *v*,[11] the dropping or aspiration of which is

---

[1] D'Arbois, **CCCI**, ii, p. 273.

[2] Consentius, in Keil's *Grammatici Latini*, v, p. 394 ; Dottin, **CXCVI**, p. 96.

[3] Philipon, **CCCLXIX**, pp. 193 ff.

[4] Ibid., p. 194 : Virido-mârus, cf. Greek ἐγχεσί-μωρος ; Gaulish *gnatos*, Greek γνωτός, Latin *notus*.

[5] Ibid., p. 195 : Teutates and Toutos, Toutiorix ; p. 196, Caunus and Counus.

[6] Dottin, **CXCVI**, p. 100 : *essedum*, from *en* and *sed*, " to sit " ; *carrus*, from *carsus*. Cf. Pedersen, i, p. 25.

[7] J. Vendryès, " À propos des groupes initiaux dentale $+ v$," in *Miscellany presented to Kuno Meyer*, Halle a. S., 1912, pp. 286 ff.

[8] Dottin, op. cit., p. 101 : Cevenna and Cebenna, *vertraha* and *vertragus*, *arcanto* and *arganto*, *verco* and *vergo*, Carpento.

[9] Ibid., p. 123.

[10] Pedersen, **CCXXVII**, i, pp. 532–3.

[11] Ptolemy, 2, 9, 1. The evolution of *s* into an aspirate, which is characteristic of Welsh (Irish *sét* " road " ; Welsh *hynt*), was not completed before the Saxon conquest of Britain, but it is possible that the group *sr* had already become *fr* both in British and in Gaulish. With Φρούδις, the R. Bresle (Ptol., 2, 9, 1), cf. Welsh *ffrwd* " torrent ", and Irish *sruth* " river ". The dropping of intervocalic *v*, attested by the Vienna Glossary (*brio* for *brivo*), doubtless appears in the Gallic *druida* (*druvida*). Dottin, op. cit., p. 237.

characteristic of Irish and Gaulish. So, too, the development of *ṵ* into *gw* (*f* in Irish), which is characteristic of Brythonic (Gaulish *vindo-*, Welsh *gwynn*, Irish *find*), went on in Gaulish in spite of the spelling, since it appears suddenly in French words like Gande, the name of a stream, from Vinda (the White), which was Vuinda or Vuanda in the tenth century, or the River Gartempe, from Vertimpa, Vuartimpa (A.D. 825).[1]

In their vocabulary the Celtic languages present a very great number of peculiarities, which cannot, unfortunately, be made into a system. They are negative facts. Certain Indo-European words and roots are lacking in Celtic, and their place has been taken by others. Before we compare the Celtic languages with the other Indo-European groups, can we at this stage obtain any light on the history of the Celts from these peculiarities ?

One postulate of the earliest comparative studies of the Indo-European languages was that there were unmixed peoples, just as it was postulated that there were unmixed races ; such changes as had taken place in these peoples were supposed to have occurred in each independently, as a consequence of its growth. On this assumption every fact revealed by comparison of their languages was used in a kind of genealogical classification, many parts of which are still useful. But the postulate has been abandoned. There are no unmixed peoples, and doubtless there never were any. But in that case a comparative study of languages may reveal their heterogeneous elements, and consequently those of the peoples which spoke them. We may, therefore, hope to find in the Celtic languages traces of the languages previously spoken by peoples, Indo-European or other, which had dealings with the Celts or were absorbed by them. One would expect them to have passed on to the Celts some part of their vocabulary and some of their ways of speaking. So the innovations which appear in Celtic would come from its associations with foreign tongues.[2]

So far as vocabulary is concerned, the hypothesis leads nowhere, for the Western associates of the Celts spoke languages which have been almost entirely wiped out or

[1] Philipon, **CCCLXIX**, pp. 199 ff.   [2] Zimmer, **CLXXXI**, ix, pp. 87 ff.

cannot be compared to any known stock, except Basque (which has yielded nothing) and Indo-European. There were probably other Indo-Europeans in the West before the Celts. The contribution which they left in the Celtic vocabulary cannot be identified.

Another thing postulated in the earliest comparative studies of vocabulary was that the Indo-European roots had very definite meanings, and therefore strictly determined uses. Consequently, great attention was paid to the absence or the replacement of a word. Ultimately it was admitted that the meanings of the roots were vague, and continued to be so save for a few words. We ourselves are constantly describing concrete objects by abstract words (e.g. " rule "), giving special meanings to words whose meaning is general (" chalk "), and, more frequently, generalizing words of special meaning or giving them a new sense, by analogy (" rubber sponge "). It is not surprising that a vocabulary consisting of such indefinite words should not have been used consistently. That one approximate term should have given place to another approximate term is of no importance. The moral is that we must not exaggerate the importance of negative facts when comparing vocabularies. In the case of the Celtic tongues such comparison reveals nothing but accidents of speech, which are quite common and are chiefly due to chance. Let us see some examples.

There was an Indo-European word for a house, which Celtic has lost. It was a word with a definite meaning. It is found in Sanskrit *véçaḥ*, in Greek [Ϝοῖκος], and in Latin *uīcus*.[1] This word, as is shown by the Sanskrit and Latin forms, meant the great house, the house of a great family, in which there might be several establishments. It is not found in Celtic. This is not because the Celts did not have great houses ; we shall see that the case was quite the contrary. It is not because the great family had broken up among them ; on the contrary, the Celtic family was a great family of people descended from a common forefather, in which several generations, several branches, and swarms of individuals lived a common life. It was a typical Indo-European family. In Irish the property on which the family lives is called *baile*. Is this an Indo-European word ? We

---

[1] Meillet, **CCXVII**, p. 357.

are not sure. It is even supposed to come from the root *bhu-*,
" to be ". *Baile* implies a word **balios*, which implies a pre-
Celtic *bhu-alio-*, " the place where one is ". In any case,
the word must be an old word kept in Irish alone, or
a suppletory term of general meaning.

Here is another accident. Indo-European had a root *sē*,
which meant to sow, but in a very indefinite sense. Welsh
has kept it in the verb *hau* " to sow " ; Irish has lost it as
the root of a verb, but has kept it in the substantive *sil*
" posterity ", and expresses sowing by the verb *cuirim*,
meaning " I throw ". The process is comparable to what
happened at the passing from *ponere* to *pondre*, from *trahere*
to *traire*, and from *tirare* to *tirer*. In the same way Irish lost
the Indo-European word meaning to glean, while Welsh
kept it (*medi*). Instead Irish uses *bongim* " I cut " ; *buain*,
a verbal noun, means " harvest ", and is a thoroughly Indo-
European word (Sanskrit *bhanajmi* " I break " ; Greek
φαγεῖν).

In the third example the case is different. There was an
Italo-Germano-Celtic word meaning furrow : Welsh *rhych*,
Old Breton *rec* (modern Breton *reguenn*). From it Low Latin
got *riga*, French *raie*, and Provençal *riga*. In Latin the word
existed in the form *porca* [1] " a furrow " (*porculetum* ; Umbrian
porculeta). Germanic produced modern German *Furche*
(O.H.G. *furh*, *furuh*), English *furrow*, and Old Icelandic *for*.
All these words come from one word, **prko/a*, the formation of
which is clear. It contains an element *-ko*, which is added to
prepositions or adverbs to form adjectives and nouns, as
in ἐπισσός = ἐπι-*k*-*yo* (ἔπισσαι, " younger daughters "),
and περισσός = περι-*k*-*yo*. The first element is *per*,
the preposition meaning across. The idea is of a line
drawn across a field. This word does not exist in Irish, and
perhaps it never did. The corresponding word is *etrech*,
which in modern Irish is *eitre* or *eitriach*, with plural *eitreacha*.
An ancient form *etarche* is given in the *Sanas Cormaic*.
But it has been formed in the same way as the other. It is
composed of *etar* + *k* + *yo*. *Etar* is the Irish equivalent of
inter. These two formations are absolutely parallel.

This example is most instructive. The Indo-European

---

[1] This seems to be proved by the Germanic in the concordance of Welsh
rhych, Latin *porca*, and Mod. German *Furche*.

dialects, before they were finally differentiated, were, like all primitive unwritten languages, very fluid. Out of a fairly few elements they made a great variety of fairly mobile combinations. Their needs of expression were amply supplied by comparatively humble instruments, and they doubtless used more than one equivalent for the same requirement. When dialects were improved it was not only by increase, but also by selection. Sometimes one equivalent remained in use, sometimes another.

There are other accidents of language, which are yet more obviously arbitrary, for they are intentional and deliberate. These are the disappearances of words on account of religious scruples. They have been studied by philologists for some time past. Certain names were avoided and replaced by approximations—those of the pig, the bear, the bee, certain degrees of kinship, and others.

When we study the vocabulary of the Celtic languages we find a fairly large residue of words which do not appear elsewhere. Most of them are produced by derivation from other words. A very large number are quite modern ; the ancient forms are too uncertain for it to be possible to say anything about them. Some may be vestiges of the most distant Indo-European past.[1] Still there are some left over. Are they an Iberian or Ligurian inheritance ? This remnant does not, so far, seem to me of great importance.

The facts of grammar and phonetics can be interpreted in the same way. According to one linguistic theory, that of *Lautverschiebung*, or permutation of consonants, which created some stir and will be examined in the volume of this series dealing with the Germans, the modifications to which Germanic subjected the grammatical and phonetic structure of Indo-European, are due to the fact that Germanic was an Indo-European language learned by a non-Indo-European people.

We can see examples of languages changing for ourselves. In France French is spoken by a whole part of the nation, which had another language of its own, but has adopted French as its language, namely the people of the Midi, of the *Langue d'oc.* They speak French with a pronunciation of

---

[1] Meillet, CCXVI, p. 2.

their own, different from that of other Frenchmen. If a strictly phonetic spelling were adopted for French there would be a danger of it breaking up into more than one language, with a common vocabulary but different phonetics.

French itself is a result of the changes which the phonetic habits of the Gauls brought into Latin. For example, they introduced *u*. Here is another example. The name Mézières comes from the Latin *maceria*. When the Latins came to Gaul Gaulish was in process of changing its surd gutturals, such as *k*, to *chuintantes* [1] and sibilants. I have chosen this instance because the word has also been adopted by the Brythonic of Britain. But in Britain Latin never became a popular language. Such borrowings as were effected were of a learned kind. *Maceria* produced *magwyr* in Welsh and *moger* in Breton, both meaning " wall ". These learned borrowings always show an uncertainty in pronunciation : *magwyr* comes from *măcēria*, having *a* for *ă* and *wy* for *ē* ; *moger* comes from *mācēria*, with *o* for *ā* and *e* for *ē*.

The Celts of the British Isles altered Germanic as the Gauls did Latin. For instance, the Britons imposed their cerebrals on English.

When a people adopts another language it brings some of its old habits of speech into it, or else it distorts it in its efforts to form new sounds and new associations of sounds. Thus the non-Indo-European Germans introduced curious changes, similar to those to which their descendants still subject the words which they borrow.

But if the Germans were not Indo-Europeans, we may ask whether the Celts were. They, too, altered the aspect of Indo-European phonetics, and we shall see that in more than one point the Celtic innovations coincide with the Germanic.

These new considerations of linguistic ethnography very much obscure the old picture which students tried to make of the descent and relationship of the Indo-European languages. They tend to give a much larger part to the aborigines, the associates, the vanquished, in the final result of the analysis. On the other hand, our belief in the dialectal unity of the parent languages from which the kindred languages are descended is strengthened, for we must now

---

[1] Sounds represented in French by *ch* and *j*, sometimes called " blade-point consonants " or " spirant palatals " in English. Trs.

presume that we are dealing with single languages which fell apart as their speakers came into contact with different peoples.

But to return to Celtic, we should note that its phonetic innovations are not to be compared to the chief innovation of Germanic, which started the arguments mentioned above. This consisted in the change from easily pronounced consonants—*b*, *d*, *g* (sonants), to consonants whose pronunciation requires more effort, the surds—*p*, *t*, *k*, *q*—and from these to aspirates and then to spirants—*f*, *Þ*, *χ*. All the consonants of a borrowed language are pronounced with an effort. To pronounce a language with greater difficulty than it is naturally pronounced may be the case of a foreigner who is making an effort to speak it, or already speaks a language whose sounds are less easy.[1] But the modifications peculiar to Celtic were not such as made the previous pronunciation more difficult. Far from it. Celtic was on the road of phonetic laziness, the normal cause of change in a language. We have evidence in the dropping of *p*, a perfectly articulated surd consonant being replaced by a mere breath. The intermediate stage was probably marked by the consonant being pronounced as a spirant ; *p* must have become *f*. Therefore, while Germanic, in view of the aspect of its phonetics, may be regarded as a borrowed language, it is not so with Celtic. From this point of view, the Celts show themselves Indo-Europeans by origin, not by adoption.

They evidently met on their way with peoples whose speech was not Indo-European. Some they may have assimilated. Their language incorporated non-Indo-European elements. But these elements do not appear in its phonetics, and they are hard to discover in its vocabulary. In the composition of Celtic the old Indo-European predominates enormously. This is an established fact of great importance.

We now have to consider the parent dialect which produced Celtic as it extended its domain, and, with that object, to compare Celtic with the languages of the neighbouring peoples. This inquiry cannot fail to give us valuable indications about the history of the Celts.

---

[1] Meillet, **CCXVI**, p. 6.

CHAPTER III

LANGUAGE (*continued*)

I

THE *CENTUM* GROUP AND THE *SATEM* GROUP

PHILOLOGISTS have made a first classification of the Indo-European dialects into two groups according to the way in which the initial consonant of the word meaning hundred developed. The word began with a palatal, which among some peoples became a sibilant, while with others it remained an occlusive. There are *satem* peoples and *centum* peoples. The Hindus say *çatám*, the Iranians said *satem*, and the Lithuanians *sziṁtas*, whereas the Latins said *centum*. The Goths said *hund*, the Greeks ἑκατόν. The Irish said *cét*, now *céad*, and the Welsh say *cant*. Celtic, therefore, is one of the *centum* languages.[1] The value of the distinction appears problematical and the attachment of Celtic to the *centum* group of little significance, if we remember that French, which is one of the heirs of Celtic, has transformed the Latin occlusive into a sibilant. But one should mention the matter.

But let us consider Fig. 1 for a moment. This diagram, devised by M. Meillet,[2] shows the Indo-European languages grouped according to their affinities. At the same time it shows their topographical distribution. The vertical diameter divides the *satem* peoples from the *centum* peoples. Each group is continuous. The dialects of each have been spoken by peoples which are or were neighbours. We shall see other evidences of their kinship. The symbol chosen is not perhaps the most expressive possible, but the thing symbolized is certain.

One group is missing from the diagram, namely the Tokharians of Turkestan. They, surrounded by peoples which spoke languages of the *satem* type, Indian or Iranian, spoke languages of the *centum* type. But we have more than

---

[1] S. Feist, **CCCXXVI**, p. 50.　　　　[2] **CCXVI**, p. 134.

one reason for believing that these Tokharian dialects have affinities with the Western group of Indo-European languages.

The slanting diameter which runs right across the diagram sets apart, in the same half of the ellipse, the Balto-Slavonic, Germanic, Celtic, and Italic tongues. This grouping expresses a different kind of relationship from that which associates Greek with the three last-named dialects to the left of the vertical diameter. The peoples of North-Western Europe had a certain number of roots in common, which the others lacked. They had bonds of civilization, a common life.

It may be said, without much danger of error, that the Indo-European languages have the same relationship to one another as the geographical areas which they cover. It is

Fig. 1.   The Indo-European Languages, arranged according to their affinities. (Meillet, *Dialectes européens*, p. 134.)

highly probable that the affinities of various kinds existing between these dialects fairly represent racial affinities of the peoples.

II

THE WESTERN GROUP : ITALIC, CELTIC, AND GERMANIC

As we follow up this comparison between the Celtic and the other Indo-European languages, two groups of languages seem by the nature of things to call for attention at the outset, namely the Germanic and Italic tongues.

The former covered an area which was continually in contact with that of the Celtic languages, and it is also probable that Celtic and Italic were spoken in neighbouring regions before the Italici settled in their peninsula,[1] and that the Gallic invasion of Italy merely revived contacts which had existed in prehistoric times. In view of the relationships which appear between these two groups and Celtic, one might possibly regard them as one family, the Western family of the Indo-European languages,[2] which, moreover, would show considerable associations with two other neighbouring groups, the Baltic and the Slavonic [3] (which belong to the *satem* group). Confining oneself to Celtic, Italic, and Germanic, one might suppose that these three groups formed a single unit comparable, to some extent, to that formed by the Celtic languages among themselves, but more comprehensive and differentiated earlier and more completely. But the matter is not so simple as that.

Of the phonetic and morphological facts in which the relationship of these three linguistic groups is shown, some may, perhaps, date from the remotest past of Indo-European and be features of one of its dialects.[4] But there are others which appear as absolute innovations, the most important of which is the modification of the linguistic rhythm. Now, the rhythm is a very stable element of a language, and still more so of a way of speaking and pronouncing. In Indo-European the accent of a word seems to have been very weak. It was musical ; it fell anywhere, according to the sense. In Celtic and Italic, as in Germanic, the qualitative rhythm of Indo-European deteriorated. The accent gradually became an accent of stress, fixed to a definite place, usually the first syllable, which finally assumed a preponderant position in the word. A fact of this kind may be attributed to the influence of foreign elements, probably in part the same elements, entering in different proportions into the formation of the three groups of peoples concerned. Italic, which changed its abode, resisted these tendencies at first, but finally succumbed to them. " Germanic and Celtic, on the other hand, which remained in neighbouring regions,

---

[1] Meillet, **CCXVI**, p. 12.   [2] Ibid.
[3] Ibid., 2nd ed., Avant-propos, pp. 3, 5, etc.
[4] Ibid., Avant-propos, p. 2.

developed partly along parallel lines." [1] The parallelism is most complete between Gælic and Germanic.[2]

M. Meillet, in the work from which I have taken these remarks, points to other facts which seem to tell the same story [3]—in phonetics the weakness of the final, in consequence of the strengthening of the initial, the alteration of intervocalic consonants, the sensitiveness of vowels to the influence of neighbouring phonemes [4] ; in morphology the accentuation in the verb of the notion of tense, which is shown by the creation of special forms to express the preterite and the distinction of a past subjunctive. These last observations are equally true of the Baltic languages.

Moreover, the Western Indo-European languages have drawn on a common vocabulary. They alone possess certain roots, certain forms of the same roots, or certain senses which these roots may take.

Latin *hasta* represents a Western root which appears in Irish *gas* " stalk ", Gothic *gazds* " goad ", and Old High German *gert* " rod ".[5]

Latin *ueru* " spit " represents another, which produced Irish *bir* " point ", Welsh *ber* " spear ", and Gothic *qairu*.[6]

Irish *fáith*, genitive *fátha* " bard ", " soothsayer ", corresponds to Latin *vates* and modern German *Wuth, wüthen*, and probably *wuotan*.

Here, now, is the name of an animal : Latin has *merula* " blackbird ", probably for **misula*. Welsh has *mwyalch*, which comes from a primitive **meisalko-*, and Old High German has *meisa*. Modern German *Amsel* " blackbird " has a kindred root.

A root *vē*, which means " to blow " (Sanskrit *vāti* " he blows " ; *vāyuḥ* " wind " ; Lithuanian *vajas* " wind "), assumes the form of a participle in the Western tongues, " the blowing one " ; Latin *ventus*, Gothic *winds*, modern German *Wind*, Welsh *gwynt*. Irish *feth* " breath " is probably derived from the same root, but it is abnormal.

A root *bhu*, which means " to be " and has given φύσις

---

[1] Ibid., Avant-propos, p. 5 ; Paul the Deacon, i, 325 ; iii, 788 ; Dottin, **CXCVI**, p. 103.

[2] Meillet, p. 6. [3] Ibid., Avant-propos, p. 132.

[4] Ibid., Avant-propos, p. 5 : *uolo, uolens* ; *uelim, uelle*.

[5] Feist, **CCCXXVI**, p. 217.

[6] Avestic *grâva* " staff ", and Greek ὀβελός " spit ", which have been ascribed to this root, are a long way off from it.

("nature") to Greek, has been used for the Western languages in the formation of the verb of being : Latin *fui* " I was " ; Irish *buith* (**bhuti*) " to be " ; modern German *bin* " am " ; English *be*. There is complete concordance between Irish *biu*, Latin *fio*, and Old Saxon *biu*.

Now let us look at a case where it is various forms of one same root that show its continuity. Latin *liquidus* has a root **vleiq*, which has assumed different forms, *vl̥* and *volq*, from which come Irish *flechod* " rain " (subst.), *fliuch* " wet ", *folc* " a wave ", Welsh *gwlych* " wetness ", *gwlyb* " wet. ". Modern German *Wolke* " cloud " (Old High German *wolcha*) represents a variety of this same root, **vl̥g-*.

These similarities of vocabulary form a very large mass of facts [1] which is comparable to the similarities of Iranian and Sanskrit, and it is still larger if we add to it the words which also appear in the Baltic and Slavonic languages, whose connections with the Western languages deserve to be considered all together and more closely. So, then, Celtic seems to have been taken from a linguistic mass which might be the remains of an Indo-European dialect, split into several fragments.

But in the vocabulary, as in the grammar, the philologists try to discover the influence of foreign elements, in the shape of words whose structure is not clearly Indo-European. They point to the word for " apple ", which is *abal* in Irish, *aval* in Welsh, and *Apfel* in modern German ; the name of the town of Abella and the epithet of *malifera* (" apple-bearing ") which Virgil gives it [2] suggests that Italic once had the word and then lost it. This is one of the words which also belong to Baltic and Slavonic. There is a village named Aboul on the island of Œsel, Slavonic has *jabl̆uko*, Lithuanian has *ŏbŭlas*, and Old Prussian had *woble*.

III

CELTIC LANGUAGES AND ITALIC LANGUAGES

Apart from these features shared by Celtic, Italic, and Germanic all together, Celtic has some peculiarities in common

[1] Cf. Vendryès, **XCIII**, xxi, pp. 41 ff. : Lat. *nux*, Ir. *cnu*, Mod. German *Nuss* ; Lat. *salebra*, Ir. *sal*, O.H.G. *salo*.
[2] *Æn.*, vii, 740.

with one or the other of these languages. In come cases
one language of the group has had losses or a development of
its own ; in others there have been special relations between
two languages or the peoples which spoke them.

The Italic and the Celtic tongues present similarities of
structure which compel us to think that there were once
a great many more, which only disappeared after a separation
which does not seem to have occurred very early.[1] The
resemblance is of the same order as that subsisting between
the languages of India and the Iranian languages; that is, the
two language-groups to which the name of Aryan is best
confined. Now we have very strong evidence of a common
Aryan stock about 1400 B.C. In the inscriptions of Boghaz-
Keui, Indian and Iranian gods, who afterwards became
enemies, are mentioned together in the same invocation.[2]
There was one religion, one people, a common language.
No doubt it was the same with the Celts and the Italici.
It is usual to speak of the Italo-Celtic language and of an
Italo-Celtic stock. I have only to show that the separation
took place a little earlier.

The only Italic language of which we possess a complete
vocabulary, Latin, has absorbed a whole Mediterranean
lingua franca as a result of being transplanted into
Mediterranean life. Hence comes its kinship with Greek,
obscuring its Celtic kinship. Nevertheless, many fragments
of an Italo-Celtic vocabulary remain in the Italic languages.
There remain, for example, those important words,
prepositions, and prefixes to verbs.[3] Latin *de* corresponds to
Irish and Brythonic *di*[4] ; Latin *cum* to Irish and Brythonic
com or *co-* (*Combroges).

It is a strange coincidence that both groups have two
forms of the same adjective to say " other ", one from a stem
ali- and the other from a stem *alio*. The Italic group has *alis*
and *alid* (whence *alter*) from the former and *alius* and *aliud*
from the latter. Celtic also has two words, Welsh *eil* and Irish
aile, which correspond to their Latin equivalents letter for
letter. *Eil* means " the second ", like *alter*. The very illogical-
ness of this duplication is what invites credence.[5]

---

[1] D'Arbois, **CCC**, p. 10.   [2] Moret, **CCCLX**, English, pp. 303 ff.
[3] Meillet, **CCXVI**, p. 37.   [4] Sommerfelt, **CCXXXIII**.
[5] Walde, **CCXLIII**, s.v. " alius."

There are semantic resemblances, morphological resemblances, common roots, common forms of a same root, common meanings. From a special root $\sqrt{gn\bar{e}}$, meaning " do ", Latin has kept *gnāvus* (from **gnowo-*), Irish has *gníu* " I do ", *gním* " deed ", *fogniu* " I serve ", and *fognom* " service " and Welsh has *gweini* " to serve ".[1] The root $\sqrt{g^{w}ei}$, which means " life ", has given *vita* to Latin and *bwyd* " food " to Brythonic.[2] The root $\sqrt{ner}$, which appears in Sanskrit and Greek in words meaning " man ",[3] appears in Irish as *nert* " strength " (Gaulish **Nerton*, as in Nertomarus), in Sabine as *Nerio*, with the same meaning, whence the name Nerio, the wife of Mars, and in Umbrian as *nerf* (accusative plural), the dead, that is the Strong Ones.[4] *Terra* corresponds to Irish *tir*[5]; *tellus* to Irish *talam*.[6] With *sœculum*,[7] from a stem **saitlo*, are connected Welsh *hœdl*, Old Breton *hœtl*, and the name of the Gallic goddess Setlocenia. And there are other instances.[8]

The phonetic and grammatical similarities are of even more weight.

We shall consider the chief resemblance in phonetics— the change from $p \ldots k^{w}$ to $k^{w} \ldots k^{w}$, which gave words of the *quinque* type to Latin and words of the *coic* type to Irish, and the transformation of k^{w} into p in Brythonic and Osco-Umbrian[9]—when the time comes to extract its full significance.[10]

The grammatical similarities are morphological resemblances in declension and conjugation.

The genitive of stems in *o* was formed in *i*: Segomaros, Segomari = *dominu-s*, *domini*. In Old Irish, *maqi* was the genitive of *maqos*, and in Middle Irish *fir* was the genitive

[1] Ibid., s.v. " nāvus."   [2] Ibid., s.v. " vīta."
[3] 'Ανήρ, *nar* = Skt. *nāra*.   [4] Ibid., s.v. " neriosus."
[5] Ibid., s.v. " terra " ; Vendryès, **XCIII**, xiii, p. 385.
[6] Walde, s.v. " tellus."   [7] Ibid., s.v. " saeculum."
[8] Vendryès, " Un Rapprochement celto-ombrien," in **CXL**, 1914, p. 212; Loth, " Notes étymologiques," ibid., 1917–19, p. 314.
[9] Meillet, **CCXVI**, p. 33.   Other resemblances are : The treatment of ṛ, ḷ, and ṇ before a vowel as *ar*, *al*, and *an* (ibid., pp. 33 ff.) ; the change from *bh*, *dh*, *gh* to *b*, *d*, *g* (Dottin, **CXCVI**, p. 98) ; the passing from *gw* to *b* (Philipon, **CCCLXIX**, p. 204). Cf. Windisch, **CCXLV**, pp. 390, 393.
[10] Windisch, **CCXLV**, pp. 390–4 ; cf. **XXX**, 1918, p. 71 ; Meillet, op. cit., 2nd ed., p. 9 ; Moulton, **CCXXI**, p. 6 ; Taylor, **CCCLXXXVI**, p. 192 ; Giles, **CCII**, p. 26 ; Meillet and Cohen, **CCXVIII**, p. 53. The similarities of Celtic and Italic institutions and rites will be discussed in the following volume in this series.

of *fer* (* *uiro-s*), the *i* of the root-word being due to the *i* of the lost termination, of whose existence it provides evidence.[1]

In both groups the superlative was formed by adding -*samo*-, whence come Latin -(*s*)*im*- and Celtic -(*s*)*am*- or -(*s*)*em*-, to the positive. " Nearest " is *proximæ* in Latin, *nessimas* in Oscan, *nesimei* in Umbrian, *nessam* in Old Irish, and *nesaf* in Welsh. Modern German, on the other hand, says *nächste*, and the other Indo-European languages have a formation in *st* : Sanskrit *svadiṣṭhaḥ*, Greek ἥδιστος, Old High German *zuozisto*, whence *süsseste*.[2]

The verb systems of the two groups, which are fairly different from Indo-European and are in part refashioned from new sources, present the same innovations. Both have the future in -*bo* and two forms of the subjunctive. *Amabo* and Faliscan *carefo* are like the Irish futures in -*f* and -*b* : *legfa*, *ni legub*, from *legaim* " I read ".[3] *Feram* is equivalent to Irish *bera*,[4] *faxim* to Irish *tiasu*, *teis*.[5]

The forms of the middle voice with a reflexive meaning (cf. Greek λύομαι " I wash myself ", λύει, λύεται) disappeared in Latin [6] and in Celtic, whereas they survived to some extent in Germanic.[7] To take its place, Latin and Celtic created what is called in Latin grammar the deponent, the inflexion of which in certain forms is marked by final *r* and is the same in both languages down to the smallest detail : *loquor* = *labrur* ; *loquitur* = *labrithir* ; *loquimur* = *labrimmir*.[8]

---

[1] D'Arbois, **CCC**, p. 10 ; Meillet, op. cit., p. 35 ; id., " La Forme du génitif pluriel en ombrien," in **XCIII**, 1922, p. 258 (gen. plur. in *o* : Umbrian *fratrom* ; Irish *fer*, from *uiron*, whence oghamic -*a*) ; Pedersen, **CCXXVII**, i, p. 248 ; ii, p. 84 ; Windish, **CCXLV**, p. 395.

[2] Meillet, op. cit., p. 37. Suffix -*tei* broadened by a nasal suffix : *natio*(*nis*) ; Irish *toitiu* (gen. *toimten*) " thought " (cf. *natine*, an Umbrian ablative). Windisch, op. cit., p. 395. Suffix -*tāt* : *unitās* (*tātis*), Irish *oentu* (gen. *oentath*).

[3] Meillet, op. cit., p. 37 ; Vendryès, **CLXXXI**, p. 557, and **CXL**, xlii, p. 387.   [4] Meillet, op. cit., p. 36.   [5] Ibid.

[6] Ibid., p. 35 : Except in the first person singular of the perfect.

[7] Gothic *bairada*, from *bairan*.

[8] Vendryès, **CXL**, xxxiv, pp. 129 ff. Gaulish had the same conjugation (Loth, **LVIII**, 1916, p. 175 ; Dottin, **CXCVI**, p. 123). The deponent, like the Greek middle, is used as an active for a certain number of words which express psychical operations, and so imply some reflexion of the subject about his own action, such as *reor*, *arbitror*. The semantic distinction between the deponent or middle and the active is a delicate thing, which tends to fade out. It disappears in Celtic. Moreover, as the semantic distinction goes, the corresponding forms disappear likewise. While they are more or less preserved in Old Irish, only a few scant traces of them remain in Brythonic (*gwyr* " he knows ").

In Latin the conjugation of the deponent is indistinguishable from that of the passive. Moreover, there are traces in Latin of an impersonal passive : *itur* " people go " ; *quom caletur* " when it (the weather) is hot " (Plautus, *Captivi*, 80). Umbrian had *ferar* " let someone carry " ; so, too, Oscan had *sakrafir* " let sacrifice be made ". This is the only passive that Celtic has. The Irishman, for example, says *berir* " it is carried ", " someone carries ". To express the first or second person passive the personal pronoun is added, either before or after the verb, in the accusative, as a complement : Irish *no-m-berar* " it (is) me is carried " ; *glantar mé, thú, é,* " it (is) me, thee, him is purified." It is the same in Brythonic : Middle Welsh *ym, yth gelwir* for " I am, thou art, called " ; in Modern Welsh one can still say *fe'm dysgir, fe'th dysgir,* as well as *dysgir fi, di* for " I am, thou art, taught ".[1]

The impersonal passive indicates that the action of the verb is being done or has been done. In this respect it resembles another form, whose termination also contains an *r*, namely the third person plural of the preterite (*fecere* " they made "). Celtic has the equivalent of this form. It has two preterites—a sigmatic preterite, with a sigmatic *s* added to the stem (*legsit* " they read ", from *legaim*), and a radical preterite, formed directly on the root-word, which is either reduplicated or lengthened. This latter preterite makes the third person plural by adding *r* to the termination *nt* ; for example, *lingim* " I leap ", *roleblangatar* " they leaped " (*nt* + vowel + *r*). But here we find ourselves on wider ground, for there is a similar plural in Sanskrit : *asthiran* " they held themselves ", the aorist plural of *sthā* " to hold oneself ". This usage, and its extension, constitute a fairly large system, but one which is on the decline ; and the fact that it survives in more complete form in Italo-Celtic than elsewhere is one of our best evidences of Italo-Celtic unity.[2] There is, however, one other language which presents the same features, with a few differences, namely Tokharian.[3]

[1] Rowlands, **CCXXXI**, p. 86.

[2] Dottin, **CXCVI**, pp. 122–3 ; Meillet, " Sur les désinences en -*r*," in **XLVII**, 1924, pp. 189 ff., shows that there is evidence for these terminations in Phrygian, Pseudo-Hittite (3rd pers. plur. of the preterite), and Armenian.

[3] Vendryès, **CXL**, xxxiv, pp. 129 ff.

Again, Italic and Celtic are at one in the formation of the passive preterite. It is composed of the same noun-form, the adjective in -to- : Latin *cantatus est* (cf. Oscan *teremnatust* = *terminata est*). So, too, Irish said *rocét*, from *canim*, " it was sung ".[1]

These are facts of great significance, these common innovations in the mechanism of the verb (that chief element in the sentence) and common loyalties to obsolete forms. The kinship and life together attested thereby must be regarded as an established fact before we start to look for the first home of the Celtic peoples and to study how they divided. We shall come across it more than once in the course of this work.

IV

CELTIC LANGUAGES AND GERMANIC LANGUAGES

The special affinities of Celtic and Germanic are quite different. Here agreements in vocabulary are far more interesting than phonetic or grammatical similarities. Indeed, examination of the grammar reveals a considerable gulf between the two groups of languages.

There are capital differences in the declension of the substantive and adjective.

(i) In Indo-European, nouns whose stem was formed by the addition of *o* or *a* to the root had their plural in *s*, while the *o* or *a* became long ; for example, *equŏs, equōs* (Sanskrit *açvaḥ, açvāḥ*). For this termination Greek, Slavonic, Latin, and Celtic substituted the old termination of pronouns : *poploi* (*populī*) ; Gaulish *Tanotali-knoi*. Germanic, alone of European languages, remains faithful to the ancient form : Gothic *fiskōs* " fishes " ; Anglo-Saxon *fiscas*. Hence come the plurals in *ar* (= *as*) of Old Scandinavian and those in *er* of Danish (*kjökkenmöddinger*).[2]

(ii) Germanic and the Slavonic languages have different inflexions for the adjective according as the adjective is, as it is called, determinate or indeterminate.

---

[1] Meillet, **CCXVI**, p. 35.
[2] D'Arbois, **CCCI**, ii, p. 330. Note, too, that Germanic has not the genitive in *i* of Italo-Celtic.

(iii) Old Slavonic, Lithuanian, and Germanic agree in marking the dative plural of the declension by a termination of which *m* was the characteristic feature : Gothic *vulfam* " to wolves " ; Lithuanian *vilkum* ; Old Slavonic *vlŭkomŭ*.[1]

(iv) The superlative in the Germanic languages was formed in accordance with the Indo-European type, as we have seen above. Old High German had *suozisto* (modern German *süsseste*),[2] like the Sanskrit *svádiṣthaḥ*, whereas Italic and Celtic had adopted a form in -(*s*)*amo*.

Germanic, therefore, is distinguished from the Celtic languages by peculiarities, some of which it shares with no other European language, while others connect it with the Balto-Slavonic languages of the North.

It has also peculiarities which mark it off from all the Indo-European languages. There is its famous permutation of consonants (*Lautverschiebung*),[3] and there is the quite special poverty of its verb forms. Germanic, while expressing the notion of time very vigorously, like the other Western tongues, has cut down the Indo-European verb to two tense-forms, one for the present and one for the past, sufficient to supply words for the singular and plural and for the indicative and subjunctive (*nehme, nahm, nähme*). It is a cut-down language, a language which has been learnt. The same hypothesis satisfactorily explains the two facts.

But if we must accept this hypothesis of the adoption of an Indo-European language by the ancestors of the Germans, it is not possible, as those who adopted it thought at first, that the language borrowed was Celtic,[4] or even Italo-Celtic. Really the Germans borrowed from more than one Indo-European language, Italo-Celtic among them.

Yet, different as they are in grammatical structure, the two families of languages show the most significant likenesses in their vocabulary. These have been frequently pointed out and interpreted.[5]

---

[1] Ibid., p. 333.

[2] Kluge, **CCX**, pp. 481–4.

[3] On *Lautverschiebung*, see above, p. 50.

[4] Feist, **CCCXXVI**, pp. 482 ff. Van Ginneken, in **CCIV**, pp. 475 ff., maintains that the change of surd explosives and aspirated sonants in Germanic into fricatives began inside words after vowels, liquids, and nasals, under the influence of the ancient Celtic, from 700 to 600 B.C. Cf. Loth, " La Première Apparition des Celtes dans l'île de Bretagne et en Gaule," in **CXL**, 1920–1, p. 261.

[5] D'Arbois, " Les Témoignages linguistiques de la civilisation commune

The name of the sun is common to both. In modern German it is *Sonne* (Old High German *sunno*), in Welsh *huan*, which, like *Sonne*, is feminine.[1] The Coligny Calendar gives a word *Sonnocingos*, which clearly contains the same word.[2] Celtic and certain Germanic dialects also had the root of *sol* in common with Latin.

An important group of common topographical terms meaning the ground, accidents of the ground, the adaptation of the ground to human life, is of some interest, because it may tell of a life lived in common in the same region[3] : English *floor*, modern German *Flur*, is the same word as the Irish *lár* and Welsh *llawr*. It is from an ancient *plāros*. Gothic *waggs*, used to translate παράδεισος, and Old Icelandic *vongr* " field " seem related to Irish *fagh*, meaning " territory ". Gothic *sinps* " road " (whence *Gesinde* " servants ", " the people who accompany you on your way "), is the same as Irish *sét* and Welsh *hynt*. Modern German *Rain* " ridge " (Old High German *rein*, meaning " rampart of earth ", " boundary between field and wood "), is the same as Irish *roen* " road ", and Gaelic *raon* " field ". It gives us a vision of rather swampy country, where roads could only be on raised embankments. English *wood* (Old High German *witu*, which is found in the name Widukind) is the same word as Gaulish *vidu-*, which appears in Viducasses, *vidubion*, Irish *fid*, and Welsh *gwydd*. These words mean " trees ", " timber ", " a forest ".

There are many technical terms, the names of materials, such as metals and instruments.[4] Modern German *Eisen*, Gothic *eisarn*, is the same as Gaulish **isarno-* (in *isarnodori*, glossed by *ferrei ostii*), Irish *iarn*, and Welsh *haiarn*. Old High German *lôth*, English *lead* (the metal), is the same as Irish *luaidhe*. Modern German has another word, *Blei*, of uncertain origin.

So one can make up a long list of words which are both

aux Celtes et aux Germains pendant les V⁰ et IV⁰ siècles av. J.-C." in **CXLI**, 3rd ser., xvii, p. 187 ; id., " Unité primitive des Italo-Celtes," in **LVIII**, 1885, pp. 316 ff. ; id., **CCCI**, ii, p. 330 ff. ; Kluge, **CCXI**, i, pp. 234 ff. ; Bremer, " Ethnogr. der germ. Stämme," in Paul, **CCCLXVII**, ii, pp. 787 ff. ; Pedersen, **CCXXVIII**, i, pp. 21 ff. ; Dottin, **CXCVI**, p. 128 ff. ; Meillet, *Lang. germ.*, pp. 208 ff. ; Munsch, s.v. " Kelten ", in Hoops, ii, p. 26 ; Meillet and Cohen, **CCXVIII**, pp. 65 ff.

[1] Kluge, **CCX**, s.v. " Sonne ". [2] Dottin, op. cit., pp. 175, 191.
[3] D'Arbois, **CCCI**, ii, pp. 359 ff. [4] Ibid., p. 362.

peculiar and common to Celtic and to Germanic, or, more correctly, to the whole extent of the Germanic world. These words are substantives.

Do they come from a common parent-tongue ? Were they borrowed by one language from the other ?[1] There are words which Celtic borrowed from Germanic, but that happened quite late, and we need not linger over them. They are, in particular, the words which Irish took from the Scandinavian tongues in the time of the Vikings. There are authenticated cases of borrowing by Germanic from Celtic.

First of all there is a series of words which have not undergone the Germanic permutation of consonants, and were probably borrowed after that practice had ceased, or, at least, after it had ceased to affect spelling.[2] Gaulish *carruca*, whence comes French *charrue* (" plough "), gave to Old High German *charruh*, modern German *Karch*. Gaulish *keliknon* " tower ", " upper storey ", was taken over unchanged by Gothic. Modern German *Pferd*, Old High German *pferfrit*, comes from Gaulish *paraveredus*. We should note that a great number of words dealing with horses and vehicles are common to Germanic and Celtic, and there is every chance in the world that the former got them from the latter.

English *breeches* (Old Icelandic *brok*) comes from Gaulish *braca*.[3]

Other words were borrowed by Germanic after Celtic had lost *p*.

German *Land* comes from a Celtic **landâ*, which produced Irish *lann* and Welsh *llan*. In the Middle Ages it meant both waste land and the ground surrounding a church. It comes from the root of **plānus*.

German *Leder* " leather " comes from a Celtic word represented by Irish *lethar* and Welsh *lledr*. The root contained the *p* of Latin *pellis* and English *fell*.

In the presence of these facts some scholars, like d'Arbois de Jubainville, have been led to suppose that many

---

[1] The question is discussed systematically in Kluge, **CCXII**, p. 325.
[2] Ibid., ii, p. 324 ; Feist, **CCCXXVI**, p. 482.
[3] Here the derivation may have happened the other way round. Vendryès, **CXL**, 1912, p. 377.

words were borrowed before the Germanic permutation of consonants took place or the Celtic languages lost *p*.[1]

Among the terms common to both groups of languages, there is a whole series of political, legal, and military words. Some of them were certainly borrowed from Celtic, and it is hard to deny that all were.[2] The Gaulish *ambactus*, meaning " servant " (ἀμφιπόλος), but in a sense which tended towards that of " minister ", gave O.H.G. *ambaht*, with the same meaning, and German *Amt*. Gothic *reiks* " prince " and *reiki* "kingdom" come from Gaulish *rīx* and -*rigion* (Irish *ríge*), not from Indo-European *rēx* and the associated words. The Indo-European *ē* would have become *â* in German. The resemblance of the following words is explained in the same way :—

Irish *oeth*, German *Eid*, English *oath*.

Irish *luge* " oath ", Gothic *liuga* " marriage ". Here the borrowed word has been given a more special meaning.

Irish *fine* " family ", Old High German *wini* " husband ". Old Scandinavian *vinr* means " friend " (the same specialization).

Welsh *rhydd* " free ", modern German *frei*.[3]

Irish *giall* " hostage " (*geislos*), modern German *Geisel*.

Irish *orbe* " inheritance ", modern German *Erbe*.

Irish *air-licim* " I lend ", represents a Celtic word corresponding to Gothic *leihvan* and modern German *leihen* " to lend ".

Old Breton *guerth* " value ", " price ", represents the prototype of Gothic *wairþs* and modern German *Werth* " value ".

Modern German *Bann* " order ", comes from a Celtic word represented by Irish *forbanda* " legal order ".

Now for terms of warfare :—

Modern German *Beute* comes from a Celtic word *bōdi*, which is found in the name of Boudicca (Boadicea), Irish *buaid* " victory ", and Welsh *budd* " prey ", " booty ".

Modern German *Brünne* " breastplate" comes from a Celtic word represented by Irish *bruinne* and Welsh *bronn* " chest ".

---

[1] Feist, op. cit., pp. 170, 482 ; Kluge, **CCXI**, p. 787.
[2] D'Arbois, **CCCI**, ii, pp. 335 ff. ; id., **CCXCIX**, p. 170.
[3] From an Indo-European form *prijo-s* ; cf. Skt. *priyaḥ* " loved ". D'Arbois, **CCCI**, ii, p. 337.

The war song of the Germans, the *barditus*, bears a name, the origin of which can be perceived through Welsh *barddawd*, the science of the bards. It was a song sung by the Germanic bards. In all ages, as we know, the best equipped and best ordered troops have supplied others with their military vocabulary.[1]

The similarities of the Celtic and Germanic vocabularies bear witness to a long period during which they lived together. If we suppose that the Celts and Germans ever spoke the same language their intercourse went on long after their dialects were separated. But it is hard to believe that they were ever brothers in speech, in view of the different structures of their languages.[2] Probably they were only brothers by adoption. The most characteristic instances quoted may be explained as borrowing by Germanic from Celtic. They are the borrowings of a people which goes to another for things and ideas of civilization, for things and ideas designated by substantives. The Celts seem to have been for long ages the schoolmasters of the Germanic peoples. Perhaps one may go further still ; I am very much inclined to believe that one cannot dismiss the hypothesis which has already been put forward, particularly by d'Arbois de Jubainville, that some political relations existed between the Germans and Celts, whatever may have been their nature—alliance, domination, or the formation of a common *Reich*—and whatever their extent.[3]

So the relations of Celtic and Germanic are of a very different kind from those of Celtic and Italic. In the latter case we have two languages born of a parent tongue which lies not very far behind, and in the other the formation of a common stock of words due to the contact of two peoples, one of which was much influenced by the other, at different times, in any case from an early period, and without their ever ceasing to be neighbours.

In this influence of Celtic on Germanic it is not possible to determine the proportionate share of each of the Celtic

[1] We may add some religious terms : e.g. Old Saxon *nimid* (*de sacris silvarum quae nimidas vocant ;* cf. d'Arbois, op. cit., p. 377 ; Feist, op. cit. p. 354) = Gaulish *nemeton* ; and the name of Velleda among the Bructeri = Irish *ban-file* " prophet-woman " (see the following volume in this series).

[2] Kluge, **CCXI**, p. 324 ; Mansion, **CXXXI**, lvi, pp. 191–209 ; **CXL**, 1914, p. 387.

[3] D'Arbois, **CCCI**, ii, p. 323 ; Bremer, in **CCCLXVIII**, iii, p. 787.

dialects. The ancestors of the Irish may well have been in contact with the Germans, no less than the Britons and the Gauls. Secondly, the borrowed words are found in the Eastern and Northern dialects of Germanic, such as Scandinavian and Gothic, as well as in the Southern and Western.[1] All the Celtic world influenced all the Germanic world. Its influence extended even beyond and through the Germans to the Balto-Slavs and the Finns.

V

CELTIC LANGUAGES AND BALTO-SLAVONIC LANGUAGES
THE VOCABULARY OF THE NORTH-WEST

It has already been observed above that the signs of kinship with the Western languages extend in part to the Slavonic and Baltic tongues. But philologists have been especially struck by the fact that these languages have in common a great number of words which are lacking in Indo-Iranian, Armenian, and Greek. They therefore infer that all North-Western Europe had a vocabulary of its own, as opposed to the Mediterranean vocabulary.[2] These represent two areas of civilization, two areas of intercourse. It is needless to demonstrate that one of them was the Mediterranean basin. The belt in which the North-Western vocabularies are supposed to have been used was the scene of cultural events of a general nature which are revealed by prehistoric archæology—the spread of the rite of incineration in the Bronze Age, the diffusion at the same time of pottery of the Lausitz type,[3] and the amber-trade.[4] All these mean

---

[1] Fischer, **CC**, 1909, No. 85. Cf. **CXL**, 1912, p. 377. As we see, Celtic cannot be shown to have supplied Germanic with all its Indo-European words. Germanic has words in common with Latin which are lacking in Celtic ; perhaps it got them from Italo-Celtic. But it also has words which are part of the common stock of the Indo-Europeans and are lacking in Italic and Celtic. It has even some which it shares with the Indo-Iranian languages alone ; e.g. such a religious word as the Old Icelandic *draugr* " ghost ", which is the same as the Vedic Sanskrit *druh* and the Avestic *druj* (Feist, op. cit., pp. 189, 191, 195, 214, 223 ff., 263).

[2] Meillet, **CCXVI**, i, p. 17, on the vocabulary of the North-West.

[3] Déchelette, **CCCXVIII**, ii, i, p. 385 ; Hubert, " La Poterie de l'âge du bronze et de l'époque de Hallstatt dans la collection de Baye," in **CXLIII**, 1910, pp. 5 ff.

[4] Déchelette, op. cit., ii, i, pp. 623-7.

intercourse within a given belt, the climate of which, more-over, is much the same throughout, suits the same crops, and bears the same flora. Communications of this kind are calculated to encourage interchange among languages; some words correspond to the features of civilization which are found in the two different parts of the belt, while others are picked up by men going about in it. We may suppose that there was a lingua franca for North-Western Europe as there was for the Mediterranean.

The Italic languages extended their domain southwards, and the Celtic languages south-westwards, of the great plain of Northern Europe, to which the North-Western vocabulary belonged, but they had their share in it. In its Mediterranean evolution Italic drew close to Greek, but many similarities prove that it is connected with the languages of the North. So, too, Celtic contains many words which have equivalents in the Slavonic languages on the one hand, and in the Baltic tongues—Lithuanian, Lettic, and Old Prussian—on the other. It is an interesting fact that both Italic and Celtic preserve, as records of their origin, their share of the Northern vocabulary.

Long lists have been drawn up, from which we shall draw with due caution. Of the words contained therein, some are shared only by Celtic and the languages mentioned (the question of borrowing has even been raised, as in the case of Germanic), and the rest appear also in Germanic and in Latin.

All these languages had one same word for the sea. They pronounced it differently—Celtic with an *o, mori* (Morini, Aremorici), Irish *muir*, Breton *mor* ; Latin with an *a, mare* ; Germanic and Balto-Slavonic with an *ŏ* or an *ă*, Old Icelandic *marr*, modern German *Meer*, Slavonic *morje*, Lithuanian *maris*.[1]

Some of the words in which these languages agree refer to social life, such as the word for " people ", which appears in the following forms : Irish *tuath*, Oscan *touto*, Gothic *þiuda*, Lithuanian *tauta*. A root *val-vla*, meaning " power ", " greatness," " territorial dominion," " territory," comes into Latin *valere*, modern German *walten*, and Slavonic *vladi*, and is represented in Celtic by Irish *flaith* " dominion ",

---

[1] Meillet, op. cit., p. 22. For the following words, see ibid., pp. 18 ff. ; Berneker, **CXCI**, s.vv.

" territory ", and Welsh *gwlad,* whence comes *gwledic* " prince ".

Most of the common words deal with agriculture, plants, and animals. Old Slavonic *zrŭno* " seed " and Lithuanian *zirnis* " pea " correspond to Latin *grānum,* Irish *grán,* Gothic *kaurn,* and English *corn.* Russian *bórošno* " rye-meal " corresponds to the Gothic adjective *barizeins* " of barley ", Latin *farina,* and Welsh *barra* " bread ". The word for apple has been discussed above.[1] The pig, Latin *porcus,* was called *orc* in Irish, *farah* in Old High German, *pârszas* in Lithuanian, and *prase* in Old Slavonic. Latin *faba* " bean " corresponds to Old Prussian *babo.*

Naturally Celtic and Germanic present more similarities to the Baltic dialects, shared with them alone, than Italic does. The resemblances in Latin are survivals. Those in Germanic have been kept up by the relations of the two peoples as neighbours, and this is also to a great extent true of Celtic. The Baltic and the North Sea united the peoples which dwelt on their shores just as the Mediterranean did. It is possible, too, that in the centre of Europe the Celts had once been neighbours of the earliest Slavs as of the Germans.

The following words are found only among the Celts, Germans, and Slavs. There is a plant-name, variously used for the yew and the willow : Welsh *yw* " yew ", Old High German *iwa, Eibe* " yew ", Old Slavonic *jiva* " willow ". The word for the metal lead, *luaidhe* in Irish and *lôth* in Old High German, is found in Russian in the form *luda,* meaning tin.

The Balto-Slavonic languages have more likenesses to Celtic than to Germanic. This may be due to the loss of words by Germanic. But the resemblances may also be special and typical. Some of them consist of terms of abstract or general meaning relative to qualities, to manners of being, and bear witness to a common past, perhaps a remote one. Thus, Irish *cotlud* (gen. *cotulta*) " sleep ", " to sleep ", is a compound of a verb which Lithuanian possesses in its simple form *tuleti* " to be quiet ". Irish *gal* " worth ", " power ", is found in Lithuanian *galeti* " to be able " and Old Slavonic *golemŭ* " great ". Others are names of concrete

[1] P. 57.

things or social notions. For example, Irish *mraich*, *braich*, Welsh *brag*, Gaulish *brace* " malt ", correspond to Russian *braga*, with the same meaning. Irish *sluag* " troop ", corresponds to Slavonic *sluga* " servant " and Lithuanian *slauginti*. Mr. Shakhmatov [1] has drawn up a long list of words of the common Slavonic tongue, which he holds to have been taken from Celtic, but it is open to criticism. We must, however, suppose that some of the similarities between Celtic and Balto-Slavonic are due to the latter language borrowing words through Germanic or over the head of Germanic.

Even the Finnish languages borrowed some words from Celtic. But here there is no question of a common past. We only note these borrowings because they give an idea of the distance to which Celtic civilization shed its influence.

Some of the political and legal terms which Germanic took from Celtic were passed on to Slavonic and Finnish.[2] Such are : the word for debt, Old Irish *dliged*, to which Slavonic *dlŭgŭ* [3] corresponds, through Gothic *dulgs* ; the word for inheritance, *arbe* in Finnish ; the word for worth, *verta* in Finnish ; the word for kingdom, *rikki* in Finnish (these last two words were borrowed fairly late) ; the word for office, *ammatti* in Finnish.

In the above words it was probably the intermediate Germanic form that was borrowed. Celtic influence was only transmitted ; the connection might be quite close, but it might be very distant. As an instance of direct borrowing, on the other hand, we have Finnish *tarvas* and Celtic *tarb* " bull ". Here there is no intermediate Germanic word.

These facts show how Celtic civilization circulated and expanded in the cultural area of the north-west.

[1] In **XXIV**, xxxiii, pp. 51–99 ; **CXL**, 1912, pp. 391 ff. The author connects Russian *bojarinu* " leader " with Irish *bo-aire* " cattle-owner, landowner " ; Slavonic *otici* " father ", with Irish *aithech* " master of the house ". Many of the words in his list are common, not only to Celtic and Slavonic, but also to Germanic and Latin. Cf. Meillet, in *Revue des Études slaves*, i (1921), p. 190, n. 1 ; Lubor Niederlé, **CCCLXIV**, i, pp. 24 ff.

[2] D'Arbois, **CCCI**, ii, p. 348.

[3] Old Slavonic *dlugu* and Russian *dolgu*, from the root *dhlegh*, which gave *dliged* " duty, law ", to Irish, *indulgere*, *indultum* " authorization ", to Latin, and *dulgs*, " debt ", to Gothic, are derivatives from Germanic. See Vendryès, " La Racine occidentale *dhlegh*," in **CXL**, 1923, p. 429.

CHAPTER IV

Language (*concluded*)

I

CELTIC LANGUAGES AND INDO-EUROPEAN LANGUAGES OF THE EAST AND SOUTH-EAST. CONCLUSION

CELTIC came into contact with other languages than Germanic, Slavonic, and Italic. When the Latins and Umbrians went down into Italy they left the Celts uncovered on the east. In that quarter, various Indo-European languages were spoken, which it would be interesting to know, in order to have a complete notion of the affinities of Celtic. These were Illyrian, Thracian, Dacian, and Getic. The Illyrians had historical relations with the Greeks, and so did the Dacians, but how far did they go back ? There were certainly religious resemblances between the Thracians and the Greeks which may have come down from very ancient cultural relations. These various languages did not vanish without leaving a trace. Something of their vocabularies remains in those of the Slavonic tongues, Rumanian, Albanian, and Greek.

This last language is highly complex. It inherited something from the languages which were spoken on Greek soil before the Hellenes, properly so called, arrived there, and among these there were Indo-European tongues which we cannot classify. It also picked up many words from neighbouring dialects. The scholars of Greece were interested in these foreign elements in their speech, and faithfully collected them in their dictionaries.

Greek has a certain number of words in common with Celtic—either with Celtic alone or with it and other of the languages which we have been considering. Usually they are rare words,[1] or, to be more accurate, the most striking cases are rare words, that is, foreign words. Thus Greek, which is

---

[1] *Βρένθιξ*, Hesych., *Βρένθος*. Cf. Welsh *bryn* " hill " ; Gaulish, *ex monte Brenno*. Holder, **CCVII**, i, p. 525.

only distantly related to Celtic, has preserved words which
bear witness to languages which were much closer to it. For
example, the name 'Ακράγας contains a word κράγος, which
does not mean " cry ", but " rock ", like Welsh craig.[1]
The word may be Sicel or Ligurian ; now Celtic, like Sicilian
Greek, absorbed some of the Ligurian vocabulary. There are,
too, reciprocal borrowings, for which Greek travellers and
colonists were responsible. Greek πρῖνος " ilex " is Gaulish
prenne (Irish crann).[2] Old Irish meccon " root " and Gælic
meacan " carrot " recall Greek μήκων " poppy ", as do Old
Slavonic makŭ and modern German Mohn.[3]

Greek has also preserved some relics of the ancient
tongues of Asia Minor, some of which, such as Phrygian,
which is a form of Thracian, belong to the group of European
languages enumerated above, while the others are at least
in part Indo-European, such as Hittite. Here we can glean
a few similarities to Celtic.[4] Another descendant of these
tongues is Armenian, which is difficult to place exactly in
the body of Indo-European languages. It seems to be even
more distant from the Celtic group than Greek. The further
apart dialects lie on the map the fewer similarities do we
seem to find.[5]

Nevertheless, the two groups of Indo-European languages
whose areas are furthest removed from Celtic and which lie
at the opposite pole of the Indo-European expansion have
very singular affinities with it, the systematic nature of which
calls for attention.

---

[1] Pedersen, **LXX**, xxiv, p. 270.
[2] Boisacq, Dic. étym. lang. gr., s.v. πρῖνος ; Pedersen, **CCXXVIII**, i,
pp. 44, 159.
[3] Macbain, **CLXXXIX**, s.v. " meacan." Other resemblances which exist
between Greek and Celtic alone are so singular that they must be merely
apparent ; e.g. the similarity of Welsh cerd " art " to Greek κέρδος, and
that of Irish cian " long " to Greek κεῖνος (i.e. " distant "). Cf. Boisacq,
s.v. κέρδος ; Macbain, s.v. " cian."
[4] e.g. Δίνδυμος ; cf. Irish dind ; Old Icelandic tindr ; modern German
Zinne.
[5] The Celts of the British Isles have preserved several types of boats
made of hides over branches, which are called by the generic name of currach
or coracle—Irish curach, Welsh cwrwg, Low Latin curucus. These coracles
are exactly like the gufas of the Tigris and Euphrates, and many Assyrian
monuments portray these ancestors of the modern coracle. The various forms
of this vessel were used in Armenia, as appears from the accounts of the
Armenian campaigns of Assyrian kings. In Armenian, kur means boat.
This very striking coincidence does not seem to be mere chance. It is tempting
to connect the word with an Indo-European root, that of corium " leather "
(Macbain, **CLXXXIX**, s.v. " curach." See below, p. 195, n. 2).

The kinship of Celtic and Indo-Iranian is shown by a common vocabulary, but this only contains a very few words which really count—a few craft-terms, if any, the feminine forms of the nouns of number " three " and " four ", and a considerable group of religious or politico-religious words. In this domain, Italic has much in common with Celtic, and both with Indo-Iranian ; institutions have even been preserved which correspond to this vocabulary or explain its preservation.[1]

Celtic has two words to designate religious belief, Irish *crabud* (Welsh *crefydd*) and Irish *iress*. There is nothing corresponding to them except in Indo-Iranian, namely Sanskrit *viçrabdhah*, meaning believer, and Pahlavi *parast* " worshipper ". Sanskrit *çraddha* " confidence in the virtues of the offering " has equivalents in Latin *crēdō* and Irish *cretim*.[2] Latin *jus*, preserved in Irish *huisse* (**justiios*), corresponds to Zend *yaoš* (Sanskrit *yoḥ*). The word for king is the same in both groups : Sanskrit *rāj* (stem *rāj*) and *rājan-*, Latin *rex*, Celtic *rix*. The root meaning " drink " has kept the same form : *pibāmi*, *bibo*, Irish *ibim*. To drink the sacred liquor is an essential part of worship. Lighting the fire is another, and here, too, the roots reappear and can be recognized by their nasals : Irish *-andaid* " to light ", Sanskrit *inddhé* " he lights ". Greek says *αἴθω*. For milk, a religious drink, Irish has two words, both of Indo-Iranian kinship : *gert* " cream ", which recalls Sanskrit *ghṛtam* " rancid butter ", and *suth*,[3] Sanskrit *suláḥ* " pressed ", that is the *sómaḥ*. The root **bhewd* has given *bhāvayati* " he causes to prosper " to Sanskrit, the name of the god Faunus to Latin, and that of the goddess Buanann to Irish.

The Latin name Neptunus, which recalls the Irish Nechtan, one of the secondary names of the sea-god Nuada Necht, has often been connected with Sanskrit *napta-*, and the Irish *triath* or *trethan* " sea " with the Sanskrit name of the god Tritaḥ (Tritaḥ Āptyaḥ, Trita of the Waters), Zend *Þraētaonō*.[4] M. Vendryès adds to these names of water-gods,

---

[1] Vendryès, " Les Correspondances de vocabulaire entre l'indo-iranien et l'italo-celtique," in **XCIII**, xx (1918), pp. 265–285.

[2] Id., **CXL**, xliv, 90.

[3] On *suth*, see **XCIII**, p. 277. The word is preserved in a gloss of Cormac (*Sanas Cormaic*, ed. K. Meyer, p. 111, No. 1283).

[4] Pedersen, i, pp. 132, 179 ; cf. Greek Τρίτων.

the only divine names corresponding in the two groups, those of the rivers Sionann (Shannon) and Sindhuḥ, and that of the Danuvius and Zend *danuš* " river ".[1]

The affinities of the dialects now called Tokharian [2] with Celtic are grammatical, like those of Celtic and Italic. It has a medio-passive or deponent with verb-forms in *-r-*.[3] It also has, like Latin and Celtic, a subjunctive in *-a-*, taken from a stem different from that of the indicative.[4] I have already said that it belongs to the *centum* group of languages, and other analogies of structure have been pointed out.[5] These analogies, which are very unlike those of Celtic with Indo-Iranian, suggest a relationship something like that between Celtic and Italic, only blurred by time. The Tokharians lived in the Indian orbit, and were fed on Indian thought and literature, and their vocabulary shows the effect. It is the structure of their language which tempts one to seek kindred for them in the West. But are we to suppose that they travelled from Europe to Asia ? Prehistoric archæology has noted many traces of migrations from Europe to Asia, at dates which do not agree with that which can be assigned to the breaking up of any Western group to which the Tokharians could have belonged. I am convinced that there were other migrations, from Asia to Europe, at that very date.[6] I also believe that the discovery of Tokharian, like that of the Hittite inscriptions, compels us to move the cradle of the Indo-European tongues eastwards, and that they were to some extent differentiated before they expanded towards the West.

Some little contact with the Greeks or the peoples whose languages are unknown save through Greek forms ; frequent intercourse with the Balto-Slavs, either by immediate contact

[1] I shall return to the parallel between Celtic and Indo-Iranian institutions in the following volume.
[2] Meillet, **CLXII**, i, pp. 1–19 ; Lévi and Meillet, **XCIII**, xviii (1914), pp. 1 ff. ; Meillet, **CXXXVII**, Aug., 1912, pp. 136 ff. ; Pedersen, **CCXXVIII**, ii, pp. 396, 673 ; Feist, **CCCXXVI**, pp. 428 ff.
[3] Vendryès, " Les Formes verbales en *-r* du tokharien et de l'italo-celtique," in **CXL**, 1913, pp. 129 ff. : *aikemar* " I know " ; *dhatmasdhar* " thou art born " ; *ayitr* " he attributes to himself ". We may contrast the Latin line, *tunicaque inducitur artus* (Virg., *Æn.*, viii, 457), with the Tokharian sentence, *wastsi* (cf. *vestis*) *yamassitr*. Cf. Meillet, **LXXV**, 1911, i, p. 454.
[4] **LXXV**, p. 142 : *wärpnātr* " he admits " ; subjunctive *wärpatar*.
[5] Meillet, **XCIII**, xviii, p. 24.
[6] Feist, **CCCXXVI**, pp. 423 ff.

in the centre of Europe or through the Germans ; contact on a very wide front on the Germanic side ; more or less complete unity with the Italici at a fairly recent date, broken, however, as we shall see, before the Celts finally moved away to the West—these are the facts which first emerge from a comparative examination of the Celtic languages and the Indo-European tongues of Europe. The region in which these complex relations can have existed almost completely and simultaneously during the time when the Italo-Celtic community was breaking up is near the centre of Europe, probably round about Bohemia. The comparisons which have been made between Celtic and the Eastern branches of Indo-European—Indo-Iranian and Tokharian—open vistas into a more distant past ; they forbid us to place the separation of the groups which are geographically furthest from each other too far back, and suggest that the point of junction of the neighbouring groups should be shifted eastwards, where I shall not try to locate it exactly.

In defining the Celtic peoples by their speech, I based my definition on a factor which holds good for peoples which are completely constituted, however they may have been formed and whatever elements they may have absorbed, and it is so that I prefer to consider them. The brief comparative study which we have just made has given us much information about the element which supplied the language, or the bulk of the language, and the very definite affinities which it presents with the most distant groups of Indo-European leave no doubt that that element was of the same stock as the speakers of those tongues. But it has shown from the very first, unfortunately not in at all a clear manner, that the composition of the Celtic peoples was complex, and that in the differentiation of their languages a share must be ascribed to the alien tribes which they absorbed.

II

IBERIAN, LIGURIAN, AND RÆTIAN

The ancient Greek and Latin writers from whom we obtain some of our information about the Celts mention them in the West of Europe in opposition to two peoples which inhabited

large areas, the boundaries of which changed from time to
time and are very problematical—the Iberians and the
Rætians—and these peoples themselves evidently stand
for many others.

The ancients speak of the Iberians as being in the British
Isles. Is this because of the likeness of name between the
Iberians and the people after which Ireland was called, the
Hibernians ? Or is it on account of the great number of dark-
skinned folk in the West of England, which struck Tacitus ? [1]
In the time of Cæsar the Iberians were spreading very much
into Gaul in Aquitania.[2] In another direction they are said
to have occupied the whole of Italy and also Sicily, the earliest
historical inhabitants of which, the Sicani, are supposed
to have been Iberians.[3] In the Iberian Peninsula, which they
had long shared with the Ligurians,[4] the Iberians appear
to have been so long established that we can hardly take them
for anything but aborigines.

But the problem is quite clearly presented, and admits
of several solutions. One consists in identifying the Iberians
and the Basques, who are supposed to be the inheritors of
their language in modern Europe. Although this view has
its adherents, it is hardly tenable from the point of view of
language,[5] and indefensible from that of archæology.[6] The
Basques are the remnants of prehistoric populations confined
in the Pyrenees. We have already seen that the comparison
of Basque with the Celtic tongues leads to nothing. If
Iberian were represented by Basque we should evidently
learn nothing about the part played by the Iberians in the
constitution of the Celtic societies from philology.

Next, the Iberians have been connected with the Berbers
of North Africa, whose languages had already been compared
to Basque.[7] Herr Schulten and his Spanish pupils and
colleagues, Sr. Bosch Gimpera among them, have given
a scientific form to this solution of the problem [8] in a series

[1] Philipon, **CCCLXIX**, p. 296 ; Tac., *Agr.*, 11.
[2] Caes., *Bell. Gall.*, i, 1 ; Strabo, iv, 1, 1 ; 2, 1 ; Philipon, **DXVI**, p. 302 ;
cf. d'Arbois, **CCXCIX**, p. 91.
[3] Philipon, **CCCLXIX**, pp. 304, 160, 305.
[4] Schulten, **DXVIII**, i, p. 54 ; Bosch Gimpera, **DIII**, p. 49 and passim;
Avien., *Ora Maritima*, 195 ff.
[5] Philipon, **DXVI**, pp. 1 ff. ; **CCCLXIX**, pp. 158 ff.
[6] Bosch Gimpera, op. cit.
[7] Philipon, **DXVI**, pp. 1 ff. ; Boudard, **DVI**, p. 92.
[8] Schulten, **DXVIII**, i, pp. 50–1 ; Bosch Gimpera, **DIV**.

of important works, in which they have supplemented these linguistic data by archæological arguments of great value.[1] In this way they have reconstructed a very convincing picture of the expansion of the Iberians in Spain.

M. Philipon, a pupil of d'Arbois de Jubainville, has on two occasions put forward another theory,[2] based on absolute distinction between the Tartessians and Iberians [3] and the elimination of the Ligurians from the Peninsula.[4] According to his view, the Tartessians occupied a large part of Gaul,[5] and the Iberians almost the whole country, at different but fairly recent dates. Both peoples were Indo-Europeans [6] who came from Asia, the former by way of the sea and Africa, the latter by land and the North.[7] M. Philipon has drawn up for the Iberians a vocabulary which is distinct from the Tartessian. It is based on geographical names and proper nouns in which he finds words which are plainly Celtic, like gurdus,[8] and others which have usually been assigned to Ligurian, such as Rhodanus (the Rhone), Sequana (the Seine), Isara (the Isère), Alba, and Albion,[9] and even Albis (the Elbe), which is certainly Germanic.[10] His vocabulary, therefore, is very like Celtic and not very different from Ligurian. The consequence would be [11] that Iberian left place-names all over France,[12] even the names of towns,[13] and also in Western Germany to the Elbe,[14] in Britain,[15] and throughout Italy, to say nothing of the traces of their journey from east to west.

Unfortunately, M. Philipon supports his ethnological conclusions with no archæological fact and very little chronology. To my mind, accepting as I do, with reservations,

---

[1] See below, pp. 282 ff.
[2] Philipon, **CCCLXIX**, pp. 151 ff.
[3] Ibid., p. 51.
[4] Ibid., p. 133.
[5] Philipon, **DXVI**, p. 53 ; **CCCLXIX**, p. 154.
[6] **DXVI**, pp. 50, 57 ff. ; **CCCLXIX**, pp. 155, 163, 165, etc.
[7] This would explain the red-haired Iberians of Silius Italicus (16, 472).
[8] Philipon, **CCCLXIX**, p. 159. See above, p. 37. The question of *briga* will be discussed below, pp. 293–4.
[9] Ibid., p. 299.
[10] Ibid., p. 300.
[11] M. Philipon also attributes words in -*asc*-, -*osc*-, to Iberian (see below).
[12] Ataravus, the Arroux ; Vesera, the Vézère. Philipon, op. cit., p. 300.
[13] Agedincum, Avaricum. Ibid., p. 303.
[14] Ambra, the Ammer ; Visera, the Weser ; Leisura, the Lieser. Ibid., pp. 295, 300.
[15] Tamaros, Isca. Ibid., p. 296.

many of M. Philipon's views, and regarding the ethnological testimony of the ancient authors as most important, the only set of archæological remains which could correspond to the area which may be defined with the aid of these selected data, is the series of tombs containing bell-shaped vases adorned with incised bands,[1] bored flat objects known as bracers or bowman's wrist-guards, conical buttons, and daggers of flint or copper, which are found from Sicily to the north of Italy, in Sardinia, in the Peninsula from Catalonia to Baetica and the neighbourhood of Lisbon, in France from the Pyrenees and Provence to Brittany, in the British Isles, in Holland, in the valleys of the Rhine and Danube, in Bohemia, and on the middle Elbe. It is just to these tombs containing bell-vases that the Sican period in Sicily may correspond.[2] Their area of expansion coincides in part with that of the megalithic monuments, but it is wider. The Iberian name is the last left to us to attach to that civilization of Western Europe, chiefly on the coasts, of which the megalithic monuments are the most distinguished representatives. If this is the case, the Iberian element must have formed a considerable ingredient in the composition of the Celtic peoples. It is therefore possible that in what survives of Celtic there is some Iberian, but it is difficult to place one's finger on it.

[1] Déchelette, i, pp. 549–552 ; A. del Castillo Yurrita, CCCIX.
[2] CCCIX, pp. 126 ff.

CHAPTER V

THE ARCHÆOLOGICAL EVIDENCE

I

ARCHÆOLOGICAL TRACES OF THE CIVILIZATION OF THE CELTS. THE CIVILIZATION OF LA TÈNE. THE GALATIANS AND THE GAULS OF ITALY

ARCHÆOLOGY has often been mentioned in the preceding chapters, for it is next to impossible to separate archæological and ethnological data completely in the history and prehistory of ancient peoples. Each set of facts helps to explain the other, and each fills gaps left by the other. Archæology brings together the scattered data of the ethnography of peoples whose civilization is known chiefly by remnants which it has left in the ground. These are legitimate indications of vanished peoples, like their place-names, to the full extent to which the postulate of ethnography, which represents and distinguishes peoples by their civilizations, is justified. Unfortunately they are incomplete indications, since from the period in which they help us to find traces of the Celts nothing has come down to us but somewhat scattered objects and ruins.

We must now take a general survey, as we did with the language, and run over all that it is strictly necessary to accept as known, in order to visualize the Celts on the archæological map of Europe, at least at the height of their greatness and expansion, before we can follow the whole of Celtic archæology in the order of its obscure periods. It is, it is true, begging the question to describe archæological finds as Celtic before we have tried to lay down the limits of the area covered by the Celts at the date of the objects discovered. But we can do so, starting from a certain point.

In drawing up the scheme of periods and ages by which time is measured with reference to prehistoric archæology, archæologists have distinguished a second Iron Age, which is also known as the Marne or the La Tène period,[1] after the stations or groups of stations taken as typical, and corresponds to a civilization which by common agreement is attributed to the Celts. We shall see presently that the attribution is justified. During the time when that civilization flourished, that is from the fifth to the first century before Christ, we know roughly the area over which the Celts extended. The area of the La Tène civilization coincides with it, or goes beyond it only to testify to the influence exercised over their neighbours by the Celts, who at the time were the ruling power of barbarian Europe.[2] That that civilization should be attributed to the Celts is as self-evident as that the language of the region should, and requires no proof.

But if proof is wanted, the data collected on the southern and south-eastern borders of the Celtic world, where the Celts came late and did not maintain themselves as a people, where they were in contact with peoples which have a history and whose civilization is known, are certainly decisive. Galatia would furnish the best, if it supplied many. We must wait on the excavations, which will one day show results.[3] In the meantime, the Galatians have given us the orthodox portrait of the Gaul. All the ancient monuments depicting Gauls are derived, more or less directly, from those which commemorated the great Gallic inroad of 279 B.C., the victories of the Kings of Pergamon over the Galatians settled in their neighbourhood, and various episodes in the wars of the East.[4] They represent Gauls of the La Tène epoch, with typical ornaments and arms—the characteristic torque and the horned helmet which tradition ascribes to them. The Dying Gaul of the Capitol has sunk down on

[1] General bibliography : Déchelette, **CCCXVIII**, ii, 3 ; Dottin, **CCCXXII**; Lindenschmit, **CCCXCIX** and **CCCCVI** ; Vouga, **CCCCXCIV** ; Allen, **CCXCVIII** ; Hoernes-Menghin, **CCCXXXIX** ; Smith, **CCCLXXXIV** ; Reinach, **CCCLXXIII** ; Morel, **CCCCLXXXIV** ; Montelius, **CCCLVII** ; Holmes, **CCCCXXXIII** ; Schumacher, **CCCCIX**, i.

[2] Siret, **DXXIII** ; Bosch Gimpera, **D** ; Pič and Déchelette, *Le Hradischt de Stradonič en Bohème* ; Parvan, **DXLVIII**.

[3] Reinecke, **CCCCVI**, v, p. 293, n. 2 ; R. Zahn (in **CLXIII**, 1907, pp. 638 ff. ; **XX**, 1907, p. 225) is endeavouring to find Galatians in the pottery of Gordion, Boghaz-Keui, and Priene.

[4] In this connection it is most important, for the study of Gallic weapons, to take into account the trophies and other monuments on which they are represented in Asia and Gaul. They add to what we already know, and they supply dates. Cf. Couissin, in **CXXXVIII**, 1927–8.

a shield with metal-work like that of the shields from the Marne cemeteries, especially those of that date ; his horn might have come from Gaul or Ireland ; his sword, unfortunately, is merely fanciful (see Plate I).

The excavations which have been systematically conducted in Italy for some years in the neighbourhood of Ancona have given results which are of great importance for the identification of the Gallic civilization. The first discoveries were made at Montefortino, two miles from Arcevia and twenty-five miles from Sinigaglia (Sena Gallica). This was in the territory of the Senones, who settled there after 390 B.C., but departed (or at least their chiefs did) after 285 B.C. Here there was found a cemetery of rectangular graves, lying east and west, in which the dead were buried stretched on their backs, surrounded by a whole paraphernalia comprising weapons, ornaments, and funerary vessels. A large number of the objects found in these tombs are of Etruscan make. But the tombs themselves are different from those of the country ; they are like those of Champagne, and contain exactly the same weapons as they.[1] It is a Gaulish cemetery, a Senonian cemetery, and, what is more, a dated cemetery.

Moreover, it is not an isolated case, for there is a whole series of cemeteries, from the Alps to the Apennines, which resemble those north of the Alps, period for period, in the funeral rites which have been observed in them or in part or all of the grave-goods.[2] Some lie in country which was actually occupied by the Gauls, others in Ligurian country which was subject to Gallic influence,[3] or in Venetian country which they encroached on or visited frequently.[4] The information furnished by the graves corroborates the picture which the ancients drew of the Gauls.[5]

---

[1] For Montefortino, see Déchelette, **CCCXVIII**, p. 1088 ; Brizio, in **CVI**, ix, 3 (1901), pp. 616 ff. ; cf. Déchelette, in **CXXXVIII**, 1902, i, p. 245. Later excavations have yielded gold objects adorned with figures just like those of the Gundestrup cauldron.

[2] Cf. Déchelette, pp. 1086 ff.

[3] Giubiasco, Ornavasso.

[4] Alfonsi, " Tomba pre-romana di Este del IV periodo," in **LIII**, 1911, p. 125.

[5]   *Aurea cæsaries ollis atque aurea vestis ;*
     virgatis lucent sagulis ; tum lactea colla
     auro innectuntur ; duo quisque Alpina coruscant
     gaesa manu, scutis protecti corpora longis.
          Virg., *Æn.*, viii, 659–662 ; cf. Sil. Ital., iv, 154–6.

In short, we know the civilization of the Gauls of Italy, and that gives us a certain foundation for ascribing to the Gauls a similar civilization which we find elsewhere—namely, the civilization of La Tène. There are compelling reasons for ascribing it to the Gauls of the fourth and following centuries, and strong grounds for supposing that it was peculiar to them. The remains of that civilization, from its beginning onwards, will be described in this chapter as archæological indications of the Celts.

With regard to the La Tène civilization, certain archæologists and historians have made a mistake which must be corrected. The Celts have been the subject of a false argument in archæology similar to those committed with regard to them in anthropology. Such indications as we possess have been given a too general significance, and they have been taken to mean that La Tène civilization and the Celts were one and the same thing. One school[1] has in this way abbreviated the history of the Celts in Ireland in the most misleading way, making it begin with the earliest La Tène objects found in the island. It is necessary here, at the outset, to state, as a matter of principle (we shall have to prove it later), that the civilization of La Tène really corresponds to only one of the groups of the Celts, who had split up long before the fifth century before Christ. It is the culture of the Continental Brythons,[2] who afterwards became leaders of the other groups. It is not that of the Goidels of Ireland. The civilization of the Celts became uniform later, in consequence of the overflow of the Brythons over the whole Celtic world.

Moreover, the Celts left relics of civilization in the ground before the La Tène period. But these cannot be defined *a priori* as Celtic ; they do not bear the recognizable stamp of a Celtic civilization, and before we can attribute one or another series of objects to the Celts it will be necessary to examine systematically all the historical and linguistic evidence which leads one to look for the presence of that people at the places where the objects have been found. It does not seem to have been until the fifth century B.C.

---

[1] MacNeill, **CCCXLI** ; Macalister, **CCCCXXXIX**.
[2] Déchelette, p. 575.

that Celtic society attained the degree of development and self-consciousness implied by the production of a distinct and complete style for every kind of tool, weapon, and decoration. The finds of the La Tène period present just the homogeneity and originality that one would expect in such a civilization and such a stage in the life of a people. When, therefore, we inquire whether some set of earlier remains is to be put down to the Celts, we have to arrange in chronological series all that preceded the La Tène civilization in certain regions and led up to it. Thus, the exposition which follows in this chapter will serve as a basis for our inquiry into the archæological materials for the history of the Celts.

In the course of it we shall make an analysis, as we did with the language. The material which makes a civilization for the archæologist is made up of elements ; it is a compound, like the civilization itself. The La Tène culture, homogeneous and original as it is, has clearly been influenced from outside and has its foreign ingredients. Thus it reveals some of the relations which the Celts had with their predecessors and their neighbours.

Lastly, this civilization displays variations which are certainly not due to mere chance. We may try to attach them to one or another group of the Celtic peoples, or to one or another Celtic nation. In this respect archæological research is one of the methods by which we may resolve the problems which history will put to us. We shall take due note of these variations when the time comes to do so.

II

THE LA TÈNE CULTURE AND ITS SUBDIVISIONS. THE STATION OF LA TÈNE

The civilization with which we are dealing is now most usually known by the name of one of its chief centres.[1]

The station of La Tène has been known for a long time,[2]

[1] Id., pp. 911–941 ; E. Desor, " Les Constructions lacustres du lac de Neuchâtel," in **CIX**, 1864, p. 63 ; Vouga, **CCCXCIV**.

[2] It was brought to light in 1857 by the level of the lake falling. The first excavations took place in 1874.

but quite recent excavations [1] have made our knowledge of it very complete. It stands at the outflow point of the Lake of Neuchâtel, by the side of an ancient bed of the Thielle. At first, since it was covered by the waters of the lake, it was taken for a lake-village. Really it was a post on the edge of the water, with bridges and store-houses on piles, guarding the lake and the river, a military post, and one where there had been fighting. There were found many fragments of harness and vehicles, weapons of all kinds, the tools needed in the station, and skeletons which told of tragic episodes in its history. It was probably a toll-station.[2] The Gauls made

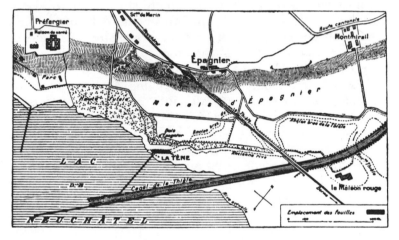

MAP 2. La Tène. (Vouga.)

profit from the trade-routes,[3] and La Tène commanded that which led from the Rhone to the Rhine and another connecting the valleys of the Rhone and the Doubs. Tolls may have been paid in kind, and the proceeds piled up in

[1] V. Wavre and P. Vouga, " La Tène. Fouilles de 1907," in **CIX**, 1908, pp. 59–69 ; " Fouilles de 1908," ibid., 1909, pp. 229–237 ; Vouga, " Troisième Rapport. Fouilles de 1909," " Quatrième Rapport. Fouilles de 1910–11," and " Cinquième Rapport, 1912–13," ibid., 1910, pp. 183–9, 1912, pp. 7 ff., and 1914, pp. 49–68 ; " Note sur les fouilles de 1917," ibid., 1917, pp. 94 ff. ; id., **CXVIII**, 1912, p. 218 ; **XVII**, 1915, pp. 196–222 ; Heierli, **XLVIII**, iv, p. 105.

[2] Déchelette, p. 939.

[3] Thus, Dumnorix levied tolls for the Æduan country (Cæs., *Gall. War*, i, 18).

the store-houses, unless the post contained an entrepôt for other purposes.

The choice of the name of La Tène for the civilization in question is not altogether happy, for the site only represents one period of that civilization. Nor is it any better to call it, as some do, after the hundred and ninety-one cemeteries of the Marne.[1] These have yielded earlier types, but not the whole series. No one site covers the whole range of those few centuries. As for the expression " Late Celtic ",[2] used by British archæologists, which suggests the idea of the latest developments of Celtic civilization in the British Isles, one does not know at what moment to start using it, and it leads to hopeless contradictions about the date of the first Celtic settlements in that region. In spite of the disadvantages of the terms, therefore, I shall speak of the " La Tène period " and the " La Tène civilization ".

I should mention, before proceeding further, that its chronological development falls into a system of periods regarding the definition of which there is general agreement. There are three periods, known as La Tène I, II, and III. This system was instituted by the German archæologist, O. Tischler.[3] For some years another system, distinguishing four periods, one of which is intermediate between the so-called Hallstatt epoch (first Iron Age) and that of La Tène, has come into favour.[4] This first period is called by the letter A, and the other three, which correspond to the old classification, are likewise marked by letters. The arrangement is based on the observation of data in Germany. At the end of the development of the Hallstatt civilization, the appearance of the objects changes, and they assume forms which announce the coming of the later culture. This latter, which we shall continue to call La Tène, appears earlier in Germany than elsewhere. This observation takes us a step nearer one of the conclusions to which we are moving.

---

[1] Déchelette, p. 929.
[2] CCCLXXXIV, p. 83. Similar ambiguities arise from the use, in German, of such terms as *Früh-La-Tène*, *Spät-La-Tène*, as in Forrer's " Früh-La-Tène-Gräber bei Blosheim," in LIV, 1919, p. 983, which deals with La Tène II.
[3] Tischler, in LXI, 1885, p. 157 ; Reinach, in LIX, Monaco, 1900, p. 427.
[4] Reinecke, CCCCVI, pp. 1, 7, 11, 13 ; CCCXCIX, v, pp. 50, 57, 8, 15, 51.

The forms assumed in succession by the objects of each of the classes which we are about to examine can be classified chronologically according to these periods.

III

WEAPONS OF OFFENCE

The objects to which the civilization of La Tène has given a style are weapons, jewels, and other articles of wear, and vases of earthenware and metal. We shall examine them in turn, starting with the weapons.

Of offensive weapons the most characteristic is the sword. Moreover, the sword seems to have been the chief weapon of the men of this civilization.[1] It is fairly frequent in the tombs, although economy may have been exercised with regard to it.[2] Moreover, these swords seem to be good, well-forged weapons,[3] in spite of the contrary remarks of Polybios in his account of the campaign of the Consul C. Flaminius against the Insubres in 223.[4] The swords of the Gauls, he says, bent at the first stroke, and had to be straightened with the foot. The Gallic sword of La Tène I was so good that it was probably adopted by the Romans. Those of the third century had defects, but these were tactical, not technical.[5]

The tactics of the Gauls, like those of the Romans, consisted in the close combat with the sword, the attack being prepared by volleys of javelins. It was *infantry* fighting, at least at the beginning. In any case, the infantry were always more numerous than the cavalry. In Cæsar's time there were in Gaul large forces of mounted nobility, but these

---

[1] Jullian, **CCCXLVII**, ii, p. 195. On the divine nature of the sword, see d'Arbois, **CCXLVIII**, i, p. 73.

[2] To tell the truth, many tombs of armed men contain no sword. That means that it was so precious that the survivors did not always sacrifice it for the sake of an uncertain future life. Chiefs may have been regularly buried in battle-gear or state costume. Common men were probably content with scanty funeral furniture. Here, as elsewhere, I attach more importance to positive evidence than to negative.

[3] Déchelette, ii, 3, p. 1129.

[4] ii, 53 ; Plut., *Cam.*, 41. Cf. S. Reinach, " L'Epée de Brennus," in **XV**, 1901, p. 344.

[5] Livy, xxii, 46 : At the battle of Cannæ the Iberians and the Gauls had the same weapons, but the Gauls cut, while the Iberians thrust.

were not the mass of the army.[1] The use of chariots, which preceded that of cavalry and still existed in Britain when Cæsar came, did not affect tactics. Troops engaged with

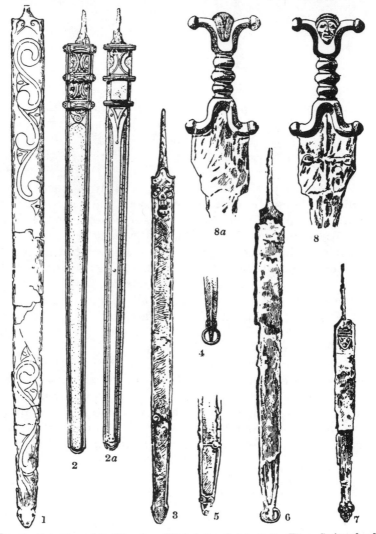

Fig. 2. Swords and Scabbards. (Déchelette, ii, 3.) 1, La Tène, Switzerland (fig. 463). 2, R. Witham, Lincs (fig. 645). 3, La Tène (fig. 459.) 4, The Rhine at Mainz. 5, Castione, Ticino. 6–7, Marson, Marne (fig. 457). 8, Chaumont, Hte.-Marne (fig. 474).

[1] The army of Vercingetorix contained only fifteen thousand horse in the last rising of Gaul. Cæs., *Gall. War*, vii, 64 ; cf. Cic., *Pro Font.*, fr. 12.

the sword, and the chariots were mingled with the infantry.[1]
It was the same with all the Celts, for the old Irish poems
describe the same tactics.[2]

This form of fighting, common to the Celts and Latins,
was very different from that of the Greeks. The Greek
phalanx was a body armed with long, heavy spears. For the
Greek hoplite, the sword was an auxiliary weapon, not the
chief one. Like the medieval knight, he only resorted to it
when his spear was broken.

The swords of La Tène are of quite a peculiar kind.[3]
They are derived from the latest type of Hallstatt sword.
This was a dagger, from 16 to 24 inches long, the hilt of which
branched out into antennæ of various shapes. The edges
were sharp and straight, and to a certain point parallel.
The scabbard ended in a chape, which took two forms :
sometimes it terminated in a ball, and sometimes in a crescent
or fish-tail. In the history of weapons one sees alternately
the dagger lengthening into a sword and the sword con-
tracting into a dagger. Some La Tène swords still have the
remains of the antennæ of the Hallstatt dagger. But the
kinship of the two types is chiefly shown by the chape of
the scabbard. The earliest La Tène swords have an open-
work chape (Fig. 2, Nos. 4, 6). The ends of the crescent of
the Hallstatt chape have grown longer and come round to
meet the edges of the scabbard. The Gauls were in the habit
of giving life, as it were, to structural forms, and the horn
of the crescent, curving like a swan's neck, was given a swan's
head, often with a piece of coral for the eye. The early swords
are still fairly short ; the average length is from 24 to
26 inches. The scabbards were of metal—first bronze, and
then iron. The mouth curved upwards in the shape of an
arch, and fitted into the guard, the shape of which we do
not know.

The sword grew longer steadily. Those of the second
period of La Tène are about 96 inches long. The handle

---

[1] Tacitus gives a description of a typical battle of this kind (without,
however, properly understanding it) in *Agr.*, xxxvi. The cavalry was at first
employed in the same way, mixed with the infantry.
[2] d'Arbois, **CCXLVIII**, vi, pp. 332–3, 340.
[3] Déchelette, ii, 3, pp. 1107 ff. ; **CCCLXXXIV**, p. 58, fig. 56 ; p. 59,
fig. 58 ; Nicaise, **CCCCXXXV**, pl. iv ; Vouga, **CCCCXCVI**, coll. 31–45 and
pl. i–viii.

remains as before. The scabbard still has an arch-shaped mouth. It is usually of iron. Whether it is of iron or of bronze, it is often adorned with fine engravings (Fig. 2, No. 1). The chape has altered ; the horns of the crescent have been flattened right down on to the scabbard, and the open-work has gone (Fig. 2, Nos. 1, 3).

The latest swords are still longer. The scabbard has a straight mouth, and is often made of wood. There is no trace of the original form of the chape. The scabbard has no ornament, and is bound with a network of wire which is a development of a transverse bar which existed on earlier types. The point of the sword has been rounded off (Fig. 2, No. 2). It is a wholly different weapon from that of La Tène I.

When the weapon intended for close combat can only be used for cutting, the warrior needs a second weapon with which he can thrust. This is almost a general rule. So we find the dagger with antennæ reappearing, this time with an " anthropoid " handle (Fig. 2, Nos. 8, 8a). This weapon is derived from the earlier swords, in which the end was still pointed, and the mouth of the scabbard and the chape recall the swords of La Tène II.[1]

The sword was slung on the right, not the left, and from a waist-belt, not a baldric.[2] The strap which held it ran through two rings and a metal loop at the upper end of the scabbard. The belt did not consist of a metal chain, as Diodoros says ; it was only partly of metal, being a leather strap ending in bronze or iron chains which formed the two sides of a clasp. These belt-ends are often found in Gallic tombs.

The late La Tène swords found in Britain, which were made locally after the conquest of Gaul by the Romans, have the suspension-loop about the middle of the scabbard. They must, therefore, have balanced differently. There are other peculiarities about them. The hilt sometimes ends in a globular pommel, like those of the Hallstatt swords. The chape spreads out into a winged form, and is derived from

---

[1] Déchelette, ii, 3, pp. 1137 ff. ; S. Reinach, in **XV**, 1895, pp. 18 ff. It is hardly probable, as M. Reinach supposed, that these daggers, which are found far apart but are not numerous, are of Helvetian origin.

[2] Diod., v, 30 : ἀντὶ δὲ τοῦ ξίφους σπάδας ἔχουσι μακρὰς σιδηραῖς ἢ χαλκαῖς ἀλύσεσιν ἐξηρτημένας παρὰ τὴν δεξιὰν λαγόνα παρατεταμένας.

those of La Tène II.[1] They were, too, pointless swords, used
only for cutting.[2]

These swords are quite different, not only from the straight
sword and κοπίς of the Greeks,[3] the iron sword used in Italy
before the country was united,[4] and the curved sword which
the Iberians are commonly supposed to have used [5] at the
time when the Roman army might have adopted it, as it is
alleged to have done, but also from the Germanic imitations
and adaptations with two cutting edges or one single one.[6]

Heads of spears and javelins [7] are much more frequent
in the stations and tombs than daggers and swords. It is
difficult to tell spear-heads from javelin-heads, and it is not
always possible to distinguish them from those used in other
periods and by other civilizations. The oldest resemble the
Hallstatt types,[8] being long and shaped like a willow-leaf,
sometimes with a not very pronounced midrib. Some are
very long, measuring from 16 to 20 inches. In La Tène II spear-
heads become broader [9] and assume fanciful shapes. Some
are flame-shaped, with sinuous edges, others have crimped
edges, and others have pieces cut out of the edge or middle.
Some are very finely decorated. The heads of spears and
javelins are either socketed or tanged.

One often hears of a javelin which was peculiar to certain
Celtic nations, namely the *gaesum* ; its shape is not known.[10]

A recent find of arrow-heads in a Marne burial has settled
the much disputed question as to whether the bow was used
in Gaul.[11]

[1] Déchelette, ii, 3, p. 1123 (cf. figs. 466, 464).
[2] Tac., *Agr.*, xxvi. It should be noted that the late La Tène sword of
the British type is shorter than its predecessors, probably in imitation of the
Roman *gladius*.
[3] Daremberg and Saglio, **CCCXV**, s.v. " Copis " ; Déchelette, ii, 3, p. 1125.
[4] Déchelette, p. 1137, n. 1.   [5] Ibid., p. 1134.
[6] Ibid., pp. 1126, 1132.   [7] Ibid., pp. 1143 ff.
[8] Ibid., ii, 2, p. 744.
[9] Diod., v, 30, says that the Gauls had spears with heads a cubit long
and nearly two spans broad.
[10] A. J. Reinach, " L'Origine du pilum," in **CXXXIX**, 1907, i, p. 424.
The Gaulish cemeteries of the Pyrenees and Spain have yielded javelins
with long shafts of iron, the σαύνια ὁλοσίδηρα, *soliferrea*, which, according
to the ancient writers, the Iberians used (Déchelette, ii, 3, p. 1151). A more
frequent type of javelin has a long prolongation of the socket (ibid., p. 1147 ;
cf. A. Blanchet, " Note sur le *gaesum*," in **CXL**, 1904, p. 229, on a Roman
denarius bearing the figure of a Gallic warrior casting a broad-headed javelin).
[11] A. J. Reinach, " La Flèche en Gaule," in **XV**, 1909, p. 14 ; Vouga,
CCCCXCIV, pl. xiv.

IV

DEFENSIVE ARMOUR

The commonest arm of defence was the shield, which is represented by a great number of bosses and a few plates found at La Tène.[1] For a long time the Celts, like almost all the peoples of Northern and Central Europe, used round targets of wicker or metal.[2] The shield of the Celts of history, Gauls and Irish,[3] was a large, long buckler, oval or oblong in shape, and sometimes fairly narrow. They were recognized by this shield.[4] Except the square shield with double bosses found in the Hallstatt tumulus at Huglfing, near the Würm-See in Bavaria,[5] our oldest evidence for it consists of artistic representations—a sword-sheath of La Tène I, found at Hallstatt (Fig. 19), on which warriors carrying shields are engraved,[6] Italic vases adorned with figures, like the Certosa *situla*,[7] and a stele at Bologna,[8] all dating from just before the great Gallic invasion of Italy. But no trace of a shield has been found in the tombs of La Tène I.[9]

The shields of La Tène II had the " trigger-guard " boss, consisting of a strip of metal rising into an ellipsoidal half-cylinder, the flat wing on each side being riveted to the surface of the shield. Another type had in addition a brace running in a ridge down the axis ; this is the shield of the Dying Gaul (Plate I), and it appears in the monuments commemorating the Galatian wars and in works derived from them. A more useful representation from this point of view is a statue found at Mondragon, in Vaucluse, now

[1] Vouga, op. cit., pls. xv–xviii. Shields similar to those of La Tène have recently been found in Denmark, in a boat of that period (" Oldtidsbaaden fra Als ", in **CCCCI**, pp. 21–3, figs. 11–12). These are Celtic shields adopted by the Germans.

[2] On these shields, see Déchelette, ii, 3, pp. 1167 ff.

[3] Joyce, **CCCCXXXIV**, p. 124. This is the shield to which the Irish word *sciath* and Welsh *ysgwyd* are applied.

[4] In the reliefs of Osuna, in which warriors appear, some bearing round targets and others large oblong shields, the latter represent Gauls (P. Paris and A. Engel, " Une Forteresse ibérique à Osuna," in **CXIII**, xiii). The auxiliary at Borgo San Dalmazzo is shown to be a Ligurian by his target.

[5] Déchelette, ii, 2, p. 719 ; Naue, **CCCCII**, pp. 46, 100, pl. xv ; id., in **CXXXIX**, 1895, 2, p. 55.

[6] Déchelette, ii, 2, p. 770, fig. 297.

[7] Hoernes, **CCCXXXIX**, p. xxxii.

[8] **CVI**, ix (1901), p. 56 ; cf. Grenier, **DXXIX**, pp. 455 ff.

[9] Déchelette, ii, 3, p. 1167.

PLATE II

WARRIOR FROM MONDRAGON
Avignon Museum

[face p. 92

at Avignon (Plate II).[1] This shows that the shield of
La Tène II must have been still in use at the time of the
Roman conquest. Most of the bosses found in the trenches
at Alesia are of this form.[2]

But a new type had been introduced, with a conical boss,
attached to the surface by a circle of metal, rivetted on.
This is represented on the arch at Orange,[3] on an altar found
at Nîmes,[4] and in the statue of a Gallic chieftain found at
Vachères (Basses-Alpes) (Plate III).[5] It has lately been
put forward that these bosses should be regarded as
Germanic, because the Germans adopted and developed
them.[6] Cæsar's German cavalry are supposed to have left
some at Alesia. It is more likely that the Gauls copied them
from the armament of the Romans, which they readily
imitated, than from the Germans, who were still subject to
Gallic influence.

The British shields of the first centuries before and after
Christ still recall that of La Tène II by their pointed oval
boss.[7] The round boss also appeared in this country, but with
the wealth of decoration peculiar to British art.[8]

These Gallic shields were richly ornamented and bore
emblems [9] ; for example, those represented on the arch at
Orange and that found in the River Witham with the emblem
of a boar. The Gauls were organized in clans, and clans have
always had their own colours and emblems. The Scottish
clans still have colours ; those of the other Celts must have
had them once.

The rank and file wore no breast-plate. It is part of the
gossip of ancient history that the Gauls fought stark naked.[10]
The Gauls of the East, however, adopted the Greek breast-

---

[1] Espérandieu, **CCCXXV**, No. 271 ; cf. the frieze at Nîmes, ibid.
[2] Déchelette, ii, 3, p. 1172 ; S. Reinach, **CCCLXXIII**, ii, p. 121. For
contemporary finds in Germany, see **CLX**, 1897, p. 348 ; 1899, p. 400 (grave
at Weisenau, peat-bog at Mainz).
[3] S. Reinach, op. cit., i, p. 45, fig. 36 ; cf. id., in **CXXXIX**, 1889, i, p. 201.
[4] Espérandieu, op. cit., i, No. 431.
[5] Ibid., No. 35.
[6] M. Jahn, in **LXXXV**, 1913, p. 75.
[7] Déchelette, ii, 3, p. 1175 ; **CCCLXXXIV**, pp. 104–6, figs. 114–115 ;
Kemble, **CCCL**, pl. xiv, 1 (shield from the R. Witham).
[8] Déchelette, p. 1176 ; **CCCLXXXIV**, frontispiece ; Kemble, **CCCL**,
pl. xv, 1.
[9] Diod., v, 30 ; Livy, vii, 10, etc. ; Dottin, **CCCXXII**, p. 213 ; Déchelette,
p. 1174 ; Joyce, **CCCCXXXIV**, i, pp. 127 ff.
[10] Diod., loc. cit.

plate.[1] The leaders wore it.[2] What is more, ancient Celtic had a word for it—Irish *bruinne*, French *broigne*. It can be seen on trophies and some other monuments. The ancients mention coats of mail.[3] Varro says that these were invented by the Gauls,[4] and their skill in metal-work makes this likely, but only late fragments of them are known.[5] The Vachères statue (Plate III) shows that these coats of mail had broad shoulder-pieces of the Greek type. Breast-pieces of scales are represented on the arch at Orange, and fragments of them have been found at La Tène.[6]

One usually thinks of the Gauls in helmets with plumes and horns. The arch at Orange shows these,[7] but only one actual specimen exists, and it is not like them. It is a bronze helm found in the Thames at Waterloo Bridge (Fig. 4, No. 4),[8] and consists of a plain metal cap with two conical horns. The helmets represented on the Gundestrup cauldron have analogies with this specimen.[9]

Most of the Gaulish helmets of the La Tène period are Italo-Greek helmets, either imported into Celtic countries or copied with the addition of elaborate Celtic decoration. The finest was found at Amfreville-sous-les-Monts (Eure).[10] It is covered with bands of ornament, some in embossed gold and the others inlaid with enamel. The decoration includes palmettes, more or less modified, at the level of the chin-strap, and a band of triskeles, standing for a vine-tendril motive (Fig. 4, No. 2). These helmets consisted of a head-piece of varying height, with a very short neck-guard and cheek-pieces which are often missing, but must always have been of the triangular type.[11] Sometimes the

---

[1] Lucian, *Antioch.*, 8. The Galatians who fought against Antiochos Soter wore breast-plates of bronze.
[2] Plut., *Marcel.*, 7, 8 ; *Cæs.*, 27.
[3] Diod., loc. cit.
[4] *De Lingua Lat.*, v, 24, 116.
[5] De Bonstetten, CCCCLXVIII, p. 3, n. 2.
[6] Vouga, CCCCXCIV, col. 57.
[7] Déchelette, pp. 1156 ff. ; monument of the Julii at St.-Rémy (Espérandieu, CCCXXV, i, p. 93) ; relief from La Brague (ibid., i, p. 31) ; trophy in the Vatican (Déchelette, p. 1157) ; bronze in the Berlin Museum (Schumacher, CCCCX, fig. 5).
[8] CCCLXXXIV, p. 107, fig. 116.
[9] C. Jullian, in CXXXIV, 1908, pls. 1–10.
[10] Déchelette, p. 1164 ; *Gaz. archéol.*, 1883, pl. 53 ; Coutil, *Le Casque d'Amfreville*, pp. 2 ff.
[11] Déchelette, p. 1161.

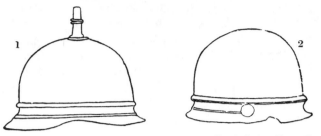

Fig. 3. Iron Gallic Helmets of La Tène III. (Déchelette, ii, 3, fig. 491.)
1, *Oppidum* of l'Hermitage near Agen. 2, Alise-Ste.-Reine, Côte d'Or.

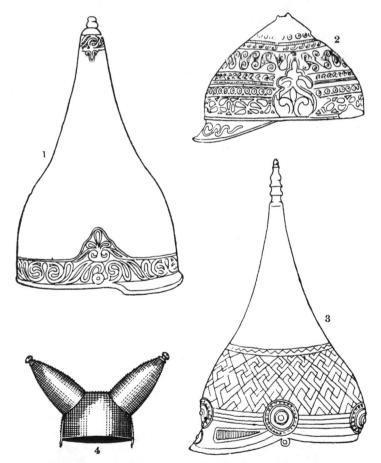

Fig. 4. Celtic Helmets of La Tène. (Déchelette, ii, 3.) 1, Berru, Marne.
2, Amfreville-sous-les-Monts, Eure. 3, La Gorge-Meillet, Marne (fig. 490).
4, Bed of the Thames (fig. 487).

head-piece was of a plain spherical shape, and sometimes it rose to a cone, with a knob on the top. These helmets with a terminal knob grew longer and were developed into a particular type of which the cemeteries of the Marne furnish some examples. The finest specimens, those of La Gorge-Meillet and Berru (Fig. 4, Nos. 1, 3), were adorned with studs of coral.[1]

The Gauls had a helmet of another kind, having a spherical head-piece round which ran a line in relief, with a concave band below it, from which the rim spread out, and asymmetrical cheek-pieces like those of the Roman helmet (Fig. 3). This helmet and its cheek-pieces have been found in the circum-vallations of Alesia. It is the helmet of La Tène III,[2] and it is also an Italic helmet; indeed, it is derived from bronze Italic models which are earlier than those from which the preceding Celtic types were copied, namely the great Hallstatt helmet with a double crest or its variant with a plain ridge.[3]

In fact, in the La Tène period as before, the helmets of Central Europe were always importations or copies. It must have been very difficult in the Gallic Wars to tell the helmet of a legionary from that of a Gaul. Moreover, helmets were rare. Most warriors fought bare-headed or in leather caps.[4]

V

ORNAMENTS AND ACCESSORIES OF DRESS

Brooches.—The Gauls were fond of ornament.[5] The finds of the La Tène period show this, although almost all the gold is gone and little but the copper remains of their jewellery. They made delightful things out of the hooks of their belts and the pins with which they fastened their

---

[1] Ibid., p. 1163. A helmet of the Berru type is shown on the Pergamon trophy (S. Reinach, s.v. " Galea " in Daremberg and Saglio).

[2] Déchelette, pp. 1165–6.

[3] The statuette of a warrior found in the necropolis of Idria in Istria wears a helmet of this type (Szombathy, in CIV, 1901, p. 6, fig. 9). Others have been found in that of Giubiasco. Gallic warriors were not all equally up-to-date in their armour, and one may occasionally have seen, as in the romances of chivalry, dinted old armour and, doubtless, ancient swords of forefathers.

[4] But all the warriors on the Gundestrup cauldron seem to have helmets.

[5] Diod., v, 27.

PLATE III

WARRIOR FROM VACHÈRES
Avignon Museum

cloaks (*sagum*).[1] Their *fibulæ* or brooches are of an originality and variety which make them especially instructive for deciding questions of date and race.

The La Tène brooch is derived from the Hallstatt brooch which immediately preceded it. This latter had a very arched bow, which tended to become slenderer than in the old types. The foot had grown much longer, and had a knob which kept the catch pinched together. The spring, formed of only a few coils, was on one side of the bow only.[2] At the very end of the Hallstatt period the spring had grown longer; it had been made to coil on both sides of the bow, and, at once leaping to the extreme of the fashion, was made so long that the brooch looked like a cross-bow.[3] At the same time the foot had been curved back, first slightly and then at a right angle. Such is the type named after the Certosa (Charterhouse), near Bologna (Fig. 5, Nos. 1–2), and it seems to be the point from which the La Tène brooches started. The Certosa brooch seems to have been native to Italy.[4] That of La Tène originated in a country which was in frequent communication with Northern Italy and was influenced by the fashions prevailing there.

The oldest La Tène brooches often have a highly arched bow. The foot is sometimes slightly turned up, and sometimes tends to curl back to the bow. There is a great variety of shapes. The makers experimented, and displayed ingenuity.[5]

Among the brooches with a slightly raised foot some have a fairly thick bow, moulded in quaint reliefs, the chief element in which is a human head. The knob is in the shape of a head (Fig. 5, No. 5). In some cases the decoration is carried beyond the head of the bow over the spring, on a broad tongue (Fig. 5, No. 7). Other brooches, of the same early period, have a curling-up piece on the head of the bow, and

---

[1] Sometimes brooches are found in pairs, joined together by a chain. In this case they fastened a cloak which hung over the shoulders and left the chest bare.

[2] Déchelette, ii, 2, p. 847.

[3] Ibid., p. 849.

[4] Ibid., p. 848.

[5] Ibid., ii, 3, pp. 1247 ff. ; Viollier, **CCCXC**, pls. iv, v, xi. All these brooches belong to La Tène A. Recently M. Viollier has selected them, with others of a simpler form, as characteristic of a first subdivision of La Tène I. P. Reinecke, " Fibeln der La Tène Zeit aus der süd- und nord-deutschen Zone," in **CCCXCIX**, v, pl. xx ; Beltz, in **CLXIX**, 1911, p. 665.

this portion and the turned-up foot become absolutely symmetrical. Sometimes these ends are shaped like the heads of birds (Fig. 5, No. 6).

Among the brooches whose foot turns back to the bow there is a whole series in which it has the form of a hollow

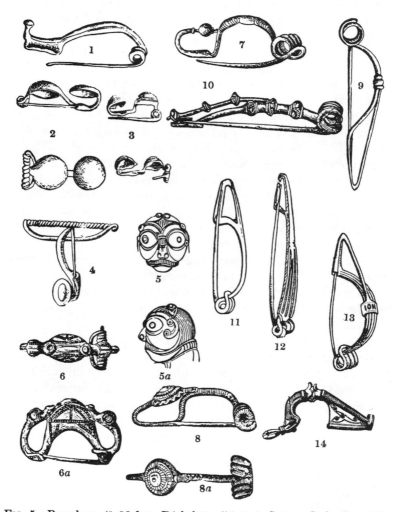

FIG. 5. Brooches. (1–13 from Déchelette, ii.) 1–3, Certosa, Italy (figs. 348, 350). 4, Heiltz-l'Évêque, Marne (fig. 350). 5, 5a, Parsberg, Upper Palatinate. 6, Nierstein, Rheinhessen. 7, Ciry-Salsogne, Aisne. 8–9, Vevey, Switzerland (fig. 533). 10, Dühren, Baden (fig. 535). 11–12, Stradonitz (fig. 537). 13, Puech de Buzeins, Aveyron (fig. 538). 14, Backworth (B.M. Guide to the Iron Age, fig. 102).

kettle-drum. The main part of the bow is broadened so as to form the same shape.

After these there comes a type with a spring formed of only a few spirals and a thick depressed bow, adorned with motives in relief. The foot ends in a broad disc set with coral (Fig. 5, No. 8).

The brooches which come next are simpler. The foot ends in a complicated knob, which recalls the birds' heads mentioned above, and the spring generally has one more coil.

So much for the brooches of the first La Tène period. In the second period the foot comes closer to the bow, until at last it is attached to it by a ring. This ring is at first near the centre of the bow, and then it shifts towards the head. The knob is at first recognizable, and then ceases to be. Both bow and foot have more than one knob. At the same time, the spring tends to become longer. At this date brooches of iron and also of silver are made (Fig. 5, Nos. 9, 10).

As time goes on the brooch of La Tène II comes to receive its shape in the casting. The bow and the turned-back foot are made in one open-work piece (Fig. 5, Nos. 11, 12). This type continued to be in use after the Roman conquest of Gaul, at which time it presented a great number of varieties. The La Tène II brooch was also developed in a form which is fairly easy to recognize, in which the connecting ring comes close to the head of the bow and the latter is surrounded by the wire of the spring (Fig. 5, No. 13).[1]

The succession of types was the same in Britain. There it continued in various kinds of brooch, differing from the Roman brooches in the style of their decoration (Fig. 5, No. 14).

In the family tree of the brooches we find occasional " sports "—disc-shaped brooches,[2] the earliest of which are the kettle-drum brooches, in which the whole mechanism is covered by the drum-shaped bow, and the ring-brooches of the Pyrenean and Iberian stations, which are mounted on a ring passing through the head and the foot.[3]

Torques.—After the brooch the torque, or collar, is the

---

[1] Almgren, " Fibules d'Alésia et de Bibracte, deux dates fixes dans l'histoire de la fibule," in **CLXXXV**, p. 241.

[2] Déchelette, ii, 3, p. 1251 ; Kropp, **CCCXCVIII**, p. 16 (a brooch found at Ranis).

[3] Déchelette, p. 1269.

most characteristic article of Gallic adornment and that
which presents the greatest number of classified and dated
varieties. *Torques* is the name which the Latins gave to it,
because it was often made of a twisted strip of metal, with
very sharp edges. The Greeks have preserved the Celtic
name for it in the form μανιάκης.[1] Irish *muince*, Old Welsh
minci (modern *mynci*) " collar ", may come from the same
root. The torque is not peculiar to the civilization of La Tène.
At the end of the Bronze Age magnificent gold torques with
hooked ends were made in England.[2] But in Western Europe
the torque was still rare in the Hallstatt period, and came
into general use immediately afterwards.

Perhaps it was not merely an adornment. We have
figures of Gaulish gods, holding a torque in the hand and
apparently elevating it ritually (Fig. 7, No. 1). Another
figure of one of these gods, in Paris, bears a torque on his
horns.[3] It was an ornament with which, it seems, representations of the gods had to be provided. It was even added
to the figures of Roman gods.[4] It was an offering. Quintilian
tells us that the Gauls offered to Augustus, who was a god,
a gold torque weighing a hundred pounds.[5] On an altar
dedicated to Tiberius, found in Paris, we see armed Gauls
bearing a huge circle or hoop before a seated personage.[6]
Perhaps this was a torque of the kind.

Except in three instances,[7] torques have been found only
in the graves of women.[8] On the other hand, the monuments
regularly show them on the necks of men, and the whole of
written tradition, Irish included,[9] confirms their evidence.
The Gauls who invaded Italy may have worn it already, if
we are to believe the story of Manlius Torquatus,[10] and their
successors always wore it.[11] There may be differences of
race ; there are certainly differences of date. The torques

---

[1] Polyb., ii, 31 ; cf. Dottin, **CXCVI**, p. 269.
[2] E. Toulmin Nicolle, in **XLVI**, 1912. Cf. Déchelette, ii, 1, p. 316.
[3] Espérandieu, **CCCXXV**, No. 3653.
[4] The Hypnos in the Besançon Museum (S. Reinach, **CCCLXXII**, fig. 102).
[5] vi, 3, 79.
[6] The monument of the Nautæ (Espérandieu, op. cit., No. 3132).
[7] Déchelette, ii, 3, p. 1209 ; Brizio, in **CVI**, i, ix (1901), pp. 724 ff.
[8] Déchelette, loc. cit.
[9] *Táin Bó Chuailgné*, xxii; **CXL**, 1910, p. 10 ; Joyce, **CCCCXXXIV**, i, p. 99.
[10] D'Arbois, **CCXLVIII**, xii, p. 126 ; cf. Déchelette, p. 1210.
[11] Déchelette, p. 1208 ; Armstrong, *Celts*, 24.

found in female burials date from La Tène I ; the monuments are of La Tène II. The fashion had changed. Women ceased to wear the collar of rigid metal ; men, and perhaps only the chieftains, wore it.[1]

The earliest torques are very simple, some being formed of a hollow tube of bronze bent into a hoop, and others of a solid rod, plain or twisted, and ending in hooks for the

FIG. 6. Torques. (Déchelette, ii, 3, fig. 515.) 1, Bussy-le-Château, Marne. 2, Schirrhein, Alsace. 3, Étrechy, Marne. 4, Courtisols.

clasp or in buffers (Fig. 6, Nos. 1, 2). These are attributed to the beginning of the first period. Gradually the ornamentation grew richer.   There were buffer-torques,

[1] This is the explanation of Déchelette, with which I fully agree.   He adds (p. 1210) that the Celts of the Danube took the practice of wearing the torque as a national emblem from the Scythian chiefs.   He suggests that they even imported Scythian torques, or at least models ; see below.

the hoop of which was thick with relief decoration (Fig. 6, No. 1), sometimes including human faces (Fig. 6, No. 4). Then there was a whole series of torques, completely closed or having a movable segment, the ornament on which was similar, but was distributed symmetrically in three groups (Fig. 7, Nos. 2, 4) or asymmetrically on one part of the hoop

FIG. 7.   Torques.   (2–5 from Déchelette, fig. 516.)   1, Horned God on the Gundestrup Cauldron, elevating the Torque (*Mémoires de la Soc. des Antiquaires de France*, 1913, p. 259).   2, Aube.   3, Schlettstadt, Alsace. 4, Pleurs, Marne.   5, Marne.

only. This decoration consisted of discs set with coral alternating with bosses adorned with spirals. In some cases it might be open-work and consist of separate pieces fixed on to the collar (Fig. 7, Nos. 3, 5).[1]

From La Tène II we have a few torques, such as the plain wire type with the ends bent into an S. The torques which warriors were beginning to wear as badges were of precious material, gold,[2] and have therefore usually disappeared. There is, however, a group of torques of this date, most of them in the Toulouse Museum and found in that neighbourhood,[3] with a voluminous decoration of bosses bearing scroll-work distributed all round the hoop or beside the terminal buffers. The buffers were fastened together by T-shaped tenons. A torque of this family has been found in Hungary, at Herczeg-Marok (near Baranya),[4] and two others, with less violent decoration, come from Clonmacnoise and Broighter in Ireland.[5]

From La Tène III we have thick torques with a quadrangular section, ending in large knobs.[6]

Bracelets.—It is not always easy to distinguish La Tène bracelets from those of the preceding period.[7] But there are quite special types, and these can be classified chronologically. Their classification follows that of the torques, and they have the same characteristics.[8]

Like the torques of the tombs of the Marne, bracelets were almost exclusively worn by women. But, like the torques, they were sometimes worn by men, especially chieftains. In that case they were valuable objects, like the gold bracelet found on the arm of the warrior buried in the grave at La Gorge-Meillet.

Corresponding to the simple early torques, there is a series

---

[1] Déchelette, ii, 4, pp. 1211 ff.
[2] Id., ii, 3, p. 1208 ; Roget de Belloguet, CCCLXXIX, iii, p. 89 ; Dottin, CCCXXII, p. 133 ; S. Reinach, s.v. " Torques ", in CCCXV.
[3] At Cordes, Montans, and Lasgraïsses in Tarn, Fenouillet in Hte.-Garonne (Déchelette, ii, 3, pp. 1339 ff.), and Serviès-en-Val in Aude (P. J. Cros, in XCI, iv, p. 143).
[4] Costa de Beauregard, in LX, Autun, 1907, p. 826 ; Coffey, CCCCXXVIII, p. 80, pl. ix ; Sir A. Evans, in XVII, 1897, p. 400.
[5] Déchelette, pp. 1208, n. 1, 1217.
[6] CLXIX, 1904, pp. 54 ff. ; analogies between the bracelets and rings of La Tène and the earlier forms of the Caucasus and Hungary.
[7] Déchelette, pp. 1218–1230 ; Viollier, in CLXXX ; Brizio, in CVI, 1901, p. 30.
[8] Heierli, in XLVIII, iv, pp. 126, 131, 137.

of bracelets found in the same tombs—tubular bracelets, open or closed, bracelets formed of a sharp-edged rod ending in knobs, ribbed bracelets, and others with slight bosses (Fig. 8, Nos. 1, 2).[1]

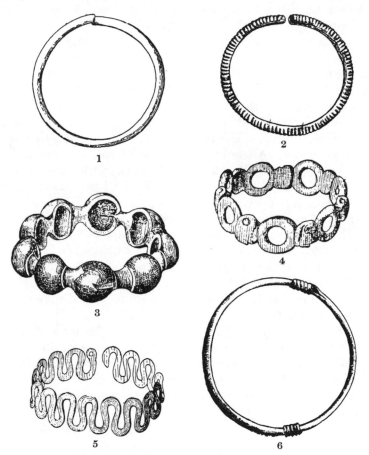

FIG. 8. Bracelets. (Déchelette, ii, 3.) 1, Marson, Marne. 2, Caranda, Aisne. 3, Bydžov Novy, Bohemia (fig. 517). 4, St. Rémy-sur-Bussy, Marne. 5, Marne (fig. 519). 6, Stradonitz (fig. 520).

Another series corresponds to the second series of torques and presents many of the same characteristics. The bosses become larger, they are arranged in groups, and they have additional S-shaped ornamentation.

[1] Allen, **CCXCVIII**, p. 113 ; Anderson, **CCCCXIV**, p. 141.

When the torque disappears the bracelet continues to develop. It is now that the bracelets formed of hollow semi-ovoid bosses with *appliqué* or relief ornamentation appear. Some of these are fairly heavy, having the clasp made in a separate piece. There are also types containing open-work and others formed of an undulating wire (Fig. 8, Nos. 3–5).

All this series belongs to the second period of La Tène.

In the third period a type appears which lasted long afterwards. This consists of a plain wire with the ends twisted round each other and some way along the hoop. At the same time bronze comes to be used less frequently in the making of bracelets. Glass bracelets become more numerous, especially in Switzerland. Some are of white or transparent glass ; others of blue glass, sometimes relieved with yellow or white enamel. They are of native make, or, at least, come from Cisalpine Gaul (Fig. 9, Nos. 1–3). The Gauls also made use of Kimmeridge shale, or lignite, but the lignite bracelets of the La Tène period are narrower than the Hallstatt lignite bracelets of barrel form.

At the end of the development of La Tène civilization heavy bronze bracelets are found in Scotland, which are adorned with reliefs or enamels and look as if they were made of three bracelets stuck together.[1]

Belts.[2]—The belts with iron chains of which I have spoken date from La Tène II. Before that time the Gauls wore belts of leather or cloth with clasps.

These clasps are derived from Hallstatt types, and keep their general form. They consist of a metal tongue, usually not decorated, sewn on to the material, and one or two cross-bars, forming tags, attached to it. The hook springs from a plate of bronze, or iron, or even gold, attached to the last bar. It is triangular, like that of the Hallstatt clasp, but it often has rich open-work ornamentation, derived from the Greek palmette or composed of confronted animals (Fig. 9, Nos. 6, 7).

The later we come down the more massive these hooks become, just like the torques and the bracelets. There are balls and bosses and reliefs (Fig. 9, No. 4) ; and finally, at the end of the La Tène period, they are simplified into thick rings. In this last type the hook is at the end of a triangular

---

[1] Déchelette, ii, 3, pp. 1230 ff.   [2] Ibid., pp. 1263–1270.

piece, mounted on a ring which is supported by two crescents (Fig. 9, No. 6), or it is concealed under a palmette, the base of which is an oblong slot (Fig. 9, No. 5). Belt-hooks are found in the graves of both men and women.

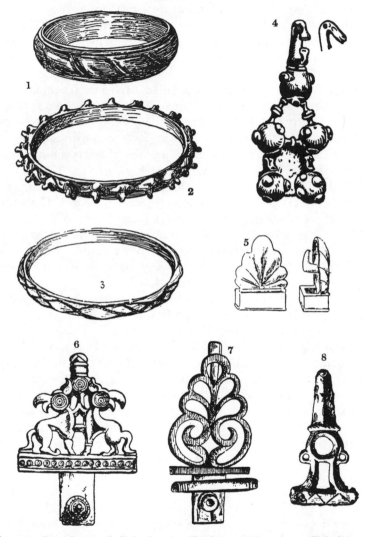

FIG. 9. Bracelets and Belt-clasps. (Déchelette, ii, 3.) 1, Val d'Aosta. 2–3, Münsingen, Switzerland (fig. 580). 4, Gröbern, Saxony (fig. 526). 5, Stradonitz (fig. 528). 6, Somme-Bionne, Marne. 7, La Motte-St.-Valentin, Hte.-Marne (fig. 524). 8, Stradonitz (fig. 527).

Hooks of this kind are found on very beautiful chain-belts of bronze which women wore at the end of La Tène II. These are made of circular rings or of rings alternating with ornamented oblong bars, and have pendants hanging from them.

Various Objects.—To obtain a complete picture of Gaulish adornment in the La Tène period we must note, in addition

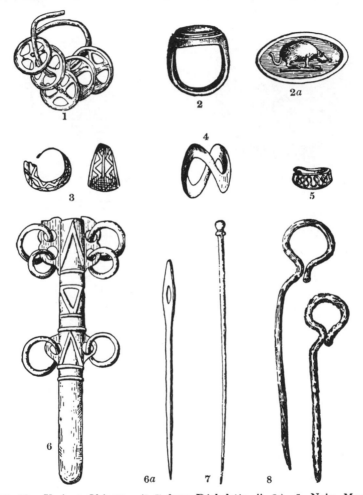

FIG. 10. Various Objects. (1–7 from Déchelette, ii, 3.) 1, Naix, Meuse (fig. 560). 2, Stradonitz (fig. 546). 3, Étrechy, Marne (fig. 542). 4, Steinhausen, Switzerland (fig. 544). 5, Münsingen (fig. 545). 6, 6a, La Tène (fig. 559). 7, La Motte-St.-Valentin, Hte.-Marne (fig. 541). 8, Bonchester Hill (*Proc. Soc. Antiq. Scotland*, xliv, p. 235).

to the brooches, torques, bracelets, and belts, the earrings
of bronze and of gold, shaped like boats,[1] and the rings,
most of which are small bracelets (Fig. 10, Nos. 3, 5).[2] In
La Tène III seal-rings appear (Fig. 10, No. 2). These were
borrowed from Italy and Greece. Some rings have a bent
form (Fig. 10, No. 4). But we also have silver rings with
this saddle-shaped bend, which must have gone on the

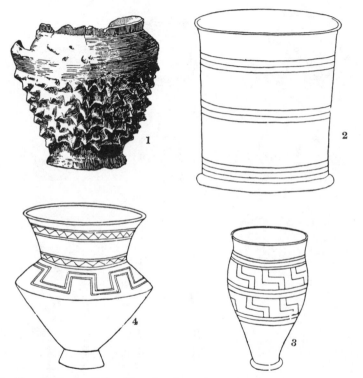

Fig. 11.   Pottery of La Tène I.   (2–4 from Déchelette, ii. 3, fig. 659.)
1, Caranda vase (Moreau, *Album Caranda*, i, pl. xxxix, fig. 1).   2, Aisne.
3, Aisne.   4, Marne.

shoulder and been used as brooches.[3] We must not forget
the buttons, those used for actual buttoning and those
merely sewn on, which were often decorated with enamel[4];
the pins, which recall the Hallstatt pins, with button and
swan's neck heads (Fig. 10, Nos. 8, 9), the buckles, the

---

[1] Ibid., p. 1264.   [2] Ibid., p. 1244.   [3] Ibid.   [4] Ibid., p. 1289.

needle-cases (Fig. 10, No. 6),[1] the mirrors,[2] the combs,[3] and the amulets of all kinds, especially those consisting of wheels (Fig. 10, No. 1).

VI

POTTERY [4]

The pottery of La Tène, although unequally distributed,[5] is very abundant and varied, and includes many forms which certainly show their origin, but also show how freely the people of that time made use of the heritage of the past.

The first types which strike one in a collection of vases from the cemeteries of the Marne are those with straight sides and angular shoulders. These " carinated " vases, as they are called, have necks either high or low. They belong to the first period (La Tène I), as do the beaker-shaped vases, sometimes small and sometimes very large, and others which are cylindrical (Fig. 11, Nos. 1–4).

These vases are of a fairly fine paste, covered with a brown or blackish burnished slip. They are engraved with patterns of straight lines, filled with red or white paint.

Some of the short-necked vases have the belly covered with a decoration like the heads of nails.[6] These curious vessels look as if they were made of metal, and, indeed, they are copied from metal originals.

The carinated vases are derived from the Italic pails (*situlæ*) of riveted bronze, which are frequent in Hallstatt tombs (Fig. 12, No. 1).[7] The cylindrical vases are modelled on the cordoned buckets known as *ciste a cordoni*, and their incised decoration recalls the cordons of the buckets.[8] Nor

---

[1] Ibid., pp. 1286–9.   [2] Ibid., pp. 1284–6.   [3] Ibid., pp. 1292 ff.
[4] Ibid., pp. 1258 ff. ; Morel, **CCCCLXXXIV** ; Moreau, **CCCCLXXXIII.**
[5] It is completely absent in Central and Southern Gaul (Déchelette, op. cit., ii, 3, p. 1459) and at La Tène (Vouga, **CCCCXCIV**, 26–8). It is very abundant in the Marne cemeteries, especially for the first period. In the Cisalpine cemeteries Italic pottery to a great extent took the place of the native ware.
[6] Déchelette, ii, 3, p. 1467. Similar vases are found in the Cisalpine cemeteries. Cf. Schumacher, in **CCCXCIX**, v, pl. lxx, 1320.
[7] There are many examples of similar imitations in the earlier Italian pottery.
[8] The handles even of late buckets were reproduced in earthenware. Cf. vases from the tumuli of the plateau of Ger (Pothier, p. 57, fig. 11).

are these the only La Tène vases derived from metal prototypes. A vase found at St. Pol de Léon bears, no doubt in an exaggerated form, the palmette which adorns the junction-point of the handle in the corresponding Italic

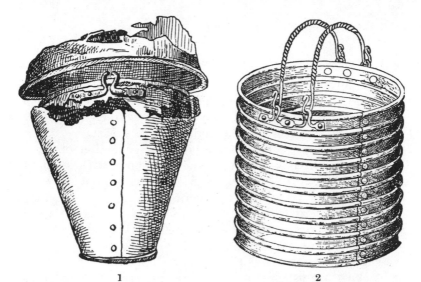

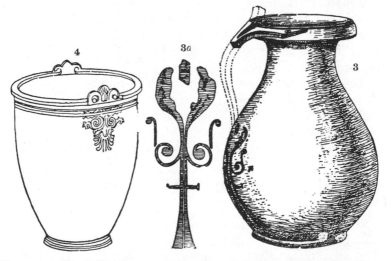

FIG. 12. Metal Prototypes of La Tène Pottery. (Déchelette, ii, 3.) 1, Pail from Plougoumelen, Morbihan (fig. 292). 2, Cordoned bucket from Reuilly, Loiret (fig. 299). 3, 3a, Aylesford, Kent (fig. 652). 4, Montefortino (fig. 646).

buckets (Fig. 13) ; compare, too, the ornament on the metal jug from Aylesford (Fig. 12, Nos. 3, 3a). Another, from Lann-Tinikeii, in the commune of Plœmeur, in Finistère,

FIG. 13. Vase from Saint-Pol-de-Léon. (Déchelette, ii, 3, fig. 663.)

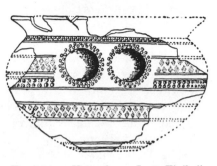

FIG. 14. Vase from Lann-Tinikeii, Morbihan. (Déchelette, ii, 3, fig. 665.)

is an imitation of a vessel made of riveted metal bands (Fig. 14). Others, by their incised decoration of *pointillé* arches and large dots, recall the Veneto-Illyrian bronzes.[2] There are

FIG. 15. Vase from Mané-Roullarde, Morbihan. (Déchelette, ii, 3, fig. 666.)

not many vases copied from prototypes in riveted metal-work in Gallic countries, but some have been found, for example, in Brittany (Fig. 15). There the cordoned bucket

---

[1] Déchelette, **CCCCLXXXVIII**, ii, 3, p. 1468 ; Du Chatellier, **CCCCLXXI**, pl. xiv, 1, 2 ; pl. xvi, 1.

[2] Reinecke, **CCCXCIX**, p. 24.

produced local imitations richly decorated (Figs. 15, 16, No. 4). While the prototype of the carinated vases has not yet been discovered among Celtic remains, buckets of cast metal are fairly frequent.

The tombs of the Marne have yielded many examples of a baluster-shaped type of vase which is much more widespread. The proportions of the elements in this " pedestal urn " vary a good deal. It is derived from the typical Hallstatt vase in two portions ; indeed, the most remarkable peculiarity of the Hallstatt vases, the sagging of the belly under the weight of the upper part, can still be seen in it. It is, therefore, contemporary with the beginnings of La Tène. These vases almost always have a moulding round the foot and their decoration regularly contains cordons in relief.[1] Their forms vary much between two extremes—on the one hand a long-necked bottle which is characteristic of the earliest La Tène sites in South Germany (Fig. 16, No. 1), and, on the other, a kind of jar with a wide mouth surrounded by the same cordon-moulding and a foot which tends to be very simple (Fig. 16, No. 3). In Germany these vases sometimes have an incised decoration which recalls the Hallstätt metal vases (Fig. 16, No. 1a). In France they are often covered with a very broad curvilinear pattern, painted in brown on red or incised.[2]

The pottery of the second La Tène period seems to be especially rich in vases of this family,[3] and they continue into the third period.[4] Either they are monochrome, and plainly decorated with their relief cordons or lustrous lines put on with the burnishing point, or they are painted with red or brown motives on a smooth white ground (Fig. 17, Nos. 4, 5, 8).

This ware is more varied than the preceding one, because it is not only a funerary ware. It comprises all the usual crockery, great jars for provisions, plates, vases with handles, etc. Many are adorned with hatchings or dots, put on with the punch or the comb (Fig. 17, Nos. 1–3). Most of the pottery

---

[1] These cordons are sometimes distributed down the whole body of the vase, dividing it into regular bands as in the pottery of the Venetian area.

[2] Cf. vases of the Glastonbury type (Déchelette, ii, 3, p. 1473 ; **CCCLXXXIV**, p. 137).

[3] Déchelette, pp. 1460 ff., 1480 ff.

[4] Ibid., pp. 1481 ff. ; Laville, " Sépultures marniennes de Valenton (Seine-et-Oise)," in **XLI**, 1910, p. 571.

FIG. 16. Pottery of the Marne, Brittany, and Central Europe. (Déchelette, ii, 3.) 1, 1a, Matzhausen, Upper Palatinate (figs. 671–2). 2, Beine, Marne (fig. 660). 3, Manching, Upper Bavaria (fig. 675). 4, Plouhinec, Finistère (fig. 663). 5, Praunheim, Hessen-Nassau (fig. 673).

at Mont Beuvray is like this, but painted pottery is also plentiful there.[1]

The painted decoration of pottery develops especially in the area of the southern expansion of the La Tène civilization,

FIG. 17. Pottery of La Tène III. (1–7 from Déchelette, ii, 3.) 1–3, Mont-Beuvray (fig. 677). 4, Montans, Tarn. 5, Lezoux, Puy-de-Dôme (fig. 683). 6, Shoebury, Essex (fig. 681). 7, Stradonitz (fig. 677). 8, Celles (Pagès-Allary, in *l'Anthropologie*, 1903, p. 402).

[1] Déchelette, pp. 1485 ff.

in the south of Gaul and in Spain. In the south of Gaul very curious vases were manufactured, with a flower or fruit ornament on a slip.[1] But painted ware spread all over Gaul, and was manufactured at more than one place.[2] Sometimes its decoration includes relief friezes which were kept up in the pottery of the Empire.[3]

Arms, ornaments, and vases—that is what constitutes the main part of the furniture of the graves of La Tène. It is also what constitutes most of the finds made in the dwelling-places. It does not, of course, represent the whole material side of the civilization of the period.

Many remains of vehicles have been found. The Gauls had a reputation as cartwrights. There are also many portions of harness and horse-trappings, the interest of which for this chapter lies not in their form but in their decoration. Fire-dogs have been discovered, and keys, and a fair number of iron tools.

This is not the place to present a systematic picture of the whole civilization of the Celts and all the things which they produced or used in the La Tène period, but to point out those objects and characteristics of objects which allow us to attribute one or another series of finds to the Celts or their influence and to date them. To this end some facts still remain to be noticed.

VII

DECORATIVE ART

Many of the objects of which we have been speaking are decorated, and some very richly. The taste, the style, the fashion to which they bear witness are expressed, not only

---

[1] Ibid., pp. 1488 ff. ; cf. R. Zahn, in **CLXVIII**, 1907, pp. 338 ff. ; **XX**, 1907, p. 226. For Galatian sherds with painting on a slip, see Déchelette, **CCCCLXXIII**, i, p. 130 ; Mazaurie, " La Céramique polychrome des Celtes ", in **CXXXIV**, 1901, p. 82.

[2] Carlier, " Vases peints du Musée archéologique de Genève," in **CXXXIV**, 1908, p. 257 ; Marteaux and Leroux, **CCCCLXXXIII**, p. 417. For painted vases from the Æduan district, see Déchelette, ii, 3, p. 1491 ; Abbé Philippe, **CCCCLXXXVIII**, p. 23 ; Lindenschmit, **CCCXCIX**, i, vi, pl. 6.

[3] Painted La Tène vase with frieze of birds in relief, at Lochenstein, near Balingen (G. Bersu, in **LXV**, 1924).

in their form, but in characteristic ornament. In particular there is no mistaking the decoration of metal objects of La Tène for that of any other period. Moreover, it is certainly Celtic, for the tradition of it continued in Celtic countries after the conquest of the Continental Celts and was perpetuated in the Christian art of Ireland.[1]

It is purely an ornament of line, in which the zoomorphic

FIG. 18.   Bracelet from Rodenbach, Rhenish Bavaria.   (Déchelette, ii, 3, fig. 583.)

elements, human heads, etc., mentioned above, take a predominant place, and indeed these are distorted so as to fit into the linear decorative scheme (Fig. 18).[2] The type of stylization which was the result was quite new in ancient art.

Needless to say, the La Tène decorators often got their effects with less trouble.   They had preserved, at least in

[1] Allen, **CCXCVIII**, p. 125 ; Déchelette, ii, 3, pp. 1525–7.
[2] Lindenschmit, op. cit., iii, i, and suppl.

pottery, the rectilinear patterns of Greek frets, chevrons, zigzags, and crosses practised in the preceding period. Metal objects are often adorned with plain ribs and grooves,

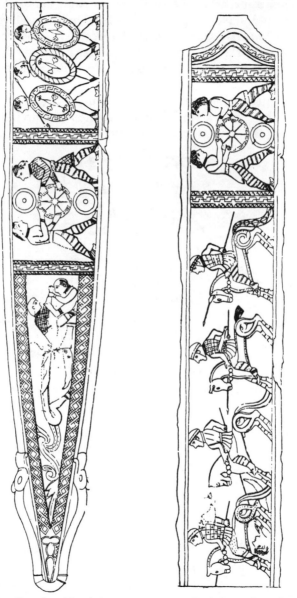

Fig. 19.   Sword-scabbard from Hallstatt.   (Déchelette, ii, 2, fig. 297.)

and some of them are not always easy to tell at first sight from things made earlier, later, or elsewhere.[1]

But in every series of manufactured objects the decoration approached at one time or another to the ideal type which I have roughly defined. The decorative art of La Tène evidently turned in that direction. The people for whom the works of art were produced found that type satisfying to their taste, and they had a distinct preference for curved lines.

The chief element in this curvilinear decoration is the double volute with a thick stem and ends curling in opposite directions, the symbolic S of Celtic ornament.[2] It is found

FIG. 20.   Bracelet from Montsaugeon.   (Déchelette, ii, 3, fig. 697.)

isolated, and also in close combination with other volutes and other decorative elements (Fig. 21). The triple volute, sometimes called the triskele, is equally frequent (Fig. 20).[3] The combination of these elements forms a rich pattern of curves (Fig. 22).

Just as the art of the first Iron Age is derived from Græco-Asiatic art, and reproduces its decoration of bands of animals, the ornament of La Tène is derived from a later Greek art.   Of that first style Celtic art keeps only the

---

[1] Déchelette, pp. 1505 ff.
[2] Ibid., pp. 1514 ff.
[3] Ibid., p. 1518 ;   CCCLXXXIV, pp. 17 ff. ;   Hœrnes, CCCXXXIX, p. 662, figs. 197–8.

confronted animals.[1] The palmette, which is its favourite motive, is the source of the Celtic volutes.[2] It is certainly the

FIG. 21. Bracelet from Bologna. (Déchelette, ii, 3, fig. 519.)

FIG. 22. Triskele-pattern on Gold Plaque from the Tumulus at Schwarzenbach. (Déchelette, ii, 3, fig. 698.)

Greek palmette, with its long, wide-spreading leaves, first stiff and then drooping (Fig. 23, No. 1), and not the more softly curving Egyptian or Oriental palmette which is one

FIG. 23. Palmettes. 1, Drooping palmette on a pail from Waldalgesheim (B.M. Guide to the Iron Age, 1925, p. 19, fig. 10). 2, Detail on a torque from Waldalgesheim (ibid., p. 20, fig. 12). 3, Classical palmette (ibid., fig. 13). 4, Stiff palmette on the handle of an oenochoë from Somme-Bionne (Déchelette, ii, 3, fig. 641).

of the most ancient motives in decorative art.[3] The Celtic artist broke up the palmette and simplified it (Fig. 23, Nos. 2, 4). Moreover, he took his inspiration from the two

[1] CCCLXXXIV, p. 17.
[3] Montelius, CCCLVII, i, pp. 77 ff.
[2] Déchelette, pp. 1513 ff.

FIG. 24. Ornament of the Bronze Vase from Saulces-Champenoises, Ardennes.
(Déchelette, ii, 3, fig. 655.)

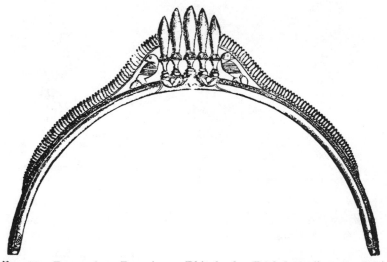

FIG. 25. Torque from Besseringen, Rhineland. (Déchelette, ii, 3, fig. 584.)

types of Greek palmette, that of the sixth century and the classical type (Fig. 23, No. 3).

The Greek palmette is a somewhat complex ornament. It is composed of petals, spreading from a stylized calix represented by volutes. From these volutes spring accessory ornaments—the palmette in bud, the palmette seen sideways on. The palmettes and buds may be enclosed by the network formed by the volutes.

Celtic art took the volutes chiefly and made them into its S decoration and, by combination, its triskeles. It reduced the number of petals of the palmette, which was from nine to eleven, to three. It adopted the profile palmette (Fig. 24), the bud (Fig. 25),[1] and the encircling of the palmette by volutes (Fig. 26). Having

FIG. 27. Sword from
Lisnacroghera.
(Déchelette, ii,
3, fig. 469.)

FIG. 26. Disk from Auvers, Seine-et-Oise.
(Déchelette, ii, 3, fig. 694.)

[1] The grouped balusters on the Besseringen torque (**CCCXCIX**, ii, ii, pl. i) are, in my opinion, palmette-buds, and so are those on the Rodenbach bracelet.

broken up the elements of its models, it spread them out along its sword-scabbards (Fig. 27).

Celtic ornament is incised, or embossed in relief, or cast in relief, or cast and then treated with the engraver. It favours bosses. It also favours very sharp ridges, producing definite shadows. It also favours open-work, and has left

FIG. 28. Horse-trappings from Somme-Bionne. (Déchelette, ii, 3, fig. 506.)

very strong and graceful examples of this method in metal (Fig. 28). One at once compares this art to French Gothic art, but there is no transition between them. The execution of this decoration varied much in the course of the period, in the manner indicated in the preceding paragraphs. The ornament of La Tène I is more varied, more mingled with

FIG. 29. Coral Boss from the Marne. (S. Reinach, *Catalogue du Musée de Saint-Germain*, ii, p. 245, fig. 133.)

zoomorphic motives, and generally slenderer than that of La Tène II. The art of this period tends to approach to the classical models, imitating, for example, the bands of vine-tendrils, which had hitherto not been attempted.[1] No really local style was produced except in the British Isles.[2]

[1] On the Gundestrup cauldron, for example.
[2] Déchelette, ii, 3, pp. 1526–7 ; CCCLXXXIV, p. 29.

One peculiarity of La Tène art is the use of other materials in the decoration of metal. Two are of especial interest—coral and enamel.[1] The people of this age had at first a marked liking for the red of coral. The coral was set in sunk beds on the surface of an object (Fig. 29), or affixed by small nails or rivets to a support of iron or bronze, as in the brooches adorned with coral knobs. Sometimes the coral was carved.

The objects adorned with coral belong to the first La Tène period. Either taste changed, or supplies were cut off; at a certain date they vanish from Celtic jewellery.[2] Pliny states [3] that the coral-producing countries one day started to send such large quantities of it to India that it became rare in the centres of production. M. Salomon Reinach explains

Fig. 30.   Cross with enamel inlay from La Gorge-Meillet.   (Déchelette, ii, 3, fig. 508.)

that this must have happened after the expedition of Alexander, that is, at the end of the fourth century. It is just at this time that coral disappears from Celtic lands.

Its place was at once taken by enamel. This was a red enamel, the colour of blood, which is described by Philostratos.[4] It seems to have been a Celtic invention. Enamel was at first used as a substitute for coral, and in the same way, being either riveted [5] or fixed in a setting in small solid pieces, while cold (Fig. 30). The fusibility of enamel allowed of greater liberty of treatment. The *champlevé*

[1] Déchelette, pp. 1547 ff. ; Allen, **CCXCVIII,** p. 94.
[2] Déchelette, pp. 1330 ff.
[3] *N.H.*, xxxii, 2 ; S. Reinach, " Le Corail dans l'industrie celtique," in **CXL,** 1899, pp. 24 ff.   [4] *Icones*, i, 28.
[5] This process continued in vogue in Britain after the Roman conquest, as in the Battersea shield (fig. 31, below ; **CCCLXXXIV,** pp. 101 ff.).

process was invented. The enamel was poured hot into sunk beds, which were made larger as time went on. Finally the whole surface to be decorated was covered with enamel and the sunk parts were separated from one another only by a slender net-work of metal. Enamelled decoration of this kind appears on the Amfreville helmet. These different methods were practised during the second La Tène period.[1] Later the Gauls came to use enamel yet more freely. They made objects entirely covered with enamel, held on a grooved ground.[2] They used it in particular for buttons, especially at Mont Beuvray, at Bibracte, where enamellers' workshops have been excavated.

It is not certain whether enamel-work continued without interruption in Gaul after the Roman conquest.[3] In Britain it certainly developed, particularly in adding blues, yellows, and reds to its range of colours.[4] The use of enamel to cover large surfaces is one of the characteristics of the art which developed in Britain while Roman art was taking the place of Celtic in Gaul.

The popularity of enamel did not preclude a liking for glass and a certain skill in making it. I have already spoken of glass bracelets, and many glass necklace-beads have been found.[5] The Celts at first went to Italy for their glass-work, but they soon made their own. Later the Gallo-Romans were remarkably skilful and inventive in this craft.

We have chiefly to do with a purely ornamental art decorating useful articles. The richness of the ornament and the freedom with which it was used makes some of these useful articles real works of art (Fig. 31).[6] But plastic art properly so called is very poor.[7] Nevertheless, it shows a taste and a style of its own. The most remarkable specimen of it that we have, the silver vessel found at Gundestrup in Jutland, outside the Celtic countries,[8] is adorned with divine figures and symbolical scenes which make it an ethnographical document of inestimable value for the history of the Celts (Plate IV).

---

[1] Déchelette, ii, 3, p. 1549. [2] Ibid., pp. 1551–5. [3] Ibid., p. 1547.
[4] **CCCLXXXIV,** pl. viii. [5] Déchelette, pp. 1314 ff.
[6] e.g. a plaque from Auvers (Seine-et-Oise), a bracelet from Rodenbach, and the Battersea shield.
[7] Déchelette, ii, 3, pp. 1531–9 ; De Gérin-Ricard, **CCCCLXXVI,**
[8] Drexel, " Über den Silberkessel von Gundestrup," in **LXXIII,** 1915, pp. 1–96.

PLATE IV

THE GUNDESTRUP CAULDRON

Denmark (Sophus Muller, *Dei store sølekar fra Gundestrup i Jylland*, frontispiece)

[face p. 124

FIG. 31. The Battersea Shield. (B.M. *Guide* to the Iron Age, frontispiece.)

VIII

CHRONOLOGICAL SUMMARY AND CONCLUSIONS

The characteristics of the La Tène periods, including the intermediate period which Herr Reinecke's arguments compel us to take into account, may be summarized as follows :—

La Tène A : Tumulus-tombs, with cremation and with inhumation ; swords like the Hallstatt sword with antennæ ; very varied brooches, closely derived from the Certosa types, and, in particular, kettle-drum brooches.[1]

La Tène I (B) : Inhumations under tumuli and in flat-graves ; swords with curved scabbard-mouth and open-work chape ; brooches with turned-up foot ; torques, except at the end ; pottery like the Hallstatt types or carinated ; coral ornament.[2]

La Tène II (C) : Flat-graves ; cremation is practised again ; tumuli rare ; long swords, without open-work in the chape ; long brooches, with the foot attached to the bow by a ring ; pedestal vases ; enamel decoration.[3]

La Tène III (D) : Cremation ; long swords with blunt point ; scabbards with a straight mouth ; cast brooches ; pedestal vases ; lavish use of enamel.[4]

Each period is represented by typical sites—La Tène A, by the rich tumuli of Bavaria and the Middle Rhine ; La Tène I, by the cemeteries of the Marne ; La Tène II, by the station of La Tène itself ; La Tène III, by Mont Beuvray and the Hradischt of Stradonitz.

This series of periods is conventionally taken to end with the conquest of Gaul. But La Tène civilization lasted longer in Britain and Ireland. We can distinguish a La Tène IV, the Late Celtic of British archæologists, the characteristic of which is the extreme development of the decoration,

---

[1] Reinecke, **CCCCVI**, pp. 2–6, pl. vi ; id., **CCCXCIX**, v, p. 50.
[2] Id., **CCCCVI**, p. 7 ; **CCCXLIX**, v, pp. 8, 57.
[3] Id., **CCCCVI**, p. 11 ; **CCCXLIX**, v, pp. 15, 57 ; Déchelette, ii, 3, p. 931 ; **CCCLXXXIV**, p. 71.
[4] Reinecke, **CCCCVI**, p. 13 ; **CCCXCIX**, v, p. 51 ; Déchelette, ii, 3, pp. 931–2 ; **CCCLXXIV**, pp. 74, 76 ; **XV**, 1903, pp. 385 ff. (tumulus at Celles) ; **XXXVIII**, 1897, pp. 553 ff. (tomb at Cernon-sur-Coole) ; **CCCCLXXXIII** (Presles, St.-Audebert).

the main features of which we have been considering.[1] The last heir of that art, which was crossed about the sixth century with Germanic art, is the art of Ireland of the time of Charlemagne, with its illuminated manuscripts covered with twining decoration and its gorgeous gold-work.[2]

The positive dates of the first four of these types of culture are established, like all positive dates in prehistory, by reference to the historical civilizations of the Mediterranean, in virtue of the various contacts which took place between them and of dated objects which were imported into the regions which have no written history. The Celts were visited by traders of Marseilles,[3] and later by others from Italy.[4] Meanwhile the Gauls had descended at historically known dates into the peninsulas of the Mediterranean, and the areas which they occupied varied in a manner which is of great interest from a chronological point of view.[5]

The extreme terms are supplied by the excavations at the camp of Château-sur-Salins and those at Mont Beuvray. At Château, the presence of red and black Attic pottery similar to that found on the Acropolis among the rubbish resulting from the burning of 480, gives a date to a fairly complete series of cross-bow and kettle-drum brooches. La Tène I brooches, of the earliest type, were found above this layer.[6] So La Tène A corresponds to the fifth century, and to the whole length of it. Later Greek vases, such as the ovoid pail with movable handles, are found with objects of La Tène I.[7]

The finds from Mont Beuvray give another term, for the site was abandoned for that of Autun in the year 5 B.C. The series of coins stops at this date, which may be taken as the final date of La Tène III.[8]

---

[1] Déchelette, ii, 3, pp. 934, 1525–7.

[2] Allen, **CCXCVIII**, pp. 163 ff.

[3] List of Greek vases found in La Tène burials, in Déchelette, pp. 933–4 ; list of objects of Greek, Italo-Greek, or Etruscan manufacture found north of the Alps, ibid., pp. 1599–1607.

[4] Vases of the potter Aco, ibid., p. 1579.

[5] See above, pp. 1 ff.

[6] M. Piroutet and Déchelette, " Découverte de vases grecs dans un oppidum hallstattien du Jura," in **CXXXIX**, 1909, i, pp. 183, 201 ; Piroutet, " Essai de classification du hallstattien franc-comtois," ibid., 1928, ii, pp. 266–7 ; Déchelette, ii, 3, p. 697 ; Reinecke, **CCCCVI**, pp. 2 ff.

[7] Reinecke, op. cit., p. 7 ; tumulus at Waldalgesheim, near Bingen.

[8] The finds at the Hradischt (*oppidum*) of Stradonitz, in Bohemia, give another term. But the site was first abandoned by the Boii in 58, and then

Intermediate terms are supplied by Italy. M. Viollier has observed that his first subdivision of La Tène I (La Tène I*a*) is not represented in that country. That period, therefore, came before the great Gallic invasion of 390. The excavations at Montefortino have yielded objects belonging to the last phase of La Tène I (La Tène I*c*), but none of La Tène II. Now the country was recovered from the Gauls in 283.[1]

But from this point onwards coins come to our aid— coins of Marseilles, Greek coins from Europe and Asia, Roman coins.[2] The cemetery of Ornavasso, near Novara, has yielded a series from La Tène II and La Tène III, some of which are dated quite closely by Roman consular coins.[3]

From all this evidence we obtain the following scheme :—

La Tène A	500–400
La Tène I*a*	400–375
La Tène I*b*	375–325
La Tène I*c*	325–285
La Tène II	285–100
La Tène III	100–1

The civilization of La Tène begins with the Golden Age of Greek civilization. The innovations which mark the former were stimulated by those of the latter.[4] From then onwards the surfaces of contact steadily increased, and, in spite of some appearances to the contrary, the influence of the Mediterranean peoples and the amount of things imported increased likewise, until the civilization of La Tène was absorbed by that of Rome.

Italic influence, which seems to have been that to which the Hallstatt culture was chiefly subject, continued to affect the succeeding civilization ; the zone of intercourse and

conquered by the Marcomanni in 12–10 B.C. There is, therefore, an uncertainty of nearly fifty years. It is true that some hold that it was the Marcomanni that brought the series of La Tène civilizations to an end at the Hradischt, but this is quite wrong. The civilization of the Hradischt is too like that of Mont Beuvray to be that of another people. Cf. Déchelette, **CCCCLXXII.**

[1] Viollier, " Giubiasco," in **CLXXX**, pp. 229 ff.
[2] Reinecke, op. cit., p. 11 ; **CCCXCIX**, v, p. 15 (burials at Dühren in Baden, La Tène II) ; Blanchet, **CCCVI**, ii, p. 531.
[3] Déchelette, pp. 1093–4.
[4] Furtwängler, in **XX**, 1889, pp. 43 ff. ; Reinecke, **CCCCVI**, pp. 3 ff. ; Déchelette, p. 1508 ; E. Maassen, " Die Griechen in Südgallien," in *Œsterr. Jahrhft.*, ix (1906), p. 181. See below.

exchange seems to have extended between Venetia and Bavaria.[1] Later, the presence of Celtic settlements in Italy must, until Cisalpine Gaul was conquered by the Romans, have contributed to the influence of Italic civilization over that of La Tène.

Lastly, the wanderings of the Celts and their extension eastwards brought them into touch with the Scythians and the Hellenized Asiatics of Asia Minor. Here they got the torques with heads of serpents, the animal-headed torque of Vieil-Toulouse, the similarity of the torques of Lasgraïsses to that of Herczeg-Marok, and, what is still more significant, certain figures on the Gundestrup cauldron.

But what the men of La Tène borrowed they usually adapted and transformed in a fashion quite their own. Never before, among all the arts borrowed by the civilizations of Central Europe from the more advanced cultures of the South, had such originality been displayed. The development of such a strongly marked style implies a society which is populous, united, prosperous, and full of life—and perhaps more than a society, a nation.

Besides, the art of La Tène is not all borrowed from foreign peoples. It is derived directly from what it inherited from the Hallstatt civilization, as it was in the fifth century before our era in Western Germany, Upper Austria, Switzerland, Lorraine, the Franche-Comté, and Burgundy. The civilization of these regions, which I shall show to have been the heart of the Celtic world, had for long ages been steadily growing more united and homogeneous.

The constancy, the homogeneity, of the La Tène civilization all over the area which it covered is one of its most striking features. That is why one should pay the greatest attention to any local variations which it shows at one same date, and need not make too much of the many lacunæ in our archæological maps.[2] In archæological ethnography most negative facts are inadmissible.

---

[1] Reinecke, **CCCXCIX**, v, p. 284.
[2] Déchelette, ii, 3, pp. 1120–1 (the distribution of La Tène swords in France) and map iv.

PART TWO

MOVEMENTS OF THE CELTIC PEOPLES

CHAPTER I

THE ORIGINS OF THE CELTS

I

THE SEPARATION OF THE GOIDELS AND THE BRYTHONS

WE now have to try to find out whence they came, where they went, how they expanded, and where they stopped—in short, to trace their history—and that will be the second part of our inquiry.

The fact which dominates the whole history of the Celts, and apparently starts it, following as it did closely upon the breaking-up of the Italo-Celtic community (if that abstract concept ever corresponded to the existence of a definite social group), is their separation into two groups of peoples, whose languages became different as has been explained above—that is, the Goidelic, or Irish, group, and the Brythonic group, which includes the Gauls.

The separation of the Celtic dialects is a fact of far greater importance than the supposed distinction between the Celts and the Gauls.[1] It implies a fairly deep division between the peoples which spoke these two groups of dialects, and also a fairly long separation,[2] a fairly long interval between the migrations of the two Celtic bodies, a rhythm in those migrations not unlike that assumed by those historians who speculate on the distinction between Celts and Gauls, but much ampler. In other words, it leads one to believe that the occupation of the British Isles by the Celts and of Ireland by the Goidels took place long before—centuries before— the historical movements of the Brythonic peoples. These latter expanded about the sixth century before Christ. We must go back to the Bronze Age for the earlier invasion.

---

[1] Dottin., **CCCXXII**, pp. 12 ff.
[2] Sir John Rhys once tried to explain the phenomenon of labialization by the absorption of the Continental Celts by non-Aryan peoples (**CCXX**). Cf. S. Reinach, *Origine des Aryens*, pp. 108–112. D'Arbois has refuted this theory (**CXL**, 1891, p. 477).

Many historians and archæologists ignore this cleavage, or do not attach enough importance to it.[1] But Celticists and philologists are as divided over its importance as over its date. Mr. Eoinn MacNeill,[2] after making the mistake of identifying the Celts with the La Tène civilization, and making the movements of the Celts, all the Celts, date from the beginning of that culture, is obliged to conclude that the Goidels and Brythons arrived in Great Britain and Ireland together, and in the fourth century B.C. at the earliest. Had they become different before that ? Did they become so after their settlement in the British Isles ? The question does not seem to have occurred to him. In any case he does not think that the facts on which the distinction of the Celtic dialects is founded are important. Phonetic changes of this kind, he says, are not necessarily bounded by racial frontiers. They propagate themselves in some mysterious way, and stop equally without apparent reason.[3]

It is true that many of the things which make the difference between the two groups of Celtic dialects are of fairly late date. But that is not the case with the most characteristic of all, the labialization of velar consonants,[4] our chief indication of the softening of the consonants in Brythonic, which has given Welsh its present form.

Labialization had already become general at the time when the Goidels and Brythons accomplished together, according to Mr. MacNeill, the Celtic colonization of the British Isles. The name of the islands, Πρεττανικαὶ νῆσοι, which dates from the voyage of Pytheas, would be valuable evidence of this, were it not that it is derived from the name

[1] Continental archæologists seem quite unaware of this distinction between the two groups of Celts, although they admit in a general way that Britain was occupied by Celts long before the historical migrations (Déchelette, ii, 2, p. 573). The historians pay no more attention to it than the archæologists. M. Jullian (CCCXLVII) does not trouble about it. Niese (in Pauly and Wissowa, CCCLXVIII, vii, p. 611) holds that the distinction between Goidels and Brythons appears only at the end of ancient times.

[2] CCCCXLI.

[3] J. Loth, in CXL, 1922, pp. 4 ff. Mr. MacNeill is an admirable Celticist, and his learning gives great authority to his opinion. His theory was, however, greeted with some surprise. It is, of course, true that phonetic facts, like archæological, have no absolute racial significance. Their significant value follows from their circumstances, their context, the chronological indications attached to them, their recurrence in similar conditions, or some other adventitious element in their definition. It is from these that conclusions must be drawn.

[4] See above, pp. 39–42.

of the Picts (*Pretanni, Prydain*), the Celtic origin of which is doubted. It is hard to believe that two peoples which spoke very similar tongues, which may be supposed to have lived fairly close to each other in the country from which they started, should have engaged in similar adventures, perhaps together, at any rate with the same object, in the same direction, and at the same time—adventures such as would bring them closer together, and, indeed, mingle them inextricably—and yet have had no influence on the phonetic development of each other's speech. Yet, when we do find such influence at work in Ireland it is only in the case of particular words, which Irish quite definitely and consciously takes over. The *p* of Brythonic,[1] and even that of Latin,[2] is carefully changed to *k* in Irish, although the Latin *p* is sometimes kept.[3]

While always remaining the same language, Irish did, no doubt, in the long run take something from the neighbouring tongue. It only resisted it as well as it did because its own characteristics were already quite definitely established, and it had had time to fix them; this always implies a fairly long separation. In fact, while all the Celtic dialects which make up Gaulish for us, without exception, as we shall see, underwent labialization, Irish alone escaped because it was cut off from the rest for a long time.

But how far must we go back to find the date of labialization, considered as the chief indication of the distinction of the dialects, and the date, doubtless far earlier, of the separation of the peoples [4]? The close kinship of Celtic and Italic will serve us as a guide, and will give us

[1] Welsh words transcribed with *k*.

[2] From *purpura* they made *corcur*; from *pascha*, *case*; from *presbyter*, *cruinther*; from Patricius, Cothraige. We see that this last transcription dates from before the dropping of *qu*; Cothraige comes from Quatricius. But the process was not quite universal, for to some Latin words they applied the dropping of *p*, as in *saltir* (*saltir na ram*), from *psalterium*.

[3] A great road in Middle Irish is called *prim roen*; a sin, *peccad*; a parish, *parche*; etc. The same thing had already happened in Old Irish, but, except where it was used for *b*, it was not used to transcribe Latin words.

[4] M. J. Loth, who, in a reply to Mr. MacNeill's book, has assembled most of the reasons for believing that the Goidels settled in the British Isles at a very early date, nevertheless declares that the differentiation of the two groups of languages does not date from more than a few centuries before our era (in **CXL**, 1920–1, pp. 282 ff.). In the preface to his vocabulary of Old Breton, emphasizing the close kinship of Gaelic and Brythonic, he explains that their differentiation must date only from the first centuries of our era, that is, from the conquest of Brythonic lands by the Romans.

means to interpret the data of the problem. We shall also find archæological data coming to confirm those of language.

For the Italic dialects present exactly the same cleavage with the same chief indication,[1] but in circumstances which entitle us to interpret it boldly as I have proposed above for that of the Celtic dialects. From this point of view the parallel between the two groups of dialects is quite remarkable. It has not failed to impress philologists strongly.[2] The most cautious and critical try to keep their conclusions within modest bounds.[3] But the similarity of the facts is too marked and the languages are too closely allied for their agreement in this particular case to be fortuitous. Celts and Italici doubtless lived near enough to each other for the same linguistic fashions to spread from one group to the other. On each side a body broke off which remained faithful to an ancient condition of its language. The groups of men among whom the velar was labialized had certainly remained very close to each other, unless they were brought together by some chance. A good scientific method makes as little use of chance as possible.

It should be noted that the same thing happened in the Greek dialects and in the Illyrian dialects. Greek ἵππος ousted an older ἴκκος, which corresponds to Latin *equus*. The word is known from the *Etymologium Magnum*.[4] The Homeric language, the literary Ionic, keeps the guttural in cases where the common Greek has lost it : κοῖος, κῶς, instead of ποῖος, πῶς. The Athenians gave the name of Πυανόψια to a feast which the Samians called Κυανώψια, the Beanfeast. Among the Illyrian dialects, Venetian kept the velars (Liquentia, Aquileia, Mogiancus, 'Αρουκία),

---

[1] See above, p. 57.
[2] Cf. Meillet, in **XLVII**, 1918, xxi, 1.
[3] Meillet, loc. cit. ; id., **CCXVI**, p. 53 ; J. Loth, in **CXL**, 1920–1, p. 278, n. 1 ; Philipon, **CCCLXIX**, p. 204 ; J. Vendryès, in **CXL**, 1923, p. 174. These do not allow that the similarities between Italic and Celtic mean very much ; they hesitate to compare the breaking-off of the Goidels and the Latins from their respective groups, and they hold that labialization occurred independently in Brythonic and Osco-Umbrian. MM. Meillet and Vendryès allow, however, that there are more connections between Celtic and Osco-Umbrian than between Celtic and Latin (Meillet, in **XCIII**, xv, p. 161 ; Vendryès, **CXL**, xxxv, p. 212).
[4] Ridgeway, **DLIII**, p. 672. Boeotian had πέτταρες and Æolic πίσυρες for " four ", like Umbrian *petora*, whereas the form τέτταρες prevailed in Greek.

whereas the dialects of the Balkans labialized them (Pempte, Λυππείος, Ἀρελάπη, Arupi).[1]

It is not likely that the fact is to be explained in exactly the same way in Greek and Illyrian as in Italic and Celtic. It is equally unlikely that it did not occur, where it is observed, in comparable conditions. In any case, if we can take it as proved that the Greeks came from the North, that is from Central Europe, we may suppose without unlikelihood that they were once neighbours, not only of the Illyrians, but of the Italo-Celts, and even of the Celts, and that contact was not completely broken at the time when the labialization of the velars took place, that early indication of the cleavage of the Celtic dialects. Now it is certain that the Greeks did not leave their original home all in one body,[2] and yet labialization took place in the mainland dialects of Greek— Doric, Attic, the common Greek. Ionic merely gutturalized the velar, like Goidelic, but much earlier. The Dorians were evidently the latest of the Greeks to come south. The Ionians, who were the first to settle on the eastern fringe of the Greek world, came before them. In fact, everything seems to have happened as if labialization was the work of the last wave of Greeks, the last who remained in contact with their Indo-European neighbours of Western Europe, among whom labialization also took place.

Roughly the Dorian invasion coincides with the disappearance of the Mycenæan civilization, with the Middle Ages of ancient Greece, and with the beginning of the Iron Age. Its true date is probably not far off the traditional date.[3] Ionic was probably the dialect of the Greeks who settled in Greece in the Mycenæan period, or even before it, whose remote history is beginning to be revealed by the Hittite records.[4]

Things went on in exactly the same way among the Italici and at about the same time. The position of one part of them, the Umbrians, can be determined very exactly in relation to the Etruscans [5] from the moment when they descended

---

[1] Philipon, **CCCLIX**, p. 99. Cf. the variation between dentals and gutturals pointed out by Kretschmer, 259 : Ἰάποδες = Ἰάπυγες.

[2] Jardé, **CCCXLV**, English, pp. 71 ff.

[3] Ibid., English, pp. 75–7 ; Fougères, Contenau, Grousset, Jouguet, and Lesquier, **CCCXXXI**, i, pp. 292 ff.

[4] Meyer, **CCCLIV**, i, 2, pp. 800 ff. ; H. R. Hall, in **CLXXXVI**, pp. 297 ff.

[5] Grenier, **DXXIX**, pp. 460 ff., 500 ff. ; Homo, **CCCXLI**, English, pp. 50 ff., 54 ff. ; H. Hubert, in **CXL**, 1914, pp. 20 ff.

into Italy. Between the Umbrians and Etruscans there were relations, not only of immediate proximity, but of intimate penetration. The Etruscans were strangers to Italy, and won their land from the Umbrians. Historical tradition, at least, says that they took from them the northern part, the region of Bologna. In brief, the Umbrians and the Etruscans were two elements, and the two chief elements, of the population north of Central Italy and south of the plain of the Po. Now we know quite well the archæological remains which represent the Etruscans.[1] There are tombs in Etruria which resemble those of Asia Minor, whence the Etruscans came. In these, pottery and other objects of Eastern origin are found. At Bologna [2] a part of the cemetery which extends from the town to the Certosa contains tombs similar to those of Etruria and equipped with Etruscan furniture. Nearer to the town there are tombs of another type, small pits with ossuaries of a characteristic shape, and older objects of various kinds. All this is also found in Etruria, side by side with the remains of the Etruscans. These objects mark the civilization called after Villanova, where a similar cemetery was found. It is the civilization of the Umbrians.

This culture has very many affinities with that which prevailed on the other side of the Alps, in the valley of the Danube. Its most significant feature is the ossuary, which is like that of the tumuli and tombs of Hallstatt.[3] This latter has its ancestors in the common pottery of the end of the Bronze Age, north of the Danube Valley.[4] From the route followed by these technical developments we may infer that of the advance of the peoples which had that civilization in Italy, if they really were newcomers in that country. Now in Italy, in Northern Italy, there had formerly been a fairly dense population, which had built, on both sides of the Po, rectangular villages reared on piles, the remains of which are known as terremare.[5] The terremare had disappeared. Were the Villanova men descended from their inhabitants ? Certainly not.[6] The people of Villanova took the place of

---

[1] Grenier, op. cit., passim ; Homo, op. cit., English, pp. 55 ff.
[2] Grenier, op. cit., pp. 160 ff., 127 ff.
[3] Ibid., pp. 133–5.
[4] H. Hubert, in **CXLIII**, 1910, pp. 5 ff.
[5] Homo, op. cit., English, pp. 30 ff. ;   Montelius, **DXXXV**, pp. 55–89, pls. v–x ; Modestov, **DXXXVI**, pp. 156–215.
[6] Déchelette, ii, 1, p. 23, n. 1 ; ii, 2, p. 537, n. 2.

those of the *terremare* ; they were not descended from them.

There is, therefore, reason for believing that the Umbrians arrived in Italy about the beginning of the Iron Age.[1] They came from north of the Alps, and it was in that region that they had been in contact with the Celts.[2]

Where, then, do the Latins come in ?[3] Latin and Irish being in the same position in relation to Italic and Celtic respectively, the Latins and Goidels must have been in like positions with regard to the larger groups of which they formed part. The Goidels had advanced furthest west of the Celts (ἔσχατοι ἀνδρῶν), and the Brythons seem to have followed in their footsteps (but this has still to be proved). The Latins, then, should be those of the Italici who first moved away from the common cradle of the race and first settled in Italy.

At the date of the foundation of the first villages which were to unite to form Rome, Latium was evidently the centre of the Latins. Their archæological domain is distinguished fairly clearly, save on the Etruscan side, from that of the Umbrians. Its characteristics are the hut-urn and the funerary *dolium*.[4] Other urns are found, covered with helmets or with caps, crowned by the *apex* of the Roman priests.

The Sabellians, whose language has the same differential characteristics, were their neighbours on the south-east.[5] But where had they been before ? Must we not give a place to the Iberians and Ligurians in the prehistoric civilizations of Italy in the Bronze Age and before it ?[6]

Several important features of Roman civilization, such as the form of the city (*Roma quadrata*) and of the camp, with its quadrangular plan and its two main streets crossing each other and aligned on the cardinal points, and the College

---

[1] Cato, quoted by Pliny, *N.H.*, iii, 114, says that the Umbrians founded Ameria 963 or 964 years before the war of Perseus, i.e. about 1134 B.C.

[2] Hence the theory of some ancient grammarians that the Umbrians were a branch of the Gauls ; Solinus, ii, 11 (according to Bocchus, a historian of the first century) ; Isidore of Seville, *Orig.*, ix, 2, 87 (Dottin, **CCCXXII**, pp. 25–6). This error is the foundation of Bertrand's hypothesis (**CCCIII**, pp. 27–32) on the first Celtic invasion of Italy. Cf. Thierry, **CCCLXXXVIII**, i, xlii.

[3] Homo, op. cit., English, pp. 41 ff.

[4] Ibid., English, pp. 75–80 ; Modestov, **DXXXVI**, pp. 248 ff.

[5] Walde, **CCXLIV**.

[6] Déchelette, ii, 1, p. 23, n. 1 ; Homo, op. cit. ; Philipon, **CCCLXIX**.

of Pontifices, recall the *terremare*, with their ritual regularity of plan, their moats and bridges.[1] Did the Latins, then, once live in the *terremare* of the plain of the Po ? It is probable that they did, and that they there mingled with the Ligurians, with whom historical tradition represents them as associated down to the foundation of Rome.[2] When we look among the remains of the *terremare* for signs of the arrival of the Latins we are faced with an *embarras de richesses*—handles with crescent-shaped projections,[3] vases with wart-ornament,[4] tanged swords,[5] pins with ring-heads, coin-necklaces.[6]

So the Latins descended into Italy some time before the Umbrians. Since they were separated from the rest of the Italic peoples, their language did not share in the evolution of their dialects. That was how Latin became different from the other Italic languages. All this gives us at least a presumption to explain what happened to Celtic.

But we must go further. The Villanovan civilization was introduced into Italy almost at the same time as the successors of the Mycenæans entered Greece. About the beginning of the first Iron Age, at the end of the second millennium before Christ, a certain stirring took place in Europe, which is revealed in prehistoric archæology by many novelties,[7] and the result of it was that new Aryan bodies descended into the Mediterranean world. A similar agitation had occurred earlier, at the end of the first period of the Bronze Age, and had had the same effects.[8]

The movements of the Celts were, in my opinion, likewise in two waves, and must have been governed by the same demographic laws, by the same general facts in the history of civilization. In other words, the breaking-off of the Goidelic group, and probably the first Celtic colonization of the British Isles, must have occurred at the same time as the descent of the Latins into Italy, and that of the first Greek invaders into Greece. The differentiation of the

---

[1] Peet, **CCCCXLVII** ; Homo, op. cit., English, p. 50.
[2] Homo, op. cit., English, pp. 45 ff.
[3] Ibid., English, p. 50. See also Pigorini, in **LII**, 1900, pp. 21 ff. ; Modestov, op. cit., pp. 156–225, 288 ff. ; Peet, in **CLXI**, 1910, 2, pp. 386–7 ; Grenier, in **CXXXIX**, 1914, i, p. 328.
[4] H. Hubert, loc. cit.
[5] Modestov, op. cit., pl. xix, and pp. 187 ff.
[6] H. Hubert, in **CLIII**, 1925, p. 25, n. 3.
[7] Déchelette, ii, 3, p. 1289.
[8] Id., ii, pp. 2, 6 ff.

Brythonic, Umbrian, and Doric dialects took place afterwards at some time unknown, among the groups which had
remained behind and in contact with one another.   The
migratory movement of the peoples speaking these dialects
occurred about the same time, but after their dialects had
become differentiated, and the result of it was that they
became definitely different languages.

In short, the dividing of the Celtic peoples into two groups
is an ancient event, of very great importance, connected with
the great facts of European prehistory.   It is the consequence
of the breaking-up of the Italo-Celtic community.

This demonstration is based mainly on three hypotheses,
which it may be as well to state here.   The first is that
linguistic affinities indicate at least the proximity of the races
concerned.   The second is that certain concordances must
have originated not only in one neighbourhood, but about the
same time.   The third is that each separate set of archæological
facts is a set of ethnographical facts, which may correspond
to one or other of the ethnographical facts implied by the
various dialects concerned.

There is nothing extravagant in these hypotheses.

II

THE CRADLE OF THE CELTS.   VARIOUS THEORIES

Before we inquire what sets of archæological facts
correspond to the breaking-off of the Goidels and the separate
existence of the Goidels and the Brythons, we must determine,
if it can be done, the place from which both bodies set forth.
The cradle of the Celts was, no doubt, quite close to the cradle
of the Italici.   Now these latter came to Italy from the north
and north-east, not from the west or north-west, of the
Alps.   It is, therefore, north of the Alps, whether close to
them or far away, that we must look for the Celts.

There are two contradictory traditions regarding the
origin of the Celts.   One places them where the ancients knew
them ; the other, further east, along the North Sea.   In the
time of Tarquin the Proud, we read in Livy,[1] the Gauls were
strongly established in the centre of what is now France.

[1] v, 34.

They centred round the Bituriges and their king, who at that time was called Ambicatus. Besides the Bituriges, the confederation comprised the Arverni, Senones, Ædui, Ambarri, Carnutes, and Aulerci, that is, the peoples which in Livy's time occupied the very centre of the Celtic world. " Gaul," he says, " was so fertile and populous that the immense multitude threatened to be hard to rule. So the King, being old and wishing to relieve his kingdom of its excess population, declared that he would send his sister's sons, Bellovesus and Sigovesus, who were energetic youths, to whatever country the gods should indicate by omens, and they could take as many men as they wished, so that no people should be able to resist their advance. The omens assigned the Hercynian Forests to Sigovesus, and to the much more fortunate Bellovesus the road to Italy."

The ancient historians were fairly clear as to the limits reached by the Gauls. They were so well established in Gaul in the first century before Christ that it required an unusually critical spirit to doubt that Gaul was the cradle of the race. The invasions by which they extended their frontiers were supposed to have started from Gaul.

But the tradition recorded by Livy is by no means to be despised. The names are good Gallic—Ambicatus " He-who-gives-battle-all-round ", Bellovesus " He-who-can-kill ", Sigovesus " He-who-can-conquer ". They may be fancy names, but the fancy is native. Therefore the tradition must be a Gallic one, which Livy doubtless got from Cornelius Nepos, that is, from the Gallic historian Trogus Pompeius.

Cæsar says as much [1] : " There was a time when the Gauls surpassed the Germans in valour, carried war into their country, and sent colonies across the Rhine to relieve their own territory of its excess population. It was in this way that the Volcæ Tectosages came to take possession of the most fertile districts of Germany, near the Hercynian Forest, which seems to have been known to Eratosthenes and some other Greeks under the name of Orcynian. There that tribe has maintained itself to this day, and enjoys a great reputation for justice and courage. Even now they live in the same poverty and with the same frugality as the Germans ; they have adopted their manner of life and their dress " (Cæsar

[1] *Gall. War*, vi, 24.

is seriously misleading as to the poverty of the Volcæ). Tacitus, in his *Germania*,[1] repeats Cæsar's opinion, and mentions other peoples east of the Volcæ—the Boii in Bohemia and the Cotini in Silesia.

But there were other traditions which are echoed in the ancient historians. Ammianus Marcellinus, in a long passage about the Gauls, writes as follows : "*Drasidæ memorant revera fuisse populi partem indigenam* (the Druids relate that part of the population was really indigenous), *sed alios quoque ab insulis extimis confluxisse et tractibus Transrhenanis* (but that others had come in from the outermost isles and the regions beyond the Rhine)."[2] The aborigines are the Ligurians or other races, and the newcomers are the Celts. Ammianus Marcellinus or his source, Timagenes, says a word on the reasons for their migration. "They were," he says, "driven from their homes by the frequency of wars and violent rising of the sea—*Crebritate bellorum et adluvione fervidi maris sedibus suis expulsos.*" So the Celts had come from beyond the Rhine, but more especially from the low countries washed by the North Sea.

Further evidence for the marine upheavals of which the Celts are reported to have been victims was furnished by the historian Ephoros [3] ; it is quoted by Strabo, who is, however, sceptical. Ephoros described the Celts as obstinately remaining in their threatened lands, and losing more lives in the floods than in war.[4] The legend of the Celts advancing against the waves with their weapons probably goes back to this tradition,[5] to which there is an allusion, of still more respectable antiquity, in the *Ora Maritima* of Avienus.[6] The passage must be quoted, for it resumes some centuries of Celtic history in ten lines.[7]

The voyager who has left Britain on his left and sails northwards comes to the land of the Ligurians, *cæspitem*

---

[1] xxviii.
[2] xv, 9, 2. Ammianus's source is Timagenes of Alexandria, a valuable historian who gave most of the classical traditions about the Gauls their accepted shape. O. Hirschfeld, in **XXXVII**, 1894, p. 36.
[3] In *F.H.G.*, i, 243–4 ; Dottin, **CCCXXII**, p. 300.
[4] Strabo, vii, 2, 1.
[5] Arist., *Eth.*, ii, 7.
[6] See above, p. 3.
[7] 140–5. In Pytheas's time there had long been no Celtic peoples on the coast, but the Germans of Jutland and the Danish islands, where the amber-trade was conducted, were very much Celticized.

Ligurum subit, which is empty of inhabitants, emptied as a result of the attacks of the Celts. They, too, were a fleeing people, *fugax gens hæc quidem.*

> *Diu inter arta cautium duxit diem*
> *secreta ab undis. Nam sali metuens erat*
> *priscum ob periclum ; post quies et otium,*
> *securitate roborante audaciam*
> *persuasit altis devehi cubilibus*
> *atque in marinos jam locos descendere.*

Avienus's source, better informed than Ephoros and Timagenes, made the Celts move backwards and forwards between the sea and the mountains.

Pytheas found the Celtic country on the coast, some days' sailing from Cantion, that is Kent, but his valuable evidence needs to be interpreted.

We are treating the ancient writers with a respect which they do not quite deserve if we rely on the documents which we have just been considering to place the Celtic cradle either in Gaul or on the very shores of the North Sea. Nevertheless, modern theories of the origin of the Celts, whether based on the observation of archæological facts or on the interpretation of historico-linguistic facts, are falling into line with the ancient beliefs.

Three of these theories must be discussed separately and set aside. The most learned of Rhenish archæologists, Herr Schumacher, maintains that the movements of the Celts went from west to east. The Celts who peopled the Rhineland, he says, came from Gaul.[1] A general shifting from west to east set up among the Celtic peoples during a period which, in his view, begins in the middle of the Hallstatt age. The Sequani, starting from the Seine, reached the Franche-Comté ; the Mediomatrici left the Marne to settle on the Meuse ; the Helvetii were Helvii from the banks of the Allier ; the Volcæ, the Bituriges Cubi, and the Turones were spread out from the Danube to Thuringia. The Treveri

---

[1] Schumacher, " Die Erforschung d. röm. u. vorröm. Strassennetzes in Westdeutschland," in **XXIX**, 1906, p. 25 ; id., in **LXXXIV**, ii, pp. 16, 18 ; id., in **CXVIII**, 1916, p. 133 ; id., in *Nassauische Annalen*, 1917, p. 175 ; id., in **LXV**, N.S., i, 1917–1922 ; id., **CCCCIX**, i, pp. 214 ff. ; H. Hubert, in **CXL**, 1925, pp. 254–7.

were of the same origin.[1] Their arrival in the valley of the Rhine is attested by a type of Hallstatt urn common in the region centring on the mouth of the Main, which resembles more southern types save in the poverty of its decoration. Herr Schumacher calls this the Mehren type.[2] The Celts, he says, reached the Rhine through the Palatinate and the Hunsrück. Crossing the river they came to the Taunus, the Westerwald, and the Vogelsberg. He follows them in the valley of the Tauber and the Odenwald. They stopped on the line of Hagenau, Rastatt, and Stuttgart. Later contingents, coming up, reinforced the first settlements, and introduced and established the civilization of La Tène. The name of the Roman Province of Rætia points to the resistance of the old Hallstatt population. This latter was Ræto-Ligurian, and had been reinforced by Illyrian elements.[3] Herr Schumacher, who has spent his life following the traces of prehistoric man on the map, has very justly remarked that the oldest roads climbed the hillsides and followed the watersheds. It was by these upland roads that the Celts advanced. He likens their movements to the treks of the Boers. They were pastoral folk, extending their grazing-grounds.

But when one starts pricking out routes on a map one is too easily led into imagining movements and directions. The discovery of groups of similar objects on a line which may have been a route does not show in which direction the route was followed. In reality the proofs are but slender. No doubt the pottery of Haulzy may resemble that of the Hunsrück. Herr Schumacher errs as to the direction in which Celtic civilization spread, because he has not seen the poverty and the wealth of the French Hallstatt period for himself. To him the immense mass of tumuli in the Franche-Comté perhaps represents the Celts in their original home. But if we look closely we can only regard that district as a jumping-off point.[4] Herr Schumacher's hypothesis, based on such a complete knowledge of the archæological evidence and such a sure judgment in matters of detail, only shows what

---

[1] Schumacher, in **LXXXIV.** 1916, pp. 133 ff.
[2] Id., in **LXVII,** 1918, pp. 98 ff. ; **CCCCIX,** p. 89.
[3] A. Schliz, in **CLXV,** 1908, pp. 426 ff. ; id., in *Heilbronn. Festschr.*, 1911, pp. 41 ff. ; Schumacher, **CCCCIX,** p. 109.
[4] Cf. certain pages of Schumacher, following on Helmke's work on the excavation of tumuli in **CLIX,** i, ii, 1918–19.

a delicate matter the racial interpretation of prehistoric archæology is.

M. Camille Jullian, after having followed the tradition of Ephoros and Timagenes,[1] propounds an entirely new theory of the origin of the Celts which, if it were accepted, would change the ground of part of the problems which we have still to settle.[2] He would obliterate all frontiers between Celtic and Ligurian.[3] In his view Ligurian is the pre-Celtic language, or, rather, a common language spoken alike by Celts and Italici, in fact, Italo-Celtic. The undivided Italo-Celtic body, instead of having been confined to Central Europe north of the Alps, as I have suggested, covered the whole of Western Europe. One fine day it resolved into its divergent elements ; M. Jullian does not tell us how. It is, indeed, difficult to imagine this dissolution if one adopts M. Jullian's theory, for, pursuing his theory as far as it will go, he makes the Italo-Celtic world a sort of united empire, the unity of which alone made possible the cultural developments which took place in it. He is thinking particularly of the trade in bronze. It is a plausible theory, for there were Italo-Ligurians in Italy, just as much as there were Celto-Ligurians in Gaul, but, although it is advancing in favour, it is only a surmise.

It must be dismissed as non-proven in the present state of our knowledge, for several reasons. First, there is not one single word attributed to Ligurian with good reason which has any one of the characteristics peculiar to Italic and Latin. We can suppose, from its wretched remnants, that it was something like Italic and Celtic, but we are not in a position to regard it as their original source. Secondly, the area covered by place-names in *asco, osco,* and *usco* does not correspond on its eastern border with that which I shall show reason for assigning to the earliest Celts. Thirdly, the ancient writers, who seem to be perfectly well acquainted with the Ligurians and use the name of Ligurian, not for an enormously spread-out nation, but as the generic name of an immense number of tribes—Salyes, Taurini, Sicels, Ambrones—always distinguish them from the Celts and the

---

[1] Jullian, **CCCXLVII**, i, pp. 227 ff.
[2] Id., in **CXXXIV**, 1917, p. 124 ; 1918, p. 43.
[3] Sir John Rhys made a similar attempt, but made Ligurian a Goidelic language of Gaul.

Italici. There were Ligurians in Rome, but they were driven out of Reate by the Sabines,[1] that is to say, by Latins. The Celto-Ligurians of Gaul are evidence of the almost generic difference between the two elements of which they were composed. Lastly, the fact remains that Ligurians were left over who did not become either Celts or Italici. Therefore the whole area covered by the Ligurians cannot be regarded as the domain of the Italo-Celts before they split ; that must be defined on its own account.

This new theory has not provided a solution, but a new and unnecessary name for the old problems. It has introduced into archæology a most vexatious tendency, which has been too readily accepted [2] ; namely, that notion of a prehistoric empire which has the air of a sociological or historical interpretation of facts. Now nothing in the prehistoric archæology of the Celtic world or the Ligurian world gives the least suggestion of an empire, even in the nature of the Aztec Empire.

A third theory has lately been put forward by Mr. Peake.[3] This is based on the interpretation of a piece of archæological evidence and of one only, namely the so-called flat-tanged sword. The hilt of this sword consists of a metal tang springing from the base of the blade and shaped to fit the hand, with pieces of other material rivetted on to its two faces.[4] Swords of this type were first used as a sign of race by Herr Kossinna,[5] who regarded them as evidence of the expansion of the Germans. He drew up a chronological classification of them which still holds good.

The early swords have only one or two rivets at the guard and none on the hilt. Most were found in Schleswig-Holstein (about thirty in all), and the rest not far off. They date from the middle of the second period of the Bronze Age.[6] The next type, belonging to the end of that period, has rivets on the hilt and, without exception, more than two pairs of rivets on the guard. The swords of the third period of the Bronze Age are distinguished from their predecessors by the fact that the edges of the hilt and guard form one continuous

---

[1] Dion. Hal., ii, 49.   [2] Homo, **CCCXLI**, English pp. 46–7.
[3] **CCCCXLVII**, pp. 81–103.   [4] Déchelette, ii, 1, pp. 208–9.
[5] Kossinna, in **LXXXV**, 1912, pp. 275 ff.
[6] H. Hubert, in **XV**, 1920, pp. 575–6.

concave curve. Most of the examples of this type also come from Schleswig-Holstein. Here Herr Kossinna stops, but the history of these swords went on much longer, well into the Hallstatt period. Hallstatt swords of this class have at the base of the blade notches to which a guard was probably attached.[1]

Mr. Peake has no difficulty in showing that Herr Kossinna's statistics are incomplete. He adds a long series of swords from Hungary and the north of Italy.[2] He concludes that the Celts originally came from the middle valley of the Danube. Thus he is opposed to both the other theories which I have discussed. But it is evident that he confounds the area of extension of the Celts with that of the Indo-Europeans of Europe.[3] In trying to settle the question of race by examining one single indication, he has taken a cultural fact of far too general a kind as the indication of a particular race.

The problem of the origin of the Celts can only be solved by following the data given in the preceding chapters. They were allied to the Italic peoples in language, and their routes crossed. They rubbed shoulders with the Germans, lived in the same climate as the Slavs, and perhaps encountered the Illyrians and Greeks near their cradle. Furthermore, the main body of the Celts and the leading nations among them were certainly settled in the region where the civilization of La Tène was formed, that is, where it could receive the decisive influences of Greece and Italy direct, where industry displayed the greatest inventiveness and the relics of human life bear witness to wealth in the most settled condition.

---

[1] I have called attention (ibid.) to the fact that the area in which these swords were found stretched far further, but westwards (Western Germany, France, Spain, the British Isles), than Herr Kossinna made it do ; so much so, that I regard it as one indication of the extension of the Celts. In proof, I only cited the collection in the Saint-Germain Museum, which is large and very representative (Déchelette, ii, 1, pp. 208–9). I am of opinion that this type of hilt is not of Northern origin, but was used in Ægean and Hungarian daggers. If so, the flat-hilted swords of Mycenæan type are not imports from the North. For the significance of these swords with regard to the ethnology of the Celts, see below, p. 177.

[2] **CCCCXLVII,** pls. x, xiii.
[3] Same work.

III

Western Germany fulfils these conditions exactly. It is full of place-names of Celtic origin, quite especially in the south-west. A very large number have survived in recognizable form.

First there are the *names of towns*.[1] In Bavaria, Carrodunum (Karnberg), Cambodunum (Kempten),[2] and Locoritum (Lohr); in Wurtemberg, Virodunum (Wirtenberg); in Baden, Tarodunum (Zarten), near Freiburg-in-Breisgau, Bragodunum or Bragodurum (Brännlingen), and Lopodunum (Ladenburg) on the Neckar, near Mannheim; in Hessen and the Rhine Province, Tredentus (Trans) near Mainz,[3] Bondobriga (Boppard), Vincum (Bingen), Valandra (Vallendar), Vosavia (Wesel), and, right in the north, Mediolanum (Meteln-an-der-Vichte).[4]

All these names have been changed and Germanized in different degrees. Others have been completely altered, or cannot be identified exactly with the names of towns now existing. Near the Main, Segodunum is doubtless Würzburg; Bamberg was Devona; Rottenburg on the Neckar was Sumelocenna. In Bavaria, Boiodurum has become Innstadt, a suburb of Passau, which was Batava Castra, and Ratisbona has become Régensburg (Ratisbon). Stranting was Sorviodurum. In the south-east of Bavaria there was a town of Artobriga, which may be Burgerwald, between Teissendorf and Traunstein, and in the Taunus, near Frankfort, there was an Aretaunum.

It is needless to demonstrate the Celtic character of all these names. It is apparent at first sight. It is due to obviously Celtic elements—*dunum, durum, bona, ritum, briga, cenna, lanum, are*.[5] Moreover, many of these names are found also in Gaul.[6]

[1] D'Arbois, **CCXCIX**, pp. 9 ff., 127–131; Müllenhoff, **CCCLXII**, ii, p. 227; Grupp, **CCCXCIV**, p. 69; Cramer, **CXCV**.
[2] P. Reinecke, in **LXI**, 1912, p. 4.   [3] D'Arbois, **CCCI**, ii, p. 324.
[4] Schumacher, in **CX**, 1917.
[5] I have not mentioned the names in *-acus* (Abudiacus, Eppach; Cassiliacus, Kisslegg : Lauriꞈcum, Lorch), which may be Gallo-Roman place-names of the time of the Empire.
[6] Tredentus or Tridens (Trans) = Tredentus or Tridens, in the diocese of Le Mans = Tridentum (Trent) in N. Italy (D'Arbois, loc. cit.).

The Celtic place-names of Western Germany include, too, a series of names of mountains and a still larger number of names of rivers.

Names of Mountains.[1]—Ercynia Silva, the Erzgebirge ; Gabreta Silva, the Goat Mountain, the Böhmer-Wald, also in Bohemia. In Gaulish, the word for goat was *gabros* (Irish *gathar*, Welsh *gafr*, Breton *gabr*). The Finne, a range in the basin of the Saale north of Saxe-Weimar, south of the Harz, has a name of Celtic origin, *pennos*, head (Welsh and Breton *pen*, a Brythonic word, the Irish form being *ceann*).[2] The name of the Taunus is not Germanic, and may be Celtic. I do not venture to suggest a derivation. Some have connected it with *dunum*.[3]

Names of Rivers.[4]—First of all the Rhine (Rēnos) and Danube (Danuvius) have Celtic names. In Irish *rian* corresponds to Rēnos exactly, the Irish diphthong standing for an *e* in ancient Celtic ; the word means the sea. The name Danuvius is applied to the upper course of the Danube, which flowed through a Celtic country ; in Irish *dana* means swift. Ister is the Illyrian, eastern name of the river.

The Danube has tributaries and sub-tributaries with Celtic names. The Laber (Labara), which flows into the Danube on the left bank, near Ratisbon, is the Talking River (Irish *labrur*, Welsh *llafar*, Breton *lauar*). The Lauterach, a sub-sub-tributary, flowing through the Vils and the Naab into the Danube near Ratisbon, has a name in which the Celtic *lautron* can be recognized.[5] Near Salzburg, in the valley of the Inn, there is a Glan. Glan is Glana, the Pure (Old Irish *glan*). There is another in Rhenish Bavaria. A tributary of the Upper Danube, the Brege, gets its name from a Celtic Bragos.[6] We should note that river-names, which were masculine in Celtic, were made feminine by the Germans. It is supposed that the name Licus, the Lech, is likewise Celtic.[7]

---

[1] W. Krause, **CCCXCVII**, p. 39.
[2] Doubts have been cast on the Celtic origin of the name Finne. Vendryès, in **CXL**, xlii, p. 194.
[3] Holder, **CCVII**, s.v. " Taunos ".
[4] D'Arbois, **CCXCIX**, p. 6 ; Grupp, **CCCXCIV**, p. 69.
[5] Endlicher's Glossary : *lautro = balneo*. Dottin, **CXCVI**, p. 265 : Ir. *loathar* " basin " ; Breton *louazr* " trough ".
[6] Bragodunum, in the Rhine valley, stood on another Bragos.
[7] Licorix, 'Ἀμβιλικοι, in Pannonia.

In the basin of the Rhine, Celtic names of rivers are still more numerous. That of the Neckar, Nicer, may be Celtic. That of the Main, Mœnus, probably is ; in any case, the diphthong is not Germanic.[1] That of its tributary, the Nida, is certainly Celtic ; it is shared by the Scottish Nith and the Nied, an affluent of the Saar, in Lorraine. The Tauber, a tributary of the Main on the left bank, was called Dubra, the nominative plural of *dubron*, a Celtic word meaning water.[2] Near the Tauber there was a Vernodubrum ; that is, an Erlenbach ; now there is an Erlenbach just there, and there are some others in the same district, whose names may perhaps have the same origin.

The name of the Lahn, Logna,[3] is not Germanic, and may be Celtic. In any case, Nassau, through which it flows, has a name which recalls Nasonia (Nassogne in the Belgian Luxemburg) and Nasium (Naix-sur-Ornain, in the department of the Meuse). The Ruhr, Raura, has the same name as the Hérault, Arauris.[4] The Embscher, which is called Embiscara in tenth-century documents, was once Ambiscara, in which one can see two Celtic elements, *ambi* and *isca*, a word for water which has furnished river-names in Britain, to which a suffix *ara* or *ala* has been attached. So, too, we have Iscara, Iscala, from which come the Ischar in Alsace and the Ischl in Austria, near Salzburg. The Lippe (Lupia or Lupias) has a name of uncertain origin, but it flowed by Aliso, the name of which is very like Alesia.[5] There is the same proportion of Celtic names on the left bank of the Rhine.

So much for the valley of the Rhine. The origin of Amisicus, the name of the Ems, is uncertain.[6] In the valley of the Weser, the Wümme had the name, perhaps Celtic, of Uimina, which was also borne by the Visme, an affluent of the Bresle. But some have regarded it as Ligurian.[7]

---

[1] It recalls the Irish *muin* "neck" (Welsh *mynci* "collar"; see above, p. 38).

[2] Ir. *dobor*, Welsh *dubr*, *dwfyr*, Bret. *dubr*, *daour*.

[3] Laugona, Loucona.

[4] The Sieg (Sigina) bears the name of the Seine (Sequana) Germanized. But it is not certain that the latter is Celtic ; it may be Ligurian (Jullian, **CCCXLVII**, i, p. 115) or Iberian (Philipon, **DXVI**, p. 128).

[5] Alesia may be explained by Old Irish *all*, gen. *aille* (from *als-* ; cf. Germanic *fels* " rock ") ; Alesia would mean Rocky Hill.

[6] H. M. Chadwick, in **CLXXXII**, p. 318, n. 2.

[7] Müllenhoff, **CCCLXII**, ii, p. 232.

The Leine, further south, seems to have the same name as the Lahn.[1] The Weser itself has an indubitably Germanic name, Visurgis, which may, however, conceal a Celtic name.[2] The name of the Elbe either is Germanic and the same as the Swedish word *elf*, meaning river, or belongs to the family of the Aubes, Albes, Albion, which is pan-European. The names of its tributaries are probably Germanic, except, perhaps, that of the Saale ; and this, like the other names of rivers in Western Germany, may equally well be Celtic or Germanic.[3] In Thuringia three Wippers have a name, the Celtic origin of which has lately been revealed, as in the case of the Wupper in the Rhine basin.[4]

The list of Celtic river-names in Germany has been extended by the incorporation of a long series of names (mostly of streams) ending in -*ef*, -*pe*, -*p*, and -*ft* (Olef, in the Eifel ; Wörpe, an affluent of the Wümme ; Erft, near Neuss), the Latin name of which end in -*eva*, -*efa*, -*apa*, -*afa*, -*affa*.[5] For these names have equivalents in Britain,[6] such as Ἄβος (the Humber) (Ptolemy), Abona (the Avon) (Tacitus), Αὔσοβα, Τοίσυβις, Τουέροβις. This makes it probable, if not certain, that they are Celtic.[7] They are very frequent in Flanders, Brabant, Holland, and the German provinces west of the Rhine, and extend north-eastwards to a line which runs up the Weser valley, goes through Hanover, and stops at the ridge of the Harz, embracing the greater part of Westphalia. They become very rare and finally disappear south of the Harz. So, if we add this series of names, they extend the area of Celtic place-names towards the north-east and give us its limits in that direction more accurately.[8] But on the whole, Celtic names, which are

---

[1] Ibid. Its Latin form, *Laina*, may be a Germanization of a Loina, Logna (cf. Mœnus).

[2] Cf. La Vesdre, a tributary of the Ourthe, which then became Liez, and the Wear in Durham.

[3] Müllenhoff, op. cit., ii, p. 213. Cf. Salzach, which flows into the Plattensee, Seille (Salia), and Selse, near Alzey (Salusia).

[4] Ibid., ii, p. 214.

[5] Ibid., ii, pp. 207 ff. ; C. Tauber, in **LXIX**, 1910, 2, p. 333 ; Chadwick, same article, p. 315 (cf. **CXL**, xxxviii, p. 283). Many of the names in this series now have a termination in -*er* ; e.g. Hesper (Hesapa), on the Ruhr.

[6] Abusina (Abens) near Ratisbon ; Apala (Appel) near Kreuznach (Müllenhoff, op. cit., ii, pp. 227–230).

[7] Ibid., ii, p. 231, comparing Olef, Olpe, Oleve, with Ὀλίνας (the Orne), Olario, Oléron.

[8] Ibid., ii, p. 232.

very frequent in the valleys of the Rhine and Danube, grow scarce before we reach the Elbe, and are almost wholly absent in Frisia and the northern part of Hanover. If the Celts ever were in those parts they were driven out at a very early date.

What do these Celtic place-names mean ? That the Celts set out from Germany, or that they conquered it ? There is

MAP 3. Northern Germany.

strong reason for believing that the names are aboriginal, or, at least, very ancient, since there are so many names of rivers and mountains among them. We know that such names are almost rare in Gaul.[1] Many names of French rivers and mountains come from the Ligurians, if not from still further back.[2] Now the names given to the land and its natural features are the most enduring of place-names. The

[1] Dottin, **CXCVI**, p. 74.　　　[2] Jullian, **CCCXLVII**, i, p. 114.

first occupants of a country always pass them on to their successors. These latter sometimes add a name of their own. The Gauls did this in Gaul. To the Araris, a tributary of the Rhone, they gave the name of Souconna, Saône. But the new name has not always won the day. In Germany, likewise, we find some Ligurian or Iberian names, perhaps even east of the Rhine [1]; but among the non-Germanic names a very large number, and those very ancient, are Celtic.

There is one which bears in itself evidence of its great antiquity, and that is the name of the Hercynian Forest. It is a relic of a very ancient state of the Celtic world. It had probably remained attached to the place which it designated ever since it took its earliest form. At that time the Celts were neighbours of the Italici in that region. The name appears in different forms—Hercynia, Ἀρκύνια, Ἑρκύνια, Ὀρκύνια, Ἑρκύνιον ὄρος.[2] The initial h is uncertain. In any case, the etymology seems clear.[3] The word is derived from a name of the oak, common [4] to Celtic, Italic, and Germanic, $perq^w$, which is preserved unaltered in the name of the Lithuanian god Perkunas. Old High German forhe attests it equally, although it has changed its meaning. Latin made $perq^wos$ into quercus, following the rule which I have explained before. Celtic, following the same rule, should have produced first *Querqunia and then *Perpunia in Brythonic. But, before the rule took effect, the velar in the second syllable was probably changed, as in a certain number of words, to k. The p, having then escaped assimilation, maintained itself (Gothic Fairguni [5] may, perhaps, be evidence of this stage in the history of the word), and was later dropped, as p usually was in Celtic. In short, the name of the Hercynian Forest dates from an age before the Celtic dropping of p and the Italo-Celtic assimilation of p to the velar in two-syllable words of the form $p \ldots q^w$. Now, it is a fossil,

---

[1] Even if Sieg is Ligurian or Iberian, in any case, the Beybach, near Neumagen on the west bank of the Rhine, was called Rodanus (Venantius Fortunatus, 3, 12, 7 ; cf. M. Müller, in **CLVII**, 1906, pp. 51–9) ; not to mention a tributary of the Upper Danube on the right bank.

[2] Holder, **CCVII**, s.v. " Ercunion ".

[3] The Welsh verb er-chynu " to rise " has been mentioned in this connection ; but the prefix was are in Gaulish (Müllenhoff, op. cit., ii, p. 243).

[4] D'Arbois, in **CXL**, 1890, p. 216 ; Kluge, in Pauly and Wissowa, i, col. 325.

[5] Wiedenann, in **CCXXXVIII**, xxviii, 1904, i.

for the Celtic languages took the common name of the oak from other roots ; and the fossil is *in situ*.

D'Arbois de Jubainville has extracted from the names of German rivers indications regarding the direction in which the Celtic peoples moved.[1] He has observed that many of these peoples were called after places, and particularly after rivers, which seem to have been in their neighbourhood.[2] In Italy there were the Ambisontes, who were Gauls settled astride of the Isonzo ; in Illyria, the Ambidravi on both banks of the Drave ; in Gaul, the Ambarri on both banks of the Arasis, or Saône.[3] The Taurisci were the Gauls of the Tauros, that is, the Tauern ; the Scordisci, those of the Shar-Dagh ; the Sequani, those of the Sequana. This kind of name was especially suitable for groups which had broken off from larger groups and had not yet got a name of their own, or chance groups whose unity, while they were still settling, was chiefly geographical. Now, we always find them in process of forming or of breaking off.

Some of these names taken from places show that their bearers had changed their abode. The Sequani, for example, who lived in the Franche-Comté were nowhere near the river to which they owed their name, the Sequana, or Seine. We shall see how they came to leave it.

Now, we know Gallic peoples whose names recall those of rivers in Germany which have kept their Celtic name.[4] Near Basle there dwelt the Raurici ; the Raura is the Ruhr, and there is no other river of the name. Avranches is the town of the Abrincatui ; the Abrinca is the Vinxtbach, which flows into the Rhine on the left bank, south-east of Cologne. D'Arbois de Jubainville [5] adds to these the Salassi or Salluvii of the Alps, who perhaps came from the banks of a Sala in Saxony or Lorraine. But it is not certain that they were Celts. At the very most they were Celto-Ligurians.

The same reasoning would lead one to suppose that the Volcæ, Cenomani,[6] Turones, Santones,[7] and Lemovii or

---

[1] D'Arbois, **CCXCIX,** p. 129.

[2] Philipon (**CCCLXIX,** p. 153, n. 7) declares that the Iberians can be recognized by these names of peoples taken from names of rivers ; e.g. Iber and Iberes, Astura and Astures.   [3] Pauly and Wissowa, i, col. 1795.

[4] D'Arbois, op. cit., p. 130.   [5] Ibid., p. 154.

[6] A subdivision of the Volcæ ; cf. Cenomanni (ibid., p. 153).

[7] On the Main, in the Odenwald (Zangemeister, in **I,** xiii, 2, i, p. 283, No. 6607 ; Norden, **CCCCIV,** p. 257).

Lemovices,[1] who appear distributed between Germany and Gaul in Cæsar's time, originally came from Germany, not from Gaul.[2] This was what the Helvetii did, who left behind them, on the right bank of the Rhine, the desert of the Helvetii. One part of them, the Tigurini, has left place-names

MAP 4. Germany between the Rhine and Elbe.

in Bavaria to tell of their former presence in that country. Another, the Raurici, were once, perhaps, on the Ruhr, and their last migration was the cause of Cæsar's intervention in

[1] Tac., Germ., 43 ; **CLXVIII**, 1930, p. 153.
[2] Cf. Jullian, **CCCXLVII**, i, p. 251, n. 8. According to him, the Volcæ lived in the valleys of the Doubs, Saône, and Marne, and joined in the migration to the Danube.

Gaul, as was that of the Boii, who followed the same route at the same time. The Helvetii and Boii were the last of the Celtic peoples to move, and their movement, related in some detail by an eminent contemporary, can be regarded as the last wave of the general movement in which the Celtic peoples were involved.

With regard to the Volcæ, one of the oldest groups and one of the first to leave their old homes, bodies of whom went to the ends of the Celtic world and were in the position of an advanced guard in Gaul, a recent conjecture corroborates our hypothesis regarding their original habitat. That very ingenious philologist, M. Cuny, has compared the name of the Volcæ to that of the Volsci of Latium,[1] and suggests that the two peoples had the same name, having the termination -*co* in one case and -*sco* in the other. Both terminations were used alternatively in what was apparently the old name of the Oscans, Opisci, or, as the Greeks said, 'Οπικοί. If M. Cuny is right we have to do with a name which was common to the vocabularies of the Italic and Celtic groups. Since racial names do not seem to turn up in two neighbouring racial spheres by mere chance, the Volcæ or Volsci may be a people divided between the two groups, belonging to one and having sent out emigrants to the other. Their presence in Bavaria and their obstinacy in remaining there are most significant facts. The Volcæ did not go to Bavaria ; they were there, and quite close to the probable point of contact between the Italici and the Celts.

To sum up, the names of places and peoples which have been enumerated cover the south-western corner of Germany. The area in which they are found is a vast irregular triangle with one point on the Rhine near Cologne and another beyond Bohemia.[2]

Between Bohemia and the Rhine we have definite trace of a frontier. It lies in Thuringia. Along the ridge of the Thüringer Wald a very regular grassy track runs through the trees. It is called the Rennstieg, and marks the present

---

[1] In **CXXXIV**, 1911, p. 178.

[2] The Boii held an advanced position on this side down to the first century. Their domain is marked on the east by the towns of Mediolanum (Wolkersdorf, north of Vienna), Eburodunum (Brünn in Moravia), Meliodunum on the border of Moravia and Bohemia, Budorigum (Brieg in Silesia), and Lugidunum (Liegnitz). To the north-east there are still some names, but they are very infrequent and doubtful (Müllenhoff, op. cit., ii, map 1).

frontier of Gotha. It has always been a frontier, and its name has been supposed to come from the mounted wardens who guarded it, as if it was derived from *rennen* and *steigen*; not a very satisfactory explanation. Now, it is the name of a road.[1] Further west, running roughly north and south, is a small range, once the frontier between Franconia and Thuringia, called the Rhön, a name for which Germanic furnishes no plausible explanation.[2] Celtic, on the other hand, gives us two words, which may be one and the same. First, there is Middle Breton *reun*, Irish *roen* " a hill ". *Run* implies a Gaulish **roino*. In Irish *roen* means a road, that is, a raised road, and in Gaelic *raon* means a stretch of land (cf. *céte* " hill " and " road "). Secondly, Gaelic *roin* or *rann*, corresponding to Welsh *rhan*, Cornish *ran*, and Breton *rann*, means a division. Now both the Rennstieg and the Rhön are at once heights and boundaries [3]; and, what is more, these parallel ranges, running in two successive lines across the horizon from the Elbe to the Rhine, are crowned with prehistoric forts, for here Celts and Germans were for a long time in conflict.

We can, then, have some idea how far the Celtic domain extended northwards and eastwards at a time which is not so remote that all memory of their occupation is gone and over a period which was long enough for it to leave permanent traces.[4]

Did that domain not extend further ?

Beyond the Boii, in the time of Tacitus, it seems—at least, Tacitus is our informant—there was a Celtic people, the Cotini,[5] speaking its own language, between the Quadi, who were Germans, and the Sarmatians, who were Slavs or Indo-Iranians. They must have been somewhere near Galicia. They paid tribute, and, what should be noted, were the people who worked the iron mines. Whether they were

---

[1] Bædeker, *Mittel- und Norddeutschland*, p. 419 (Leipzig, 1885).

[2] Krause, **CCCXCVII**, pp. 8 ff.

[3] Müllenhoff, op. cit., ii, pp. 207 ff. ; Goetze, in **LXXXV**, Erganzgsb., ii, 1910–11, p. 91.

[4] Reinecke, **CCCCVI**, p. 9, draws the line, at the beginning of the La Tène period, along the Thüringer Wald, Frankenwald, and Erzgebirge, taking in Silesia. Bremer, in Paul, **CCCLXVII**, iii, p. 774.

[5] *Germ.*, 43 : *Cotinos Gallica . . . lingua coarguit non esse Germanos et quod tributa patiuntur. Partem tributorum Sarmatæ, partem Quadi ut alienigenis imponunt.*

a remnant left by the Celts in a region which they had abandoned, or the lost outpost of a Celtic expedition into north-eastern Europe, we should have no means of deciding (even if we have to accept blindly the statements of the ancient interpreters on which Tacitus's information is based), did ethnographical archæology not here furnish its decisive testimony.

Another piece of linguistic information, apparently less valuable, also supplied by Tacitus, has in recent years given rise to a number of rather adventurous theories. In the south-east corner of the Baltic lived the Æstii, or Esthonians.[1] Through the amber trade they had dealings with the Teutons of the Cimbric Peninsula, or Jutland, and the coasting traders of the West. Tacitus says that they were akin to the Celts in language—*lingua Britanniæ propior*. This is possible, but they were not Celts. The Celtic etymology ascribed to the Polish, Lithuanian, Lettish, and Esthonian names of rivers and other place-names is purely fanciful, where they are not derived from pan-European roots.[2] The similarity of Ptolemy's name for the Oder, Οὐιαδούα, to that of the Irish river Οὐίδουα,[3] is deceptive. The likenesses between Celtic, Balto-Slavonic, and even Finnish do not compel one to conclude that the Celts dwelt for hundreds of years on the Vistula.

The most serious argument is the resemblance in name between the Wends, the Veneti of Morbihan, and the Veneti of Venetia.[4] But here again, as in the case of the Volcæ and the Volsci, we may have an old name which survived in differentiated branches of the Indo-Europeans, or even the name of an old people which split up among differentiated linguistic groups. Neither history nor archæology allows us to suppose that Europe was divided racially into clearly defined, watertight compartments. Movements, larger and smaller, were always taking place, raids of varying amplitude, which broke down frontiers, obliterated distances, and threw up unexpected colonies in the remotest quarters. These incidents upset the composite picture of the Europeans which we laboriously try to put together by assembling the remains of their cultures and their

---

[1] *Germ.*, 45.
[2] Niederlé, **CCCLXIV**, i, p. 24.
[3] Bremer, in Paul, op. cit., ii, p. 774.
[4] **LXXXV**, 1922, p. 59.

languages. We must accept that disorderliness, and regard
the past, like the present, in all its complexity.

The question whether the Cimbri and Teutons were
Celtic is of quite a different kind. Their chiefs have Celtic
names, and in their country the most important specimen of
Celtic plastic art was found—the Gundestrup cauldron.
They held in their hands the amber trade, that favourable
soil for racial cross-breeding. The ancient geographers dispose
of the problem by describing the Teutons and the peoples
who traded in amber between Esthonia and the mouth of the
Elbe as Celto-Scythians.[1] We have not advanced much
further than they. Are these folk Germanized Celts ? Are
they Celticized Germans ? And from when does the mixture
date ? The question will arise again, when we have to study
the fluctuations of the Celto-Germanic frontier.[2] As for the
question whether the Celts at some time occupied the seaboard extending from the root of Jutland to the mouth of the
Rhine, it must remain open until further arguments have
been examined.

On the west and south, the original domain of the Celts,
or of those Celts of whose domain we can at this stage have
any idea, comes to an end where names of the Ligurian
or Ræto-Ligurian type begin.

These are the ancient place-names of Liguria properly
so called, names which have the same terminations ; names,
particularly of rivers, which are found (on the Italian side,
for instance) outside the limits ever reached by the Celts,
names also of physical features which are unintelligible
in Celtic (though this method of determination is not trust-
worthy), and names found in Celtic lands which present
phonetic peculiarities which are foreign to Celtic.

Names ending in -*usco*, -*asco*, -*osco* are the most typical.
They appear in numbers in the oldest documents regarding
the geography of the Ligurian country (Neviasca, Tulelasca,
Veraglasca, Vinelasca, streams in the neighbourhood of
Genoa) and wherever the ancient historians mention the
presence of Ligurians.[3] Peutinger's Map gives a station
of Caranusca (cf. Carrara and Caria, now Chieri) on the road

---

[1] Strabo, xi, 6, 2 ; cf. i, 2, 27 ; Plut., *Mar.*, ii.
[2] See the following volume in this series.
[3] D'Arbois, **CCCI,** ii, pp. 68 ff.

from Metz to Treves. In the Eifel there were a Pagus Carouuascus,[1] a Carascus (now Karsch) near Treves, and an Yvasco ; near Malmédy, a Via Masuerisca, mentioned in a Merovingian document ; in Luxemburg, a Villa Marisca. In Bavaria, south of Munich, probably near Tolz, there was in the ninth century a Radinasc.[2] These names mark the extreme north-east frontier of names in -asco, -osco, and -usco. That frontier is important.

But it is not the extreme limit of all Ligurian names.[3] Names of rivers have been found beyond.[4] Certainly more have been found than ever existed.[5] We must, too, distinguish Ligurian names from the Iberian names which also came so far. For example, the various rivers called Dore, Dorre, etc., have their counterparts in the Rhine Valley, such as the Thur, a tributary of the Ill, which was once Dura.[6] Fortunatus mentions a Rodanus, an affluent of the Moselle.[7] The name of the Drôme, Druna, reappears in Bavaria in the Traun, a sub-tributary of the Inn.[8]

The Isar (Isara) has been regarded as having a Ligurian name no less than the Isère, and so have the Isen (Isana), Ammer (Ambra), and Lieser (Lesura).[9] The valley of the Moselle, down to the neighbourhood of Treves, and a great part of the left bank of the Rhine were Ligurian country ; the right bank of the Danube, all that constituted Vindelicia, had been Ræto-Ligurian and doubtless remained so in part. If we are tempted to recognize Ligurian names beyond, we must examine them very critically.

It is probable that the Celts took a great part of their domain in Germany from the lands of the Ligurians and Iberians, but that was doubtless at a very early date. It is also probable that their advance for a long time halted on

---

[1] Ibid., p. 70.
[2] Cf. Livy, xlii, 7 : *In Liguribus . . . ad oppidum Carystum* (or Caruscum).
[3] Cramer, **CXCV**.
[4] The Celtic name of Worms, Borbitomagus, contains a non-Celtic element. This is found again in the name of a god, who is sometimes called Bormo and sometimes Borvo. He was the god of hot springs. The variation between *m* and *v* is not Celtic. It only appears in the name of the Cevennes. Cf. above, p. 50.
[5] e.g. the name of the Vimina and that of the Albis (Philipon, **CCCLXIX**, p. 300), which is certainly pan-European.
[6] Holder, **CCVII**, i, p. 1378.
[7] M. Müller, in **CLVII**, 1906, pp. 451–550.
[8] Holder, op. cit., i, p. 1331.
[9] Philipon, op. cit., pp. 295, 300.

a line running through Treves, the Vosges, and Upper Bavaria.[1] That, roughly, is the south-western limit of the oldest Celtic domain that can be determined by the method which we have so far followed. It would, moreover, be rash to try to make the line too straight and simple.

IV

THE DOMAIN OF THE CELTS IN GERMANY. ARCHÆOLOGICAL DATA [2]

On the north-east the frontier of the Celtic civilization of La Tène coincides roughly with that which we have obtained from the linguistic evidence. We shall now see that on that line, from the end of Neolithic times, there was established a fairly stable archæological frontier, which can only be the frontier of the Celts and the Germans.

It ran at the beginning of the La Tène period a little to the east of the ridge of the Thüringer Wald, between the upper valleys of the Saale and the Weisser-Elster.

Excavations conducted in this region near Ranis, east of Saalfeld,[3] have revealed a certain number of contemporary cemeteries belonging to that time. Some are composed of inhumation-tombs and others, known as urn-fields, were confined to cremations. Their distribution is somewhat confused. The inhumation-cemeteries belong to the Gauls, although that race continued to practise cremation at the beginning of the period ; the urn-fields are, at least chiefly, the work of the Germans, who adhered to the old rites.

At the level of Weimar the urn-fields are found west of the Saale. Below the mouth of the Saale the cemeteries contemporary with La Tène I are urn-fields (Map 5).

---

[1] It should be observed that the name of the Argonne may be connected with that of the Hercynian Forest (Wiedemann, in Bezzenberger, xxviii, 1904).

[2] See recent publications of Herr G. Kraff, *Die Kultur der Bronzezeit in Süddeutschland* (Augsburg, 1926) ; " Beiträge zur Kenntniss der Urnenfelderkultur in Süddeutschland," in **XXXVII**, cxxxi, 1927, pp. 154 ff. ; " Urnenfelder in Westeuropa," ibid., 1929, pp. 47 ff.

[3] Déchelette, ii, 3, pp. 1074 ff. ; Reinecke, **CLVIII**, p. 480 ; Kropp, **CCCXCVIII** (cf. H. Hubert, in **CXL**, 1912, p. 364) ; K. Jakob, " Die La-Tène-Funde der Leipsiger Gegend," in **LXXIV**, ii, 1907 ; H. Busse, *La-Tène-Gräberfeld bei Schmetzdorf* ; W. Hindenburg, " Neue Funde der La-Tène-Zeit aus dem Kreise Tetlow," in **LXXXV**, ii, pp. 194 ff. ; K. Wasse, " Möritzer Funde," ibid., i, pp. 273 ff. ; E. Wahle, " Ein Grabfund der Spät-Latènezeit von Zahna," ibid., 1912, pp. 306 ff.

Objects of a Celtic type of manufacture are found in the Germanic cemeteries, but are less and less frequent the further away one goes. Also cultural differences in craftsmanship appear on the racial frontier. For instance, the copies of pottery-types are less well executed, and hand-made vases are more frequent. The shape of objects, too, is altered; for example, that of swords and scabbards. Scabbards of the Germanic type have been found in the upper valley of the

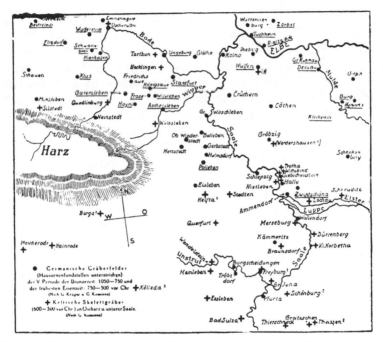

MAP 5. The Frontier between Celts and Germans in La Tène. Legend: ● Germanic urn-fields of the fifth period of the Bronze Age, 1050–750, and earliest Iron Age, 750–500. ✛ Celtic inhumations, 600–500, in the Eastern Harz and on the lower Saale (Kossinna, *Ursprung und Verbreitung der Germanen in vor- und frühgeschichtlicher Zeit*, Mannus-Bibliothek, No. 6, Leipzig, Curt Kabitzsch, p. 32, fig. 45).

Saale, at Grossromstedt in the Kreis of Apolda.[1] This is as far as they reach towards the south and west.

On the Lower Rhine the boundary was at the level of Cologne.[2] Below that the La Tène civilization is confined

---

[1] See Kossinna, **CCCXCVI**; for brooches, see R. Beltz, in **CLXIX**, 1911 pp. 664 ff.; 1912, pp. 660 ff.; Motefind, ibid., 1913, pp. 101 ff.

[2] Rademacher, in **LXXXV**, i, pp. 83 ff.

to the left bank. Upstream it is not really well represented on the right bank until one comes to the Neuwieder Becken, near Coblenz.[1]

Between the Rhine and the Elbe, it is absent in Westphalia and Hanover, where the previous civilization persists, very little influenced by the new fashions.[2]

In the south-western corner of Germany the La Tène culture was particularly rich and brilliant. It is represented by especially numerous and especially ancient finds.[3] It is on account of these German discoveries that we have had to recognize a La Tène period prior to that of the Marne burials.[4] The map (Map 6) drawn by Déchelette to show the finds of Greek and Italo-Greek objects in Celtic tombs brings out the frequency of these tombs in the district between the Lower Moselle and the Upper Danube, of which the Middle Rhine forms the axis, in contrast to their rarity in regions lying further west. The Hallstatt finds indicated by Déchelette are late Hallstatt,[5] and some of them might be ascribed to this La Tène A period, the existence of which is generally accepted. Most of them were made in the south of the region which we are considering.

To these late Hallstatt objects we must add the majority of those, scarcely later, which have been found in the region of the Middle Rhine. They come from tumuli, similar to the Hallstatt tumuli—those of Klein-Aspergle, Dürkheim, Rodenbach, Armsheim, Waldalgesheim, and Schwarzenbach—which were most certainly the tombs of chiefs, and have been found here in greater numbers than anywhere else.

A map showing the distribution of gold objects would look very much the same,[6] but with one addition, namely, an important group of finds in the country of the Volcæ Tectosages in France, at Cordes, Montans, and Lasgraïsses in the department of the Tarn, and at Fenouillet in the Haute-Garonne.[7] Here there was, without any doubt, a very wealthy

---

[1] Gunther, ibid., iii, pp. 1 ff. ; Schumacher, **CCCCIX,** pl. viii.
[2] W. Schulz, in **LXXXV,** x, pp. 108 ff., 226.
[3] Déchelette, iii, 3, pp. 1063 ff.
[4] See above, p. 126.
[5] Kappel-am-Rhein, Vilsingen, Pisek (Déchelette, ii, 3, pp. 1597, 1596, 1599). The finds marked in the east (the Vettersfelde treasure and the Vogelsang bracelet) are Scythian.
[6] Ibid. pp. 1332 ff.   [7] Ibid., pp. 1339 ff.

colony, the colony of a wealthy people. But the bulk of
the gold objects were in Germany, and it was between the
Moselle and the Danube that the axis of the Celtic world
still lay in La Tène I. It was in this region that the wealthiest
aristocracy remained established. The Volcæ and still more

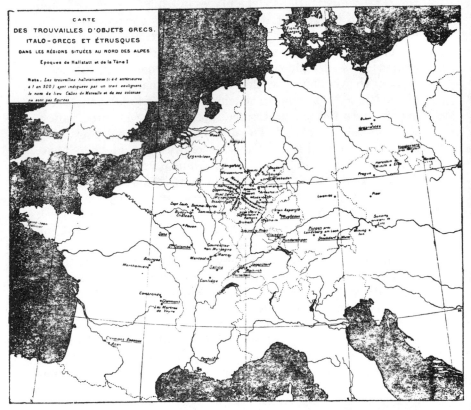

MAP 6. Finds of Greek, Italo-Greek, and Etruscan Objects north of the
Alps in Hallstatt and La Tène I. Legend : Hallstatt finds (i.e. earlier
than 500 B.C.) have the name of the place underlined. Those of
Marseilles and its colonies are not given. (Déchelette, iii, map v.)

the Helvetii, who for a long time occupied the south-western
corner of this region, left behind them a reputation for
riches, riches in gold, which they doubtless obtained by
washing the sand of the Rhine.[1]

[1] For the collection of gold in rivers among the Celts, see Athenæos,
vi, 233, following Poseidonios ; for the wealth of the Volcæ in gold, see
Strabo, vi, 1, 13.

The great tumuli of which I have spoken contained either skeletons or ashes. But inhumation, which came to prevail in La Tène I, even in this part of Germany, had not yet become general, and still less had burial in flat-graves. Therefore the great majority of the Greek objects found were early importations. The places in which they were found lead one to think that it was just in this region, under the influence of Greek or Italo-Greek art, that the La Tène culture became different from that of Hallstatt. For an archæologist like Déchelette they are proof that the main body of the Gauls was at that time in Germany, on both sides of the Rhine.[1] Déchelette concluded from his map that Greek imports into Celtic country had come by the Danube valley. Here he was mistaken.[2] The map itself shows that they came either by the valley of the Aar or by that of the Saône, and that they doubtless started from Marseilles. But it is likely that the Italian objects which maintained the fashions of Northern Italy in Celtic countries came in by the passes of the Central or Eastern Alps.[3] The conjunction of Greek and Italic influences which produced the style of La Tène took place at the meeting-point. The style and workmanship are mixed, no doubt, but they are Celtic and not Ræto-Celtic. One single people made the mixture into something new with a character of its own. The distribution of La Tène finds in Bavaria—some north of the Danube and in the north-eastern corner of the country [4] and the rest south of the Danube [5]—does not make it possible to trace a Ræto-Celtic frontier. If at this time there were Rætians and Celts living side by side in what was afterwards Vindelicia, the former were assimilated or the settlements of the two groups of peoples were inextricably interspersed.[6]

So in La Tène I the archæological map still coincides, on the whole, with the linguistic map. The movements of the Gauls westwards and southwards had not yet shifted the former balance of their settlements. Their old homes were in Germany. There they remained for a long time yet. Afterwards, when the Celtic body had extended indefinitely,

---

[1] Déchelette, ii, 3, p. 913.
[2] Piroutet, in **XV,** xxix, pp. 213 ff. ; xxx, pp. 31 ff. ; cf. Hubert, in **CXL,** 1925, pp. 252 ff.
[3] See above, pp. 128–9.
[5] Ibid.
[4] Reinecke, **CCCCVI,** p. 5.
[6] Mehlis, **DXLV.**

examination of their funeral rites, failing other information, shows that one of its chief centres was there. For it was there that they introduced the new and there that they maintained the old. There they continued to build tumuli until La Tène II ; there they began making them again in La Tène III ; and it was probably there that the practice of cremation, which had long been preserved there, was revived.[1]

In Bohemia the Celts did not yet occupy more than the south-western corner of the country at the beginning of

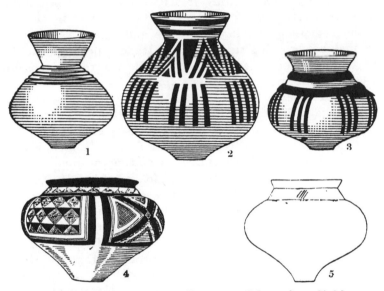

FIG. 32. Hallstatt Pottery from Germany. (Schumacher, *Siedelungs- u. Kulturgesch.*, figs. 28, 31, 33.) 1–3, Gündling type. 4, Salem type. 5, Koberstadt type.

the La Tène period.[2] Their La Tène burials are there found in tumuli ; at Pisek, an early Greek *œnochoë* and a basin, also Greek, have been discovered. Then, in the course of the first La Tène period, they expanded towards the line which I have indicated. The cemeteries which they have left there are like those of the Marne.

---

[1] Schumacher, **CCCCIX**, pp. 144 ff. For tumuli of La Tène II, see P. Horter, in **LXXXV**, x, p. 231 ; H. Hornung, in **LXVII**, v, pp. 19, 102. For tumuli of La Tène III, see Reinecke, in **LXXXI**, 1919, p. 12.

[2] Déchelette, p. 1078.

In the Hallstatt period the same state of things already obtained all over this region. From Bohemia and Bavaria to the neighbourhood of Cologne we find the same tumuli, with some local differences in construction which are hard to reduce to a system.[1] In these tumuli there are the same urns, shaped like tops, which are unlike the Hallstatt urns of the Middle Danube and are, on the whole, decorated in the south and plainer in the north (Fig. 32), their differences perhaps corresponding to tribal divisions, but to divisions inside one same group of peoples.[2] The urns are accompanied by grave-gear which varies greatly between the beginning of the Hallstatt period and the end, being richer in pottery at the beginning and in ornaments and arms at the end,[3] but includes brooches related to the Italic types [4] and unlike the two-piece brooches common to the centre and coastal districts of Germany, and iron swords.

The north-east frontier is the same. The urn-fields of Westphalia and Hanover lie outside it.[5] Hut-urns extend as far as it, and there stop.[6] The deposit discovered at Wahren, near Leipzig, in 1915,[7] is a typical find. It includes an engraved iron collar with buttons set at right angles on the ends. This is a type of collar which is found in Eastern Germany as far as the Baltic, but doubtless comes from the Illyrian countries. The deposit also contained an ingot of iron in the shape of a double pyramid. This is the easternmost find of an ingot of the type, which is very frequent in the southern angle of the Rhine. It is probable that the Celtic countries supplied the Germanic lands with iron at the time, and this would agree with the fact that the Germans took the word for " iron " from Celtic.

On the western side there are the same outlying sites as in La Tène I,[8] but again the great majority of tumuli are in Western Germany.

In relation to the culture of Western Germany the superiority belongs to that of the Middle Danube, which had

---

[1] Ibid., ii, 2, pp. 606 ff.
[2] Schumacher, op. cit., p. 86 ; Hubert, in **CXL**, 1925, p. 125.
[3] F. Kaufmann, **CCCXLVII**, i, p. 196.
[4] D. Viollier, in **CCCCXC**, pp. 26 ff. ; Beltz, in **CLXIX**, 1912, pp. 660, 26 ff.
[5] Schulz, in **LXXXV**, x, pp. 108 ff.
[6] Schumacher, **CCCCVIII**, p. 38.
[7] M. Næbe, in **LXXXV**, 1915, p. 83 ; G. Kossinna, ibid., p. 84.
[8] See the following volume in this series.

a different history. This alone would suffice to explain how
Illyrian elements entered into the population of Southern
Germany with the Illyrian civilization.[1] It seems, too, to
be as difficult to trace a Ræto-Celtic frontier in Bavaria
in this period as in La Tène I.[2] In Bohemia the area of the
tumuli, which I have regarded as coinciding with that of the
Celts, was the same.

If it were possible to use the argument of permanence of
habitat there would be no doubt that the same men lived all
over this region in the Hallstatt and La Tène periods. But
habits of life changed much in the course of the Iron Age,
and the population shifted accordingly.[3] Only in a few
places can one definitely say that it stayed where it was—
about Hagenau, at Grossgartach, on the Heiligenberg near
Heidelberg, on the Hennenberg near Riedlingen.[4] But it
moved within only a small area. The archæological maps of
the Hallstatt and La Tène periods coincide in great part.[5]
Herr Schumacher has made the continuity of population all
over the Rhineland quite plain.[6]

If we go back yet further in time we find the archæological
map of the third and fourth Bronze Age periods [7] much like
that of Hallstatt, but with narrower extensions westwards.
Again there are tumuli and special types of pottery from
Bohemia to Cologne and from Cologne to Switzerland, with
changes in fashion [8] ; the same weapons and the same bronze
objects appear in tombs and deposits.[9] The same line
forms a rough frontier, not between an area of tumuli and
one of urn-fields, for funeral practices were generally much
the same on both sides, but between two kinds of metal-
working, with distinctly different characteristics. The thick-
hilted Germanic swords, the Baltic axes, the gorgets, the

[1] See above, pp. 128–9.
[2] J. Naue, in **CXXXIX**, 1895, 2, p. 40 ; **XV**, 1897, p. 641 ; M. von Geyer
and P. v. Goessler, in **X**, 1917, p. 29.
[3] T. Voges, in **LXXXV**, i, p. 288.
[4] For Hagenau, see Schumacher, **CCCCIX**, i, p. 66, n. 33 (see also
Schæffer, **CCCCVII**) ; for Grossgartach and the Heiligenberg, ibid., p. 135 ;
for the Hennenberg, G. Bersu, in **LXV**, 1917, p. 22. Herr Schumacher does
not raise the question, and that is perhaps why he does not answer it ; my
own personal notes are also unsatisfactory.
[5] Maps : For the Forest of Hagenau see Schumacher, op. cit., i, p. 67,
fig. 21 ; for Grossgartach, ibid., p. 44, fig. 14 and pls. iv–x.
[6] Ibid., map, pl. x.
[7] Cf. Lissauer's maps, in **CLXIX**, 1904–7.
[8] Schumacher, op. cit., i, p. 61.   [9] **CCCXCIX**, v, p. 38.

large cast brooches, hardly extend beyond Thuringia, on the one side ; the axes, swords, pins, and general knick-knackery of Western Germany hardly pass it, on the other.[1] On the one side industry is connected with that of Switzerland, Eastern France, and Italy ; on the other, with that of the Danube valley and Hungary.

An archæological map of the second period of the Bronze Age would present an utterly confused picture. Moreover, it is difficult in the archæology of the beginning of the Bronze Age to say how much is due to native settlements, to trade, to itinerant craftsmen, and to the influences of other civilizations.

Meanwhile, something happened which adds much confusion to the picture of the archæology of the West, namely, the spread of the civilization which is chiefly represented by the curious pottery known as Lausitz or Lusatian ware.[2] This culture stretched in a belt, narrowing west of the Rhine, from Galicia to France, where traces of it are found in Normandy and Dordogne,[3] leaving pottery with relief decoration in countries where pottery was incised and urn-fields in countries of tumuli and inhumations. The phenomenon may be the result of one of those abnormal movements of peoples, as we may call them, which are known to have occurred several times in the history of the world, which, without altering the racial maps permanently, have upset them considerably. This movement had a great effect on the civilization of Western Europe, and it must have brought very large bodies of settlers to the west of Germany, for at the end of the Bronze Age their funeral practice prevailed everywhere, and it persisted into the Hallstatt period.[4]

In the region which has thus been defined archæology reveals nothing corresponding to the separation of two groups of peoples, related yet having linguistic differences which imply a real separation. On the contrary, everything points to unity, concentration, and increasing concentration. In that region there was only one group of Celts, that of the Brythonic Gauls. Also, as we have seen, the place-names show that *p* was used, as in Lopodunum (Ladenburg), Lupias (the Lippe), and the Finne, from *pennos*.

---

[1] See map in Kossinna, **CCCXCVI**, fig. 17.
[2] H. Hubert, in **CXLIII**, 1910, pp. 5 ff.   [3] See below, p. 251.
[4] H. Horter, in **LXXXV**, 1913, p. 307.

V

But whence did the Goidels come, and when did they come ? Where must we look for their earliest home on the Continent and their starting-point ? Probably they came from north of the Brythonic domain, and it is to them that tradition refers when it tells that the Celts used to live on the low coasts of the North Sea. They must have left those shores very early, for hardly a trace of them remains there.

Such was not the opinion of the great Celticist, Zimmer.[1] He maintained that the Goidels came from France, and probably by the Atlantic coast, starting from south of the mouth of the Loire. He has set himself to study the relations of the British Isles with the Continent. He had collected a great number of facts about the trade which went on at the beginning of the Middle Ages between Ireland and the French coast, especially the wine-trade, and he held that men had gone to Ireland by the same route as goods. But there is not only one route by which goods or men could have gone from the Continent to Ireland. There are at least two others, one by which the Angles and Saxons went from the mouth of the Elbe to the east coast of England and over England to Ireland, and one which the Vikings of Denmark and Norway took round the north of Scotland and past the Isles to the north of Ireland and the gates of the Irish Sea.

But at what date did the Goidels cross over ?

An orthodox but unfortunate answer is supplied by the use of the word κασσίτερος in Homer to mean " tin ".[2] The tin which was worked up in Greece came from the Cassiterides Islands, which may have been Scilly and were, in any case, a Celtic country[3] ; it was Celtic tin, τὸν κασσίτερον τὸν Κελτικόν, according to the author of the

---

[1] In **IX**, pp. 1–59.
[2] D'Arbois, **CCXCIX**, p. 19 ; S. Reinach, in **XV**, 1892, p. 275.
[3] L. Siret (in **XV**, 1908, p. 129) places the Cassiterides in Brittany ; G. Bonsor (in **XXXIV**, 1921, p. 60), in Bætica (Mons Casius, in *Avienus*, 259–261). Cf. J. Loth (in **CXL**, xxxviii, p. 260), on ancient tin-working in the Scilly Isles. Carty (in **LXXXVIII**, 1924, pp. 166–7), commenting on a very troublesome passage in Pliny (vii, 119), supposes that the sea-route to the tin countries was discovered in the sixth century by a Phocæan navigator named Midacritus.

Marvels attributed to Aristotle.[1] If tin is Celtic its name may be. D'Arbois de Jubainville saw in it a Celtic stem, *cassi-*, meaning " pleasant ". The Irish noun *caise*, containing this stem *cassi*, means " esteem ", " love ", while the adjective *cais* means " elegant ".[2] M. Salomon Reinach has suggested that *kassiteros* got its name from the Cassiterides ; d'Arbois was of opinion that it was a Celtic comparative.[3] So the Celts and, at least, the Goidels, must have held the Western tin-mines about 800 B.C., and doubtless had done so for a long time.[4] The reasoning is satisfactory, but the premiss is doubtful. Its chief weakness is that there is no equivalent for the word at all in Celtic. Tin is called *stan* in Irish and *ystaen* in Welsh.[5] These may have been borrowed from the Latin ; but it is not likely that a word describing an important product which was almost peculiar to the Celts would have disappeared, particularly since it was supported by Greek usage.

A preferable etymology [6] makes κασσίτερος a Greek comparative, and connects it with κασίγνητος, a close relation. It is a term of kinship which belongs to the dialects of Asia Minor, attested by the lexicographers in the forms κάσις, κασσᾶς, κάσας, κασύας, and κασσύας, and meaning very close relationship. So κασσίτερος refers to the kinship of tin and lead, which are always brought together and always compared to each other. Tin was called *plumbum album*.[7]

We must turn to archæology in order to go back so far, and even further, in the history of the movements of the Celts. The Hallstatt period is out of the question. Except at the end it is hardly represented in the British Isles, and

---

[1] Ps.-Arist., *De Mir. Ausc.*, 1, 834a, 6.

[2] **CCXCIX**, p. 19. The stem is very well represented in Celtic. The Gauls had gods called Casses, there was a British people of the Cassi, and it appears in many compound names—Cassivellaunos, Cassignatus, etc.

[3] A comparative of equality. The comparative of superiority is in -*yos*-, like the Latin comparative, and the Greek comparative in ιων.

[4] Mr. MacNeill (**CCCCXLI**, p. 47) believes that the word is Celtic, but that it does not prove that the Celts were in possession of the country where tin was extracted.

[5] Middle Irish also said *cred* (O'Curry, **CCLXXVIII**, p. ccccix).

[6] S. Reinach, in **XV**, 1892, pp. 275 ff.

[7] Pokorny (in **CLXXI**, 1913, pp. 164 ff.) derives the word from the Elamite *Cassi*, which appears in the name of the Kassites, *Kassi-ti-ra*, whence Sanskrit *Kastira*. Cf. Hüsing, in **CXIV**, 1907, p. 25 ; Bork, in **CLXIII**, 1917, p. 541 (*Kassitú*, the name of an Elamite god).

what we know of its last phase is not enough for us to imagine a Celtic colonization of any magnitude distinct from that which took place in the La Tène period. But the archæology of the Bronze Age presents two series of facts which must be considered. Apart from those scholars who do not think that there were any Celts in the British Isles before the La Tène period, opinions are divided between two hypotheses which place the arrival of the first wave at the beginning and at the end of the Bronze Age respectively.[1]

In the first period of the Bronze Age there arrived in the British Isles, coming from the Continent, people with very marked characteristics.[2] The old Neolithic inhabitants (among whom I include those of all the beginning of the

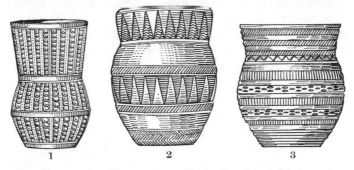

FIG. 33. Bronze Age Pottery from England. Zoned Beakers from the Round Barrows. 1, Lambourn Down, Berks. 2–3, Goodmanham, Yorks (Ebert, *Reallexicon*, 2, pl. 248 ; B.M. *Guide* to the Bronze Age).

Bronze Age) were long-heads of Mediterranean type, who built for their dead, or, at least, for the more distinguished of them, tumuli with a funeral chamber known as " long barrows ", in which one sometimes finds those curious bell-shaped beakers adorned at regular intervals with bands of incised or stamped decoration, of a very simple and austere type. The newcomers were of quite a different type, and had other funeral practices.[3]

They buried their dead under round tumuli, known as

---

[1] D'Arbois (**CCC,** p. 16) says that the Goidels imported metal-working into the British Isles, but did not arrive there until between 1300 and 800, i.e. at the very end of the Bronze Age or well within the Hallstatt period. Cf. Allen, **CCXCVIII,** p. 21.

[2] A. Keith, in **LXXVI,** 1915, p. 12 ; J. Loth, in **CXL,** xxxviii, p. 271 ; Holmes, **CCCCXXXIII,** p. 119.

[3] Keane, **CCCXLIX,** p. 527.

"round barrows ", in graves in which the body was placed in a crouching position on one side and enclosed in stone flags or woodwork.[1] Later they burned them. In their graves there were zoned beakers (Fig. 33), but of a late type in which the neck is distinguished from the belly, or vases derived from these beakers.[2] The funeral urns descended from them. The grave-goods comprised buttons with a V-shaped boring, flint [3] and copper daggers, arrow-heads, and flat perforated pieces of schist which are " bracers ", or bowman's wrist-guards.[4] The skeletons were of a new type : tall, with round head of a fairly constant shape, the brow receding, the supraciliary ridge prominent, the cheek-bones highly developed, and the jaws massive and projecting so as to present a dip at the base of the nose. I have already described them as one of the types represented in Celtic burials.[5]

The association of the physical type of this people with the beaker has led British anthropologists to call it the Beaker Folk. Some of the invaders landed in Britain on the east, in the region of York and about the Firth of Forth ; others landed in the south and established themselves on the Downs, where they were very densely grouped about Salisbury.[6] In Scotland they were accompanied by other brachycephals, with a higher index and of Alpine type.[7] In general they advanced from south to north and from east to west, and their progress lasted long enough for there to be a very marked difference in furniture between their oldest and latest tombs. As they advanced they scattered, and they are comparatively few in the north of Scotland and in Wales.[8]

---

[1] Holmes, op. cit., p. 179. For variety in the construction of tumuli, ibid., p. 175.

[2] Abercromby, in **LXXVI**, 1902, p. 373.

[3] For the chronology of the flint daggers, see Smith, in **CXXXIII**, 32. It must not be forgotten that all these things are later than the introduction of metal, and that the flint daggers are contemporaneous with the bronze ones.

[4] Evans, **CCCCXXIV**, pp. 420 ff. ; del Castillo, **CCCIX**, pls. cxcv ff., p. 185.

[5] See above, pp. 29 ff. ; Loth, loc. cit., p. 272 ; Keith, loc. cit. Index, between 68 and 88 ; average height, 5 ft. 7½ in.

[6] O. G. S. Crawford, in **LXVI**, xl, 1912, p. 184. Loth (loc. cit., p. 275) notes about 2,000 tumuli in Wiltshire alone. A. Dote, in **CXXIV**, 1911–12, p. 15.

[7] Loth, loc. cit., p. 273 : Index, between 82 and 92 ; height, 5 ft. 5 in. ; Keith, loc. cit. ; Fleure, **CCCXXVIII**, p. 51.

[8] List of beakers found in Wales in *Bull. Bd. Celt. Soc.*, i, p. 182 ; ii–iv, p. 389 ; E. M. Wheeler, in **XVI**, 1923, p. 21.

Their progress was a conquest. It is evident that they subdued and assimilated the previous occupants of the country. It is true that they did not come in sufficient numbers [1] to alter the average type of the population, whose descendants still formed a considerable minority,[2] but they were strong enough to impose certain important and predominant features of their civilization down to the end of the Bronze Age and later still.

But whence came these invaders ? The beakers and their very ancient forms are found in Sicily, Sardinia, and Italy, but above all in Spain,[3] and it has become the practice to regard them as having originated in that country.[4] In any case, they are one of the relics of the civilization which produced the megalithic monuments. The diffusion of the bell-beaker in Western Europe is a sign of the unity of that civilization. It is the typical vase of the megalith-builders, and in the greater part of France all their pottery recalls it more or less. With the beakers, one finds in this part of the area covered by them the bowman's bracers, the daggers of flint and copper, and the buttons with the V-shaped boring, which are found in the round barrows of Britain. But they do not accompany the same type of skeleton. The beakers themselves are more like those of the British long barrows than those of the round barrows. Between these last no transitional form has yet been reported, and the difference between them, in spite of their indisputable kinship, is what has first struck all observers.

The bell-beaker spread in the seaboard region of Northern Europe, in the area of the megalithic monuments, and, though no perfectly normal specimens are found in Denmark, variants of it are found in many Danish burials.[5] But others are found elsewhere, outside the region of the megaliths. The German archæologists call them zone-beakers,

---

[1] Abercromby (**CCCCXII**, p. 69) places the number of invaders very low, basing his calculation on the number of tombs found, and gets a figure of about 600. Keith rightly objects to this method of reckoning.

[2] Keith, loc. cit. : 20 per cent of a West End club, representing civil servants, squires, and professional men, were found to be of the round-headed type of the invaders.

[3] Del Castillo, **CCCIX**.

[4] H. Schmidt, in **CLXIX**, 1913, p. 235 ; Åberg, **CCCCXCV** ; Bosch Gimpera, **DII** ; del Catillo, op. cit., pp. 29 ff.

[5] Del Castillo, op. cit., pls. ccv, ccvi, 1, 3, p. 191.

Zonenbecher,[1] to distinguish them from the bell-shaped vases.
They have a flat bottom, sometimes a foot, and are taller.
Sometimes they have been manufactured in the country.
The zones are treated differently, tending to fall into groups
on the neck of the vase and on the belly, the curve of which is
broken, sometimes near the top and sometimes near the
bottom.

These zoned vases seem to have come into the Rhine
valley from the west. The agricultural peoples of the Rhine,
who were very peaceful folk, found themselves at the
beginning of the Bronze Age face to face with bowmen,
probably coming from the Vosges or the Ardennes, whose
armament and dress must have been the same in every detail
as those of the Beaker Folk of Britain. They had, too, almost
exactly the same funeral practices. They were also round-
heads of a particular type, very ancient in Western Europe,
which has been compared to the type of Grenelle and that
of Ofnet, but certainly resembles the British type of the
round barrows.[2]

The map of the distribution of the zoned vases [3] and other
objects which go with them is most interesting to study.
They are crowded in the Dutch provinces of Guelderland and
Drenthe, and along the Rhine from Coblenz to Cologne and,
especially, from Mainz to Spire. They have been found in the
Taunus, in Hessen, in Hessen-Darmstadt, along the Main,
in the valley of the Neckar, and in Bavaria. They appear in
Bohemia, crossing it from north-west to south-east. They
are, indeed, so numerous there, and the pottery which accompanies them is so varied, that one may ask whether they did
not originate there, or come there direct through Italy and
across the Danube. Both suggestions seem doubtful. The
first, indeed, seems hardly possible, for the zoned vases found
in Bohemia appear in a belt, marking the line of a movement
which cuts across the settlements of the aborigines.[4] North
of Bohemia and the Thuringian mountains, they are numerous
in the valley of the Saale and north of it, between Magdeburg

---

[1] Bosch Gimpera, s.v. " Glockenbecherkultur," in Ebert, **CCCXXIV**,
del Castillo, op. cit., pp. 141 ff.
[2] A. Schliz, in **XXIII**, 1909, p. 263 ; A. Stocky, in **CXV**, 1919–1920.
[3] Del Castillo, op. cit., map i.
[4] Cervinka, in Ebert, op. cit., s.v. " Böhmen-Mähren " ; del Castillo,
op. cit., p. 149.

and the Harz. Further east, in the basin of the Oder, they have been found in Silesia along the Sudeten and about Breslau, and northwards they appear in Westphalia, the province of Osnabrück, Mecklenburg, and the island of Rügen. They are concentrated along the Rhine, in Bohemia, and in Saxony, and scattered in all the rest of Germany west of the Elbe. They are still more thinly spread between the Elbe and the Oder. We must imagine warlike bodies moving fairly fast, for their cemeteries are generally small, ravaging the country but holding it, for the cultures which they found in possession have vanished while theirs has lasted.

This tremendous journey of the bell-beakers and the zone-beakers is still full of mysteries. It was clearly not the same men who used them in Spain and in Bohemia, and one mystery which we should be glad to solve is the origin of the Continental branch which covered Germany and flourished there. We do not find it commencing in France, and the type of man which accompanies it is absent from the normal French series of Neolithic skulls.[1]

It is at least certain that the Beaker Folk went from Germany to Britain, and not from Britain to Germany. The typical round-heads of the round barrows are a Nordic type, which may have grown up on the plains of Northern Europe. No doubt the state of things revealed by British remains of the beginning of the Bronze Age is complex, and one must not draw too close a comparison between the round barrows and the German and Bohemian tombs containing beakers. Other things are found in the round barrows besides beakers and brachycephals. But, apart from these two features, three things have to be considered, which point in the same direction ; first, the comparatively large number of cremations ; secondly, the similarity of the British barrows to the tumuli of North Germany at the beginning of the Bronze Age and the constant practice of burying the dead, when inhumation is practised, in a contracted position, as in Central Germany ; and, lastly, the similarity of many of the urns of the round barrows, which are late developments of the zoned beaker, and of other vases found there, to the so-called Neolithic pottery of North Germany in the region

---

[1] Cf. Poisson, in **CXXXVIII,** 1929.

of the megaliths.[1] They are a development or a degradation of the same species.

At this point it is legitimate to ask what became of all the people who set up the megalithic monuments in the north-west of Germany, and what became of the tribes of bowmen who were mingled with them, for it is a dogma of German *Siedelungsgeschichte* that all the north-west seaboard, Westphalia, and Hanover were emptied of their inhabitants before the second period of the Bronze Age.[2]

Many scholars, British, German, and French, have accordingly thought that the mixed population of this part of Germany, which one day set off and emigrated, was the original stock of the Goidels.[3] Others have denied this[4] because very few beakers have so far been discovered in Ireland.[5] Their contention is plainly absurd, for there are two chances out of three that the Goidels crossed Britain in order to reach Ireland, and if the beakers themselves are rare in the country their derivatives are plentiful.[6] But the positive statement requires further proof.

It is not likely that North-Western Germany was depopulated and part of its inhabitants went over into Britain all at once. It is certain that the movement of trade connecting the British Isles with the Continent across the North Sea was not at once affected. At that same time objects manufactured in Ireland—which was rich in metal, especially gold, and much visited by sailors—were travelling as far as the Danish archipelago : axes with very slightly flanged edges and incised and hammered decoration, and gold lunettes.[7] In the period when metal-working was spreading the British Isles had been a half-way house on the route to the north, and now things went on as before.

From the second period of the Bronze Age onwards this current seems to have flowed in the opposite direction.

---

[1] Del Castillo, op. cit., pp. 161 ff. For the *Trichterbecher*, cf. **LXXXV,** 1921, pp. 13 ff., 143 ff., 239 ff.

[2] Kossinna, **CCCXCV,** iii.

[3] J. Loth, loc. cit.

[4] Holmes, **CCCCXXXIII,** p. 195.

[5] **CXXXIV,** 1904, pp. 316–17 ; Armstrong, **CCCCXV** ; **CXVIII,** 1911, p. 184 ; A. del Castillo, in **LXXXV,** 1915, p. 34 (Knockmaa, co. Galway) ; W. J. Dargan, ibid., 1916, p. 77 (co. Wicklow).

[6] Holmes, op. cit., p. 187 ; **CCCLXXXIV,** p. 44 ; J. Loth, op. cit., p. 273.

[7] Montelius, **CCCC,** p. 79 ; Déchelette, **CCCXVIII,** ii, 1, pp. 354 ff.

Objects have been found in Ireland and Great Britain which are or may be derived from prototypes in Northern Germany and the Danish archipelago. Does this stream of imports point to a movement of men ? Messrs. Crawford [1] and Peake [2] believe that it does, and that those men were the Goidels.

Their attention is chiefly directed to the flat-tanged swords of which I have spoken above, which are represented in the British Isles by some specimens of their early types.[3] But swords were not the only imports. The great symmetrical brooches of cast bronze passed from Germany into Ireland, where they were made in gold, without pins, and became a kind of clip, used as a fastening.[4] The great torques with turned-back ends of the fifth period of the Germanic Bronze Age followed the same road,[5] as did the breast-ornaments of the same time, formed of several torques set edge to edge, which were imitated in gold wrought in one piece.[6] The curved, broad-headed pins of Eastern Germany are found in Ireland and Scotland, with their characteristic annulations and curved ends.[7]

The Western German pins with the bulge in the middle are found in England.[8] While many of the bronze tools of the British Isles are like those of Western Europe, Spain, and even the Mediterranean countries, some of the latter are noticeably lacking, such as the sickle with a lateral button, and as time goes on a fair number of Northern types and objects come in.

Is all this the consequence of the exodus of the populations once established in Frisia, Hanover, and Westphalia ? It cannot be denied that the facts brought forward are, after all, very meagre,[9] and might be explained without supposing great shiftings of peoples. The practice of cremation, which was general in the British Isles, prevents

[1] O. G. S. Crawford, " A Prehistoric Invasion of England," in **XVI**, ii, p. 27.
[2] See above, pp. 145 ff.　　　[3] Peake, **CCCCXLVII**, pl. xiv.
[4] Coffey, **CCCCXXVIII**, pl. v.　　[5] Ibid., pl. viii.
[6] Ibid., pl. ii.　　　　　　　　　[7] Childe, *The Bronze Age*, 1930, fig. 14.
[8] Ibid.
[9] Messrs. Crawford and Peake also argue from the appearance in England, at the end of the Bronze Age, of large vases surrounded by lines of finger-prints, which were very common on the Continent at the time. But these are too common objects and too vague characteristics to be used as indications of race.

us from identifying the new invaders, if there were any. Moreover, the British barrows and pottery of the end of the Bronze Age appear to be developments of the barrows and pottery of the beginning.

VI

A VIEW OF THE ORIGINS OF THE CELTS AND ITALO-CELTIC RELATIONS. TRACES OF THE GOIDELS AT THEIR STARTING-POINT

In working up to the origins of the Continental, Brythonic branch of the Celts, we had to stop at the second period of the Bronze Age. At this time, according as one adopts one or the other of the hypotheses set forth above, either the migration of the Goidels was beginning, and their establishment in the country from which they started was much earlier, or else it was over, and we must go back in our search for an undivided Celtic race, to what many still call the Neolithic Age, that is, the long succession of centuries during which metal was slowly coming into use in Western and Northern Europe.

The picture presented, at this approximate date, by the prehistoric archæology of the region which we are considering, is very involved. An attempt has been made to bring some order into the facts revealed by the excavations by distinguishing different civilizations by their pottery. For the pottery (Fig. 34) is very plentiful and varies greatly, whereas this cannot be said of other objects. For types of pottery students have sought corresponding types of man, not without contradictions ; behind civilizations they have tried to detect peoples.[1]

The pottery has been classified in types—that of the megaliths of Northern Germany, that of the lake-dwellings, that which is adorned with incised bands, the beakers on which a pattern has been impressed with cords, the zoned vases, and a number of wares adorned with deeply impressed dots, called after Schönfeld, Rössen, Nierstein, Grossgartach, and other sites.

The pottery of the lake-dwellings and the hill-stations

---

[1] A. Schliz, in **XXIII**, 1909, p. 263 ; **CXVIII**, 1912, pp. 36 ff., 220 ff. Wilcke, ibid., 1909, 3, p. 336 ; Kossinna, in **LXXXV**, 1911, pp. 313 ff.

FIG. 34. Neolithic Pottery of Germany. (Schumacher, *Siedelings- u. Kulturgesch.*, p. 58, fig. 18.) The types, reading down, are: Pile-dwelling; megalith; Rössen, Grossgartach, etc.; Hinkelstein; spiral; cord-impression; zoned.

which have the same furniture may be set on one side.[1]
The people who used it, after advancing as far as Mainz,
retreated, and doubtless did not enter into the final amalgams
except in the south of Bavaria and perhaps in Bohemia and
Austria.

The banded ware [2] belongs to a civilization with very
clearly-marked features, which spread from the Lower
Danube to France, passing north of Switzerland, almost
certainly from east to west. The people of this culture came
into contact with many others, as we see from the mixtures
revealed by the excavations and by the frequent appearance
of local types, not at all regularly distributed, alongside
of the banded pottery. Such in the Rhine valley is the
Hinkelstein ware.[3]

The pottery of the megaliths of North-Western Germany [4]
is quite different from the corresponding wares of Western
Europe, although it has copied some shapes of vase from the
latter, applying its own style of decoration.[5] It is not
fundamentally different from the local wares of Central
Germany. It is another mixture with some new elements
added, brought by the sea or the coast, and perhaps some
elements lacking.

The wares decorated with impressed dots bear witness
to a taste common to all the peoples of Northern Europe.
Some (the Schönfeld [6] and Rössen [7] types) seem to be
descended from the pottery of the megalithic monuments,
while others (the Nierstein and Grossgartach types) seem
to be the result of a crossing of the banded ware with the
Rössen type. They are found in a limited area, except
the Rössen type, which was first made in Saxony and
reached the valley of the Rhine.[8]

A not very dense population of agriculturalists, attracted
chiefly by the good soil of the belts of loess, clearing the
ground as they needed it, exhausting the soil and moving
on ; or a pastoral population, without reserves of fodder

---

[1] Schumacher, **CCCCIX**, i, pp. 21 ff.   [2] Ibid., p. 31.
[3] Ibid., p. 34.   [4] Ibid., p. 30.
[5] Kossinna, **CCCXCVI**, pp. 155 ff.
[6] On Neolithic pottery, see Reinecke, in **CLX**, 1900, p. 232 ; Kossinna,
in **LXXXV**, i, 26, 255 ; ii, 59.
[7] Kossinna, **CCCXCVI**, p. 164.
[8] Schumacher, op. cit., i, pp. 39 ff.

and therefore scattered—such was the bulk of the people. Among them tribes of hunters, fishermen, or brigands went about—warlike, conquering tribes, drawn by the woods and the high ground, or by the rivers. These were the men who

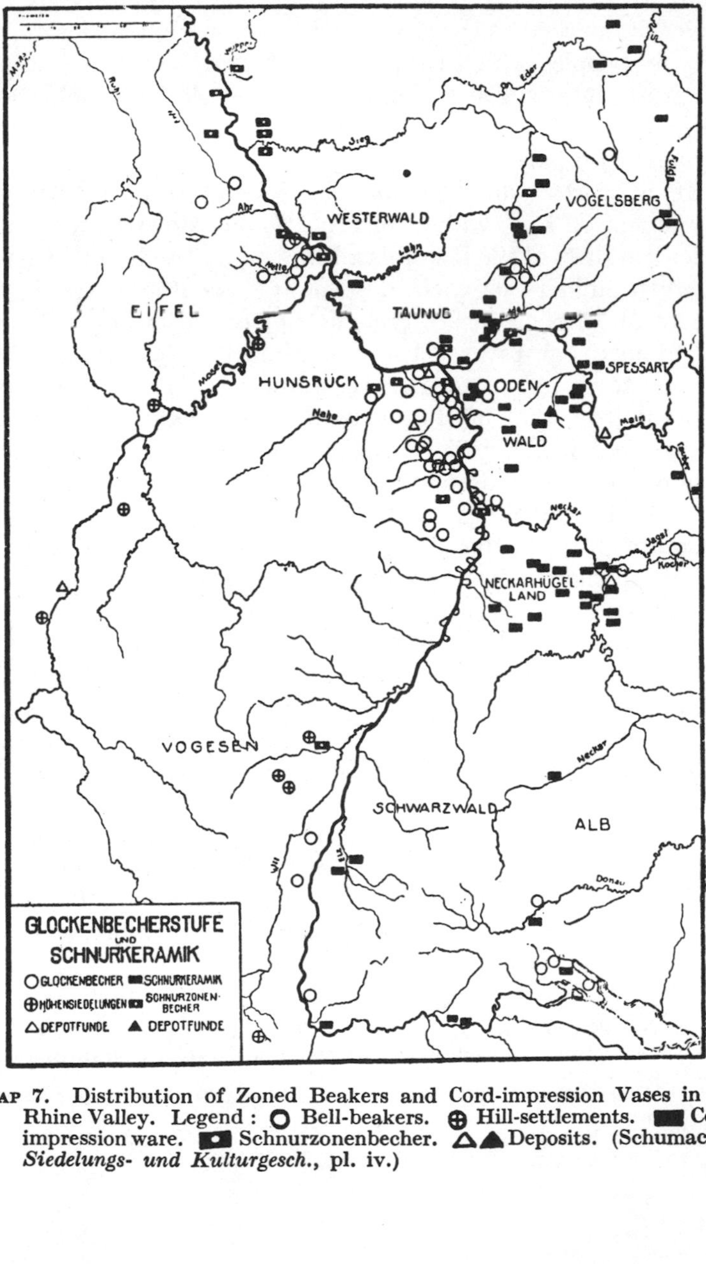

Map 7. Distribution of Zoned Beakers and Cord-impression Vases in the Rhine Valley. Legend : ○ Bell-beakers. ⊕ Hill-settlements. ■ Cord-impression ware. ▣ Schnurzonenbecher. △▲ Deposits. (Schumacher, *Siedelungs- und Kulturgesch.*, pl. iv.)

produced the zoned pottery,[1] or the cord-pattern pottery which is very like it.[2] (Map 7.)

This state of things prevailed roughly in all the districts between the North Sea and Switzerland, and between the Meuse and the Oder. The western and eastern limits are not so clearly marked as those which I have previously described, and the peoples which they bounded were less concentrated and more interwoven. This was the world in which those Celtic societies came into being, round which the whole population finally crystallized.

It is worth while to consider the eastern frontier for a moment. The valley of the Elbe, down which the agriculturalists of the Danubian Plain came [3] and up which the megalith-builders or their descendants went, was, probably as a result of their meeting, a district of variations. But we should note that it was at the same time a line of demarcation. The pottery of the megalithic tombs of the east is very different from that of Hanover and Westphalia.[4] The types of ware found side by side in Anhalt spread, some to the west (Schönfeld, the Rössen type), and the others to the east through Brandenburg and Pomerania (balloon-amphoræ, Molkenberg type, Bernburg type). Local types of culture sprang up there which spread out in opposite directions, and the human groups turned opposite ways, those who were to be Celts and those who were to be Germans, and the archæological map of Europe shows their progressive differentiation.[5]

But if we can talk of Celts at this early date we must look in the racial hotchpotch of Western Germany for the element which formed them.[6] In our search we must place the people of the cord-pattern pottery [7] side by side with the people of the zone-beakers. The typical cord-pattern vase is a round-bellied beaker like the zoned vase, but taller. The decoration usually consists of horizontal lines impressed with

[1] Ibid., p. 49.
[2] Ibid., p. 47.
[3] Kossinna, op. cit., pp. 165 ff.
[4] Åberg, CCXCVII, pp. 151 ff.
[5] These facts will be studied in more detail in the volume on the Germans in this series.
[6] G. Wilcke (in LXXXV, 1918, pp. 1–54) regards the Rössen-Nierstein ware as an indication of the Celts.
[7] Schumacher, op. cit., i, pp. 46 ff. ; Åberg, op. cit., pp. 97, 178, 182, 190, and maps iv, xi ; Schuchardt, CCCLXXXIII, pp. 108 ff.

cords on the fresh paste and (only in late or degenerate specimens) of bands of engraved herring-bone pattern, sometimes vertical. It is an almost general rule that this ware is chiefly of a funerary nature. It is found in tumuli erected in a few cases over cremations and usually over graves in which the body was laid out at full length. These tumuli are generally in high, wooded places.

This cord-pattern ware is most frequent in the valley of the Saale. It is very common all over Saxony, from the Elbe to the Thuringian mountains. (Further north, between Magdeburg and the Harz, a few specimens have been found, and also on the right bank of the Elbe and even in Jutland [1]; but this was the domain of another people.) There is hardly anything between the Elbe and the Oder, and nothing between the Oder and the Vistula. East of the Oder two objects only, one in Silesia and the other in Volhynia, have been assigned to it. It is very frequent in the north of Bohemia. Westwards it appears beyond the mountains of Thuringia, and extends through Hessen and along the Taunus to the Rhine and Neckar. Specimens are found as far as Switzerland in the lake-villages. In South-Western Germany the men who made this pottery seem to have lived alongside of other groups without either colliding with them or mixing with them. Perhaps they lived a different manner of life. They were warriors or hunters. But if they lived side by side with the agriculturalists of the plain their relations must, on the whole, have been peaceful.[2] What were their relations ? We are free to imagine them as we like. Certainly they were very considerable.

The makers of the zoned vases and those of the cord-pattern beakers lived in the same districts in Saxony, in Bohemia, and in Western Germany. If maps showing their distribution were placed one over the other they would fit, and each would complement the other. We now have to inquire whether they came into contact and, if they did so, whether either side influenced the other. We have only one proof of their meeting. In a burial at Hebenkies,[3] near Wiesbaden, a zoned vase has been found together with

---

[1] Åberg, op. cit., p. 182.
[2] Schumacher, op. cit., i, pp. 44–5 ; A. Schliz, in *Heilbronner Festschr.* pp. 10 ff. ; Kossinna, op. cit., pp. 173, 180, 183.
[3] Åberg, op. cit.

cord-pattern vases, and the decoration of this zoned vase is produced by the impression of cords. A certain number of these *Schnurzonenbecher* have been found along the Rhine.[1] They may be hybrids, and Herr Schumacher believes that it was under the influence of the people of the cord-pattern beakers that the tumulus was adopted by the tribes of the zoned vases.[2] In any case, the two ceramic types crown the development of the so-called Neolithic pottery of Western Germany.

Thus, as early as this time, in this region two groups of warlike tribes insinuated themselves concurrently among the old inhabitants, and formed a kind of network round and between them. It has been suggested that one of the two groups was Celtic, because it sent out to the British Isles the only large colonies which they received before the La Tène period.[3] The relative position of these two groups in Germany, which reveals, even before that colonization, the principle of a differentiation comparable to that of the Goidels and Brythons, affords a very strong argument in favour of that hypothesis.

But two points remain to be considered.

A certain number of Scandinavian and German archæologists have held that the people of the beakers with stamped decoration had also crossed over the Lower Elbe into Jutland, and there formed a very large colony, which exerted a considerable influence all round and is certainly one of the chief elements in the formation of the Germans.[4]

The racial mark by which this Jutland folk is known is the round tumulus covering a pit, in which the dead man was laid in a contracted position, which is called the single-burial tomb in contrast to the megalithic funeral chambers. In it we find beakers, sometimes similar to those of Saxony, some amphoras of the same type as those which almost always accompany the cord-pattern beakers, and asymmetrical perforated axes, the most perfect of which is the boat-shaped axe, well known to prehistorians. If the hypothesis mentioned above were true, either the people

---

[1] Schumacher, op. cit., i, pl. iv and p. 49.
[2] Ibid.
[3] Kossinna, in **LXXXV**, 1913, pp. 31 ff. ; Schumacher, in **XXXI**, x ; Wilcke, in **LXXXV**, 1918, p. 50.
[4] See the volume in this series on the Germans.

of the cord-pattern beakers was itself an element of the Germanic race, its western extensions being submerged in the mass of the Celts, or else it split and produced a nucleus of Celts and a nucleus of Germans.

Our previous examination of linguistic relations does not fit well with this hypothesis. But there are positive reasons for rejecting it. The national weapon of the people of the cord-pattern beakers was an asymmetrical perforated axe like the battle-axes of Jutland, but shaped in longitudinal facets. It went with its bearers when they expanded towards the Rhine. It is entirely absent north of the Elbe. It is unlikely that the Jutland battle-axes are derived from the faceted axe. It is equally unlikely that a people, whose remains are remarkable for their uniformity, and thereby bear witness that it expanded rapidly, as conquerors, should, where it is found to have been, have kept only part of its characteristic gear, and that not its weapons, in one particular region into which it advanced. The culture of the single-burial tomb and the culture of the cord-pattern vase are mixed formations of the same kind, the former being probably older than the latter, and are composed of the same elements, which were supplied, some by the megalith-builders of the seaboard (axe, type of beaker, tumulus), some by the aborigines of the Baltic plains, and some (funeral rites and part of the pottery) by the peoples which came from Central Europe.

The second point concerns the kinship of the Celts and the Italici.

The cultures of the cord-pattern beakers and the zoned beakers were succeeded in Bohemia by what is called the civilization of Aunjetitz, or Unetice,[1] which corresponds to a more advanced stage of the Bronze culture, extending considerably beyond its first period. This civilization extended its frontiers greatly in all directions. Later the migration of the folk who had made it left the actual centre of their habitat empty. The main movement was to the south. The culture is found, complete and unaltered, south of the Danube. The civilization of Northern Italy presents such close similarities to it that one is justified in looking here for the ancestors of the Italici and, more particularly, of the

---

[1] L. Niederle, in **LV**, i, 1907 ; cf. Déchelette, **CCCXVIII**, ii, 1, pp. 89–90.

Latins. But this culture also spread between the Saale and the Oder, in the Saxon area of the cord-pattern beakers, and then westwards along the upper valley of the Danube and to the Rhine, where its collars and pins with rolled heads and racket heads are found, together it is true, with a pottery derived from zone-beakers (Adlerberg type).[1]

Was it descended from the two cultures whose place it took ? In that case these would represent the undivided stock of the Celts and Italici. Does it itself represent that undivided stock ? Neither supposition is probable. The people of Aunjetitz was itself a mixed people, containing a smaller proportion of Nordic types than the people of the cord-pattern beakers, and other types than the people of the zoned vases ; it had taken some features from the cultures between the Elbe and Oder and it kept the funeral customs of the Danube valley. It is, then, as it were, parallel to the two others, and not derived from them.

Furthermore, since there is nothing recalling it in the archæology of the British Isles, it is probable that the Italici and Celts had parted before it appeared. The Italici had begun to develop on their own lines in the south-east of Bohemia, in Moravia, and perhaps in Silesia [2] ; the Celts did likewise between the Upper Danube, the Saale, and the North Sea, where they already formed a community divided into two sections. But they were not so much separated as to have no intercourse and never to borrow from one another. Above all they were not so firmly settled down that parties could not cross from either side of the vague frontier to the other. We must not imagine these prehistoric peoples as keeping strictly within neat frontiers.

Dim and hypothetical as this reconstruction of Italo-Celtic origins still remains, it can be traced with some probability to the beginning of the Bronze Age. We can see that the formation of distinct groups, the concentration of the Celts on the border of Thuringia, the departure of a first Celtic migration to the British Isles, and that of a first Italic migration to Northern Italy, happened roughly at the same time, as has been indicated at the beginning of this chapter.

---

[1] Schumacher, op. cit., i, pp. 63–5 ; **CCCCVIII**, p. 89.
[2] Meillet, **CCXVII**, p. 376 ; Peet, **DXXXIX**, pp. 509–510 ; Homo, **CCCXLI**, English, p. 48.

Another result of our archæological inquiry is to show, as our linguistic inquiry might already have made us foresee, that the elements of which these societies were composed were very fluid and themselves composite.

The most obscure point in the hypothesis adopted is the original position of the future Goidels, for if the zone-beaker folk was the nucleus which organized them it is very hard to determine where it was itself formed.   Moreover, it spread over almost the whole of the Celtic domain and left

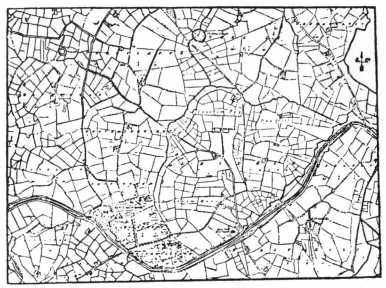

Fig. 35.   Distribution of Cultivated Land and Dwellings in Ireland.   (Meitzen, *Siedelung und Agrarwesen*, fig. 19.)

descendants there. In any case it occupied all the seaboard districts between the Rhine and Elbe which remained outside the frontiers previously mentioned.   These were the districts which were emptied by the migration of the Goidels to Britain. It is possible that the consequences of this migration affected peoples dwelling east of the Elbe. But it is certain that it did not cause any movement on the part of the interesting culture which developed in the Bronze Age in the Cimbric Peninsula, the Danish islands, and Pomerania.

Was it a total or only a partial emigration ?   It was probably partial, for there remained what is usually left behind by peoples which have been a long time in a country where they have been engaged in adapting the ground to human life, namely the distribution of dwellings and the shape of villages and fields. In the western part of North-Western Germany, in Western Hanover, and Westphalia, cultivated land and dwellings are arranged in a manner which is foreign to Germany, or has become so. It is the arrangement found in Ireland (Fig. 35), part of England, and France. The houses stand alone in the midst of their fields, and the villages are of the simplest kind. It is a system suited to the raising of horned cattle or pigs. The typical German village, on the other hand, is a large village, very irregular, with gardens behind the houses and fields, very regular, all round. Meitzen [1] designated the former type of occupation of the ground as the Celtic type, and his map shows it extending to the Weser and the Sieg.

This disposition of men and lands is not peculiar to the Goidels alone. Perhaps they inherited it. In any case, they had it, and where they have remained they have kept it. They have left it in part of their old German domain. The Germanic inhabitants of this part of Westphalia and Hanover have retained it, either because they stepped into the place of the Goidels without altering the arrangement which they found, or because they left a large number of the old occupants where they were ; probably both things happened.

Agricultural peoples never change their abode entirely. This is an indication that the Goidels did not leave in one body, and that they did not all leave.

What was the reason of their emigration ? It was certainly not weakness or poverty. Perhaps there was some encroachment of the sea on a coast which has altered much. Perhaps some invention in the matter of navigation was discovered. The megalith-builders whom the Goidels surrounded were certainly sailors who were not afraid of crossing the North Sea.

[1] CCCLIII, i, pp. 174–232 and fig. 19. Beyond the zone of the Germanic villages he places the villages and cultivated lands of a type very familiar to us, which, indeed, is like the Germanic type ; it is that of the Brythonic Celts, where the villages are large, but there are also big isolated farms and houses.

CHAPTER II

The Expansion of the Celts in the British Isles

I

THE BRITISH ISLES BEFORE THE COMING OF THE CELTS

IN the following chapters we shall consider how the various elements of the Celtic population emigrated in succession and made new Celtic countries. In this respect the British Isles, where we saw the Goidels landing in the last chapter, give a condensed picture of the Celtic world and the clearest picture of it. They must, therefore, be studied separately and before the other Celtic countries. It is, moreover, here, and here alone, except in Brittany, that the Celts survive otherwise than in a diffused condition, for they here form communities, one of which is to-day a nation. Here the two first Celtic groups can be distinguished, not by mere conjecture but by their still living languages. Here the chain of facts is complete. But we shall find in the ethnology of the British Isles other races which I have not yet mentioned, and the Belgæ in particular. All the groups of Celtic peoples which we shall find playing their part on the Continent reappear in the British Isles, and in circumstances which are favourable to study.

Furthermore, we can see here, thanks to data which are lacking for the study of the Continental Celts, the natives whom the Celtic peoples absorbed. Once these were assimilated, they certainly went for much in the making of the Celtic peoples and their civilization. The two strains had for some time remained distinct. They appeared so to foreigners, and the natives were conscious of their different origin.

In relating his first expedition to Britain Cæsar wished to say a few words about its population, and he gives us a first brief account of the races of the country. " The interior of Britain," he writes, " is inhabited by people who, according to their own tradition, are aborigines. The coast is occupied

189

by others, who came from Belgium on looting or warlike
expeditions, and have almost all kept as tribal names those
of the tribes from which they are descended. Brought in
by war, they settled down and proceeded to cultivate the
land." [1] So Cæsar knew that the population of Britain
comprised at least two different elements, and that the later
comers were distinguished by their relationship to the Celtic
peoples of the Continent, and particularly by their names,
which bore certain testimony to their origin.

Unfortunately he is not as clear as he is concise and
positive. He knew the peoples of Belgium well, and he must
have seen for himself that their names recurred in Britain.
It is a pity that he has not told us those which attracted his
notice. Ptolemy [2] mentions a *civitas Belgarum*, which covered
eastern Somerset, Wiltshire, and the north of Hampshire.
One of their towns was called Venta Belgarum, now
Winchester. North of the Belgæ, in what is now Berkshire,
was the *civitas* of the *Atrebates*. From the Thames northwards
to the Wash, in what are now the counties of Hertford,
Bedford, Cambridge, Huntingdon, and Northampton, were
the Catuvellauni, in whose name we can, without much strain
on our goodwill, see that of the Catalauni, of which it was
probably the older, uncontracted form. Further north
the Parisii occupied part of Yorkshire between York and the
sea. But the Parisii were doubtless not Belgæ.[3] This does
not amount to much in all, and the Belgæ no longer existed
in distinct communities on the coast where Cæsar could have
come across them. It is probable that the people of the British
Belgæ was formed by the union of scattered elements which
had kept their tribal names for a time and, when they
combined, contented themselves with their race-name.

Cæsar has given us another piece of information about
the adventures of the Belgæ in Britain. Before describing
his campaign of 57, he gives a brief history which he had
obtained from the Remi about their neighbours [4] : " Their

---

[1] *Gall. War*, v, 12, 1–2 ; MacNeill, CCCCXLI, p. 54 ; A. Mahr, " Das
frühe Inselkeltentum im Lichte neuerer Ausgrabungen," in Archäol. Inst.
d. Deutschen Reiches, *Bericht über die Hundertjahrfeier*, pp. 310–12 (Berlin,
1930).
[2] 3, 13 ; Holmes, CCCCXXXIII, pp. 232–3.
[3] See below, p. 214.
[4] *Gall. War*, ii, 4, 6–7.

neighbours were the Suessiones, who owned a very extensive and extremely fertile territory. At a time within recollection they had a king named Diviciacus, who was the most powerful man in Gaul, and established his supremacy over a great part of the land on this coast and over Britain." The Belgæ of England may have been remnants of the forces of Diviciacus. Their number had increased even in Cæsar's time.[1]

But what were the aborigines ? Were they the first Celtic colonists or the predecessors of the Celts ? Were they Brythons ? Or Goidels ? Or Picts ? Or still earlier inhabitants ? Scholars are divided. Cæsar's expression is probably very comprehensive, but it leaves us wondering.

II

THE MYTH OF IRISH ORIGINS

Ireland has always liked to make out that her origins are mixed, and her latest national historians are quite enthusiastic in proving that she is not thoroughly Celtic,[2] and only became so very late in the day.

The Irish have imagined their island as peopled by a series of invasions. The *fili*, the official bards, corresponding to the *vates* of Gaul, developed this tradition into a theory. The catalogues of the poems which the *fili* had ready for the entertainment of their hearers give the titles of the principal works into which these various parts had been crystallized. The poems are lost, but they are found again in a compilation of the eleventh century, entitled the *Leabhar Gabhála*, or *Book of Invasions*.[3] It is a composition of theorists and mythographers. But it was accepted. Local tradition (the

---

[1] Holmes, op. cit., p. 232, n. 3.

[2] In the Middle Ages a legend of British origins was developed, of which it would be unnecessary to speak, if it had not been cited by an anthropologist of the learning of Mr. H. J. Fleure (**CCCXXVIII**, pp. 65–71), who gives it an appearance of truth. This legend connects the history of Britain with that of Rome and the Trojan cycle. The myth of Irish origins is of the same class, but of better quality. It has the merit of having been made by Irishmen for Irishmen, and of expressing a part of the national beliefs. The legend of British origins was in part made by foreigners for foreigners.

[3] On the mythical invasions of Ireland, see Czarnowski, **CCCCXXIII**, pp. 97 ff.

Dinnshenchas) and heroic epic show that the mythical invaders of prehistoric Ireland were familiar characters in Irish mythology, or at least some of them.

The *Leabhar Gabhála* tells the story of five invasions.

The first was that of Partholon. Partholon left Spain after killing Bel, the king of the country, and arrived in Ireland on the very day of Beltane, the Feast of Bel, on the 1st May. Ireland was at that time occupied by a race of spirits or demons from the sea, the Fomorians (Fomóraig),[1] and Partholon fought them. His race was, however, carried off by a pestilence, which broke out on the day of Beltane and lasted a week. The scene of the death of the sons of Partholon was a plain called Sen Mag, the Old Plain, where the whole tribe had gathered to bury its dead. Sen Mag is a mythical plain ; but another version of the story places the event in the plain of Breg near the east coast, that is, in the religious centre of pagan Ireland, where the most famous graves are.

The second invader, Nemed, also came from Spain, and also landed on Beltane day. It was the great spring festival. Nemed and some of his people were slain by a pestilence ; the rest were subdued by the Fomorians, who made them pay a tribute of two-thirds of their children, harvests, and milk. The sons of Nemed rose and besieged the Fomorians in a tower of glass in Tory Island (Tor Inis, the Isle of the Tower). The revolt failed, and the remainder of the sons of Nemed were wiped out.

Then came the Fir Bolg, with the Fir Domnann and the Galians (Gaileoin), who are included under the name of Fir Bolg. We shall meet them again. These people sided with the Fomorians, and we are given a most unpleasant picture of them.

The following wave brought the Tuatha Dé Danann, that is, the Tribes of the Goddess Danu. They were amiable gods, doing good and bringing civilization, and among them were Nuada, the sea-god, Manannán mac Lir, another sea-god, and Lugh, the sun-god. There were other gods in Ireland who are classed among the Fomorians and are associated more or less closely with the Tuatha Dé Danann. The Tuatha Dé

---

[1] *Fomóraig* means " deep, submarine " ; *fo = ὑπο* ; *mor = mare.*

Danann, arriving at Beltane, engaged in battle with the Fomorians, whom they defeated at Moytura in Connacht on the day of the feast of Samhain, the 1st November, six months, or two seasons, later.

Fifth came the Goidels, or, more accurately, the sons of Mile, son of Bile, from Spain, like Partholon and Nemed. But Spain had been only a previous stage on their journey, and they came from much further away. Arriving in Ireland, they fought and did business alternately with the Tuatha Dé Danann. In the end they had the better of them and the Tuatha Dé Danann retired into the *sidhe*, the great megalithic tombs, such as New Grange and Brugh-na-Boyne.

But this was not all, for in the second generation of the Milesians (as the sons of Mile came to be called), the Cruithnig, or Picts, appeared. The Milesians had encountered them already on their way, and we shall come back to them later.

We might regard this whole story as a curious attempt to fit the mythical prehistory of Ireland into the history of the world as it was conceived by the last Latin writers and the Christian Church.[1] Possibly it was so. But the learned author or authors of the work of which the *Leabhar Gabhála* is the latest edition found the materials of their compilation all there, waiting for them. They did not invent the Fomorians or the Fir Bolg or the Tuatha Dé Danann. Most of the episodes revolve round the great seasonal feasts of the Irish year. They are myths, subjected to various degrees of euhemerization. But among these myths there are traditions of a historical kind, and names which belong to history. Two facts, at least, should be kept in sight. One is that the Goidels did not regard themselves as the builders of the great megalithic funerary chambers, which became the dwellings of the gods. The second is that with strange insistence, the authors of these stories make the first settlers in Ireland come from Spain, and that probability is on their side. It is a pity that they have not told us equally clearly whence the last arrivals really came.

These Irish traditions have their chronology, given in annals the authenticity of which can be checked by reference to the technical inventions ascribed to the kings who appear

[1] Bede, *Eccl. Hist.*, i, 1.

there with their dates.[1] One date which interests us is that of the discovery of gold, both gold mines and the manufacture of gold objects. Ireland was a sort of Eldorado. It is possible that its wealth in gold attracted visitors and settlers. The most ancient gold objects are the crescent-shaped things called lunettes. Leinster tradition ascribed the invention of gold-working to King Tighearnmhas. The discovery is supposed to have taken place in the auriferous region traversed by the Liffey. Tighearnmhas was a Fomorian king who lived during the reign of Nuada, and also saw the coming of the Milesians. Other traditions place him among the Milesian kings. In any case, the chronicles place him between 1620 and 1036 B.C. Even the earlier date is, in my opinion, too late for the beginnings of gold-working in Ireland, but not very much so, and it is about the probable date of the landing of the future Goidels in the island. So part of the traditions survives checking.

We shall now try to see what really lay behind these tales. At the same time we shall see how much truth is condensed in the picture drawn by Cæsar.

III

THE NON-CELTIC ELEMENT IN THE POPULATION OF IRELAND, ACCORDING TO MR. MACNEILL.   THE GOIDELS AND THE SUBJECT PEOPLES.   THE ERAINN

Anthropologists have observed in the present population of the British Isles certain aberrant types, which they hold to represent the aboriginal inhabitants. These, according to Mr. Fleure, are found, at least in Wales, in the remoter and wilder districts.[2] We hear of long-headed Mongoloids, akin to the Eskimos, and these are said to appear also in Ireland, and to be descended from its first occupants.[3] But to them we must add the far greater number of descendants of the megalith-builders and the navigators, long-headed or short-headed, who first spread the knowledge of metal in Western

---

[1] Miss M. Dobbs, in **LXXX**, 1914, p. 24 ; Macalister, **CCCCXXXIX**, p. 120. The memory of Tighearnmhas is associated with the institution of the worship of Cromm Crúaich ; that is one reason for believing that something like his real date has been preserved.

[2] In **LXXVI**, 1916, p. 35.

[3] Pokorny, in **CV**, xlix, 1919 (repr.) ; **CLXXI**, 1915, pp. 231, 308–357.

Europe.[1] Attempts have been made, with varying success, to credit these forerunners of the Celts with such institutions as that of the Druids, with technical processes, and with certain weapons.[2] Certain words, too, must be ascribed to them—the names of rivers and peoples and individuals, which have survived. But one may try to see them in intact social formations. That is what Mr. MacNeill has done for Ireland, by extracting new pieces of information from the written tradition of the country, and it is worth while to examine his findings closely.[3]

He supposes that when the original inhabitants were amalgamated by the Goidels into their political organization they kept their old constitution in part and were incorporated as ready-made social units into the Goidelic system. As a sign of their incorporation and their dependence, special burdens of a political kind were laid on them, as a tribute. For there were in Ireland a great number of vassal clans—Celticized clans, speaking Celtic and ruled by Celtic lines, but keeping their old names and compelling their masters to assume them, just as, later, the Angles and Saxons imposed their names on the Norman barons. These clans were called *Aithech-thuatha*, the lower-class clans.[4]

These clans seem to have been comprised under the general name of Féni (singular Féne) in Old Irish.[5] This name may have become Middle Irish Fianna (singular Fian). The Fianna were a permanent fighting force, which might be created by a levy of subjects, for the Goidels were not liable to military service beyond certain limited contributions. Finn mac Coul, the hero of the Fianna, belonged to a subject clan of Leinster, one of Galians.[6]

---

[1] Fleure, in **LXXVI**, 1918, p. 155.

[2] For the name of the coracle, which Pokorny ascribes to the aborigines of Ireland, see J. Loewenthal, in **CLXIV**, vii, p. 177. The root must belong to the North-western vocabulary (O. Nord. *hgrunde* " skin " ; O. Slav. *kora* " bark " ; Lith. *karna* " lime-bark "). See above, p. 73.

[3] MacNeill, **CCCCXLI**.

[4] *Duanaire Finn*, introd., xxxi ; MacNeill, op. cit., p. 148. *Aitheach* " giant, soldier, peasant ", etc.

[5] MacNeill, op. cit., p. 150 ; J. Loth, in **CXL**, xli, p. 350 ; *feni* means " kinsfolk, men of the same race " (*uenioi* ; cf. Gwynedd = *ueiniia*) ; the name of the people must at an early date have become that of a social class, the clan of free tenants ; *fiann* " troop " from *ueinā*. Ptol., ii, 2, 3 : Οὐεννικνιοι perhaps comes from the same root, and may be the tribal name of a group of Féni.

[6] MacNeill, op. cit., p. 149.

The rent-paying clans have all been put down in a list like so many things in Ireland. We have several manuscripts of a treatise giving the names and positions of these old non-Gaelic communities.[1] They are so numerous and so widely spread that one grows anxious for the Goidels. One regards the latter with surprise and admiration when one thinks that they imposed their language on that great mass of subjects so easily and so completely that nothing is left but dead words to show that another tongue was ever spoken in Ireland. When an invading people has imposed its speech on the inhabitants of a conquered country it has always had some superiority over them in numbers, in civilization, or in political organization, which we do not seem to see in this case. But it appears elsewhere, in the names of divisions of the country and towns and villages, which are Celtic, whereas the names of rivers are not,[2] and also in a tradition which relates that the Goidels cleared all Ireland of forest, but that the plain of Breg, Magh n-Ealta, called the Old Plain, where the great tumuli of the lower Boyne lie, was already cleared when they arrived.[3] Moreover, non-Gaelic does not necessarily mean non-Celtic. Subject clan does not necessarily mean non-Gaelic clan. Lastly, even if the subject clans and the ruling clans are racially of different origin, the fact that some were subject does not at all imply, as Mr. MacNeill supposes, that they came to Ireland before their rulers.

Ireland, as we know her, is a kind of feudal organization, in which clans have their order of rank like individuals. But their ranks were never fixed once for all. We know, for example, that in the first half of the second century after Christ there was a general rising of the rent-payers under Cairbre Cat-head.[4] In the course of the history of Ireland many clans rose or fell in rank through force of circumstance or arms. Their very unstable order of eminence only existed *de facto*. Those which forced their way up justified their action by history and legend, inventing titles to the possession of their rank.

[1] Ibid., p. 73. One MS. of this treatise has been published in **CXL**. The treatise goes back to the eighth century.

[2] Macalister, **CCCCXXXIX**, p. 252.   [3] MacNeill, op. cit., p. 72.

[4] Ibid., p. 119 ; Macalister, op. cit., p. 290 ; E. MacNeill, *Duanaire Finn*, i, p. lvi.

This is, in particular, true of the reigning lines which gave Ireland a kind of unity at the time when St. Patrick began, or was about to begin, his preaching of Christianity. These were the lines, this was the aristocracy, gathered round the High Kings of Tara, who called themselves the Milesians, the sons of Mile. They caused a Milesian literature to come into being.[1]

The list of the subject peoples brings all the elements which, apart from the Goidels, made up the population of the British Isles before us in review. We must, however, set aside a certain number of clans which, if their names have any qualifying sense, can only be industrial castes formed into territorial clans. The list mentioned above [2] includes in the territory of the Desi in Munster, where there are copper mines, a Tuath Semon. This was the clan of the Rivet, *seim*. In the mining district of Béarra in Western Munster were the Ceardraighe, the Smiths. A Tuath Cathbarr, or Helmet Clan, was distributed over the counties of Tipperary, Limerick, Cork, and Kerry. Whether they were Gaelic or non-Gaelic we have no idea, and perhaps there is no occasion to ask. They were not racial formations, but social. We shall also set aside a clan named Fir Iboth or Ibdaig,[3] which is placed in the lower valley of the Shannon, in Counties Galway, Tipperary, and Limerick. It has the same name as the Ebudæ, or Hebrides. According to Solinus,[4] the people of those islands lived on fish and the milk of their cattle. Were there Hebrideans in Ireland ? Was it the common name of a caste of fishermen ? We have no reason for inclining to either view.

Among the subject or rent-paying peoples one of the largest seems to have been that of the Erainn, who apparently gave their name to Ireland,[5] which the Goidels continued to call by it. Ireland is called Eire, Old Irish Eriu. The Greek and Latin forms, Ἱερα (νῆσος), whence Avienus gets his Sacra Insula, Strabo's Ἱέρνη, Ptolemy's Ἰουερνία, the Iverna of Pomponius Mela and Juvenal, and the Hibernia of Cæsar, render the old root-word as exactly as possible. The Irish Erenn, the genitive of Eriu, and the

---

[1] *Duanaire Finn*, i, p. xxxviii.   [2] MacNeill, op. cit., p. 75.
[3] Ibid., p. 74.   [4] *Collectanea Rerum Memorabilium*, 22, 42.
[5] The accusative plural Erna has provided the stem of a more modern form of the word.

Welsh form Iwerddon,[1] take us back to a term containing an
n : *Iuerion, genitive Iuerionos.

The Erainn were the Iverni. Ptolemy places the people
of the 'Ιουέρνοι in the south-west of Ireland.[2]   Now this
was just where the Erainn had their principal centre in the
time of the oldest epics.   The list of rent-paying peoples
places the Erainn, or rather the Sen-Erainn, the old and
authentic Iuerni, in the district of Luachair, covering the
north of Kerry and the adjacent parts of Limerick and Cork ;
here stood Teamhair Erann,[3] that is Tara of the Erainn,
which had been the chief burying-ground and meeting-place
of the Erainn before it became one of the religious centres of
Munster.   At the beginning of our era the Erainn of Munster
were subject to the dynasty of the Eoganachta of Cashel,
a thoroughly Celtic line.[4]   But there were also Erainn in
Connacht and Ulster,[5] where they appear as the scattered
remnants of an ancient population, driven by invaders
into corners where they make a stand.

But what were the Erainn ?   It is possible that they were
not Celts.   It is tempting, on the other hand, to compare the
names of the Iverni and the Iberians.[6]   The likeness of these
names naturally leads one to infer relationship between the
peoples.   That likeness is even more complete than it first
seems.   For the *n* of the stem both of Erainn and of Ierne
is an addition.   The Erainn, like all the peoples of Ireland,
got their name from an eponymous ancestor.   Theirs was
called Iar (in two syllables).   This name is directly descended
from an Old Celtic word *Iueros*.   It is easy to conclude that
there were two race-names corresponding to the name of
Ireland—Iueri and Iuerni.   Now " Iueri " and " Iberi "
are almost identical.   Spain and Ireland lie near enough
and have always had enough intercourse for this similarity
to be at least taken into consideration.

---

[1] The *dd* represents a *y*.   The *h* in the form Hibernia, Hiberio, is
adventitious.   Rhys (**CCLXXXI**, p. 130) wrongly connects the form *ywerit*
with the name of Ireland (cf. Skene, **CCLXXXVII**, i, p. 295 :   Bran mab
Ywerit) ; Ywerit is the same as Welsh *gwerydd* and O. Irish *fairge*, " the Ocean,"
and Ywerit is the wife of Llyr, the sea-god.   Cf. Ptol., ii, 2, 5 ; 3, 2 ; vii,
3, 2, Οὐεργιουος, Οὐεργιουιος.   In Mela, ii, 78, the name of Ireland appears
in the form Bergyon (Hercules fights with Albiona and Bergyon), which =
Iberygon or Ivorygon.   MacNeill, **CCCCXLI**, p. 67.

[2] Ptol., ii, 2, 6.   [3] T. J. Westropp, in **LXXX**,1918, pp. 111 ff.
[4] MacNeill, op. cit., p. 65.   [5] Ibid., p. 66 ; e.g. in Antrim.
[6] Ibid.

The authors of the *Leabhar Gabhála* have found worthy successors in the scholars of our time who have endeavoured, with much learning, labour, and ingenuity, to detect the Iberian element in the racial antiquities of the British Isles.[1]

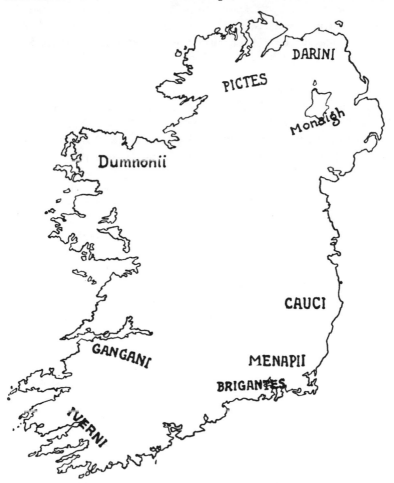

MAP 8.   Ireland about A.D. 90.   Pictes = Picts (French map).

Their pains have been ill-rewarded, for, while it is almost certain that there was this Iberian strain, and that it was considerable, anything definite to be said on the subject can be summed up in a very few words.

[1] Sir J. Rhys, in **CXLVII**, 1890.

Tacitus remarked that there were dark-skinned men in Britain who were very numerous in Wales among the Silures, who occupied the south-west of that region : " The dark faces of the Silures, their usually curly hair, and the position of Spain opposite, are evidence that the ancient Iberians crossed the sea and settled there." [1] Now it is probable that the inhabitants of Spain, particularly of the south-west, who formed large communities at the end of the Neolithic Age and the beginning of the Bronze Age, played a considerable part in the diffusion of megalith-building, which has been mentioned above, towards the north of Europe, and in the colonization of the shores of the Atlantic. In any case, the civilization marked in the British Isles by the megalithic monuments is closely related to that of Spain.[2]

During the second part of the first period of the Bronze Age and all through the second period there was constant communication between the British Isles and Iberia. A very large number of bronze objects—axes, halberts, daggers, etc.—come from Spain or are of Iberian style. Iberian, too, or rather Spanish and perhaps Iberian, is the engraved ornamentation of the Irish axes and lunettes.

It was at this time that the Beaker Folk, who may have been the Goidels, came and established themselves in these islands. The cultural exchanges which had gone on between the British Isles and Spain then became less frequent, but they never quite ceased.[3] The sea is a great road and those who dwell by it are not home-keepers ; the mariners of Galicia, Brittany, and the British Isles were quite ready to sail to each other's countries.

It is quite useless to seek further. The examination of language has yielded nothing. The sifting of the cults of

---

[1] *Agr.*, xi ; Holmes, **CCCCXXXII**, p. 398 ; Philipon, **CCCLXIX**, p. 296 (on the connections of the Silures with Spain). Avienus mentions a Mons Silurus (433), and the proper name Silur has been found in Spain (**I**, ii, 5923). MacNeill (op. cit., p. 61) maintains, over-critically, that the Iberian theory of the population of the British Isles has no other foundation than the passage in Tacitus. Cf. Dion. Perieg., *Orbis Descriptio*, 563–4, on the Hesperides, the land of tin, islands inhabited by the wealthy children of the noble Iberians.

[2] J. Loth, in **XCII**, 1925, p. 137 ; 1926, p. 1 ; Bosch Gimpera, in **CXXXIX**, 1925, 2, p. 191 ; Breuil, ibid., 1925, 1, p. 79 ; Breuil and Macalister, in **CXXII**, p. 921.

[3] Examples of ear-rings of Portuguese type, **LXXX**, 1917, p. 30 ; R. Severo, in **CXVII**, ii, pp. 405–412 ; Anderson, **CCCCXIV**, pp. 144, 149, 208, 210.

Ireland and the folk-lore of Britain has been equally fruitless,[1]
for what do we know about the Iberians, their language or
their religion ? A few rare place-names [2] add their testimony
to archæological probabilities to assure us that there were
Iberians in the British Isles. The Iverni may perhaps have
been among them. It cannot be shown that Ireland was ever
called Iberia. Indeed, there is a set of names, similar to
Eire and Erainn, which are the names of rivers in Britain—
the Scottish Earn and Findhorn [3] and the Iwerne in Dorset
(cf. 'Ιουερνία).[4] If the name of Ireland is to be explained
in the same way as those of the rivers, it does not come from
a racial name, but from an adjective of quality. Iverjon
would come from *Piverjo-, which is comparable to Sanskrit
pivari, Greek πιαρός, " fat ", and would be parallel to
Pieria, the home of the Muses.[5] It would have nothing in
common with the name of Iberia, and would even be a Celtic
word, by the loss of the radical *p.*

The name of Britain, Albion,[6] in company with which
that of Ireland appears from the earliest times,[7] tells us as
clearly as possible that it is not Celtic. The Irish kept it in the
forms Alba, Alban, Alpe, to designate the whole of the sister-
island, but more particularly Scotland. It belongs to a family
of names : Alba, Albona, Albis, Alpes, Albani, Albioeci, etc.,
the names of towns, rivers, mountains, and peoples, which is
perhaps the most numerous family of European place-names
and is certainly the most widespread. It is highly probable
that these names are Indo-European and are connected with
the same root as Latin *albus.* But Celtic has lost just this very
root. In Western Europe these geographical names seem to
belong to the Ligurian vocabulary, which is Indo-European,
or to the Iberian vocabulary,[8] if it is Indo-European, or to
the Italic vocabulary. For they appear both in Spain and in
Sicily ; in Gaul, as the names of peoples, they are confined to
Narbonensis ; lastly they are represented by several instances
in Liguria properly so called.

In my opinion the names of the two islands date from
before the coming of the Celts and are an inheritance from

---

[1] Rhys, **CCCCLI**, vii.
[2] Philipon, op. cit., p. 296, Tamaros and Isca, in Cornwall.
[3] MacNeill, op. cit., p. 67.   [4] See above, p. 197.
[5] Thurneysen, **CCXL**.   [6] Holder, s.v.
[7] Avien., *Ora Mar.*, 112.   [8] Philipon, **DXVI**, passim.

their predecessors in Western Europe, Iberian or Ligurian. While the Iverni had kinsmen of the same name in Spain, there were also Albiones in Spain, on the north coast, in Asturias. They are mentioned by Pliny.[1] These were doubtless old Ligurians. But I do not insist on this point, for I do not want to have to demonstrate against learned Spanish scholars that the islands of Ierne and Albion were off the coast of Spain, like the still vex'd Cassiterides.

IV

THE PICTS

So the Neolithic population had left remnants in the two islands, and, also in the two islands, there had been Iberian settlers. But the racial map of Britain shows nothing corresponding to the Erainn. On the other hand, there is another group of tribes which is common to both islands; it, too, was very considerable, and in the north of Ireland it formed a mass comparable to that formed by the Erainn in the south. These were the Cruithnig. The Cruithnig are the Picts, who were a distinct people in the larger island, occupying all or part (but the chief part) of Caledonia before the Scots—that is the Irish, the Gaels—came into the country and hewed a domain for themselves out of their land.[2] In Ireland the Picts held a large part of Ulster, where they were so numerous that they became the preponderant power.[3] In Connacht there were communities of Picts near Cruachain, the capital, and there were others in Munster, Meath, and Leinster. The Cruithnig of Ireland are called *Picti* in the Irish annals.[4] The Caledonian Picts are called *Cruithnii* or *Cruthini populi* in Adamnan's *Life of St. Columba*,[5] and the Irish list of the Pictish kings begins with an eponymous founder, Cruidne.[6] It is, therefore, certain that the two terms are equivalent.

[1] *N.H.*, iv, 111 : *a flumine Navia Albiones*, etc.
[2] Pedersen, **CCCXXVII**, i, p. 12 ; Windisch, **CCXLV**, p. 28 ; Nicholson, **CCXXIII**, pp. 20–97, 100–3 ; S. Ferguson, in **LVI**, 1912, pp. 170–189.
[3] D'Arbois, **CCXCIX**, p. 26 ; MacNeill, op. cit., p. 63.
[4] Holmes, **CCCCXXXIII**, pp. 411–12.
[5] Ibid., p. 422.
[6] D'Arbois, **CCC**, pp. 35–6, n. 6.

The Pictish people took up enough space to give its name to the whole of the British Isles. If we suppose that the c of Cruithnig represents a *qu*, which was destined to become *p* in Brythonic, we can go back through the forms of the sister language to a form Qurteni (Qartani) or Qretani. The corresponding name for the country was pronounced Pretani in Brythonic, from which comes Welsh Prydain. Ynys Prydain is the name of the island of Britain. Pytheas heard this name about 300 B.C., and very correctly called the two islands Πρεττανικαί νῆσοι. But it is uncertain whether he heard them called by this name in Gaul or in Britain itself.[1]

The name is intelligible in Celtic. It is generally traced back to Irish *cruth*, Welsh *pryd*, meaning " form ".[2] The Picts had a name among the Romans for tattooing themselves with animal and other forms.[3]

The word Pict has no such ancient ancestry. It is first met in a panegyric of 296 in honour of Constantius, who commanded in Britain.[4] It has been thought that it might be merely a Latin name given by the Romans, a kind of nickname afterwards consecrated by the chronicles. Cæsar, in his account of the Britons of the interior, says that they painted themselves for war with woad.[5] *Picti Britanni*, Martial repeats.[6] So the Picts would be Britons who still remained savage outside the Roman frontier. A Celtic explanation of the word has, however, been put forward. It is supposed to come from a root meaning " to tattoo ", beginning with *qu*, which became *p* in Brythonic. From the same root came Irish *cicht*, meaning " engraver ".[7] The Gaulish proper names Pictillus, Pictilus, Pistillus are diminutives of a term which may have been identical with the name of the Picts and has not been preserved.

These two doublets explain one another. All the same, the very existence of the duplication is perplexing, and the fact that that one of the two terms which seems to have

[1] Holmes, op. cit., p. 413.
[2] Ibid., p. 418, n. 5.
[3] Herodian, iii, 14, 17 ; Claudian, *Goth. War*, 416–18.
[4] Incerti Panegyricus Constantio Augusto, c. 7 : *Caledonum aliorumque Pictorum silvas.*
[5] *Gall. War*, v, 14.
[6] xiv, 99, 1.
[7] Holmes, op. cit., p. 414 ; Rhys, op. cit., pp. 215–16.

prevailed in Britain does not appear in the Irish traditions in the vulgar tongue, but only in Latin annals, would need explaining.

The Pictish question is one of those most hotly debated in the ancient history of Britain, but it does not seem to have received much illumination in the course of these unending battles. Many historians and philologists have maintained that this little-known, mysterious people, with its reputation for wildness, relegated to the north of Britain or scattered about in Ireland, was the remnant of the pre-historic inhabitants. Sir John Rhys regarded them as the chief representatives of the prehistoric population of these islands,[1] the Erainn being only a branch of them. But really the Erainn and Picts are very clearly distinguished from one another ;. in Antrim, for example, the north, Dal Riada, was Hibernian, and the rest was Pictish.

At the time when the Venerable Bede wrote his *Ecclesiastical History* the Picts, according to his statement, spoke a language which was different both from that of the Scots, who were Goidels, and from that of the Britons.[2] Moreover, Adamnan, in his *Life of Columba*, tells us that when the Saint evangelized the Picts he spoke to them through an interpreter.[3] But this separate Pictish language may have been Celtic. The six inscriptions which are said to be Pictish, found in the east and north of Scotland, afford no evidence on one side or the other, being indecipherable.[4]

The principal argument to which recourse is had is one based on the prehistoric customs of the Picts, and in particular on their law of succession. In Bede's time, that is in the sixth century, the succession in the Pictish royal families went in the female rather than in the male line.[5] Thus, a king of the Picts of the beginning of the seventh century, Talorcan, was the son of a Saxon refugee named Eanfred

---

[1] Op. cit., p. 272.
[2] i, 1 ; iii, 6 ; MacNeill, op. cit., p. 63.
[3] i, 33 ; ii, 33 ; Rhys, loc. cit. ; Holmes, op. cit., p. 421.
[4] They are in oghams or in minuscule characters ; only one is in disfigured Roman capitals ; Rhys, in **CCXIV**, xxvi, p. 263 ; **CCCCL**, ii, p. 681, 2 ; Macalister, **CCCCXXXIX**, p. 253.
[5] Bede, i, 1 ; H. Zimmer, in **CLXVII**, xv, 1894, pp. 209 ff. ; Skene, **CCCCLVII**, i, p. 232 ; Rhys, op. cit., ii, p. 682 (compare the succession of the sister's son in the royal families of the Berbers) ; Macalister, op. cit., p. 242. The last author observes (p. 244) that the same rule of succession obtained under the Irish kings.

and a Pictish princess.[1] Intermarriages between Picts and Scots, with similar consequences, are mentioned in all the chronicles. The Irish related that the Picts invaded Ireland shortly after the settlement of the sons of Mile. Herimon, the chief of the Milesians, drove them out and settled them in Alban (Scotland). But he gave them for wives, since they had none, the widows of the warriors of the race of Mile, who had perished at sea before the conquest of Ireland, on the condition that in the future inheritance should go through the woman, not through the man. The mythological explanation confirms the fact.

This mode of succession created particularly close relationships between men and their mothers' brothers. Tacitus had noticed this among the Germans,[2] and a votive inscription found at Colchester shows that it was the same among the Picts, probably even outside the royal lines. Here it is :—

> DONVM. LOSSIO. VEDA. DE SVO
> POSVIT. NEPOS. VEPOGENI. CALEDO.

" Presented at his own cost by Lossio Veda, nephew of Vepogen, a Caledonian." [3]   It is a unique thing in Latin epigraphy for a man to indicate his family by the name of his uncle and not his father. In the history of the family the right of cognates, kinsman on the distaff side, has always been opposed to that of the agnates, kinsman on the male side. The evolution of the Indo-European *gens* evidently reached a form in Greece, Rome, Ireland, and Wales in which the right of the agnate prevailed over that of the cognate, and in consequence the facts noted among the Picts have been regarded as alien to Indo-European law.

But the law to which these facts bear witness also obtained among the Goidels of Ireland, and even among the ancestors of the Welsh. Considerable traces of it are to be found in their legal texts, their history, and their epics. The Irish gods and heroes are called after their mothers ; Lugh is the son of Ethniu, Cuchulainn is the son of Dechtire.[4] The Welsh god Gwydion is the son of Don.[5] The Celtic family is a fairly complicated institution, not quite like the Latin

---

[1] This is exaçtly what Bede relates. Cf. d'Arbois, **CCI**, i, p. 265.
[2] *Germ.*, 20.   [3] Holmes, op. cit., p. 415.
[4] Rhys, **CCCCLII**, p. 15.   [5] Ibid., pp. 14, 87, 46, 56, 68.

family, and it has varied since the time at which we first know anything of it.

So there is nothing to prove that the Picts were not Celts. On the other hand, we have some reason for believing that they were a Celtic people, doubtless including a large proportion of foreigners and aborigines, but not more or less, no doubt, than the other Celtic peoples.

The names of the Pictish tribes—Cornavii, Smertæ, Cæræni, Carnonacæ, Creones, Lugi, Decantæ, Epidii, Tæzali, Vacomagi, Dicaledonæ, Verturiones [1]—contain Celtic sounds. So do the names of individuals—Argentocoxos, Togenanus.[2] Examination of the ancient and modern place-names of the Pict country leads to the same result [3] ; Albhais (Alves in Morayshire) is to be compared to Alventium (Avin in Belgium) and Alvinca. Aberlour in Banffshire gets its name from Labhair, which is the same as Labara (*labrur* " I speak "). Dea'in, the Aberdeenshire Don, which is derived from Δηούανα, the name of the town of the Tæzali, now Aberdeen, belongs to the same family as Devona in Gaul. Fuirgin (Foregin, a farm in Inverness-shire) corresponds to Vorgium, a town in the country of the Osismi in Gaul.

It is true that among the place-names of the Pictish country there are some in *ar*, of the type of Isara, Araris,[4] which might be Ligurian or Iberian, and stems which are usually regarded as Ligurian.[5] These are the contribution of the aborigines or of the previous inhabitants, whatever their position was, who survived among the Celtic tribes of the Picts.[6]

If the Picts were Celts so were the Silures. The names of their towns—Venta Silurum, Isca Silurum [7]—are Celtic. Another town, Abergavenny, was called Gobannium ; it was the town of the smiths, for *gof* in Welsh means " smith ".[8] But perhaps they were only very much Celticized.

[1] D'Arbois, **CCXCIX**, p. 21.
[2] Ibid., p. 29.
[3] Diack, in **CXL**, xxxviii, p. 109 ; H. Marwick, in **CXXIV**, 1922–3, p. 251.
[4] Ptolemy's Οὐάραρις εἰσχυσις is the same word as Farair, the R. Farrar (Inverness-shire) ; Diack, loc. cit.
[5] Diack, in **CXL**, 1924, p. 125 ; Bodotria (Tac.), Βοδερια (Ptol.), cf. Bodincus, the Po ; Turcid, cf. Nematuri (in Liguria), Furobriga, Furia (in Spain) ; ibid., 1920–1, p. 109.
[6] Windisch, **CCXLV**, p. 25.
[7] Holder, s.v.
[8] D'Arbois, op. cit., p. 30 ; cf. Zimmer, in **IX**, 1912, p. 16.

In the lists of Irish subject tribes there are other Celtic tribes—the Fir Domnann, the Galians, and even the Fir Bolg. But before we come to them we must place the Picts in relation to the Goidels and the Britons. In doing so we shall obtain information about the three groups, which we shall suppose to be distinct.

V

GOIDELS, PICTS, AND BRITONS

The Picts and Goidels seem to have followed the same route and, in general, to have gone about the extension of their settlements in the same way. Landing on the south and east coasts of Britain, they would cross the country and, coming to the opposite shore, each in turn reach Ireland, while keeping one foot on the larger island. The archæological evidence seems to confirm this view. The builders of the round barrows slowly came to Ireland, and all the successive strata of British archæology are found in their order in that country.[1]

The traditional history of Ireland shows something of the same sort. King Ugaine the Great reigned over both Ireland and Britain to the English Channel. Some annals make him a contemporary of Alexander.[2] At that time there were Britons in Britain, for Pytheas encountered them there ; but they had not been very long established. It seems doubtful that if the Britons on their arrival found a great Celtic kingdom, or something like it, spread over both sides of the Irish Sea, it was a Goidelic kingdom. But the question deserves discussion, and we have to find out whether the Picts or the Goidels established themselves in the British Isles first. M. J. Loth has recently maintained that the Picts were first, and that they were the builders of the round barrows.[3]

Why should the Britons have called their new country the island of the Picts if they found one or more Goidelic states established there ? If they heard it called Quretenion

---

[1] See above, pp. 171-2.
[2] According to the *Annals* of Tighearnach, he became king in the eighteenth year of Ptolemy, son of Lagos, i.e. in 306.
[3] In **CXL**, xxxviii, pp. 259 ff.

it was because the Picts were the predominant or the most numerous part of the population. And if this was so it was probably because the Picts had superseded the Goidels, and in that case had come later than they.

It may be argued that the Britons got the name of the island from the Goidels. But the Irish probably never used the name Cruitheantuaith for the whole island of Britain. By it they meant the land of the Picts, Scotland.[1] It is not likely they ever meant a wider region, for which they had another term, Alba.[2]

But why suppose that the Picts came before the Goidels ? For once the mythical tradition of Ireland, which makes the Goidels come after most of the foreign peoples which they conquered or absorbed, represents them as followed by another Celtic people [3] ; what need is there to reject it in this one case ?

In my view, then, the Picts were not the first, but the second body of Celts to enter the British Isles, and it is they who may be represented in the archæological remains by the series of bronze objects mentioned above.[4] But we must not draw too hard a line between the second and third wave of invaders.

To tell the truth, the archæological evidence of a second invasion of the British Isles in the Bronze Age is so elusive that at first we must try to use it sparingly. It is hardly likely that the Picts were a division of the Goidels, and arrived at about the same time as they. But it is not at all certain that they were fundamentally different from the Britons.[5]

First of all the language of the Picts, however much it may have differed from Brythonic in the eighth century of our era, had by then undergone the change characteristic of Brythonic, the Brythonic change of qu to p, which is attested in Pictish, apart from the name of the people itself, by that of the Epidii,[6] a Pictish tribe dwelling north of the Wall of Antoninus.[7] According to Bede, they called the end

---

[1] Marstrander, in **CXL**, xxxvi, 1915, p. 362. Loth (op. cit., p. 280) distinguishes between Prydyn, Scotland, and Prydain, Britain.
[2] **CXL**, xxxvi, 1915, p. 380.
[3] D'Arbois, **CCXCIX**, p. 25.
[4] See p. 177.
[5] D'Arbois, **CCC**, p. 33 ; Frazer, **CCI**, p. 9.
[6] Ptol., ii, 3.
[7] Skene, **CCCCLVI**, 4.

of that vallum Pean Fahel, while the Angles called it Penneltun.[1] So the place-names of Britain seem to have been homogeneous and free of Goidelism before the arrival of the Scots.[2]

Secondly, the Pictish kings, of whom we have a list, had Welsh names, such as Mælchon [3] and Drust.[4] Some of their names can actually be contrasted with Irish forms. One king is called Wurgust, which is Uorgost, Uurgost, Gurgost in Old Breton, and Gwrgwst in Welsh, while the Irish equivalent is Fergus. It means " superior choice ". The first part of the word is u[p]per. The initial vowel, becoming a consonant in both families of languages, tended towards *f* in Goidelic and to *g* in Brythonic.

Lastly, one tribe of the Picts, which lived in Caithness in the north of Scotland, was called the Cornavii,[5] and seems to have been the double of a much larger British tribe of Cornavii in Cheshire, on the north-eastern border of Wales.

So we have the same language and the same tribes. Are the Picts really different from the Britons ? Was Cæsar not thinking of the Picts when, in contrasting the tribes of the interior with those of the coast, whose manners seemed to him to resemble those of the Gauls, and whom, as we have seen, he described as Belgæ, he ascribed strange matrimonial customs to the former ? [6] " The women are held as wives in common by groups of ten or a dozen men, who are generally brothers, fathers, and sons. Any children born are regarded as belonging to the men who have taken the mothers into their houses as virgins." Cæsar does not express himself well, and he is translated worse. According to this account the Picts were polyandrous. Polyandry is not matriarchy. But both terms are used equally inaccurately by ethnologists, anthropologists, and archæologists to describe the facts which result from a very well-known condition of social constitution. Surely the truth is that there were exogamous clans which went in pairs, all the men and all the women of one clan being supposed to be the husbands and wives

[1] Bede, i, 12.
[2] *Parisii, Petuaria, Pennocrucium.*
[3] Welsh Mailcon (*Annales Cumbriae*, passim).
[4] Welsh Drystan (*Mabinogion*).
[5] Rhys, **CCCCLIII**, pp. 111–13.
[6] *Gall. War*, v, 14 ; cf. MacNeill, **CCCCXLI**, p. 59.

respectively of the other clan, without that legal relationship being necessarily exercised or preventing the formation of small families consisting of married couples.[1] In this state of society the children usually belong to the clan of the mother, and this gives rise to conditions which are labelled matriarchy. Cæsar was fairly well informed, and the manners which he describes have no doubt more connection with those of the Picts than that of mere oddity. It does seem, too, that in the ccntre of Britain the royal families were organized like those of the Picts. The Queen, through whom the royal blood and rank came, must have enjoyed an esteem which, when she knew how to use it, gave her considerable authority ; witness Boudicca, the Queen of the Iceni of Norfolk and Suffolk, who led the rising against Suetonius Paulinus in A.D. 61.[2]

So if we follow and interpret Cæsar there were only two bodies of organized peoples in Britain at the time of his landing—Belgæ and Picto-Britons or Picts—and in that case the arrival of the latter can be placed much nearer that of the former, that is about the time when the use of iron was introduced into the country, at the beginning of the La Tène period.

The question would be finally decided against the distinction of Picts and Britons if it could be proved that they really bore the same name.[3] But in the history of the Britons and of their name, one fact of peculiar importance stands out. At the time of the Anglo-Saxon invasions, between the sixth and eighth centuries, with the rebirth of a kind of national sentiment, the Britons felt the need to give themselves a name. They called themselves the Combroges, the Fellow-countrymen, the Kymry (Cymry).[4] That is the national name of the Britons. It has not much meaning, and it does not suggest that it took the place of another more or less obsolete name. Britanni was not a national name, but a geographical designation given to the inhabitants of South Britain, first by the Gauls and then by the Romans. The Britons themselves probably adopted it (whence would come personal names like Britto and Brittus), but not so completely as to be content with it.

---

[1] Holmes, op. cit., p. 415.   [2] Ibid., pp. 269, 297.
[3] Ibid., pp. 460 ff.   [4] Ibid., pp. 449 ff.

If this was so we have to suppose that between the settlement of the Picts, who called themselves the Qretini or Pretini in virtue of their nationality, and the first incursions of Belgæ, a mass, even a considerable mass, of Celtic invaders arrived, for whom, though we cannot give them any particular name, we shall reserve that of Britons. Cæsar, who only knew them from the other side of the line of battle, may have thought that they were the same as the Picts. But they were conscious of their difference, and they made others see it. We shall see that the Goidels did not confuse the Picts with the various groups of Britons with whom they came into contact.

As for the Picts—of whose manners and institutions Cæsar ascribed what he had heard tell to all the inhabitants of the interior as a whole—they had certainly come to Britain so long before the Belgic invasions that they had acquired the right to be regarded as aborigines.

But were they, if not *the* Britons, at any rate Brythonic, in the general sense in which I have used the word ? That is to say, had their language, when they arrived in Britain, changed *qu* to *p* ?

The Goidelic form of their name, Cruithnig, cannot be adduced as proof of the negative, since the Goidels were aware that the *p*'s of Brythonic corresponded to the *qu*'s of their own tongue. In the Irish texts which have come down to us we find them transcribing the *p*'s of Brythonic and even of Latin as *qu*, that is as *c*. Thus, *purpura* became *corcur*, and Patricius (St. Patrick) became Cothraige.

We have nothing certain in support of the affirmative. If the Picts arrived at the end of the Bronze Age, it seems to me scarcely probable that their language had not yet undergone the mutation of the velars.[1] It is certain that it offered it no resistance, either because it was already tending that way or because the Picts adopted the language of the people who came after them. The British emigrants arrived with the prestige of a superior craftsmanship and a better-armed civilization. They could impose their language. I should, moreover, be very ready to believe that there was fairly thorough interpenetration between the Pictish and British tribes. Were the Cornavii of Cheshire and those of Caithness,

[1] See above, pp. 132 ff.

living so far apart, Picts ? Were they Britons ? In any case, one fraction of them was surrounded by alien groups. The Epidii of Argyll were, perhaps, a British tribe which had pushed northwards, like the Novantæ who were opposite them across the Firth of Clyde. But, on the whole, when we come to the Celtic peoples of the Continent, we shall find reason for thinking that the Picts were probably closer to the Britons than to the Goidels.[1]

VI

PICTS, BRITONS, AND BELGÆ IN BRITAIN

So, after the settlement of the Goidels, there were three Celtic colonizations of Britain, by the Picts, by the Britons, and by the Belgæ, following each other at fairly long intervals.'

The first to come were the Picts, who followed the Goidels about the middle of the Bronze Age. Their movement had come to an end when the civilization of Hallstatt, or rather its second period, that of the large iron swords, was beginning on the Continent. The civilization of this period is hardly represented in the British Isles.[2]

When Cæsar says that the peoples of the interior of Britain, as opposed to the agriculturists of the coast, were pastoral folk, living on meat and milk and clothing themselves in the skins of their cattle,[3] he is probably speaking of the Picts. The economic life of the Continent in the Bronze Age, and still in the Hallstatt period, was pastoral rather than agricultural.[4]

They did not make a complete clearance of the builders of the round barrows of the beginning of the Bronze Age, whom I have identified with the Goidels, for down to the La Tène period and during it the inhabitants of Britain continued to erect round barrows, under which contracted skeletons have been found in graves.[5] This is a fact which

---

[1] See below, pp. 230 ff.
[2] **CCCLXXXIV**, pp. 82–3 ; Déchelette, ii, 2, p. 729 ; E. C. R. Armstrong, in **XVI**, 1922, p. 204, points to only one large iron Hallstatts word, and there is not one short Hallstatt III sword (against this, see Déchelette, loc. cit., p. 737).
[3] *Gall. War*, v, 14 ; Holmes, op. cit., p. 267.
[4] See below.
[5] Holmes, op. cit., p. 287.

we must take into account, in order to understand what sort of connections there were between the various elements composing the Celtic population of Britain.[1]

A new body of colonists arrived at the beginning of the first period of La Tène. These were the Britons,[2] and their settlement must have been completed about 300 B.C., when Pytheas made his voyage.[3] The new civilization brought a new economic life. The British settlers were agriculturists. Pytheas observed this besides practices which were new to him, such as that of threshing in barns and not out of doors.[4] In Cæsar's time things in general must have been very much as in Gaul. But agriculture did not change the face of the land so completely as in certain parts of Gaul. The Britons were not settling in a depopulated country. Agriculture took its place in a countryside which had already been adapted to pasture, and the English countryside remains the same to-day.

The first Britons seem to have arrived at the very beginning of the La Tène period, perhaps even a little earlier, between 550 and 500. In the excavations conducted in 1911 and 1912 at Hengistbury Head,[5] in a fortified settlement on the spit separating Christchurch Harbour from the sea, pottery was found very similar to that of the tumuli of the south of Gaul [6] and that recently discovered near Penmarch,[7] a squat ware, still reminiscent of those of the Bronze Age and Hallstatt. For some time past many objects of this period have been found in the south of England.[8]

[1] Cf. Nicholson, in **CXL**, 1904, p. 350. Some have connected the Picts with the Pictones of Poitou. I see no great reason for either agreeing or doubting. But I am inclined to think that a generalized designation like that of " Picts " is ancient, and everything seems to show that early racial names, like those of the Picts and the Pictones, do not recur independently.

[2] Holmes, op. cit., pp. 232–3.

[3] Ibid., p. 229.

[4] Ibid., p. 224, and, for the economic condition of Britain, pp. 357 ff.

[5] J. P. Busche-Fox, in **CXXVIII**, iii, 1915 ; cf. Hubert, in **CXL**, 1927, pp. 398–9.

[6] Déchelette, ii, 2, pp. 663 ff.

[7] Favret and Bénard, in **CXXXIX**, 1924, i, pp. 179 ff. In France, these wares are of the end of the Hallstatt period or the very beginning of La Tène. They come from Gallic settlements.

[8] See C. Hawkes and G. C. Dunning, " The Belgæ of Gaul and Britain," in *Archæol. Journ.*, 1930, pp. 150 ff. ; Hawkes, " Hill-forts," in *Antiquity*, v, 1931, pp. 60 ff. ; Hawkes, Myres, and Stevens, *St. Catherine's Hill, Winchester*, 1930 ; Bushe-Fox, **CCCVIII**, for Scarborough ; E. Cunnington, in **XVI**, 1922, pp. 14 ff., for All Cannings Cross, and ibid., 1921, p. 284, for various finds.

The oldest and largest group of barrows of this epoch is that at Arras in Yorkshire.[1] These tombs contain furniture which is very like that of the Marne burials. In particular it includes remains of two-wheeled chariots like those of Champagne.[2] But the bodies are mostly contracted, instead of being laid out at full length as in France.[3] The new culture, therefore, did not prevail in Britain in its pure form. That of the previous inhabitants did not completely disappear. It is, however, to be supposed that the newcomers were sufficiently numerous at the beginning to spread their technical methods and their tastes all over the country fairly soon.

We can judge of the numbers of the Britons from the number of their tribes. Under the Roman Empire there were about twenty *civitates*,[4] that is, British tribes, each of them a composite formation. Most of these are found in Britain alone. It follows that either they were formed in the country with a Celtic organization and native material, or they were already complete, organized social bodies when they arrived. In either case, we must suppose a fairly large number of Britons. Only three British tribes, the Brigantes, Parisii,[5] and Cassi,[6] one of which occupied the greater part of Yorkshire and Nottinghamshire, and another Holderness in Yorkshire, left a portion behind them on the Continent. There were Parisii in the neighbourhood of modern Paris. The Brigantes came from Switzerland and Upper Bavaria ; Bregenz was originally Brigantum, and Cambodunum (Kempten) was a town of the Brigantes. They founded another Cambodunum on the road from York to Chester.[7] Although the Brigantes come before us as a fraction of a people, they were one of the most numerous tribes in Britain, if we are to judge from the map, in which the names of their towns are sown thick. The Cassi must have belonged to the

---

[1] **CCCLXXXIV**, pp. 115, 119 ; Déchelette, ii, 3, p. 1102.
[2] Chariot-burial at Hunmanby near Hull ; R. A. Smith, in **CXVIII**, 1909–1910, pp. 403 ff.
[3] The previous types persist in these burials. Also, the British ingredient was composed of the same strains as the Goidelic and Pictish : round-heads and long-heads of the North, with a few Alpines. For the ethnology of Britain at this time see Holmes, op. cit., p. 234.
[4] Ibid., p. 234.
[5] D'Arbois, **CCC**, p. 26.
[6] Cæs., *Gall. War*, v, 21.
[7] Camboritum, in *Itin. Anton.*, 474, 7 ; cf. Chambourcy, Chambord.

same group as the Veliocasses, Viducasses, Baiocasses, and Tricasses ; this group perhaps gave its name to Hessen.

MAP 9. Britain at the time of the Roman Conquest. (C. Hawkes and G. C. Dunning, *The Belgæ of Gaul and Britain*, fig. 33.)

The presence of the Parisii, Brigantes, and Cassi among the Britons shows that they were related to the Celtic peoples of the Continent, and also points to the part of the Celtic world in which we should look for the origins of which they preserved the tradition.[1] Intercourse and exchanges of all kinds kept alive that likeness between Britons and Gauls which is a sign of their kinship.[2]

At a much later date new Celtic invaders landed in the British Isles. These were the Belgæ.[3]

Did the Belgæ form a body within the whole Celtic mass in any way comparable to the Goidelic and British groups ? [4]

From the linguistic point of view, no. The Belgæ spoke the same tongue as the Gauls, whose language belonged to the Brythonic group.[5] The names of places and persons, which are all we have to represent the Belgæ, are similar to or identical with Brythonic names.[6] No linguistic fact has been discovered to distinguish the language spoken by the Belgæ from Brythonic. Celtic developed in the same way among them as among the Britons. The two peoples lived close to each other and mixed with each other.

But this is only a partial answer, for in other respects the Belgæ could be regarded as a solid, distinct group of peoples, conscious of their unity and finding the principle of their destinies in themselves. We can only judge of the matter when we have formed some judgment of the size of the Belgic peoples and of the history of their migrations.

In any case, they felt the need of expressing their unity and independence by having a racial name of their own.

The passages in Cæsar regarding the ethnology of Britain,[7] properly interpreted, place their first inroads in the first half of the second century B.C. The archæological evidence confirms this. The appearance of the culture of La Tène II, followed by that of La Tène III, can be explained by the

---

[1] Many place-names are common to Britain and Gaul, and suggest the same inferences as Cambodunum. Cf. Sorviodunum (Old Sarum) and Sorviodurum near Straubing in Bavaria, also Uxellodunum, Noviomagus, Mediolanum, Condate, Segodunum.

[2] Tac., *Agr.*, 11 ; cf. Pliny, *N.H.*, xvii, 4 ; xxxii, 6 ; Mela, iii, 3 ; d'Arbois, **CCXCIX**, p. 32.

[3] See below, p. 221.

[4] See below, p. 229.

[5] Yet Cæsar declares, on the first page of his *Commentaries*, that the Belgæ differed in dialect from the other Gauls. Strabo (iv, p. 176) more accurately speaks of slight differences of dialect.

[6] D'Arbois, op. cit., pp. 25 ff.

[7] See above, pp. 210–11.

arrival of a new stratum of immigrants.[1] Cremation-tombs
of La Tène II and III have been found in the south of Britain.
The largest group of such tombs is that of Aylesford, in Kent.[2]
They are small pits, 2 or 3 feet deep, containing funeral
urns, sometimes arranged in circles.

Not all tombs in Britain contain cremations from
La Tène II onwards.[3] Even in the south cremation was not
the universal custom. The new rite, therefore, seems to be
an indication of the new race ; cremations mean Belgic
tombs.[4]

There are, perhaps, other traces of the passage of the
Belgæ besides those which I have mentioned. The *Antonine
Itinerary* gives a Blatobulgium in Scotland, which was
doubtless Blebo (representing an earlier form Blathbolg),
near St. Andrews. We shall see that it was possible for the
first vowel to waver between *e* and *o*. Bolge, or Bolgios,
has been found among Pictish masculine names. In
Aberdeenshire the name of Strathbolgin (Strathbogie)
contains the same element, which may be evidence of the
Belgæ.[5]

It is probable that the Belgæ, like the Britons, advanced
as far as they could. But they did not arrive in masses to
be compared to those of the Britons. Cæsar says that they
came on warlike expeditions, which were probably little
more than pillaging forays—either organized attempts at
conquest from a centre which remained on the Continent,
like that of Diviciacus, or else a succession of raids on a small
scale on the part of adventurers and seekers of loot. There
was no movement of a whole nation. The invaders were
bands, some organized in " cities " and some composed of
detachments from various " cities ", which were usually too
small to form complete social units when they settled in
the country. The actual peoples remained in Gaul. In the
racial make-up of Britain, then, the Belgæ were not nearly
so large an ingredient as the Britons.

---

[1] Bushe-Fox, in **CXXVIII**, 1925, p. 31 ; shield of La Tène II with elongated
boss, found at Hod Hill, in **XVI**, 1922, p. 98.
[2] Déchelette, ii, 3, p. 1102 ; **CCCLXXXIV**, pp. 124 ff. ; for tomb at Welwyn,
Herts, see R. A. Smith, in **CXVIII**, 1912, p. 170.
[3] Holmes, op. cit., p. 287.
[4] I shall have occasion to point out that the rite of cremation never ceased
to be practised by one branch of the Belgæ from the Hallstatt period onwards,
and that it spread in Gaul at the time of the Belgic ascendancy.
[5] Rhys, **CCCCL**, ii, p. 206.

Nevertheless, the Belgæ, like the Britons, added their contribution to the civilization of the country.[1] When they first landed Greek coinage was beginning to be disseminated in Britain.[2] The Belgæ doubtless helped to spread its use. At all events the culture which was theirs and that of their age spread like the previous civilization and equally widely.[3]

But the Belgæ were not the only Celts who arrived in Britain in La Tène II and III. One of the most remarkable

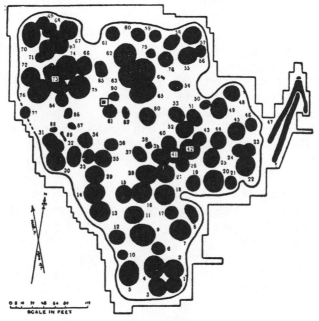

SCALE IN FEET

FIG. 36. Plan of the British Village at Glastonbury, Somerset. (Déchelette, ii, 3, fig. 405.)

Celtic settlements in Britain is the pile-village at Glastonbury (Fig. 36), in Somerset.[4] It contains the same incised pottery (Fig. 37) as is found in the Celtic cemeteries and *oppida* of Finistère (the cemetery of Kerviltré, the *oppidum* of Castel-Meur).[5] It was probably imported from Brittany; at least,

[1] For their importation of Greek and Italian objects, see Holmes, op. cit., p. 246.
[2] Ibid., p. 248.
[3] In particular, the swords of La Tène II and III. The Caledonians of Galgacus had them (Tac., *Agr.*, 36).
[4] Bulleid and Gray, **CCCCXVII**.
[5] Ibid., ii, p. 494. Cf. Déchelette, ii, 3, p. 1473. For the Brittany origin of the Marlborough bucket, see A. J. Evans, in **XVIII**, ix, 1890, p. 373.

it is evidence of relations, perhaps of a commercial kind, especially affecting the south-west of England. This pottery is found at Hengistbury Head, with coins of the Curiosolites and Andecavi.

The Glastonbury village is the largest and richest crannog known, and is the best excavated.[1] Is it to the Belgæ or to the Britons that we must ascribe the building of these curious structures,[2] standing on piers of timbers, clay, and stones

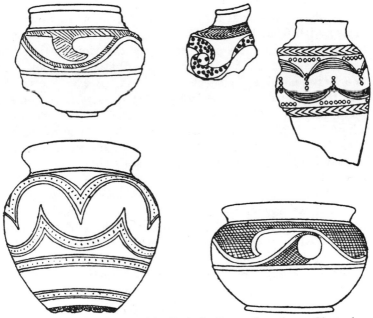

Fig. 37.   British Vases with Incised Decoration from Glastonbury.
(Déchelette, ii, 3, fig. 668.)

held in place by piles, which resemble the lake-villages of Central Europe but are quite unconnected with them? Crannogs are found all over Great Britain and Ireland. They date from the La Tène period, but they outlived it, and they reveal, with the forts, how insecure life was in the troubled times in which the Celtic settlement of the British Isles was nearing completion.

[1] Coffey, **CCCCXXVIII**, p. 103 ; Macalister, **CCCCXXXIX,** p. 50.
[2] I should ascribe them to the Belgæ, for piles have been found in the rivers of Northern Gaul, and the swampy districts from which the Belgæ of Britain came were better suited to this kind of dwelling than those occupied by the Britons.

There was, perhaps, a fourth strain in the population of Britain when the Romans conquered it, namely the Germans. Tacitus [1] ascribes Germanic origin to the Caledonians on account of their red hair and great height. It is not a very good reason, but it is quite likely that a few Germans came to Britain in the wake of the Belgæ, considering how long the Germans had lived close to the Belgæ and that, as we shall see, they started moving after the Belgæ and in just the same manner.[2] But Tacitus might well have connected what he tells us of the maternal family of the Germans in their own country with what he could have been told of the customs of the Picts.[3] If the Picts set forth after the Goidels from the German coasts of the North Sea, it is probable that they drew some Germans along with them.

If the archæology of Britain reflects, as it is reasonable to suppose, its racial vicissitudes—if, that is, the arrival of each of the elements in its Celtic population is to be connected, as has been done above, with a phase of its civilization, as revealed by the remains left in its soil, the Belgæ having contributed the culture of La Tène II and III, the Britons that of La Tène I, and the Picts that of the end of the Bronze Age—then we have nothing to ascribe to the Goidels but the culture of the beginning of the Bronze Age, and they must be identified with the Continental invasion which took place in Britain at that time.

In the preceding pages it has been sufficiently established that that first influx of Celtic population was not driven out by the succeeding waves. Indeed, traces of it are found down to the Anglo-Saxon conquest. The remnant, incorporated in the political organization of the later comers, kept its funeral customs, that is, a part of its morals. It made such a lasting impression that the face of the countryside to this day is as its ancestors had made it. If the south of England, which is so very like the French coast opposite, presents such a different appearance, that is certainly partly due to the persistence of a strong Goidelic strain in people and civilization. But these first invaders likewise allowed their predecessors to survive. There was room for these latter to live within the network of the Goidelic occupation. The

---

[1] *Agr.*, 11. For the Caledonians, see **CXL**, xxxix, p. 75.
[2] See above, p. 214.　　　　　[3] See above, p. 205.

Goidels borrowed some things from them,[1] and certain imported objects in Goidelic tombs show that they took over the Western and Mediterranean connections of the aborigines.[2]

But we have something still better, namely an evidence of the mixed civilization which grew out of the contact of invaders and invaded and implies some association between them. That is Stonehenge, the largest of the megalithic monuments.[3] The Goidels must have provided the religious idea, their predecessors the method of construction.[4] The grouping of a large number of round barrows about the monument,[5] its successive transformations, revealed by the latest excavations,[6] its constant use until after the Roman conquest,[7] and, lastly, the ancient tradition of a circular temple of the Sun among the Celts of the Ocean,[8] all compel one to ascribe its construction to the first Celtic occupants of Britain.[9] It implies the highest degree of power and organization of which prehistoric times have left a trace. It has, too, been thought that the great number of barrows surrounding Stonehenge proves that men came from far away to be buried near the holy place.[10] These funeral pilgrimages would demand roads, such as the well-known Pilgrims' Way,[11] a prestige as a sanctuary, and a social unit of vast extent and influence, something like the great Goidelic Kingdom of Britain, the memory of which has been preserved, but post-dated, by tradition.

VII

THE BRITONS AND BELGÆ IN IRELAND. FIR BOLG, FIR DOMNANN, GALIANS

The Britons and Belgæ, like the Picts, went beyond Britain and crossed the Irish Sea on their westward way.

[1] Abercromby, **CCCCXII.**   [2] Cylinders and various beads ; ibid.
[3] Hawley, in **XVI**, 1921, pp. 19 ff.
[4] Astronomical considerations tend to fix the date of the building of Stonehenge about the second millennium (Holmes, op. cit., pp. 475 ff.).
[5] Hawley, loc. cit., 47.
[6] Ibid. Romano-British pottery and coins of Claudius II Gothicus found during excavation.
[7] For stone rings in Scotland, see **CXXIV**, xlv, 1910, p. 46 ; lvii, 1922–3, pp. 20, etc.
[8] Hecat. Abd., in *F.H.G.*, ii, p. 387 ; cf. Diod., ii, 47, 2 ; Pindar, Pyth., x, 29–30 ; Olymp., iii, 16.   [9] Holmes, op. cit., pp. 475 ff.
[10] Ibid., pp. 113–14.   [11] Ibid., p. 247.

Ptolemy shows us in the south of Ireland a settlement of Brigantes,[1] in what is now Waterford, and, by the side of them, in Wexford, one of Menapii, with a capital called Menapia [2]; the former are Britons, and the latter Belgæ from the Finnish coast. He also mentions an Ἐπίδιον ἄκρον, or " Horse Promontory ", a name familiar among Celtic place-names, the π of which—certain evidence that it is Brythonic—was disguised as *ch* in the Irish name Aird Echdi.[3] On the other side of the Menapii, further north, in Wicklow, were the Cauci. These are Chauci, that is Germans from the Hanoverian coast,[4] who had followed the Belgæ over the sea.

The Menapii seem to have pushed their way forwards in Ireland, for we find later a scattered people of Monaigh or Manaigh.[5] One branch of them was established in the east of Ulster, near Belfast, and another in the west, where their name is preserved in that of Fermanagh. The Irish genealogies make them both come from Leinster, where the Menapii were settled. South-east of Fermanagh lies County Monaghan, the name of which perhaps has the same origin.

With the coming of these Britons and Belgæ, the civilization of La Tène was introduced into Ireland. The arms, pottery, and art of La Tène were imposed on Ireland as they had been on Britain. Mr. Coffey has maintained, arguing from Zimmer's hypothesis regarding the Goidels, that this civilization came direct from Gaul.[6] It probably came from both sides, Britain and Gaul. Besides, it came in two instalments, one of La Tène I [7] and one of La Tène II [8]; the former was probably Brythonic, coming from Britain, and the latter Belgic, coming from Gaul. In Ireland, as in

---

[1] ii, 3, 10. Cf. Westropp, in **CXXII**, 1918, p. 131 ; J. Loth, in **CXL**, 1914, p. 111 ; Rhys, **CCCLI**, p. 285.

[2] ii, 2 ; d'Arbois, in **CXL**, 1898, p. 249.

[3] ii, 3, 1. Aird Echdi, Height of the Echdi. Cf. Feist, **CCCXCVI**, p. 58 ; K. Meyer, " Zur keltischen Wortkunde," iii, No. 41, in **CXLVIII**, 1913, p. 445.

[4] Ptol., ii, 2, 8. Pokorny (in **CLXXI**, xi, pp. 169–188) sees further traces of the Germans in the ethnology of Ireland. He Germanizes the Galians ; according to him the Coriondi, Cuirenzige, would in Germanic be *Hariandiz, and the Cauci are Chauci, Chauchi, transformed into Ui Cuaich.

[5] MacNeill, **CCCCXLI**, p. 58.

[6] In **CXXII**, xxviii, c, p. 96, where he gives a summary of La Tène objects found in Ireland. Those which best support his view are the carinated vases of Marne type found near Dublin.

[7] Coffey, loc. cit.

[8] Ibid. The Menapians of Labraid Loingsech (see below, p. 225) arrive with spears with long, broad heads.

Britain, the Britons or Belgæ built crannogs,[1] the distribution of which corresponds to the extension of their settlements.

The Fir Bolg, Fir Domnann, and Galians are simply colonies of Belgæ, Britons, and Gauls. In the list of subject tribes they appear as foreigners allowed to remain on sufferance as metics. If they are placed before the sons of Mile in the order of invasions, it is by an artifice of what is known as Milesian literature.

The Fir Bolg, Fir Domnann, and Galians go together in the *Leabhar Gabhála* and in history.[2] Therefore, what can be proved of one group is true of the others, and even of people who are constantly associated with them, such as the Luaighni.[3] In any case, Milesian literature is equally censorious about them all. This is how they are described in the *Book of Genealogies* of Duald mac Firbis [4] : " Black-haired, talkative, treacherous, tale-bearing, a clamorous, contemptible folk ; miserly, vagrant, instable, harsh, and inhospitable ; slaves, thieves, boors ; foes of music and noble pleasures, troublers of feasts, fomenters of strife— such are the descendants of the Fir Bolg, the Galians, the Luaighni, and the Fir Domnann in Ireland." These Belgæ and Britons (for they, I believe, were the peoples in question) no doubt brought material civilization and plastic art to Ireland, but it is possible that their manners and customs did not appeal to the previous inhabitants of the country. We may suppose, too, that the portrait is not a true one, especially in the matter of the colour of their hair.[5]

The Fir Domnann,[6] to take their name literally, were the men of Domnu, just as the Tuatha Dé Danann were the tribes of the Goddess Danu.[7] They were called after a hypothetical eponymous goddess. But, while Danu is a dim

---

[1] Ibid., p. 103.

[2] M. E. Dobbs, in **LXXX**, 1916.

[3] The Luaighni were established in the east, from the Shannon to the Irish Sea. The barony of Lune in County Meath is called after them. They formed one of the chief forces of the army of Leinster. That is why they are placed with the Galians, who were so numerous in Leinster, among the Gallic or British invaders of the Iron Age. Cairbre Cat-head, who led the rising of the subject peoples, was chief of the Luaighni (MacNeill, op. cit., p. 80).

[4] *Duanaire Finn*, i, p. xxxi.

[5] The Belgæ were fair.

[6] Dobbs, op. cit., p. 168. They came after the Fir Bolg, according to the *Leabhar Gabhála*.

[7] Squire, **CCCCLIX**, p. 48 : Domnu, the mother of the Fomorian gods. Rhys, **CCCCL**, ii, p. 208.

enough figure, Domnu is only a name in the genealogies. It can only be a racial name, presented in the Irish fashion. The people were also called Domnanid and Domnannaig.[1]

Now one of the principal British tribes was that of the Dumnonii,[2] who lived in Cornwall. There was another of the same name in the south of Scotland, between Galloway and the Clyde, which Ptolemy calls Δαμνόνιοι. *Dumnonii* should become *Domnain* in Old Irish. Such proper names as Inber Domnann, River-mouth of Domnu (Malahide Bay, north of Dublin), and Erris Domnann, Land-bridge or Promontory of Domnu (in the north-west of County Mayo, in Connacht), suggest incursions of Dumnonii on the Irish coast.[3]

The similarity of the names affords valuable evidence. These people are Celts, it is true, but Celts belonging to another group than the Goidels—that is Britons. A gloss informs us that one thing remembered about the Fir Domnann was that they dug wells.[4] If they had come from the region about Devon and Dorset, to which the domain of the Dumnonii was still confined at the time of the Roman occupation, they must in many places have found it necessary to dig wells in the chalky soil in order to get water. Ireland is not so dry.

Another British tribe, the Setantii,[5] who lived along the coast of the Irish Sea, south-west of the Brigantes and north of the Cheshire Cornavii, must have made a name for themselves in Ireland. The greatest hero of the Irish epics, Cuchulainn, was really named Setanta.[6] It is a foreign name, and the foreign form of the stem is preserved ; in Irish it would have become *Setéta. It is curiously like the name of the Setantii. Moreover, according to a tradition related by Duald mac Firbis,[7] Cuchulainn belonged to a subject tribe, the Tuath Tabhaira.

So there are three Brythonic tribes in Britain, all living on the Irish Sea, of which we find settlements, or at least

[1] **CXL**, xxxi, p. 15.
[2] Rhys, **CCCCLI**, p. 298 : The Dumnonii were a political formation. Windisch, **CCXCVI**, p. 25.
[3] Rhys, **CCCCL**, ii, p. 208 ; MacNeill, op. cit., p. 79.
[4] *Coir Anmann*, **CCXCV**, iii, p. 381.
[5] Ptol., ii, 3, 3.
[6] Holder, s.v.
[7] MacNeill, op. cit., p. 79 : Ferdiad is a Fir Domnann.

traces, in Ireland. They probably invaded Ireland soon after they had settled in Britain.

The Galians were closely connected with the Fir Domnann. They had the same ancestor, and they had chiefs from among the Fir Domnann.[1] I have already shown that their name came from that of Gaul and the Gauls.

A further proof of this with a date is given by the pair of stories entitled *Longes Labrada*, the *Sailing* or *Exile of Labraid Loingsech*,[2] and *Orgain Dinn Rig*, the *Destruction of Dind Rig*. Labraid Loingsech was the grandson of King Lægaire Lorc, Ugaine Mor's son, who was murdered with his son Ailill by his brother Cobthach. Labraid Loingsech fled. " He set out eastwards and came to the isle of the Britons, and then he went among the young men with speckled hair who dwell in the country of Armenia and entered the service of the King of Armenia." Where this Armenia was is disputed. D'Arbois de Jubainville proposed the reading Fir Menia, the men of Menia, that is of the country of the Menapians. But what follows is the important part. " The Galians fed him during his exile in the land of Gall." So he went to Gaul after a stay in Britain. He came back with a band of Galians, and with their help he destroyed Dind Rig and avenged his father and grandfather.

For this series of kings the annals give dates varying between the fifth and third centuries.[3] But the story itself provides an archæological date. It tells that Cobthach, in order to take his brother by surprise, decided to sham dead, and so had himself laid out on his wagon with his weapons in his hand, and when Lægaire leant over him to embrace him he killed him.[4] The murderer was imitating one of the chariot-burials which are found in the tombs of the Marne, and are not later than the first period of La Tène, that is 300 B.C. So the usages of the La Tène civilization had entered Ireland before that date, and Britons or Gauls were certainly established there.

This story might even be a history of the arrival of the Menapii, that is of the first Belgæ, in County Wexford and Leinster. For everything happens there. Lægaire is murdered at Carman, in County Wexford. Dind Rig is the chief

---

[1] Dobbs, loc. cit. [2] d'Arbois, in **CXL,** 1909, p. 212.
[3] Dobbs, op. cit., p. 72. [4] *Coir Anmann.*

residence of the Kings of Leinster. Leinster, too, seems to have been mainly peopled by foreigners. It was there that the Galians were massed as the Erainn were in Munster, and they were the chief strength of the troops of Leinster. In the great poem of the Ulster cycle, the *Táin Bó Chuailgné*, much is made of their military organization, which may originally have been due to the superiority of the iron weapons which they had brought from Gaul. I am not sure that the people in the story of Labraid are Menapii ; we are dealing with Gauls coming to reinforce their British brethren, and they come from Gaul like the Belgæ, who, in any case, cannot have arrived long after them.

The examination of certain proper names borne by Galians or found in the district occupied by the Britons leads to the same conclusion. Finn mac Coul (mac Cumhail) belonged to a Galian clan, the Ui Tarsigh. The name of his father, Cumhal, corresponds to that of the Gallic and British god Camulos, who was worshipped by the Remi. Several ogham inscriptions from County Waterford mention a person named Neta Segamonas. This name may mean Champion of Segomo. Now Segomo is not a god of Ireland, nor even of Britain ; he is a Gallic god. These inscriptions belong to a group (all found in the same county), the proper names in which appear in the dynasty of the Eoganachta of Cashel, who ruled over Munster in the time of St. Patrick. There Neta Segamonas appears in the form Nia Segamain. It is to be supposed, and Mr. MacNeill is of this opinion,[1] that the Eoganachta were a family of Gallic origin, which had risen to importance.

But the best reason for thinking that the Galians were not Belgæ is that they distinguish themselves from their successors, the Fir Bolg. For them, too, the mythologists invented a goddess, Bolga, an even more elusive being than Domnu. But the etymologists could dispense with her, for the meaning of the name is perfectly clear. The Fir Bolg are the Men with the Bags. *Bolg* means a bag ; *di bolg*,[2] the two bags, means the bellows. Mr. MacNeill makes the Fir Bolg one of his industrial classes, the Bag-makers. There was a legend that, having emigrated to Greece and become serfs, they were employed in carrying earth in leather

---

[1] Op. cit., p. 127.   [2] G. H. Orpen, in **LXXX**, 1911, p. 180.

bags and spreading it over rocky ground. According to another they did trade with the Eastern world, and sent to it leather bags filled with the soil of Ireland, which was scattered around the cities to kill the snakes.

An opinion which is supported by the authority of Sir John Rhys [1] and d'Arbois de Jubainville identifies the Fir Bolg with the Belgæ. The first syllable of the name of the Belgæ contained a vowel which might be an *o* ; witness the name of the Galatian chief Bolgios, who, as we shall see, was a Belgian. This explanation does not exclude the other. It does not compel us to abandon the etymology proposed above. The word *bolg* is not peculiar to Irish. *Bulgas Galli sacculos scorteos appellant*, Festus says.[2] " The Gauls call leather bags *bulgæ*." In Welsh *boly* (*bola, bol*) means " bags ". It is probable that this word existed in Belgic, too, and possible that it came into the racial name of the group. Its employment in the formation of a racial name is explained in a poem attributed to Columba.[3] The author speaks of *fir i mbolggaib* " men in bags ". Here the bags are garments— trousers. So trousers are called " bags " in English. The name Gallia Braccata, applied to a people from its national garb, makes it quite credible that a name of this kind should have been adopted to describe the Belgæ. The large wide trousers in which we usually imagine the Gauls are the trousers of the Belgæ. The Gauls properly so called, those of Gallia Lugdunensis, wore another kind of trousers, which appears on the Gallo-Roman monuments, a short, close-fitting garment which was adopted by the Roman army. This is the *bracca*, short drawers not reaching below the thighs.

As for the Goidels, they wore no trousers at all. Thus the costume of the Highlander is a faithful witness to the Goidelic origin of the Scots.

The name of the Belgæ, then, is a racial nickname, and the name of the Men with the Bags of Ireland is the name of the Belgæ.

It is under their common name that the Belgæ are designated. It may, perhaps, be worth while to examine the names of the Belgic clans in detail. One clan of Fir Bolg

---

[1] Rhys, **CCCCL**, ii, p. 205.
[2] G. H. Orpen, op. cit., p. 145.
[3] Frag. 8 *b* 3. *Fir bolgg*, ibid., 131 *a* 1.

was named Clan Morna.[1] The Clan Morna were the enemies of Cumhal, and are mentioned as such in the oldest poem of the Finn cycle. Perhaps they are the Morini of the Pas-de-Calais, who are themselves Belgæ and, what is more, neighbours of the Menapii on the north.

On the whole the list of the non-Gælic tribes of Ireland is not mainly a list of non-Celtic tribes. It does not provide material for a picture of the population of the island before the advent of the Goidels, but it records the successive waves of Celtic colonization, of which that of the Goidels was the first.

But from the position of the later colonies, Gallic, British, and Belgic, in relation to the Goidels we can draw conclusions. The arrival of the new settlers did not affect, as in Britain, the racial and social balance of the country. They took their place in a system which they did not transform. If they came to conquer they failed, and were content to be received as serfs, as in the legend of the Fir Bolg in Greece.[2] They certainly did not come in sufficient force to obtain the ascendancy.

There were no migrations of whole peoples. The biggest perhaps were those of the Brigantes, the Menapii, and the Cauci, whose combined settlements covered a large area. The Dumnonii ranged the coasts of Ireland in scattered bands of pirates or traders. The Belgic and Gallic bodies probably comprised men of various races, for the names of the clans seem to be mostly new. It is possible that they sometimes arrived in armies; it is more likely that they came in bands; and one would naturally suppose that these bands consisted of men only.

Having entered Ireland these bodies of Britons, Gauls, and Belgæ went all over the country; their inroads reached far. Irish tradition is full of their exploits, and they provided its chief heroes, such as Cuchulainn and Finn, and doubtless some of its episodes. But, contrary to what happened in Britain, they became merged in the mass of the Irish; they founded no great independent settlements; they were assimilated by the first Celtic occupants of the island.

---

[1] *Duanaire Finn*, intr., xxx.
[2] MacNeill, op. cit., p. 76.

VIII

THE RACIAL COMPOSITION OF IRELAND

But there they were, and they had their own place. The bodies of Celts represented in Britain appear in Ireland. We shall see as we go on that there were no others. It would seem that each wave of invading Celts, exactly following its predecessors and tending to spread on the top of them, went as far as it could until it was forced to stop.

Let us look at our map of Ireland (Map 8) for a moment and consider the motley spectacle which it presents in the time of Ptolemy.[1] In the south-western corner are the Iverni, who are not Celts. In the north-eastern corner the Darini may likewise be a remnant from the pre-Celtic past. They lived on in the history of Ireland, but they changed their ground. They are the Deirgthene of Munster, who seem to have been a tribe of Iberians. In the south-east are the territories of the Britons and Belgæ, to which we should probably join that of the Gangani in Munster.[2] In this last name we recognize the names of Gann and Genann, who were Fir Bolg who landed in County Clare, at the mouth of the Shannon. Ptolemy's map tells us nothing about the Picts of Ulster and elsewhere, nor about the scattered groups of Fir Bolg, Dumnonii, and Galians which were to be found almost everywhere, but we must bear them in mind. The true domain of the Goidels probably covered barely half the country.

As a matter of fact, the various groups were all becoming assimilated. An expression like Erna Dé Bolgæ, the Erna or Erainn of the Goddess Bolga, which combines the name of the Iverni with that of the eponymous goddess of the Belgæ, is significant of what was happening. No less so is the way in which the ruling aristocracy took over the traditions of the subject tribes. We have seen that the chief Irish heroes, Cuchulainn and Finn, were not Goidels. The heterogeneous mass was gradually becoming a nation, which afterwards absorbed yet other elements.

Ireland gives an exceptionally complete picture of what

---

[1] **LXXX**, 1918, pp. 131 ff.   [2] Ibid., 1920, p. 140.

was likely to happen wherever the Celts established themselves—the survival and incorporation of the aborigines, the superimposition of Celts, and the amalgamation of all these various elements into new social and political bodies, which were the final form of Celtic societies. In addition, in Ireland, the organization was provided by the first invaders.

CHAPTER III

CELTIC EXPANSION ON THE CONTINENT IN THE BRONZE AGE.
GOIDELS AND BRYTHONS

I

DID THE GOIDELS TAKE PART IN THE CELTIC MIGRATIONS ON THE CONTINENT ? TRACES OF THE GOIDELS IN SPAIN

IN the following chapters we shall consider how the Celtic
domain on the Continent was constituted by the extension
of the original Celtic domain to the west and south. The
Celts met on their south-westward march the same foreign
peoples, Iberians and Ligurians, as in the British Isles. But
the first question which arises is whether the migrating bodies
contained the same Celtic elements and were composed in
the same fashion ; we already know that the great mass
consisted of Gallo-Britons and Belgæ. Did they also include
Goidels and Picts ? It is an old question which has been
revived, but with particular reference to the Goidels.

Zimmer's hypothesis as to the ports from which they
sailed [1] implies that they had advanced at least as far as the
Loire before they crossed to the British Isles. If we reject
it, as I have done, as insufficiently proved, we do not
necessarily deny that they went still further without crossing
the sea.

But whereas in Ireland the Goidels were preserved by
their isolation, and first their power and sovereignty and
then their racial character were to a great extent protected
by the sea against the encroachment or influence of the other
Celts, it could not possibly be so on the Continent, and if
any settlement or group which was originally Goidelic
survived into historical times we have no means of recognizing
it as such. Our task, therefore, is not to look for vanished
settlements, but to gather up such scattered memories as
they may have left behind them and, above all, such facts
as show that Goidelic was spoken on the Continent outside
the places of its origin.

[1] In **IX**, 1912, pp. 1–59 ; cf. J. Vendryès, in **CXL**, 1912, pp. 384 ff.

The town of Acci, in Spain, now Gaadix in the province of Granada, had a war-god who was called either Netos (genitive Neti) or Neto (genitive Netonis). His worship is attested by Macrobius [1] and also by two inscriptions in Estremadura and Portugal. He has been regarded as Celtic for various reasons.[2] Now the Goidels had a war-god named Nét.[3] *Nét* implies an earlier Netos, genitive Neti. Are these two the same god [4]? The answer is doubtful, for if the Irish Nét's name is Celtic,[5] it seems to come from a root *nant*, which appears in the name of the Gallic goddess Nantosuelta,[6] and there is no reason to suppose that the disappearance of *n* before *t* or *k* [7] had already taken place at the time when some of the Goidels reached Ireland and others of them, from some other direction, could be supposed to have invaded Spain. Nor is there any ground for imagining that the dropping of the *n* occurred among two branches of the Goidels which were not in contact with each other, whereas having become the rule among the Irish Goidels it neither spread to their near neighbours the Britons nor developed independently among them. Lastly, it is not certain that the people of Acci or the other worshippers of the Spanish Netos were Celts.

In the case of France facts can be produced which are still the subject of controversy. If they were as important as they are made out to be they would go beyond the object of our present inquiry and prove that Goidelic was not quite a dead language in Gaul when the country became Roman. Does not Cæsar state, at the beginning of his *Commentaries*, that the various parts of Gaul spoke different languages [8]? Some scholars, such as Sir John Rhys, have thought it possible to determine those of the peoples of Gaul which were Goidels [9]; for instance, the Arverni and Sequani, and

---

[1] *Saturn.*, i, 19, 5 : *Accitani etiam, Hispana gens, simulacrum Martis, radiis ornatum, maxima religione celebrant, Neton vocantes.*

[2] **I**, ii, 3386 (Acci) ; 5278 (Turgalium, Trujillo) ; 365 (Conimbriga, Condeixa-a-Velha, near Coimbra) ; Roscher, *Lexikon*, s.v. ; Holder, **CCVII**, s.v. ; Leite de Vasconcellos, **DXIII**, ii, 309 ; Toutain, **CCCLXXXVIII**, iii, 136. Schulten (**DXVIII**, p. 83) regards him as Iberian. Cf. Philipon, **DXVI**, p. 209.

[3] **CXL**, 42, 215.   [4] Hubert, in **CLXXX**.

[5] Nét is a Fomorian god.   [6] D'Arbois, in Reinach, **CCCCLXXIV**, i, 224.

[7] Pedersen, **CCXXVII**, i, 51.

[8] *Gall. War*, i, 1, 2 : *Hi omnes lingua, institutis, legibus inter se differunt;* Strabo, iv.

[9] **CCXXX**, passim, esp. p. 59 ; Nicholson, **CCXXIII**, 6, p. 116 ; Holmes, *Cæsar's Conquest of Gaul*, p. 319.

behind them all the peoples of their faction and all those of Aquitania. These were the *Celtæ*, the rest being the *Galli*. By this side-road Sir John has brought back the old distinction between the two names. The proofs adduced are a very few words, mostly proper names, which appear to contain the old *qu* of Celtic. Some are furnished by inscriptions, the others are place-names.

The principal document is the Coligny Calendar, in which three words of Goidelic appearance are found [1]—the name of the month Equos, the Horse month, which should be *epos* in Brythonic Gaulish ; the name of the month Qutios or Cutios,[2] which Sir John explains by the Welsh word *pyd* " dangerous ", and compares to Latin *quatio* ; and the word *quimon*, which he suggests is an abbreviation of a word pronounced *quinquimon* (*coic, pump* or *pimp*), comparing it to the Latin distributives *bimus, trimus, quadrimus*.[3] The Calendar also presents words for which Goidelic alone is said to have equivalents—Ciallos, which is like Irish *ciall* " collection ", " total ", and *lat*, followed by a number, which might be the Irish *láthe* " day ", for which there is no Brythonic equivalent.[4]

If these arguments hold good we have a document, and a most important one, establishing the use of Goidelic words in Gaul at the time of its Romanization. Were there considerable survivals of Goidelic in the religious vocabulary, or did the language continue to be spoken ? The district is the middle valley of the Rhone. It is likewise in the southeast and south-west of France that almost all the evidence in question has been collected. The observations made on the Coligny Calendar called attention to other documents, particularly a lead plaque, bearing on its two faces a cursive Latin inscription, found at Rom, in Deux-Sèvres,[5] and a few scattered formulæ in Marcellus of Bordeaux.[6] Little by little one-half of the Gaulish inscriptions has been grouped round

[1] J. Loth, in **CXL**, 1904, pp. 113 ff. ; S. de Ricci, ibid., pp. 10–27 ; Rhys, in **CXXI**, 1910.

[2] Rhys, **CCXXX**, p. 28 ; Dottin, **CXCVI**, p. 280. S. de Ricci compares the word to the name of the month Κούτιος in the Locrian calendar of Chalæon, in **CXL**, 1898, p. 218.

[3] Rhys, op. cit., p. 5.

[4] Ibid., pp. 6, 7.

[5] C. Jullian, in **CXL**, 1898, p. 168 ; Nicholson, op. cit., p. 127 ; Rhys, in **CXXVII**, 1900, p. 895.

[6] Nicholson, op. cit., pp. 6, 7 ; Holmes, loc. cit.

these documents. What are these facts worth? We need not pay attention to the Rom tablet or the formulæ of Marcellus of Bordeaux,[1] for the text of both is disfigured. But we must discuss the evidence of the Coligny Calendar.

Coligny lies in the ancient domain of the Ambarri, or perhaps in that of the Sequani, already discussed. Another inscription was found near Coligny, at Géligneux, in Ain,[2] which proves clearly that the same language was spoken in that part as in the rest of Gaul, namely Brythonic. It is a Latin funerary inscription, containing Gaulish words. One M. Rufius Catullus, Curator of the Nautæ of the Rhone, has built himself a funerary chapel and made provision for the maintenance of worship there by a foundation which provides, among other things, for a funeral feast to be held periodically. *Et ad cenam omnibus tricontis ponendam (denariorum binorum) in perpet(uum), sic ut petrudecameto consumatur.* This means that the banquet is to take place on the 14th day of every thirty-day month. *Tricontis* is the dative of a word meaning 30, a cardinal number; in Breton *tregont*; in Old Irish *tricha*, genitive *trichat* (= *tricos, tricontos*). *Petrudecameto* is an ordinal number, 14th.[3] But it is a Brythonic ordinal number. In a Goidelic-speaking country it would have been *quadrudecameto*. Therefore the Goidelic words in the Coligny Calendar could only be, at the most, survivals in a special vocabulary. The Calendar itself contains Brythonic words which can be recognized as such from the use of *p*—*prinni*,[4] *petiux*.[5] But its Goidelisms are

---

[1] D'Arbois, in **CXL**, 1904, pp. 351–3; 1906, p. 107.

[2] **I**, xiii, 2494; Allmer, in **III**, 753 *b*; J. Loth, in **VIII**, 1909, p. 21 ff. Loth has corrected Hirschfeld's interpretation very happily: Géligneux belongs to the bishopric of Belley, i.e. to the old *pagus Bellicensis*; just as the bishopric of Belley comes directly under the archbishopric of Besançon, so the *pagus Bellicensis* depended, under the Empire, on the province which bore the name of Maxima Sequanorum; it formed part of the *civitas Equestrium*. In the Coligny Calendar, the months of thirty days are described as *matu* " good, fortunate " (Irish *maith*, Gaelic *math*, Welsh *mad*). The only exception is the month of Equos. It is true that it is not certain whether Equos had twenty-nine or thirty days. The only day which has the indication that it is a *dies fas*, namely, *mat*, written out in full in the Coligny Calendar, is the 14th of the month of Riuros. In the matter of funeral rites, in India, the fourteenth day is set apart for banquets in memory of those who have died young or by force of arms.

[3] O. Irish *dechmad*, Welsh *degfed* " tenth ".

[4] With *prinni*, cf. *prenne* (translated *arborem grandem* in the Vienna Glossary); Welsh *pren* " wood "; Irish *crann* " tree ". Loth, in **CXL**, 1911, p. 208; Dottin, **CXCVI**, p. 279.

[5] With *petiux*, cf. Welsh *peth* " a certain amount "; O. Irish *cuit* " part ". Rhys, **CCXXX**, p. 36; **VIII**, p. 53.

doubtful. Common sense forbids us to suppose that a language which was hardly ever written should have preserved, in the spelling of certain words, sounds which it no longer pronounced. It is, on the other hand, probable that the *q* taken by Gaulish from the Latin alphabet stands for other sounds in these inscriptions than the old Celtic velar.

M. Loth supposes that the words in question are compound words, in which *qu* does not stand for a single letter, and should be expressed by the double sound *co-w*.[1] There are instances of such fusions of sounds.[2] If we break up *equos* we get an element *ek*. Now the month Equos is February ; in the Irish calendar February begins with a great feast, called *oimelc*. This word is explained in the *Glossary* of Cormac. It is the month in which the milk comes to the ewes.[3] This indication gives the key to the element *ek*. *Eko* could be the Celtic equivalent of (*p*)*ecu*, *pecus*, with the initial *p* dropped. There was an equivalent for *pecus* in Celtic, doubtless confined to religious parlance ; it is represented by the name Eochaid,[4] which corresponds, letter for letter, to Sanskrit *paçu-pátiḥ*. So Equos must have been, not the month of the Horse, but a month which affected the sheep. M. Loth has compared *quimon* with *Quigon*, the cognomen of a citizen of Treves,[5] which breaks up into *co-uigon " fellow-traveller ", Welsh *cy-waith* " fellow-worker ".[6] As for Qutios, the spelling is not certain and it is more often written Cutius. Of all the hypotheses put forward to explain the obscure passages in the Coligny Calendar, those which try to find Goidelic words in it are among the least probable.

In the same fashion M. Loth has explained the name of the Sequani, over which Celtic scholars have been justifiably concerned and which they have made out to be Ligurian,[7]

---

[1] In **LVIII**, 1909, p. 20.
[2] The name of Bituitus, the chief of the Arverni, is an excellent example. A coin found at Narbonne gives the spelling : Bito-uniotouos (Amardel, in **XXXIII**, 1906, 412, p. 426).
[3] Irish *melg* " milk " ; *oi*, *ui* " ewe ".
[4] *Eochaid* = (*p*)*e*(*ç*)*u*-(*p*)*ati*.
[5] Bulliot, in **XII**, 1863, p. 142 ; **CXXXIX**, 1863, p. 275.
[6] The country of the Treviri furnishes another example of a false velar in the name of Dinquatis (a Gallic god), which is given to Silvanus as an epithet on two inscriptions found at Géromont in Belgium (**CXLIX**, xiii, 3968).
[7] D'Arbois, **CCCI**, ii, pp. 130–3.

Iberian,[1] and Goidelic [2] in turn. He regards the name of Sequana, their eponymous goddess, as a complex stem which can be analysed into *Seko-uana* or *Seko-ou-ana*.[3] If this is so the Goidelic air of the name of the Sequani is deceptive, and it could not be otherwise, since they spoke Brythonic at least from the time when they founded their city of Epamanduodurum,[4] and they did not alter their name.

Other words found in the south of Gaul give rise to other reflections. One is the proper name Κοναδρουννία, which appears in an inscription found at Ventabren, in the Bouches-du-Rhône.[5] It is a prænomen of numerical type (like Sextus), equivalent to the Umbrian Petronia. Its Gaulish form would be Petronia. But is it certain that this name is Celtic ? And are the names Quiamelius (Antibes) [6] and Quariates (Queyras) [7] any more so ?

These names cannot be dismissed like those discussed before. But we should note that they come from the south of Gaul, where the Gauls did not arrive till fairly late, and there always remained a substratum of the native Ligurian population. That the Goidels should at a very early date have advanced further in that direction than the Brythons is highly improbable. So the words which have detained us are not at all likely to be Goidelic words. They may be Ligurian. Mixed groups of Celto-Ligurians, such as the Salyes round about Marseilles, were formed in this region. It is to be believed that the two strains in their composition appeared in their speech, and that this contained at least some proper names of Ligurian origin, correctly pronounced. The same may be said of the name Aquitania. A curious passage in Pliny seems to mean that the district was once called Aremorica.[8] *Aremorica* is Celtic, and means the country

---

[1] Philipon, **CCCLXIX**, p. 299.   [2] Nicholson, op. cit.

[3] Root *seig* ; cf. Mod. German *seihen* " to filter " ; O. Slav. *seknati* " to cut " ; Sanskr. *secanam* " pouring " ; root *sek* " to cut ", from which come Lat. *seco* and Irish *sgathaim* " I cut ".

[4] The City of Men who deal with Horses ; *-mandu-*, *-√mendh* " to deal with ". Cf. Viromandui, Manducus.

[5] Dottin, **CXCVI**, p. 149 ; d'Arbois, **CCXCIX**, p. 87 ; cf. Κοvι or *Koui* in the Cavaillon inscription (Dottin, op. cit., p. 152) ; Loth, in **CXXXIV**, 1918, pp. 38 ff.   [6] **I**, xii, 226.   [7] **I**, xii, 80.

[8] Pliny, *N.H.*, iv, 105 : *Gallia omnis Comata uno nomine appellata in tria populorum genera dividitur, amnibus maxime distincta. A Scalde ad Sequanam Belgica ; ab eo ad Garunnam Celtica eademque Lugdunensis ; inde ad Pyrenaei montis excursum Aquitanica, Aremorica antea dicta.* Rhys, **CCXXX**, p. 57.

by the sea (*are, mor*). *Aquitania* may have meant the same thing in a language in which the word for water, or the sea, was of the same form as Latin *aqua*. That language may have been Ligurian.[1] It was natural for the part of Gaul in which the natives remained distinct down to the Roman conquest to have its name from a non-Celtic language. But the supporters of the Continental Goidels do not see things so. We shall not follow them.

All the unintelligible inscriptions of the Rhone valley and all the words presenting anomalies from the Celtic point of view have been assembled round the facts furnished by the Coligny Calendar and brought forward by Sir John Rhys as witnesses to a language which he calls " Celtican ", which is at once Ligurian and Goidelic.[2] He identifies the Goidels with the Ligurians, and so gives the Goidels of Gaul a substantial reality. Thus his Ligurians spoke a Celtic language, namely Goidelic, and they were the first body of Celts to break away towards Western and Southern Europe. If so, we should have to increase the domain of the Celts by the whole domain of the Ligurians. But we should also have to be able to explain as Celtic every peculiarity of language revealed by Ligurian names and names of Ligurian type, and for that we should have to invent a pre-Celtic language, extending wider than the pre-Goidelic tongue. If we extend the limits of Celticism as much as this we shall obliterate them altogether.

One of Sir John Rhys's arguments is furnished by the name of the god Segomo. The inscriptions show that his worship extended from Nice to the Côte d'Or. He was a Mars. Now we have already met him ; in the ogham inscriptions of County Waterford the proper name Nia Segamain Segomo's Champion, appears three times. Moreover, Segomo's name recalls that of the Segobrigii, an Alpine people described as Ligurian.[3] Therefore Ireland and the south-east of Gaul had a common god, whose name had an element in common with that of a tribe situated in that part

[1] Cf. Aquincum (Budapest). Celtic also had the equivalent for *aquae*—Irish *uisge*, Welsh *aw*.

[2] Rhys, op. cit., p. 78 ; S. de Ricci, in **CXL**, 1898, pp. 213 ff. ; 1900, p. 27.

[3] Rhys, op. cit.

of Gaul where the Ligurians are placed. So far so good ; but County Waterford happened to be peopled by Gallic colonies. The Celtican hypothesis, which identifies Goidels and Ligurians, is as vain as that which regards the Ligurians as the Italo-Celts in their undivided state.

There are, then, no certain linguistic traces of Goidelic in Gaul, nor are there any in the Continental extensions of the Celtic domain. If any Goidels stayed there they have left no sign of their presence. It does not follow that the ancestors or the first cousins of the Goidels did not spread into those parts.[1] Above all it does not follow that the ancient Celtic tongue was not spoken there before its velar was transformed. There are two questions mixed together, and they should be kept distinct. They can only be answered consistently and separately by the use of other arguments which are of an ethnographic nature.

II

FRANCE AND SPAIN AT THE BEGINNING OF THE BRONZE AGE.
IS THE CIVILIZATION OF EL ARGAR CELTIC ?

We may say boldly that there is nothing in the archæology of France and the Iberian Peninsula corresponding to the invasion of England by the builders of the round barrows. Bell-shaped beakers are found there, and in great numbers, but they are of an early type.[2] They are the beakers of the megalithic monuments. There are still, perhaps, scholars who are prepared to believe that this mode of construction spread from the Scandinavian or German north to the Mediterranean.[3] But for years nobody has thought of regarding them as the work of the Celts. We have, therefore, no archæological indication of the migrations of the Celts along the western coasts of Europe before a relatively late period of the Bronze Age ; and if the Goidelic invasion of Britain is represented by the civilization of the round barrows, and particularly by its characteristic tombs and pottery, it was confined to the British Isles. But our archæological evidence is incomplete.

---

[1] D'Arbois, **CCC**, p. 12 ; Rhys, **CCCCLI**, p. 4.
[2] Del Castillo Yurrita, **CCCIX**, pp. 105 ff.
[3] S. Reinach, in **XV**, 1893, p. 731.

M. Louis Siret,[1] who was one of the founders of prehistoric archæology in Spain, has maintained that the Celts arrived in that country about the same time (in the Bronze Age), and by sea. He holds that it was the Celts who introduced bronze into Spain, and that they brought it from Bohemia, but that they came by sea, after a halt in the British Isles (for we have no trace of their transit overland), and that they founded in Spain, as in Britain, a colony of metal-workers.

He ascribes to them a series of stations in the province of Almeria, and among them the famous station of El Argar.[2] But similar sites are found from Catalonia to Portugal. They are fortified hill-stations, not having cemeteries separated from the town. The burials are in among the houses, and even in the houses. Herein they differ greatly from the earlier towns with their separate cemeteries of megalithic monuments such as Los Millares and Fuente Vermeja.

The houses and tombs have yielded a very complete series of objects. Objects of copper and bronze are very numerous.[3] In the making of tools, metal had taken the place of flint. The most characteristic object is the halbert. Since halberts are abundant in Ireland and a few have been found in Northern Germany, M. Siret makes the colonizers of Spain arrive by that route.[4]

He compares the tombs of El Argar with the Bohemian tombs of the beginning of the Bronze Age, those of what is called the Aunjetitz or Unetice civilization.[5] They are cists, some of them made of very well dressed slabs, in which the body was laid in a contracted position.[6] There are also large urns, sometimes placed in pairs, mouth to mouth.[7] The tombs are similar, and M. Siret has drawn up a list of the furniture in which the objects correspond piece by piece.[8] Not only the metal objects, but the vases are similar. M. Siret lays particular stress on the likeness of the carinated forms, with an angular profile, and of the vases with feet.[9]

---

[1] **DXXII**, i, pp. 103 ff., 195 ff.

[2] Siret, "Orientaux et Occidentaux," in **CXXXVI**, 1927, pp. 231–7; Déchelette, in **CXXXIX**, 1908, 2, pp. 244 ff. ; Schulten, **DXVII**, pp. 166 ff. ; Bosch Gimpera, **DV**, pp. 157 ff. ; J. Cabré Aguilo, in **XCVII**, i, pp. 23 ff.

[3] Siret, **DXXII**, pl. viii.

[4] Ibid., p. 194.

[5] See above, p. 185.

[6] Siret, op. cit., pl. xiii.

[7] Déchelette, op. cit., pp. 256, 260.

[8] Op. cit., p. 154.

[9] Ibid., pl. ix.

Moreover, this pottery is generally blackish, like the wares of Central Europe.

M. Siret considers that Bohemia, being supplied with tin by the deposits of the Erzgebirge and the neighbouring deposits of Lausitz, was one of the first centres of the Bronze civilization ; that it was in a position to act as distributor to countries which were less favoured in this respect, as he imagines to have been the case with Spain,[1] believing that its tin-mines were not discovered until later ; and that the peoples which had this mineral wealth in their territory (which at that time, he thinks, were the Celts) were likely to be eager for conquests and adventures.

The Aunjetitz period is contemporaneous with the time when the supposedly Goidelic invaders of Britain were beginning to cross to Ireland. But it is very doubtful, as we have seen,[2] that the Aunjetitz civilization was a Celtic culture. It is still more doubtful that that of El Argar was, and M. Siret's hypothesis has been keenly combated.[3] Even the resemblances of the two civilizations have not the significance which he attaches to them. Déchelette says that the relationship is that of cousins, not, as M. Siret holds, of mother and daughter.[4] El Argar and Aunjetitz stand on two routes from the Eastern Mediterranean, where the prototypes of their funeral customs and technical processes were to be found. The distribution of the halberts, on which M. Siret bases the route taken by his alleged Celts, is not quite what he believes it to be. The halbert was used in Italy. It is represented in carvings on the rocks of the Lac des Merveilles.[5] It was used in Hungary,[6] whence it may have come into Italy. It seems to be absent in Bohemia. Moreover, the German halberts are very different from those of Ireland and Spain. They have the handle attached by a metal socket to which the blade is riveted,[7] whereas in Ireland and the Peninsula the blade is fixed directly on to the wood, and these are probably the earlier types.[8] The resemblances in

[1] Ibid., p. 138 ; Schulten, op. cit., p. 74.
[2] See above, p. 186.
[3] In particular, by Déchelette, op. cit., pp. 261 ff.
[4] Ibid., pp. 251 ff.
[5] Montelius, **DXXXV**, ii, pl. cxxvii, figs. 1–3.
[6] Ibid., p. 93.   [7] Ibid., p. 36.
[8] G. Coffey, in **CXXIII**, xxvii, p. 94 ; H. and L. Siret, **DXXI**, pl. xxxii ; L. Siret, **DXXII**, p. 168.

culture between the British Isles and Spain can easily be explained by trade with the people of Tartessus.[1] Their differences, on the other hand, which are patent, are hard to explain if it is assumed that they were colonized about the same time by the same people.

But besides all this it is very difficult to imagine that the Celts were able at that time to send colonies to the British Isles and to Spain at once. It is enough to remember how extremely hard it is to determine their traces in the archæology of their original home at the end of Neolithic times or at the beginning of the Bronze Age, and to interpret them. They are indeed fleeting, shadowy traces ! That means that the Celts had not yet attained to unity in their first habitat. They were the most vigorous folk there, but they may not have been the most numerous. In any case they were not sufficiently homogeneous peoples, peoples sufficiently aware of themselves, to build up a single civilization of their own. Young, strong peoples have made very distant raids. Several times in prehistory we find identical remains in quite small settlements separated by great distances, and may infer that such a raid had taken place. The adventures of the Normans in the eleventh century were a repetition of many earlier adventures. But to populate a country on a large scale something more was wanted, namely numbers, mass.

At the beginning of the Bronze Age the Goidels had already grown sufficiently to found a lasting settlement in the British Isles. They were not capable of founding another in Spain.[2] Nor did they found one in France.

[1] Avien., *Ora Marit.*, 113 : *Tartessiis qui in terminos Œstrymnidum negotiandi mos est.*

[2] Nevertheless, I do not think that Déchelette has disposed of the problem raised by M. Siret. There is too much difference between the civilization of Los Millares and that of El Argar to be explained by mere development. I myself regard it as a difference of race. What can the new element be ? It is not quite true to say that there are no tombs between Spain and Bohemia like those of El Argar. There are the cists of Chamblandes in the canton of Vaud. There are those of the Valais, which contain just those objects which I have mentioned above as being identical with the Bohemian objects of Aunjetitz. Also, I am very much struck by the fact that, in stations of the El Argar type, the tombs are in the town, under the houses. It is the same in the Neolithic fortified dry-land stations of the Michelsberg type, in the pile-villages, and at Fort-Harrouard. Now, I have already admitted that the people of the Swiss pile-villages must have been Ligurians.

I wonder, therefore, whether the appearance of the El Argar civilization in the Peninsula does not correspond to the arrival of the Ligurians, whom all the ancient authorities unite in placing in that country. There were apparently Ligurians all the way to Cadiz. The resemblance of culture

III

But could the Goidels not have come later ?   Let us see the facts which we have to interpret.

The Bronze Age in Spain after the coming of the El Argar culture is very little known.[1] Axes have been found, some of Mediterranean types and others related to types in France and the British Isles. But the series of bronze tools is still very incomplete.

At the very end of the Bronze Age a series of swords appears. These are the flat-tanged swords, in which the base of the blade is carried on in a tongue, to which the two pieces of which the handle is composed is riveted.[2] The number of such swords found was greatly increased in 1923 by the dragging of the harbour of Huelva.[3] From within a small space the drag brought up over 150 bronze weapons and other objects, with a good number of swords among them. They may have been a cargo which went to the bottom. But had the ship taken them on at Huelva, or had she come there to unload them ?   The question is of importance for interpretation of this type of sword as an indication of race. Huelva is in the copper country, and near the Rio Tinto.[4] Can it have been the distributing centre for the flat-tanged swords, which have hitherto been regarded as Northern ? Nothing of the kind. The Spanish examples, including those from Huelva, are late types, with concave hilt, an oblong slit in the place of rivet-holes, and notches at the base of the blade.   If they were manufactured at Huelva they were

between El Argar and Aunjetitz which has raised the whole question would be explained at the same time. For the supposed Ligurians of the pile-villages formed one element of the population of Bohemia in Neolithic times. The pottery of Aunjetitz, which is generally compared to that of northern Germany, has as many likenesses to the pottery of the pile-villages. In bronze objects, the same relationship can be pointed out, and, on the whole, apart from one object, a diadem (which may be native), the metal objects of the El Argar tombs are not different from those of the same date found in the Swiss palafittes.

[1] Déchelette, **CCCXVIII,** ii, 2, p. 47 ; Bosch Gimpera, **CCCCXCVIII,** pp. 175 ff. ; Leite de Vasconcellos, in **XXII,** 1906, p. 179 (tombs of Bronze Age II).

[2] Déchelette, op. cit., ii, 1, p. 208 ; Cartailhac, **DVII,** pp. 221 ff.

[3] J. Albelda, in **CXXXIX,** 1923, 2, pp. 222 ff.

[4] C. Jullian, in **LVIII** 1923, pp. 203 ff.

imitations. Besides, the find as a whole was a mixed one, including Italian brooches as well as these Northern swords. If it was a cargo it can only have been the cargo of a coasting trader, putting in along the coasts of the Western Mediterranean and Atlantic. But there is in the appearance of this series of swords a suddenness, an unexpectedness, which tempts one to interpret it as the sign of the appearance of a new racial element. Unfortunately it is a very inadequate sign.

These Spanish swords come from France, where older forms of them are found and in larger numbers.[1] But there they are associated with other objects.

In the founder's deposit at Petit-Villatte (Cher) [2] we have a sword-hilt of cast bronze of a type which is found from Danzig to Silesia.[3] The same deposit includes a fragment of a blade, which must have been fitted to a hilt of this kind. It also contained two fragments of the curious bronze boxes which were made in the second half of the Bronze Age in the neighbourhood of the Scandinavian Straits. Those of Petit-Villatte are not of the latest type, but of one contemporary with the fourth period of the French Bronze Age. A similar box was found in the pile-village of Corcelettes on the Lake of Neuchâtel, which yielded two brooches consisting of symmetrical discs and an independent pin,[4] likewise from Scandinavia.

From the same region come the gold objects—vases and bracelets—of the treasure of Rongères (Allier).[5] This treasure includes a type of bracelet, with the ends splitting into two horns rolled in spirals, which was made in bronze in Bohemia in the second period of the Bronze Age and was afterwards manufactured as far away as Sweden.[6] The vases are adorned with concentric circles, which form the decoration of the latest of the bronze boxes mentioned above.[7] Their origin is revealed by their distribution.[8] The largest treasures, and far the largest, are those of Messingwerk near Eberswalde

---

[1] Déchelette, ii, 2, p. 208.
[2] Kossinna, in **LXXXV**, 1918–19, pp. 173, 185.
[3] Déchelette, ii, 1, p. 396, and fig. 157, 2.
[4] Montelius, **CCCLVII**, 57.
[5] Déchelette, in **CVII**, xix, 185, pl. xv.
[6] Ibid., pp. 187, 195–6 ; **CCCXVIII**, ii, 1, p. 315.
[7] Montelius, op. cit., p. 67.
[8] Kossinna, in **LXXXV**, 1914, p. 308.

in the Kreis of Oberbarnim in Brandenburg and Boeslunde in Seeland. A very great number of finds have been made within a line embracing Westphalia, Lower Saxony, part of Brandenburg, and Mecklenburg, with especial density in Jutland and the islands.

Another vase of the same origin, found at Villeneuve-Saint-Vistre (Marne), resembles almost in every detail one discovered at Werder on the Havel in Brandenburg.[1]

But apart from the swords the objects enumerated are rare, and, if we leave the swords out of account, they have the air among the other objects of the regions in which they are found of being exotics. But objects are not all of equal importance to ethnology, for the reason that they are used for purposes which do not all affect the consciousness of the human group to the same degree. A community will change its fashions in the matter of pottery or armament sooner than in the matter of religion or the treatment of the dead. It is more liable to go after strange drinking-vessels than after strange gods.

Among the gold objects discovered in France which are of the style of the Rongères vases there is an idol, or a fragment of one, known as the Quiver of Avanton (Vienne) (Fig. 38 b).[2] A similar object, but more complete, the Golden Hat of Schifferstadt (Fig. 38 a), was found in the Palatinate, on the left bank of the Rhine.[3] On the " brim " of this two bronze axes with the stop-ridge had been laid. A similar thing, likewise flanked by two axes, is engraved on a slab of the monument at Kivik in Skåne,[4] the other slabs of which are also covered with religious subjects or emblems. They are clearly bætyls, and they recall those which have been found in the region of the megalithic monuments in Spain at Los Millares.[5] But we cannot suppose that at that date they came from the south-west to Poitou and the Rhine. We must suppose that, in the form of the Schifferstadt Hat and the Avanton Quiver, the bætyl travelled from north-east to south-west. It is not likely that these idols were brought in by merchants. They represent a cult and a group of men who

---

[1] Ibid., p. 295.
[2] Déchelette, ii, 1, pp. 362 ff.
[3] Lindenschmit, **CCCXCIX**, i, x, pl. iv.
[4] Norden, **CCCCV**, p. 33 ; Montelius, **CCCC**, p. 68, n. 3.
[5] Siret, **DXXIII,**, p. 41.

practised that cult, and that group came from Poitou, from the Rhine, and from beyond.

So, then, in France and in Western Europe a certain number of objects dating from the end of the Bronze Age

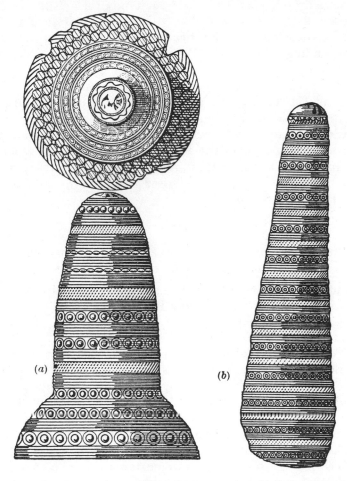

FIG. 38. The Golden Hat of Schifferstadt (*a*) and the Quiver of Avanton (*b*).
(Déchelette, ii, 1, fig. 144.)

have been found, and among them one of first importance, the Avanton Quiver, and a series of very considerable importance, the swords, which develop from originals which are found at the point where the Celtic and Germanic countries meet.

These facts can be interpreted like the similar facts presented by the British Isles. There we are compelled to look to archæological facts, which might have another significance, for evidence of additions to the population which did actually take place and have left no other visible trace. Do they, first in France and then in Spain, represent a late Goidelic invasion [1] ? Not being tempted to interpret the corresponding facts in the British Isles in this manner, we are obliged to regard them as an indication of the coming of the Picts. I have made no objection to the association of the names of the Picts and the Pictones.[2] Without disguising the meagreness of the facts which I have brought together in order to lead to this conclusion, I have no objection to regarding this people of the Pictones as one of those earliest established on the soil of Gaul, and permanently settled in its domain, whence it may be supposed to have sent out bodies of settlers into Spain.

IV

THE BRYTHONIC CELTS OF SOUTHERN GERMANY IN THE EAST OF GAUL. TUMULI OF THE BRONZE AGE

But in the course of the Bronze Age things happened in the eastern part of what is now France, the racial character of which is quite clear, and they went on in the Hallstatt period.

From the first period of the Bronze Age burial under tumuli was practised in the east of France, in the Jura.[3] These were no longer tumuli over funerary chambers but tumuli over a cist, a sort of coffin of flags, a *loculus* of stones put together more or less roughly, or merely the remains of the dead man, who at this date was laid on his back.

The objects found in these tombs are of the same family as those found, in different circumstances, in the tombs of the Valais [4] and in the Cevennes district, where, for example,

---

[1] Peake, **CCCCXLVII**, p. 164. Mr. Peake imagines the Goidels established in the region of the Swiss palafittes and attacked by the Brythons, after which they went to Gaul with the flat-tanged sword, the Sequani forming their rear-guard.

[2] See above, pp. 202 ff.

[3] Déchelette and Piroutet, in **CXXXIX**, 1909, i, pp. 216 ff. ; Piroutet, in **XV**, 1918–19, pp. 213–249, 423–447 ; 1920, pp. 51–81.

[4] Déchelette, ii, 1, p. 137 ; Viollier, in **XVIII**, pp. 125 ff. ; id., **CCCCXCII**, pp. 23 ff. ; Behrens, in Ebert, **CCCXXIV**, s.v. " Schweiz ".

the dolmen of the Liquisse (Aveyron) [1] has yielded the same trefoil-headed pins as the tumuli of Clucy (Jura).[2] But these same pins also appear in Southern Germany.[3] The fact is that the distribution of bronze objects has not really any ethnological meaning. In general they spread along trade-routes, not in areas of occupation.

Funeral rites have a very different significance. That just described is new in France. On the other hand, it had been practised in Central Germany during the vague period which is variously assigned to the Neolithic, Copper, and Bronze Ages. The beakers with cord impressions are usually found in tumuli, and under those tumuli the dead were laid on their backs when they were not burned.[4] It is therefore in the direction of Germany that we must seek the origin of the new methods of burial and the starting-point of the men who introduced them. In Switzerland,[5] where tumuli going back to the beginning of the Bronze Age, if not to the Neolithic, have been reported and excavated in certain places in the north-east, between the Aar and the Rhine, they likewise represent an encroachment by the peoples of Germany on the domain of the palafitte-builders.

On what scale was this westward movement ? It is not easy to say. The tumuli which can be referred to the first period of the Bronze Age on the strength of datable objects are not many. The systematic exploration of the neighbour-hood of Salins adds one or two to their number every year.[6] But all round these dated tumuli there are thousands which contain nothing but a few bits of flint or polished axes and shapeless potsherds. They might equally well be attributed to Neolithic times or to quite late periods. The discovery of a bronze pin in one tumulus in a group must suffice to date the group ; the proximity of a settlement of known date gives the indication needed for others.

If this is the case with the neighbourhood of Salins we are clearly justified in looking for tumuli of this date among

[1] Déchelette, ii, 1, pp. 137 ff.
[2] Ibid., p. 137.
[3] e.g. at Haberskirsch, near Friedberg (Upper Bavaria). G. Behrens, CCCXCI, p. 3.
[4] See above, pp. 183 ff.
[5] Viollier, CCCCXCIII, p. 31.
[6] See p. 246, n. 3. M. Piroutet's reports on the exploration of the country round Salins are in the *Archives de la Direction générale des Beaux-Arts*.

the countless *marchets* of the Province of Namur,[1] which
have for choice been attached to the Hallstatt series, or
further south among the tumuli without furniture of the
Haulzy,[2] Penborn, and Grossblittersdorf [3] group, and among
those of the group of the Naquée, near Clayeures (Meurthe-
et-Moselle).[4] These are sufficient to represent many others
and bear witness that the tumulus-builders who, from
Thuringia, reached the Rhine, spread widely in the first
period of the Bronze Age beyond the left bank of the river in
Switzerland, Franche-Comté, and Belgium, without leaving
any trace in their tombs (which, besides, were ill-suited to
the preservation of their contents) of the characteristic
furniture which distinguishes them in Germany.

Is it to a better method of building the tumulus, or to
the chances of the wanderings of a small, better-provided
group, that we owe the preservation in Brittany of a very
few vases with one or two handles, which, from their
horizontal ornament, can only be compared to the Adlerberg
type of pottery [5] ? Only the distance makes one hesitate
to recognize the kinship. Two of these vases were the urns
of a cremation-burial,[6] two others stood in their tumulus
beside skeletons laid on their backs,[7] one skeleton being
enclosed in a wooden coffin. These tumuli are quite different
from the round barrows of England, both in the funeral
rites to which they bear witness and in the pottery which
they contain. They are also different from the German
tumuli which yielded the zoned vases, for in them the dead
were laid on one side and contracted. In their funeral rites
they only resemble the tumuli of Saxony, Thuringia,[8] and
the Rhenish area, in which vases with cord-impressions were

[1] De Loe, *Congrès de Dinan*, i, p. 269 ; Bosch Gimpera, in Ebert, **CCCXXIV,**
s.v. " Belgien ", i, p. 401.
[2] Goury, **CCCCLXXVII**, p. 95 ; Rademacher, s.v. " Haulzy ", in Ebert,
op. cit.
[3] Beaupré, **CCCCLXII**, pp. 29, 34–5.
[4] Ibid., p. 36. Id., repr., from **LXXIII**, 1909, for three funerary sites
of the Bronze Age, at Benney, Azelot, and Bezange-le-Grand, the last two
groups being of Bronze Age I.
[5] Du Chatellier, **CCCCLXXI**, pl. xiii.
[6] Tumuli of Kerougant in Plounévez-Lochrist (id., **CCCCLXX**, p. 88)
and Run Mellou Poaz in Spézet (ibid., p. 168).
[7] Tumuli of Kervern in Plozévet (ibid., p. 282 : coffin) and Ruguellou
in La Feuillée (ibid., p. 217). Cf. J. Loth, in **CXL**, 1920–1, p. 287, for tumulus
of La Garenne at Keruzun (vase with four handles).
[8] Schumacher, in **XXIX**, x, p. 13.

found [1]; for in these tombs also cremation was found side by side with inhumation.[2] The culture which they represent contributed to the making of that of the Adlerberg. Now, we have regarded the people of this culture as the core round which the Brythonic Celts formed.[3] Must we not conclude that these were the folk who suddenly shot out a tongue as far as Brittany after advancing slowly but on a wide front stretching from Belgium to Switzerland [4]?

Some tumuli in the Jura have been attributed to the second period of the Bronze Age, and doubtless others which have no furniture are of the same date.[5] At any rate, opposite the little camp of Mesnay which overlooks Arbois (this camp probably belongs to that time), the ground is dotted with small tumuli without furniture, which may be the tombs of the people of this and the neighbouring stations. What is more, the second period of the Bronze Age seems to have been a time of great disturbance. Our best evidence of this is the discovery of almost inaccessible refuge-caves, like that hollowed in the face of the cliff overhanging the source of the Liron north of Salins. It can only be reached by rope-ladders, and it contains hearths dating from that period. The people who then lived in these parts, whoever they were, had enemies from whom they had to protect themselves in impregnable retreats.

The third period of the Bronze Age is what Rhenish archæologists call the Tumulus Period in Western Germany.[6] This was the age of unification. The tumuli become more frequent in France, too, and their area of extension becomes wider. But they are still collected, at least at the beginning, chiefly in the eastern departments of France, those of Lorraine, Burgundy, and Franche-Comté, which have been better explored or are richer. The tombs, like the famous one at Courtavant in the Aube,[7] are exactly like those on the other side of the Rhine. The various modes of erecting tumuli are

---

[1] Åberg, **CCXCVII**.

[2] Schumacher, **CCCCIX**, pp. 63 ff.

[3] See above, p. 185.

[4] Did their area of extension run out to another point in the south ? Tumuli, Neolithic or of the Bronze Age, are found in the Alpes-Maritimes and Provence. M. Piroutet (in **XV**, 1915, p. 78) is inclined to think that they are local derivatives of the dolmen-tumulus.

[5] Piroutet, in **XV**, 1903, pp. 458 ff.

[6] Behrens, **CCCXCI**, p. 93 ; Schumacher, in **XXIX**, x, pp. 39 ff.

[7] Déchelette, ii, 1, p. 148.

common to both regions, whether they cover an oblong grave with stone walling, like that at Courtavant, or a small vault of unshaped stones built over the body.[1] But the weapons and ornaments of the dead are also the same, and some of them, such as the bracelet with coiled ends depicted in Fig. 39, come from beyond Germany and must have had their origin in the wealthy industry of the Hungarian region.[2]

At the end of this period, or in the fourth period of the Bronze Age, the tumuli are found a little further west than before, except for the extension into Brittany which I have mentioned. Southward they reach to the Lozère,[3] and northward to the Haute-Marne.

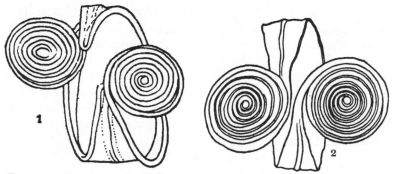

FIG. 39.   Bracelets with Coiled Ends. (Déchelette, ii, 1, figs. 47, 46.) 1, Swabian Jura. 2, La Combe-Bernard, Côte d'Or.

The funeral customs are now slightly changed. The dead placed in the tumuli were burned, not in all cases, but in some. But cremation seems to have come from the same country as the tumulus, for it was established in the Celtic territory in Germany before it reached France.

Not everything, however, that came to France from over the Rhine was Celtic. We know of cremation-cemeteries of this time which have no tumuli—those of Pougues-les-Eaux, Arthel in the Nièvre, and Dompierre in the Allier.[4] These cemeteries are rich in pottery, and their pottery is of a type which comes from a distance. It consists of carefully made

---

[1] Schumacher, op. cit., p. 73.
[2] Richly, **DLII.**
[3] Tumulus of La Roche-Rousse in the commune of Esclanèdes (Lozère) (Déchelette, ii, 1, pp. 154 ff.) ; other funerary types (ibid., p. 153).
[4] Ibid., p. 155.

vases, turned on the wheel, of fine clay, decorated with horizontal, perpendicular, or slanting grooves, cupules, and bosses surrounded by circular grooves. Similar cemeteries with the same pottery are found in greater numbers east of the Rhine,[1] but also a long way further east, even in Poland.[2] The pottery in them is the so-called Lausitz ware. It is fairly widespread in France,[3] and we shall find that it is still more so when we examine it more closely. It was imported or manufactured as far west as Dordogne and the depths of Brittany.

The Celtic settlements in Germany and Eastern France were not yet so dense but that there were gaps into which other peoples might insinuate themselves. The pottery of the Lausitz type was imported by other foreigners moving westwards, who came from further than the Celts. Perhaps this hypothesis gives the key to the problem raised by the appearance of the name of the Veneti by the Baltic, on the Po, and in Brittany.[4] In any case, we have to do with one of the groups of migrants, prehistoric or historic, of which there were many, nomadic or semi-nomadic. They contributed to the formation of the communities into which they were absorbed, and there seems to be only one left at this day, because it alone refuses to be absorbed—the Gypsies. We know so little about what goes on in our own world that we cannot ask for much more about prehistoric times.

At the end of the Bronze Age the tanged sword extended over an area which covered that of the tumuli and reached somewhat further to the west and south. This sword has been found near Paris, and in the departments of the Cher,

---

[1] Behrens, op. cit., pp. 160 ff. ; Schumacher, in **XXIX**, x, p. 45. Herr Rademacher, in Ebert, **CCCXXIV**, vi, p. 282, s.v. " Kelten ", suggests that the men of the *Urnenfelder*, being of Alpine stock, formed the Celtic race by uniting in Western Germany with the men of the tumuli. He also regards their invasion as being of a violent nature. The facts are not so clear, and one may differ entirely from his view.

[2] See above, p. 168.

[3] Hubert, in **CXLIII**, 1910, pp. 108 ff. ; Bleicher and Beaupré, **CCCCLXVI**, p. 33 (cave of la Baume, Doubs) ; Philippe, **CCCCLXXXVIII**, pp. 50 ff. (Fort-Harrouard).

[4] **LXXXV**, 1922, p. 59. The pottery with deeply in-cut decoration found in the tumuli of the Charente, the Gard, and the forest of Hagenau is to be contrasted with that of Lausitz. According to Herr Rademacher (in **LXXXV**, 1926, pp. 14 ff.), vases with this decoration are further evidence of the expansion of the Celts in the Bronze Age. If so, we must slightly increase the area occupied by them in France at that time.

Vézère, Vaucluse, Drôme, and Var.   Until we have more information we can admit that both swords and tumuli represent the area covered by the Celts in France in the Bronze Age, but that the latter alone represent the slow, age-long advance of the Celts of Southern Germany, the Brythonic Celts.

CHAPTER IV

CELTIC EXPANSION ON THE CONTINENT IN THE HALLSTATT PERIOD

I

THE CELTS IN THE EAST OF FRANCE

IN Germany it is to the third period of the Bronze Age, in France to the Hallstatt Period, that archæologists have given the name of the Tumulus Period.[1] For the practice of burying under tumuli became general in the eastern departments of France and made its way to the western departments. These tumuli,[2] which vary very much in size, and are often enlarged by secondary burials, are in the main composed of a stone erection, which unfortunately has always fallen in, formed of large rubble pieces arranged in vaulting, covered by a pile of smaller material and sometimes by a chape of beaten earth. The remains of the man for whom the tumulus was originally built were laid on a floor or in a pit. The monument was completed by circles of stones, which sometimes constituted the whole monument, unless the rest has been removed in later times.[3] The dead were interred or burned according to the place, time, tribe, and social conditions.[4] The French tombs resemble those of Germany [5] in characteristic details of construction as in contents. The invasion which had gone on through the Bronze Age seems to have continued, but without the participation of the people of the urn-fields, who still kept themselves distinct from the rest on the other side of the Rhine.

The tanged bronze swords and the thick-hilted bronze swords of the Mörigen type,[6] which we have considered above

---

[1] Déchelette, ii, 2, p. 630.
[2] Ibid., pp. 631 ff. ; Viollier, **CCCCXCI**, pp. 35 ff.
[3] Déchelette, p. 649 (Pommard), 641 ff.
[4] Inhumation seems to be prevalent in eastern France and at the beginning of the Hallstatt Period (ibid., p. 632). Cremation is general in the south-west and in Brittany at the end of that period (ibid., pp. 681–2).
[5] Schumacher, in **XXIX**, x, p. 51 ; Behrens, in **CLXXVII**, 1927, pp. 125 ff.
[6] The first phase of the Hallstatt Period (Hallstatt A), according to Reinecke, **CCCXCIX**, v, pp. 231–247.

as indications of that invasion, are already in great part Hallstatt swords (Map 10). The large, blunt-ended bronze swords with nicks at the sides of the base are even fairly far advanced in the series of products of the Hallstatt culture. Some have been found in tumuli.[1]

MAP 10. Swords and Daggers in the Hallstatt Period. + = bronze swords ; o = large iron swords ; ● = iron daggers with antennæ. (Déchelette, ii, 2, map ii.)

Tumuli which from their large iron swords must be assigned to the middle of the Hallstatt Period have been explored in Belgium [2] and in the French departments of the Meurthe-et-Moselle, Vosges, Haute-Marne, Côte d'Or, Jura,

---

[1] Those of the Combe d'Ain (E. Clerc and J. Le Mire, in **LXXXIV**, 1877, p. 471), the Barrières at Miers (Lot) (Prunières, in **XXVI**, 1887, Toulouse, ii, p. 698), the Roche-Rousse at Esclanèdes (Lozère) (ibid.), and St.-Aoustrille (Cher).   Cf. the statistics in Déchelette, ii, 2, p. 725.

[2] Court-St.-Etienne (Comhaire, in **XLIII**, 1894–5, pl. vi, pp. 53–4 ; Déchelette, p. 615).

Ain, Nièvre, Cher, Vienne, Cantal, Lozère, Aveyron, Lot, and Drôme.[1] In the Cher particularly several groups of large, rich tumuli show that there was already a considerable settlement, and not mere isolated colonies. Déchelette's map of the distribution of the large iron sword in France gives a fair notion of the extension of the tribes from across the Rhine in that country. It only differs from the map which one might make for this period in that it represents larger and more homogeneous settlements than yet existed.

But it is in the Côte d'Or and Francho-Comté, particularly about Salins, that is in the country which had long been occupied by the tumulus-builders, that we can best judge of their increase.

The Moidons forest,[2] between Salins and Arbois, is an immense cemetery of tumuli. The number has been reckoned at about forty thousand. The group of tombs at Alaise, north of Salins, is also very large. Far the most of the datable tumuli are of the Hallstatt Period. Another considerable group extended north of Dijon between the upper Seine and the upper Aube, and there were others to the south.

These huge cemeteries represent a large population. They were a people attached to the country, who had adapted it to their own practices. There were strong towns, refuge-camps, such as the camp of Château-sur-Salins, which covers about fifty acres. Here four fortified towns overlooked the ground where the small town of Salins now stands, on the hill of the camp of Château, on Mont St.-André, on Mont Poupet, and on the hill of Fort Belin. In Burgundy [3] a line of fortified enclosures ran along the heights overlooking the valley of the Saône. These Hallstatt Celts seem to have settled for choice on high ground, and as a rule in places where there are now forests or brush, for it is always there, all over France (and the same might be said of Germany), that their tumuli and their fortified towns (when these have not survived as modern towns) are found.

They evidently did not live too far away from their tombs and their strongholds. There they had their fields, sometimes overlooked by tombs, as in Bavaria in the Bronze Age, and

---

[1] Déchelette, p. 728.
[2] Piroutet, in **XV**, 1900, pp. 369 ff. ; 1908, pp. 437, 700 ; 1904, pp. 297 ff. ; **CXXXIX**, 1904, 2, pp. 52 ff. ; 1928, 2, pp. 220 ff. ; Déchelette, p. 750.
[3] Déchelette, pp. 641 ff., 693 ff.

their clearing of the fields of stones still shows the regular lay-out of the fields ; there they had their peace-time and summer dwellings. If we were to add to this picture the immense labour of clearing the forests we should have to imagine the districts in which they were in force as being at least as densely populated as they are to-day. But the Hallstatt people were pastoral, and had herds of goats which helped to keep down the forest, which only developed after their time. The country was traversed by roads or tracks of a fairly fixed kind,[1] the line of which was determined by the configuration of the land, and these have been grooved with deep ruts by the small four-wheeled chariots of which remains are found in many tombs. We can form a fairly true picture of the warriors, with shaven faces (they look their razors with them into their graves), long, broad iron swords with heavy conical pommels and wooden sheaths, seldom wearing helmets, and wearing Italic helmets when they did, seldom having breastplates, and carrying round shields of which only a very few metal specimens survive.

The disposition of their tumuli gives a somewhat vague idea of their social formations. A group like that of Magny-Lambert, with the heaps of stones which accompany the monuments and may be either houses or other buildings, the form of which we cannot restore, recalls the tribal centres, the meeting-places which were also burying-grounds, the most typical examples of which are to be found in the Irish epics. Others represent centres of only relative density.

Now just at the end of this Hallstatt Period we are able to give their true name to the inhabitants of the Franche-Comté.

Marseilles was founded about 600 B.C. About 500 the Massaliots were importing into the districts of Dijon and Salins and further north amphoras, probably full of wine, craters for the preparation of drinks, œnochoës, and painted cups from Attica. These were fragile goods which would not have stood a long journey overland, and were probably carried by boat up the Saône and, for Salins, up the Loue, which is navigable as far as Port-Lesney. The Greeks, therefore, knew something about the ethnology of the region. The

---

[1] E. Euvrard, in **XLV**, 1924, p. 103 (Gallic road from Besancon to Beures, Aveney, and Chenecey).

ancient geographers make the border-line of the Celts and the Ligurians run somewhere about the Lake of Geneva and the middle course of the Rhone. If they had been precise folk they would doubtless have told us that the Celts were already on the left bank of the Rhone in Haute-Savoie, and even further west, for tumuli have been found in the Hautes-Alpes (at Chabestan), Vaucluse (at l'Agnel in the commune of Pertuis), Bouches-du-Rhône, and Gard. But these are the remains of small isolated groups, not to be compared to those of the north and north-west. In any case, in the fifth century, if the Ligurian peoples mentioned by Apollonios and Avienus were still to be found on the shores of the Lake of Geneva they were surrounded by Celts ; and it may be that they existed only as a memory.

If the people on the right bank of the Rhone at that time were Celts, we can hardly doubt that their Bronze Age predecessors were Celts, too, at least in great part. If the persistence of the funeral rites did not prove it, the presence of Bronze Age and Hallstatt tombs side by side in groups of tumuli which appear to have been tribal cemeteries should convince us. It is, however, certain that the signs of the expansion of the Hallstatt culture are not explained by the normal growth of population. New tribes came from east of the Rhine, with the large bronze sword and with the iron sword. This latter was made on the spot in Burgundy and Berry, where iron was plentiful and easy to work. But the models came from Central Europe and with them all the Italic bronze vessels, the *ciste a cordoni*, the riveted pails, etc., which are characteristic features of the richest sepultures of the earlier Hallstatt Periods.

It was, moreover, not until the second half of the Hallstatt Period that the Celtic population of Lorraine, Franche-Comté and even Burgundy reached its maximum, if, indeed, we can yet argue from the chronological results of the latest excavations. The statistics of the discoveries made in the region of Salins show very clearly that far more tombs have been found dating from the second half of the Hallstatt Period than from the first. The population may have increased naturally in peace and prosperity. It may also have received augmentations from outside. This hypothesis fits the facts better. It seems still more reasonable, if we take into account a series of other facts which we are now going to examine. It has sometimes been thought that the hypothetical movements of peoples gave rise to violent conflicts, and that the first occupants resisted the newcomers by force of arms. They certainly had many fortresses with walls built in the Gallic fashion of a combination of beams and stones, against which the backs of their houses were set. These have been exalted by some students into scientific systems defending tribal territories. The insecurity of a disunited society is perhaps sufficient to explain the great number of these works.

II

THE CELTS IN THE DOMAIN OF THE PILE-DWELLERS

What was happening on the outskirts of the Celtic world, enlarged in the manner described above, and, first of all, what was happening on the other side of the Jura in Switzerland ? Switzerland is one of the countries of Europe whose prehistory is not only best known but clearest. Of it, as of the British Isles, one might say that the general currents of prehistory end there, but they only filter in.

During a considerable part of Neolithic times and all the Bronze Age, Switzerland was the chief home of the builders oi palafittes or lake-villages. On the shores of the Swiss lakes they had found the conditions of life which they wanted. They lived crammed between the forests, which probably came further down than to-day, and the lakes ; and their dwellings, tilled fields, and pasturages doubtless took up every scrap of habitable, cultivable, and pasturable ground in that inconvenient and unattractive country. We know that they had other settlements in France, Southern Germany, the Danube basin, and Northern Italy, which progressively broke away, shrank, and became absorbed in those of their neighbours.[1] We are almost justified in giving them a name.[2]

It would seem that in the height of the Bronze Age the people of the lake-villages enjoyed the maximum of comfort in their habitats. The level of the lakes fell, the sign of a drier and hotter climate, and it is noted that the buildings of this

---

[1] Munro and Rodet, **CCCLXIII** ; Ischer, **CCCCLXXXIX** ; Ebert, **CCCXXIV**, s.v. " Pfahlbau ".

[2] They were probably Ligurians. Déchelette, ii, 1, p. 15.

time stand at some distance from the ancient shore-line.[1]
The forests probably became clearer through the same causes,
and the grazing-grounds wider. This change of climate was
not peculiar to the region of the lake-dwellings. The Swedish
geologist Sernander has studied it in the peat-bogs of the
north,[2] which present everywhere, at the same level, a stratum
of dry ground corresponding to the same epoch. Just as
in the milder climate of the Bronze Age the civilization of the
Baltic straits rose to a dazzling prosperity, so that of the
pile-villages blossomed out, and its influence spread to Celtic
Germany and to Eastern Gaul, which was in process of
becoming Celtic.

One point in the civilization of the lake-dwellers remains
a mystery. How did they dispose of their dead [3] ? There are
not many sepultures contemporaneous with the lake-villages,
and they may be the work either of the descendants of tribes
which had previously held the country or of small groups of
newcomers which were absorbed to a greater or less extent.
Perhaps the practice was not definitely established, and
varied. But it is probable that the people of the pile-villages
kept their dead near them, as they did in their terrestrial
stations,[4] or in the late palafitte of Donja-Dolina.[5] They
could keep them on the palafitte itself, or put them in coffins
between the piles, or throw them into the water. Now, at
the beginning of the Bronze Age, there were tumulus-builders
in the north of Switzerland,[6] in the obtuse angle formed by
the Aar and the Rhine, in contact with Germany ; their
funerary ritual clearly distinguishes them from the lake-
dwellers.

At the end of the Bronze Age or, more exactly, after the
first Hallstatt Period, that of the short bronze sword,[7] the
lake-villages were abandoned, and it would seem rather
suddenly. The excavations reveal traces of burning ; but
accidental fires cannot have been infrequent. Skeletons

---

[1] Ischer, pp. 140 ff. ; Déchelette, ii, 1, pp. 112 ff.
[2] Ebert, op. cit., vii, 6 ff., s.v. " Klimatverschlechterung " ; Gerland,
Beiträge zur Geophysik, 1912, pp. 115 ff.
[3] Viollier, **CCCCXCII**, pp. 10 ff.
[4] Stations of the Michelsberg type (Schumacher, **CCCCIX**, i, pp. 26 ff. ;
W. Brehmer, in Ebert, **CCCXXIV**, s.v. " Michelsberg-Typus ").
[5] Truhelka, **DLVI**, 1902, pp. 1 ff. (Donja-Dolina).
[6] See above, pp. 247–8.
[7] This sword is found in the palafittes and is there classified as the Mörigen
sword (Ischer, op. cit., pl. xiii).

and remains of skeletons have been found, and I have given the reason. There is no patent incontestable fact to show that there was a catastrophe or a battle or violence of any kind.[1] The climate became wet and cold again, and the villages were submerged.

What became of the inhabitants ? They lived on in the mountains, where they clung to their old economic habits, tilling minute fields and raising large flocks and herds. They kept their old methods of building. The barns reared on posts which are dotted about the valley-sides faithfully repeat the construction of the lake-dwellings, of which the chalets are a more distant reproduction. When iron came into use the people of the pile-dwellings, who had had to cut quantities of wood painfully with axes of stone or bronze, found themselves in possession of an excellent stock of woodman's tools, which enabled them to move up to less damp areas in the bottoms of high-lying valleys at a level of about 3,000 feet. It is true that no trace of them is to be seen there.[2] But perhaps this objection is not fatal. For one thing, the lake-dwellers can never have been very numerous ; and when they were dispersed over an area wider than their previous habitat they must have been few and far between. For another the Swiss archæologists who have devoted themselves to the study of the palafittes and of the Gallic tumuli and cemeteries have not yet found any trace of the people, and perhaps have not sought it much. It is revealed by its work, which is the clearing of the forests on the first plateaus. Besides, history implies its existence.[3]

The second change of climate was general, like the first. The Scandinavian peat-bogs present above the dry stratum later formations of peat, which in some cases can be dated. In the north of inhabited Europe the climatic change resulted in depopulation and southward movements which determined the distribution of the Germanic peoples in the centre and east of Germany for a long time. In the west we can imagine flooded coasts, overflowing swamps, the Germans of the North Sea making for warmer climes and coming into contact with the Celts, and the latter beginning to leave the

---

[1] Schæffer, in **CXXXVIII**, 1926, p. 228.
[2] Schumacher, s.v. " Schweiz ", in Ebert, **CCCXXIV**, ii, pp. 403 ff.
[3] See the following volume in this series, *ad init.*

wet forests of Westphalia, Hessen, and the Bavarian Alps and establishing themselves in numbers on the other side of the Rhine. It has been supposed that the drying of the forests in the Bronze Age opened up those of Alsace to the Celts [1] and encouraged their expansion. The return of the cold and of abundant rainfall may have had much the same result.

At the time when the palafitte-builders were retreating new tumulus-builders arrived in Switzerland, apparently by two routes.[2] Some crossed the Rhine about Schaffhausen and advanced as far as the Reuss. The others crossed about Basle, reached the Aar, and ascended its valley and those of its higher tributaries. So they came to the neighbourhood of Lausanne. They did not, properly speaking, supplant the people of the pile-dwellings, and they seem to have stopped at the lakes of Thun, Zug, and Zurich.

Their tumuli are in quite small groups. From this it is easy to infer that the builders never stayed very long in one place. As in France, too, they stand on the medium heights overlooking the great Swiss valleys. They are the relics of tribes of stock-raisers and hunters. But those tribes never formed large, permanent settlements like those of France.

Moreover, the Hallstatt tribes of Switzerland did not comprise very large numbers. Their tumuli can be reckoned not in thousands, but in hundreds, and there are but few hundreds.

This somewhat sparse population was increasing in the second half of the Hallstatt Period.[3] Far the most of the tumuli belong to this time. In this respect the situation is the same in Switzerland as in the French Jura.

We may ask whether at least some of the Hallstatt tribes of Switzerland did not come from France. The objects found in the tumuli on both sides of the frontier are the same.[4] Fashions changed in both countries in the same way. But most of the Swiss tumuli contained cremations.[5] Among the

---

[1] Schæffer, in **CXXXVIII**, 1926, pp. 222–9 ; cf. Hubert, in **XVI**, 1929, pp. 132–5.

[2] Déchelette, ii, 2, pp. 612–615 ; Viollier, **CCCCXC**, p. 4 ; id., **CCXCII**, pp. 81 ff. For their tumuli, see the Swiss journals, esp. **XVII** : J. Wiedmer, 1908, p. 89 (near Subingen) ; von Sucy and Schultheiss, 1909, p. 1 (Gaisberg near Kreuzlingen) ; H. Breuil, 1910, p. 169 (the Murat wood near Matran) ; Viollier and Blanc, 1907, p. 93 (Niederwenigen) ; etc.

[3] Viollier, **CCCCXCII**, p. 51.

[4] Wiedmer, in **XVII**, 1909, i (tumuli, Nos. v–viii, xi).

[5] Viollier, loc. cit., and map 4.

inhumations, moreover, there is a large proportion of La Tène tombs dug in the tumuli. Again, the Swiss tombs are as rich in pottery as the French are poor. The tumulus-builders seem, therefore, to have come straight from Bavaria, where the two rites were practised, cremation being preferred.

There is no doubt that they were Celts. Although they did not come from Franche-Comté, the demonstration made in the case of the people of Franche-Comté holds equally for them. They were Celts, come direct from the cradle of the Celtic peoples.

Small as the Hallstatt population of Switzerland was, it none the less represents a migration of people from the south of Germany which, if only as an indication, is of importance. This shifting of population probably took place in more than one wave, at least in two, at the beginning of the Hallstatt period and towards the middle, like the migration into France ; but what is still only a hypothesis in the case of France can be taken as a certainty in that of Switzerland.

To perceive the full significance of these facts we must set them in their place in the whole of archæology and ancient history. At the beginning of the Hallstatt period there were movements of peoples from the centre of Europe to the south, the scale of which we can estimate. This was when the Umbrians descended into Italy. There they took the place of the people of the *terremare*, as the Celts of Switzerland had taken the place left empty by the lake-dwellers. A date for this event is provided by Cato the Elder, quoted by Pliny.[1] It took place at the time of the foundation of the Umbrian town of Ameria, which occurred, we are told, 963 years before the war of the Romans with Perseus, that is in 1134. About the same time the Dorians invaded Greece, forming the last wave of the Hellenes.[2]

Whence did the Dorians come ? From the North and from Illyria. Whence did the Umbrians come ? They certainly descended gradually from somewhere about Bohemia, in the neighbourhood of the Celts. It is impossible that movements of tribes on such a scale should have had no effect on their neighbours, setting them free to move or

---

[1] *N.H.*, 111, 114 ; Grenier, **DXXIX**, pp. 505 ff. ; Homo, **CCCXLI**, English, pp. 50–1.

[2] Jardé, **CCCXLV**, English, pp. 75–6.

encouraging them to follow, to say nothing of the change in climate, creating new vacancies and new attractions, and the migrations which it provoked. The emigration of the Celts must have been connected with the great movements of peoples which were happening at the same time, and it probably did not fall short of them in size. Moreover, about the beginning of the Hallstatt period, the Celtic peoples of Western Germany had quite emerged from the stage of incohesion corresponding to the first half of the Bronze Age. Their numbers were great. The use of iron had increased their powers tenfold. They could cut roads through the forests.[1] They had wagons, of which they have left specimens.[2] Above all, they had new and better weapons. That is why the beginning of the first Iron Age witnessed a tremendous commotion among the Celtic peoples. It did not subside altogether. The movement began again some centuries later. We shall now see how far it went.

III

THE FIRST DESCENTS OF THE CELTS INTO ITALY

By the end of the Hallstatt Period the Celts had already advanced considerably beyond the limits of the area which we have been surveying. They had crossed them on the south-eastern side and joined their Osco-Umbrian cousins in Italy. These latter had probably come in by the eastern passes of the Alps, whereas the Celts entered by the western passes, having come either through the Valais, where they had not halted,[3] or through Savoy, where they have left some traces of their stay.[4]

This was the date which Livy [5] gives to the Gallic invasion of Italy, which, he says, occurred in the time of Tarquin the Elder, between 614 and 576. Also, according to Plutarch,[6] a Greek poet named Simylos ascribed the tragic death of Tarpeia to the Celts, and not to the Sabines. Historians

---

[1] J. Fleure, in **LXXVI**, 1916, p. 143.
[2] Déchelette, ii, 2, pp. 747 ff.
[3] Viollier, in **XVII**, 1912, map.
[4] See above, p. 257.
[5] v, 33 : *Prisco Tarquinio Romæ regnante.*
[6] *Rom.*, 17.

are divided as to the amount of faith to be placed in these statements.[1]

If we adhere to the historical texts rigidly we cannot say that there were Gauls in Italy before the fourth century ; at the earliest, they can only have come a few years before the battle of the Allia.[2] Livy's story does not conflict, save in the date, with the others, but he indicates in a sentence, to which too little attention has been paid, that the invasion of Bellovesus had been preceded by another. " They crossed the Alps," he says, " by the country of the Taurini and the valley of the Dora Baltea, defeated the Etruscans near the Ticino, and hearing that the place in which they had halted was called the Plain of the Insubres (*agrum Insubrium*), that is by the very same name as a sub-tribe of the Ædui (*cognomine Insubribus, pago Hœduorum*), regarded this as an omen, which they followed, and founded a city there (*ibi omen sequentes loci condidere urbem*)." This was Milan. So Bellovesus had been preceded by a body of Insubres who had at least left, near Milan, their name, which was still known at the time of the great invasion. The passage should be borne in mind, for it gives the most ancient name of a Celtic people which we can put down on our historical maps.

The question now takes on a very different shape.

In 1827 at Zignano, in the valley of the Vara, the chief tributary of the Magra, which flows into the Mediterranean south of the Gulf of Spezia, a cippus was found surmounted by a very crudely sculptured head and bearing an inscription in Etruscan characters, running downwards, which reads *Mezunemusus*. A series of similar cippi have been found in the same region, but in these the head rises from a body, still incorporated in the block, but having arms, legs, and attributes which, as we shall see, have an ethnological meaning. A first group of four stones comes from the communes of Villafranca (the wood of Filetto and the castle of Malgrate) and Mulazzo (the parish of Lusuolo). One bears

---

[1] They have been accepted by many, including Alexandre Bertrand, who placed the descent of the first Celts into Italy still earlier, about 1000 B.C. It is true that he did not disguise the fact that these first Celts were Umbrians. The Umbrians were Celts, properly speaking. Those who came later were the Gauls. See Bertrand and Reinach, **DXLII**, pp. 43 ff.

[2] Meyer, **CCCLIV**, v, p. 153 ; Mommsen, **CCCLIX**, English, vol. i, pp. 337–8 ; Müllenhoff, **CCCLXII**, ii, p. 247 ; Jullian, **CCCXLVII**, i, p. 289 ; Niese, in **CLXVIII**, 1898, pp. 113 ff. ; id., in **CCCLXVIII**, vii, pp. 613–17.

an inscription, which is unluckily indecipherable. Three represent armed warriors ; the fourth a woman.[1] Another group of more archaic character was afterwards discovered in the commune of Fivizzano, in the parish of Cecina.[2] These stones stood in their original place and position, set in a regular row in a black soil revealing traces of animal matter. A third group also has been published.[3]

By the peculiarities of their armament the warriors of the first group have been identified as Gauls. They are naked, with the sword attached not to a baldric but to a waist-belt, and on the right, not the left. In their right hand they hold an axe which may be the *cateia*, and in their left javelins, which may be *gæsa*.[4]

If the figures are Gauls the inscription should be Gallic. Attempts were at first made to read it as Etruscan, but with no success whatever. But the Celtic appearance of the word will at once emerge if we take the various values of the Etruscan *z* into account. On the one hand it is equivalent to *ti*, *di*.[5] In that case *Mezunemusus* can be read as *Mediunemusus*, and can be compared with the place-names Νεμωσσός (Nemours, Clermont-Ferrand),[6] Medionemeton (Kirkintilloch, near Glasgow), and Mediolanum. Mediolanum probably means the Middle Sanctuary ; the cippus is a boundary-mark, not a tombstone. Secondly, the *z* may represent the dental sibilant of Celtic, which is expressed in writing by δ, ð, *d*, or *s*, either single or duplicated.[7] So *Mezu* would be *Meddu*, which appears in the names Messulus, Meddilu, Methillus, etc. The meaning of the word is indicated by Irish *midiur* " I judge ", " I measure ". *Mezunemusus*, then, would mean " he who takes care of the holy places " or " who measures them ", and would be the proper name of a man. The main thing is that the word is Celtic and that the presence of the Celts on the coast of Liguria, in the valleys of

[1] U. Mazzini, *Monumenti celtici in Val di Magra*, repr. from **LXVIII**, 1908, p. 29 ; Hubert, in **CXXXIX**, 1909, ii, pp. 52–4 ; id., in **CXL**, 1913, pp. 418 ff. ; M. Giuliani, *Di nuovi studi sui Celtici in Italia secundo monumenti recentemente scoperti in Italia*, repr. from **LXVIII**, 1923.

[2] U. Mazzini, in **LIII**, 1909, pp. 65 ff.

[3] Id., ibid., 1923, p. 73.

[4] They had no shield. Cf. Varro, *De Vita Pop. Rom.*, iii, 14 : *qui gladiis cincti sine scuto cum binis gaesis essent.*

[5] Vendryès, in **CXL**, 1913, p. 423.

[6] Strabo, iv, 2, 3.

[7] Rhys, in **VII**, 37.

the Vara and Magra, is attested by a group of monuments which are certainly akin and probably contemporaneous.

Their date is indicated by that of the sword represented on the stones of the first group. It is the Hallstatt dagger with antennæ, a number of specimens of which have been unearthed by excavation in Celtic lands.

Of these daggers with antennæ, the first origin of which was perhaps Italian, forms are known which are peculiar to Italy ; but it is not with them that we now have to deal.[1] Those on the cippi are imported weapons, and earlier than the great historical invasion of the fourth century. They had gone out of use when this took place ; the dagger with antennæ had lengthened and become the La Tène sword which is described by the ancient writers and discovered by archæologists.[2] Any Gauls who can at that time have come as far as Liguria had certainly not preserved an obsolete armament. It is almost universally agreed that the daggers with antennæ represented on our cippi were used within the extreme dates of 700 and 500 B.C. They are among the features usually taken as characteristic of the last phase of the Hallstatt culture. These dates suit the Italic buckets and bronze plaques on which much the same weapons are represented as on the cippi.[3] They also suit the whole set of objects (including the bucket) found in the famous tomb of Sesto Calende on the Ticino, south of Lake Maggiore, among which there is a short sword with antennæ.[4] Lastly they suit the late part of the cemeteries of Golasecca, Castelletto Ticino, etc., which form a large and peculiar necropolis on the plateau of Somma Ticinese, south of Lake Maggiore.[5] They must suit our cippi. From these chronological considerations one must conclude that the Gauls descended into Italy earlier than is usually supposed.

The cippi of Cecina are still older. Two of them represent men, with a dagger engraved, horizontally, below the hands. It is not the dagger with antennæ depicted at Villafranca, but one of more ancient appearance, which might be of

---

[1] Déchelette, ii, 2, pp. 740 ff.

[2] Hubert, loc. cit.

[3] On the bucket from the Certosa of Bologna, the man doing sacrifice holds a sword with antennæ.

[4] Montelius, **DXXXIV,** pl. lxii ; Hoernes, in **XXIII,** 1905, 294 ; Déchelette, ii, 2, p. 721.

[5] Montelius, op. cit., p. 233.

bronze, but which might also be a sword, a sword with a heavy round pommel like those of Hallstatt, conventionally reduced to the size of a dagger. These cippi are too crude to be used as an argument. They complete the series, that is all. If the others are Celtic these must be, and this conclusion will hold good so long as Liguria as a whole does not yield others which demand another hypothesis.

The valleys of the Magra and its tributary the Vara make passages in the Ligurian Apennines, descending from passes to which the valley of the Taro on the other slope gives access. This is a gateway into the country ; indeed, it is the most convenient entrance. One can easily understand an advanced body of Gauls establishing themselves there, in Ligurian territory. Our cippi, confined as they are to a small area, certainly look as if they had belonged to an outpost, a colony in a strange land.[1]

But an outpost implies an army. Behind the advanced guards, camping in the passes which led to the coast over the Apennines from the plain of the Po, there must have been other bodies at intervals. If there were no trace of these it would be hard to imagine a small Gallic colony established in the sixth century beside a mountain route hundreds of miles from any Gallic country. But the necropoles of the Ticino are probably traces of their main settlement.[2]

The western cemeteries of the Po valley are sufficiently unlike those of the east at this time to forbid us to ascribe them to the same peoples.[3] In each case there was a new civilization, without any very perceptible connection with that of the previous occupants of the country, who lived in

[1] Issel, **DXXX**, p. 673 ; cf. ibid., p. 594. Sig. Issel observes that the country had many attractions, including mineral wealth—the mines of Serravezza (in the Apuan Alps), il Mesco, Sestri Levante. For Celtic penetration in Liguria, see ibid., p. 670 ; on its date, Sig. Issel is as vague as can be.

[2] Montelius describes the tomb at Sesto Calende as Gallic, but we may suspect that he makes it too late. Ridgeway, Pigorini, A. Bertrand, and S. Reinach regard it and those of Golasecca as Celtic. But their definition of the Celts is rather loose, and has included, at once or alternatively, the Ligurians, Umbrians, Illyrians, and Rætians. It is not likely that when the Italici entered Italy they were already differentiated, not only from the Celts, but from one another. Montelius, op. cit., p. 64, 6 ; Ridgeway, **DLIII**, pp. 48 ff. ; Pigorini, *I Primitivi Abitatori della valle del Po*, repr. from **CXXV**, 1892, fasc. 3 ; Bertrand and Reinach, **DXLII**, pp. 57–8, 63, etc. Cf. Hubert, loc. cit.

[3] Montelius, op. cit., pp. 232 ff. ; Déchelette, ii, 2, p. 536 ; Sergi, **DXL**, passim.

the pile-villages and *terremare*.   The latter had ceased to
build their quadrangular towns in the north of Italy
at the dawn of the Iron Age, or before it.   The civilization
of the eastern side, which is called after Villanova, was that
of the Umbrians, the last Italici to arrive, since it flourished
at Bologna before the Etruscans took possession of it.[1]   The
western culture, to which archæologists attach the name of
Golasecca, may be that of the first Celtic invaders.

It is very clearly distinguished from the other by its
pottery and the construction of its tombs.   We do not find
in Lombardy the characteristic biconical urn of Villanova.
Nor do we find the pit-grave of the Umbrian country.   The
pottery consists chiefly of spherical urns and vases with
a hollow foot.   The oldest urns are adorned with parallel
bands of incised triangles.   In the latest vases these bands are
separated by cordons in relief, and are either smooth or filled
with criss-cross lines made with the burnishing-tool.   This
ware was evidently influenced by that made at the same time
in the east of the Po valley, around Este, among a third
people, the Veneti.[2]

The tombs either are tumuli of rubble, like that at Sesto
Calende, or consist of a stone cist buried not very deep but
surrounded by a stone circle, the circles being connected by
parallel lines of rubble.   These stone circles suggest tumuli
of earth washed away by rains.   Lastly, tombs of the Golasecca
type have been explored at Castello Valtravaglia, in the
province of Como, on which there were stelæ—absolutely
formless, it is true.[3]

But it is not altogether evident that the civilization of
Golasecca was not connected by some obscure links with
the autochthonous culture of the Ligurians who had
previously occupied the lake stations, at that time deserted,
at the foot of the Alps.[4]   The excavations at the Isola Virginia
by the shore of Lake Varese have yielded some fragments of
a pottery resembling that of Golasecca.[5]   It is, therefore, quite
possible that the lake-village which formed the Isola Virginia
was still occupied at the time when the cemetery of Golasecca

---

[1] Modestov, **DXXXV**, pp. 287 ff. ; Grenier, **DXXIX**, pp. 460 ff. and passim.
[2] See below, p. 275.
[3] Magni, **DXXXI** ; Montelius, op. cit., pp. 252 ff. (Castello Valtravaglia).
[4] Pigorini, in **XXVII**, 1884 ; Déchelette, ii, 2, p. 536.
[5] Castelfranco, **DXXVI**, pls. xii ff. ; Munro, **CCCLXIII**, p. 195.

was opened. But it certainly did not last so long. Moreover, except for these few potsherds, the objects found at the two sites have nothing in common. On the contrary, these abandoned villages and these tombs of a new form, grouped in new districts, mean that great changes had taken place in the country, changes of race. In Switzerland the same signs led us to infer a settlement of the Celts. In Italy (if it is admitted, for similar reasons, that the Umbrians occupied about the same time the Veronese and Emilia) we are justified in thinking, with all the reservations entailed by our ignorance, that the same Celts then descended into Lombardy and Piedmont.

What is more, the tombs and the pottery have equivalents in Celtic lands. The lines of stone connecting the tumuli

FIG. 40. Tall-footed Vase from the Tumulus of Liviers, Dordogne.
(Déchelette, ii, 2, fig. 330.)

are found in Bavaria as early as the Bronze Age, and in Burgundy and the forest of the Moidons. The stone circles are found with the tumuli in Burgundy and in the districts last conquered by the Hallstatt culture in the south-west of France.[1] The vases characteristic of the cemetery of Golasecca have their prototypes in the Bavarian tumuli of the end of the Bronze Age. It is in the West, in the pottery of the Lake of le Bourget, in the tumuli of Aquitaine (Fig. 40), and even in the Hallstatt stations of the English coast, that we see their closest kindred.[2]

This culture of the western plain of the Po had penetrated

[1] Naue, **CCCCII**, pls. xli, 1 ; xlii, 2 ; xliii, 2 ; xliv, 1 ; xlv, 2 ; Bertrand and Reinach, op. cit., 82.
[2] Naue, ibid. ; Morin-Jean, in **LX**, Chambéry, 1908, p. 600 ; Déchelette, ii, 2, pp. 815; 817 ; **CCCLXXXIV**, pp. 24–8.

into Liguria. There the same tombs have been found, consisting of chambers of badly hewn slabs containing ossuaries and other vases, without decoration save in a few rare cases, but showing distant resemblances to those of Golasecca. These tombs are not very numerous. But what is remarkable is that most of them are found in the valleys of the Lunigiana.[1]

In short, if there were any Celts in Northern Italy before the invasion of the fourth century, they lived on the plateau of Somma, and the cemetery of Golasecca holds the remains of one contingent of them. Now, if we interpret the cippi of Villafranca and the inscription of Zignano aright, there were. Behind the advanced point to which these belong the main body occupied the banks of the Ticino. If these folk were not the forces of Bellovesus, they were perhaps the first Insubres.

They probably arrived as early as the first half of the Hallstatt Period, and were armed with large swords. But it was not until the second half that they settled in any force. This first colonization of Italy took place in two waves, like that of France and Switzerland, with a greater interval between them.

At the time when the cippus of Villafranca was carved, that is not long after the opening of the cemetery of Golasecca, the Etruscans, advancing northwards, crossed the Apennines and civilized and subjugated Umbrian Emilia. Certain Etruscan stelæ found at Bologna represent foot-soldiers, naked or armed, fighting Etruscan horsemen. These are probably all Gauls. The naked ones with long shields certainly are.[2] Their appearance would not have been familiar to the people of Bologna if there had been large, unbroken masses of Veneti on one side and Iberians or Ligurians on the other between them and Etruria before their sudden irruption. Polybios was therefore right in saying that the Gauls had been in immediate contact with the Etruscans [3] long before the collision of the fourth century.

This prolonged contact, first with the Umbrians and then with the Etruscans, had a civilizing influence, the results of which are apparent. Whether the stones of the Lunigiana

---

[1] Issel, op. cit., pp. 593 ff. ; Montelius, op. cit., pls. clxiv–clxv ; Issel, in **LIII**, 1912, pp. 39 ff.
[2] Grenier, **DXXIX**, pp. 453–5.
[3] ii, 17.

were idols or tombstones, they are something quite unique among Celtic finds. They are the oldest stone monuments which the Celts have left, their oldest attempts at sculpture with their oldest inscriptions. These efforts, ancient and crude as they are, might be worse. At first they were called menhir-statues.[1] But the cippi of Liguria have nothing in common with the French menhir-statues of the Aveyron— neither the shape nor the technique, nor the things represented, nor, above all, the date. They are like the Villanovan stelæ with a human outline of San Giovanni in Persiceto or Bologna.[2] So the Celtic colony in Liguria must have taken both its writing and its art from its neighbours. That means that it had other dealings with them than fighting and pillage.[3]

Let us try to imagine this first settlement of the Celts in Italy. First of all, the invaders came from a long way off. The occupants of the plateau of Somma Ticinese were in the habit of leaving much pottery in their tombs. It was not so in the Celtic countries nearest to Italy, Franche-Comté or Switzerland, but it was so in Lorraine and Bavaria. Therefore the bands which entered Italy passed beyond the tribes which were settled down on the fringe of the Alps and in the Jura. Their advance was in no way delayed by the barrier of the mountains, over which trade had long had its tracks.

Although the cemeteries of the Somma plateau are comparatively large, these first settlers did not come in solid masses. We must think of bands of Celts squeezing into the country among the Ligurians, now as guests and now as conquerors, but so few in numbers that they were bound to be absorbed and lost.

In his description of Cisalpine Gaul, Polybios describes a pastoral people living in a very primitive fashion [4] : " They live scattered in unwalled villages. The thousand things

---

[1] Cf. Hubert, in **CXL**, 1914, p. 41, n. 3. The only objects in France to which they can be compared are some small stelæ found at Orgon (Bouches-du-Rhône), on which the same semi-cubical owl-head appears. These might belong to the same family of monuments ; apart from that, they are equally unique.

[2] Ducati, in **LIII**, 1923, 83 (Saleta, N. of Bologna) ; Hoernes, **CCCXXXIX**, pp. 218 ff., 642 ; Grenier, op. cit., p. 416.

[3] Pettazzoni, in **CIII**, xxiv, p. 317.

[4] ii, 17.

which make life pleasant are unknown to them. Their only bed is hay or straw, their only food is meat, and, in short, they lead the simplest life. Strangers to anything outside war and stock-raising, they are ignorant of all science. Their wealth consists entirely in gold and in beasts, which are the only things that they can take away with them in all circumstances and move about at will." These features contrast with the account which he has given a few lines above of the fertile Cisalpine country and its agricultural wealth and with what we know of the Gallic settlements of the fourth century. They fit the Hallstatt Celts, who were generally pastoral.

In Italy they were barbarians, but inquisitive and well-meaning barbarians. Whether they allowed themselves to become absorbed or suffered severe set-backs, their settlements must have been steadily dwindling, if not absolutely deserted, when a second wave of Celts came down.

IV

THE CELTS ON THE NORTH-EAST OF ITALY

Another inscription, which has only just been translated satisfactorily by the Norwegian Celticist Marstrander,[1] shows that the Celts had about the same time reached the eastern end of the Alps, and were flowing over into Italy on that side. At Negau in Lower Styria, a short distance northeast of Marburg on the Drave, a deposit was found in 1912 containing about twenty bronze helmets of the Etrusco-Illyrian type represented on the Italic buckets which I have mentioned above.[2] On two of them there are *graffiti*, written in an alphabet of Etruscan type, like the Zignano inscription, in which the letters common to both are the same. The wording runs from right to left. Mr. Marstrander reads on one helmet :—

Siraku gurpi sarni eisvi tubni banuabi

that is, Sittanku Chorbi ; Isarni Tisuvii ; Dubni Banuabii. All these words are proper names, and they are all Celtic. In each case a man's name is followed by that of his father ;

[1] *Les Inscriptions des casques de Negau*, repr. from **CLII**, 1925, p. 37.
[2] Giovannelli, *Antichità scoperte presso Martraj*, p. 47, pl. ii ; Mommsen, in **CI**, vii, p. 208 ; S. Reinach, in **CXXXIX**, 1883, ii, p. 272.

the first is the signature of the maker, and the two others are the names of successive owners.

The second inscription yields a more unexpected reading :

harigasti teiva . . . i . . .

This is a Germanic proper name followed by a patronymic formed from the name of the god Tiwaz.

The date of these inscriptions is clearly that of the type of the helmets. Now these spherical bronze helmets (Fig. 41) continued in use for several centuries.[1] An example appears in the tomb of Sesto Calende,[2] and is probably the earliest. A bronze statuette found in the Illyrian cemetery of Idria near Bača [3] represents a warrior wearing a helmet of the same type, and it cannot be nearly so old. Others have been

FIG. 41. Spherical Helmets. (Ebert, *Reallexicon*, v, pl. lxxxix. Naturhistorisches Museum, Vienna.) 1, Magdalenenberg, near Laibach. 2, Etruscan type. 3, Watsch.

discovered in the Ticinese cemetery of Giubiasco with swords of La Tène III, and are of the first century before or after Christ.[4] It is true that the type developed. The spherical helmet was at first forged and made of plates riveted together ; later it was cast, the crown of the earlier type serving as a model. A concave band appeared between the brim and the spherical crown. The latter was provided with one or two crests, or was pinched together at the top. The Negau helmet is intermediate between the archaic types of the seventh or sixth century and the later examples from Giubiasco. It is like the ogee-shaped helmet of the cemetery of Watsch in Carniola,[5] and is probably contemporaneous with it. One

---

[1] S. Reinach, in Daremberg, **CCCXV**, s.v. " Galea " ; E. Sprockhoff, in Ebert, **CCCXXIV**, s.v. " Helm ".

[2] See above, p. 266.

[3] Szombathy, in **C**, 1901, p. 6.

[4] Viollier, in **XXVI**, 1906, p. 97 ; **CLXXX**, p. 229.

[5] Much, **CCCLXI**, lii, 1. The incised decoration of this Watsch helmet is like that of Negau helmet No. 2.

can well believe that an ancient type of armour should have been preserved in isolated examples at the bottom of a remote valley, but twenty specimens all together, and of such a rare piece of armour, can only date from the time in which it was normally made. Whatever the nature of the deposit may be—armoury, armourer's shop, trophy—the conclusion must be the same. Besides, one of the Giubiasco helmets, too, bears an inscription, produced in the casting ; it is in Latin, and in fairly late characters.[1] The Negau *graffiti*, on the other hand, are archaic, and are certainly earlier than the inscriptions of Branio and Todi,[2] which are of the time of the great invasion.[3]

Therefore Celts came into Styria at the end of the Hallstatt period, and their presence there is attested a little later than in Lombardy.[4] Like their compatriots to the west, they were assimilated to the peoples whose guests or conquerors they had been. These folk, who fought bare-headed,[5] have left nothing behind them but helmets, and helmets which they had made themselves. This fact at least suggests that they did not pass through the country like a whirlwind, but were settled there. Their remains are merged in those of the native peoples. We do not know how far they may have advanced on this side, nor how many they were. But we do know that great changes took place in all this region comprising the Austrian slope of the Alps at the end of the first Iron Age. Cemeteries and dwelling-places were moved. The site of Hallstatt itself seems to have been abandoned. One way of explaining these facts is to suppose that foreign contingents came in, large enough to upset the old settlements and to create new ones.

---

[1] Rhys, in **VII**, p. 19.

[2] Dottin, **CXCVI**, p. 154.

[3] Marstrander, on the other hand, does not think that the inscription is earlier than the settlement of the Celts in the Danube valley in the second century. He even says first century. For he observes that in the word *banuabi*, *w* is written as *u*, as in Latin, and concludes that the inscription is later than the conquest of the Cisalpine country. The same sound is written as *f* in another word in the same inscription. I do not think that this difference in writing need be taken into account.

[4] This is what Bertrand and Reinach maintain (**DXLII**, pp. 122–144). But their argument is based on the confusion mentioned above (p. 267). They confuse Celts and Illyrians, as they confused Celts and Umbrians.

[5] On the belt-plaque from Watsch there is a scene of a helmeted horseman fighting with a bare-headed horseman ; the latter may be a Celt (Bertrand and Reinach, op. cit., p. 107).

Did the Celts descend on this eastern side as far as Italy ? We do not know. But, like the Illyrian peoples among whom they settled, they were affected by the influence of the civilizations of Italy, that of the Veneti of Este or that of the Etruscans of Bologna. One can imagine that these Celtic colonies, established in Italy or on the outskirts of it, borrowed with profit not only to themselves but to the Celtic country behind them. Their presence must have stimulated trade between the plain of the Po and Western Germany or France. It is possible that they had a great influence on the turn which Celtic civilization was to take. If we admit their existence we can easily understand how the Certosa brooch was the prototype of the Celtic brooches of La Tène.[1] Even the dagger with antennæ which has enabled us to date the Ligurian cippi, may have been borrowed from Italy, where it appears to have come directly after the bronze sword with antennæ.[2]

The second Negau inscription informs us that there were Germans among the Celts who came at the end of the first Iron Age to fight on the Italian border.[3] This is a most valuable piece of information regarding the fact, already pointed out, of Celto-Germanic collaboration, for it gives us one date for it. We must suppose that at this time, in the north-east of their domain, the Celts were the leading people of their neighbourhood. This is not clear from the archæological data, which show that the Germans were at that time subject to the influence of the Illyrian culture. But the inscription is convincing.

V

CELTIC EXPANSION IN THE SOUTH-WEST OF FRANCE AT THE END OF THE HALLSTATT PERIOD

In the south-west the tumuli of the earlier Hallstatt periods stop about Cahors, and do not reach the Garonne. They go beyond the crest of the Central Plateau, but not far.

---

[1] The Certosa brooch must have reached the Celtic world, chiefly by the east. See Reinecke, **CCCCVI**.
[2] Déchelette, ii, 2, pp. 730 ff.
[3] Marstrander suggests the Bastarnæ. But there cannot have been any Bastarnæ in this region yet, at the date which I have adopted.

There was a sudden expansion at the end of the Hallstatt Period; and there had certainly been no previous incursions

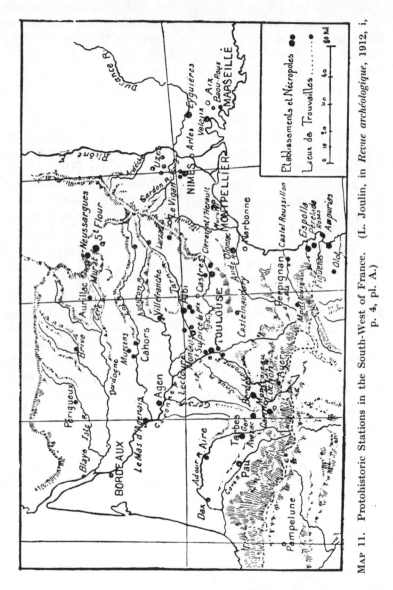

MAP 11. Protohistoric Stations in the South-West of France. (L. Joulin, in *Revue archéologique*, 1912, i, p. 4, pl. A.)

to prepare for this. We have evidence for it in the cemeteries (Map 11) which are distributed in fairly large numbers

between the crest of the Plateau and the Pyrenees.[1] It even
went a long way beyond the mountains. Most of these
cemeteries are composed of tumuli containing cremations ;
the mounds themselves may have been worn down by water
flowing down the sides, but either stone circles [2] or
recognizable traces remain. In other cemeteries the graves
are flush with the ground and arranged in regular lines.[3]

They are in three main groups, in two of which they are
concentrated in fairly large numbers. The chief group is
spread along the line of the Pyrenees from the watershed
between the Mediterranean and Atlantic, through the departments of the Ariège, Haute-Garonne, Hautes-Pyrénées, and
Basses-Pyrénées, into the Landes and Gironde. The largest
collection is on the plateau of Ger,[4] overlooking the Adour, in
the Hautes and Basses-Pyrénées. Further south there are
the tumuli of Bastrès (canton of Lourdes) and Ossun [5]
(arrondissement of Tarbes), and further north, on the plateau
of Lannemezan, is the cemetery of Avezac-Prat.[6] Behind,
east of the basin of Arcachon, the cemetery of Mios [7] speaks
for the same civilization, but the tombs in it are flat-
graves.

A second group extends from Albi to Toulouse, and
includes the cemeteries of Saint-Sulpice, of Sainte-Foy, a mile
from Castres, of the Lacam and Mons plateaus, near
Roquecourbe, of Montsalvi in the commune of Puygouzon,
of Lavène, near Montsalvi, of Saint-Roch, near Toulouse, etc.[8]

The third is a more scattered group, with Agen as its
centre.[9]

Other tumuli have been excavated farther north, at

---

[1] Déchelette, pp. 663 ff., 671 ff. ; Joulin, in **CXXXIX**, 1908, ii, 1, p. 193 ;
1912, i, 1, p. 235 ; 1914, i, p. 59 ; 1915, i, pp. 47, 259 ; 1918, ii, p. 74 ; 1922,
i, 1 ; Bosch, Gimpera, **CCCCXCIX**, 13.

[2] Déchelette, pp. 666, 669 : Stone circles at Garin (Hte.-Garonne). It
is possible that the tumulus degenerated into a circle of stones, as in Burgundy
(Auvenay road) or at Golasecca.

[3] J. Sacaze, in **XXVI**, 1880, ii, p. 877 (plain of Rivière) ; Joulin, in **CXXXIX**,
1912, i, pp. 33 (necropolis of Sainte-Foy, Tarn) and 4 (Saint-Roch, near
Toulouse) ; 1915, ii, p. 82 (Mios).

[4] Pothier, **CCCCLXXXVIII** ; Déchelette, pp. 663 ff.

[5] E. Piette, in **LXXXVI**, 1881, p. 522 (tumuli at Bastrès and Ossun).

[6] Piette and Saccaze, ibid., 1879, p. 499 (Avezac-Prat).

[7] See n. 6. Cau-Durban, in **XXVI**, 1887, ii, p. 737 (cemetery of Ayer,
Bordes-sur-Lez, Ariège).

[8] Déchelette, p. 671 ; Joulin, in **CXXXIX**, 1912, i, p. 60.

[9] Déchelette, p. 676.

Liviers near Jumillac-le-Grand in Dordogne [1] and, at the other end of that vast domain, in the environs of Nîmes.[2]

All these tombs are dated by the swords and brooches found in them. The swords are invariably of the type with antennæ.[3] But they are not the old dagger with antennæ of the necropolis of Hallstatt. They are small swords, the handle being usually of iron, and the shape of the pommel is quite unlike the model furnished by the earlier bronze sword with antennæ. The two antennæ have a right-angled bend in them, and end in fairly large knobs, which soon afterwards are all that is left of them.

The brooches are of iron, with a highly arched bow and a large cross-bow spring. They are like the Certosa type. The perpendicular continuation of the foot ends in a flat circular button. Others are of the kettledrum type, which is contemporaneous in Central Europe with the Certosa brooches, but are mounted on a ring which runs through the coils of the spring and the end of the foot ; these are a new type which is peculiar to the region and developed in it.

If we are to place these Aquitanian cemeteries in the third Hallstatt period it will be more accurate to place them at the end of it. It is even probable a priori that the Hallstatt culture lasted longer in this region than elsewhere.

The civilization represented by these tombs does not carry on that of the first Hallstatt settlements in Gaul. It is in the east of the Hallstatt area that we must seek the equivalents of certain metal objects found in the French tumuli, and, still more, of their pottery. Among the weapons there is a javelin made entirely of iron, which we shall find again in Spain. This all-iron javelin has already been reported among the arms of the necropolis of Hallstatt itself.[4] In pottery these tumuli are distinguished from those of the rest of Gaul, firstly by its abundance. There is not much in the Hallstatt tumuli of Eastern and Central France. There is more in those of Champagne and Lorraine, but it is different from the Aquitanian ware. On the whole, this latter has a curiously archaic look. With its ornament of grooves and bosses, like the Lausitz type of pottery, it might belong to

[1] Ibid.
[2] Ibid. ; Bosch Gimpera, op. cit., p. 47, n. 1.
[3] Joulin, op. cit. (Sainte-Foy).
[4] Déchelette, pp. 746, 668, fig. 254 ; Sacken, *Hallstatt*, pl. vii, 2, 3.

the Bronze Age. But there can be no mistake about it, for it includes earthenware copies of the great cylindrical bronze pails with vertical handles which must be placed between the cordoned buckets of the Hallstatt period and the British cist-type buckets of the La Tène period.[1] It also includes vases with a hollow foot shaped like a truncated cone, which cannot be placed very far back among the wares of the Continent. It is in the pottery of the Bavarian [2] and Bohemian tumuli that we find the equivalents of the Aquitanian pottery, and everything seems to suggest that large bodies of Celts from Bavaria and Bohemia had come, without halting on the way, right through France to establish themselves between the Central Plateau and the Pyrenees.

There are obviously exceptions, which do not invalidate this general conclusion. For example, the cemeteries of Roquecourbe have yielded a cup painted with red triangles on a black ground, which recalls the Hallstatt pottery of the Franche-Comté and Southern Germany.[3] Moreover, the various groups differ to some extent from one another in this or that part of their grave-gear.

One thing to note is the similarity of a certain number of vases to the early vases of Golasecca. They have the same round belly and wide neck, the same parallel bands of chevrons and zigzags, and the same high hollow foot. The construction of the tombs presents similarities of the same order. I have compared the stone circles of Golasecca to washed-away tumuli. The tumuli of the plateau of Ger and the Haute-Garonne have stone circles, sometimes several, which in some cases are all that survives, the earth of the mound having been carried away by water. Indeed, we must be in the presence of an event which is not only comparable but parallel to that of which the cemetery of Golasecca is the chief record.

In each case the domain of the Celts was extended, on the whole, suddenly. In each case I imagine that the new settlement was the work of the Celts in the rear, and not of those who had just before established themselves on the front line. History will afterwards show them established in south-western France, Volcæ and Boii—Volcæ Tectosages

---

[1] Déchelette, pp. 815 ff.
[2] Naue, **CCCCIII,** pll. xliv ff.   [3] Déchelette, p. 673.

round Toulouse, Volcæ Aricomii behind them in the Gard, and Boii or Boiates round the lake of Arcachon.[1] Both Volcæ and Boii had come from Bavaria and Bohemia. If they had not all arrived at that time, that at least shows that the Celts were capable of sending out colonies to great distances, and as a fact they were. The colonization which took place in the third Hallstatt period can be followed on its way through France by the distribution of certain types of sword.[2] It seems to have halted a moment at the foot of the Pyrenean passes, just as, in Livy's story, on the other side of Gaul, the army of Bellovesus halted at the foot of the Alps.[3] The result of this halt was the chain of settlements along the mountains. They lasted, too, perhaps because of the salt-deposits of Salies-de-Béarn and the district. But they did not last as long as the settlements beyond the crest of the Pyrenees, from which they got some of their implements and part of their civilization, as we shall see.

VI

CELTIC EXPANSION IN THE EXTREME WEST OF EUROPE

The earliest pottery of the Iron Age found in the south of England, first at Hengistbury Head near Southampton and then at All Cannings Cross Farm in Wiltshire,[4] is very like that of the Pyrenean tumuli. Did the Britons whose arrival it represents come direct from the same regions ? Did they pass through Aquitaine ? And did they take ship from the Loire, as Zimmer supposes the Goidels to have done, or from the Garonne ? They probably came from Brittany, where an exactly similar pottery has been found in the cemetery of Roz-an-Tremen near Penmarch.[5] We should note here that the pottery immediately above this stratum at Hengistbury Head consists of vases decorated with cordons in relief,[6] which are of the same type as those of the second

[1] Peynau, CCCCLXXXVI, i.
[2] Henry, " Les Tumulus du Département de la Côte d'Or," École du Louvre thesis, in " Rapport sur l'administration et la conservation des Musées nationaux " (*Journal officiel*, 24th August, 1928).
[3] Livy, v, 34.
[4] See above, p. 213.
[5] Favret and Bénard, in CXXXIX, 1924, i, pp. 178 ff. ; Bénard, *Les Deux Nécropoles de Saint-Urnel et de Roz-an-Tremen*, repr. from XLIII, 1922.
[6] J. P. Bushe-Fox, CCCVIII, pp. 34 ff.

period of Golasecca, and seem to have been made fairly soon after them. These different facts lead one to think that bands of emigrants moved at this time from the east of the Celtic world, some towards the extreme west of Europe and some towards the south-west, and that the flow, at least on the western side, was for some time continuous.

CHAPTER V

CELTIC EXPANSION ON THE CONTINENT IN THE HALLSTATT
PERIOD (*continued*). THE CELTS IN SPAIN

I

CELTIC CEMETERIES AND TUMULI

THE drive to the south-west was not exhausted when it reached the Pyrenees. Many bodies crossed them.

We must observe first of all that they never lost contact with the settlements in Aquitaine. In the tombs of that region, more particularly near the Pyrenees, objects are found which are really Spanish, invented south of the Pyrenees, where they were copied from Greek or Italic models. Such, for instance, are the belt-clasps (Fig. 42).[1] The presence of these Spanish objects helps to give the Hallstatt civilization of Aquitaine its characteristic appearance, which is so different from that of all other parts of the Celtic world. It also shows that the settlements to the north of the Pyrenees and those to the south constituted one single group, a single racial unit, the connecting links of which we may usefully consider (Map 12).

There have been found south of the Pyrenees a series of tumuli with cremations, and also cemeteries—very large ones—with cremations, dating from the end of the third Hallstatt period. The tumulus without any interior chamber and the practice of cremation were alike novelties in Spain at this time. These tumuli and cemeteries are dated by brooches of the various types already mentioned, swords with antennæ, and pottery like the Pyrenean wares of France.

---

[1] These belt-clasps are related to the Hallstatt clasps with a single hook of Central Europe ; they differ from them in having more than one hook and in having oblong holes in the base of the hooks. Clasps of this kind have been found at Olympia and in the ruins of the Greek colony of Ampurias. From this Déchelette concludes that they were Greek (" Agrafes de ceinturon ibériques d'origine grecque," in **CLXXXV**). Bosch Gimpera thinks that they may have come to these places as trophies, or that they belonged to auxiliaries (**CCCCXCIX**, p. 30). For the archæology of the Celts in the Peninsula, see Bosch Gimpera, *L'Arqueologia y l'arte ibericas*, vol. i. *Etnologia de la Peninsula iberica*, pp. 452 ff., Barcelona, 1931.

The earliest, therefore, date from the middle of the sixth century.[1]

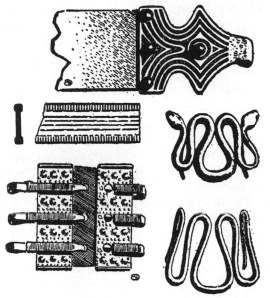

FIG. 42. Iberian Belt-clasps.
(G. Bonsor, *Colonies agricoles*, figs. 9–13.)

The tumuli are in groups on the little hills, the Alcores, which fill the great bend made by the Guadalquivir before

[1] Sr. Bosch Gimpera and some other Catalan archæologists think that the Hallstatt culture had entered Spain by the Mediterranean coast two or three centuries before. Cremation-cemeteries, without tumuli, have been explored in Catalonia (Espolla, Tarrasa, Sabadell, La Punta del Pi), where vases have been found which resemble those of the earliest Hallstatt sites of the south of France, and must date from about the eighth century (Bosch Gimpera, J. Colominas Roca, " La Necropoli de Can Misert," Tarrasa, in **XV**, vi, 1920 ; Bosch Gimpera, **DV**, pp. 175 ff. ; **DII**, p. 45 ; **CCCCXCIX**, p. 14 ; **DXVII**, p. 179 ; Péricot, **DXV**, p. 47). Sr. Bosch Gimpera at first thought that these might represent the advance of early bodies of Celts by the east coast of Spain, two or three centuries before the date assigned to the first Celtic settlements in the country. The natives maintained themselves in the more mountainous parts of Catalonia, where their archaic civilization is represented by a certain number of stations, while the influence of the Hallstatt culture, spread by the Celts, made itself felt farther south as early as this time in the province of Almeria, where, with the Hallstatt period, cremations in graves and stone tumuli appear (Siret, **DXXIII**, vii, fig. 69 ; Déchelette, ii, 2, p. 686 ; Péricot, loc. cit. ; Bosch Gimpera, **DII**, p. 53). Afterwards Sr. Bosch Gimpera talks of nothing but Ligurians. But the cemeteries in question are quite remarkably poor. There are no weapons in them which might date them beyond dispute, and the pottery is hardly older in type than that of the Pyrenean tumuli. Provisionally, I regard them as of the same date as these latter, and I do not take them into account in reconstructing the history of the Celts in Spain.

it reaches the sea, and are there contiguous to inhumation-cemeteries without tumuli. They were found to contain the pottery which we already know and brooches of the serpentine and Certosa types, all mixed with so many Phœnician objects that the excavator did not hesitate to ascribe the tombs to Carthaginian colonists. But the Carthaginians and their Libyan subjects did not burn their dead.[1]

To the Marquis of Cerralbo we are indebted for our knowledge of the great cemeteries of the two central provinces of Soria and Guadalajara, which lie side by side, one in the south-east of Old Castile and the other in the north of New Castile.[2] There, too, there was salt, which might keep the population in the place. In these two regions a dozen cremation-cemeteries are known. The largest is that of Aguilar de Anguita in the province of Guadalajara, near the sources of the Salon, the ancient Salo, the valley of which was a channel of intercourse between the Ebro and the Tagus.

In this cemetery and others the urns were arranged in several parallel rows, a yard or five feet apart. In other cemeteries, which are just the same in respect of the objects found in them, this arrangement can no longer be seen, if it ever existed. There were no tumuli. Above the urn a tombstone was set, which, with one exception, was quite plain.[3]

The characteristic objects of the grave-gear are the same as north of the Pyrenees. The sword is of the type with antennæ. There are several forms, from those with bronze antennæ and semicircular iron antennæ to that with atrophied antennæ.

The brooches (Fig. 43) are the iron brooch with a perpendicular foot and a button, the ring-brooch, and

---

[1] Bonsor, **CCCCXCVI**. He ascribes the tombs with zoned vases to the Celts. Déchelette (in **CXXXIX**, 1908, 2, pp. 391 ff.) does not hesitate to regard these tombs as Celtic. Cf. Reinecke, in **CLXIX**, 1900 ; **CLVIII**, p. 162. Recently, MM. Bonsor and Thouvenot have explored a necropolis in the province of Seville, the furniture of which presents analogies with that of the tombs in the valley of the Bætis (**CCCCXCVII**). These tombs are really native (those containing bell-beakers) or Iberian (containing painted pottery), but they show signs of Celtic influences.

[2] Cerralbo, in **LIX**, Monaco, 1912, i, pp. 593 ff. ; Déchelette, ii, 2, p. 687 ; id., in **LVIII**, 1912, pp. 433 ff. ; Bosch Gimpera, **DXVIII**, p. 189 (bibliography) ; Schulten, **DXVIII**, p. 199 ; Bosch Gimpera, **CCCCXCIX**, pp. 13 ff. ; **DII**, p. 55 ; Péricot, **DXV**, p. 47 ; **CXVIII**, 1911, p. 384.

[3] Déchelette, ii, 2, p. 688, i.

another Hallstatt brooch which is absent, as far as I know, in the series from the French side of the Pyrenees, that in the shape of a horse or of a horse with rider. This last appears at Hallstatt itself. It is of Italian origin, and it was probably from Italy that it came to Spain. It is possible that the belt-clasps, which are of quite a peculiar kind, were likewise imported direct, and developed independently in Spain.

The pottery, which consists chiefly of funeral urns, is in part related to that of the north of the Pyrenees. This

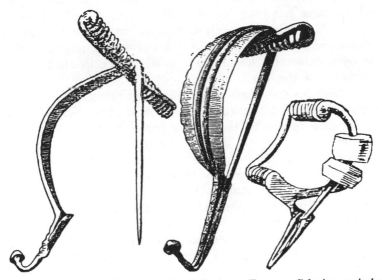

Fig. 43. Hallstatt Brooches from Spain. (Bonsor, *Colonies agricoles*, figs. 6, 96–7.)

part of the pottery of the cremation-cemeteries persists in the latest necropoles.

For not only did these cemeteries last a long time, but the communities which left their dead in them adhered, like those of Aquitaine, to ancient forms. We may merely note this in passing; we shall have to return to it later. It cannot have taken less than two or three hundred years for the Hallstatt types to develop as they did in Spain [1] and the Pyrenees. After that the civilization to which they belong outlived itself. Dates are furnished by the discovery of Greek

[1] Bosch Gimpera, **CCCCXCIX**, pp. 20 ff.

vases of the fifth and fourth centuries in a similar necropolis at Alcacer-do-Sal [1] in the south of Portugal and by that of painted Iberian vases of the third century in several others.[2]

Let us now go over the area. Brooches of the series described above and isolated daggers with antennæ, or contemporary cremations, have been discovered in certain *citanias*, ancient towns of masonry construction, in Portugal,[3] in Cantabria and Galicia in the north, and in the south at Almedinella in Andalusia,[4] and at Villaricos in Almeria, on the Mediterranean coast.[5] In the north-east the dagger with antennæ has been found in the cemeteries of Gibrella [6] and Perelada (Gerona). In Catalonia, in the provinces of Gerona and Barcelona, a whole series of cremation-cemeteries has been explored, the pottery of which recalls that of the cemeteries of the Tarn.

In fact, almost all over the Peninsula the objects characteristic of this culture, which, it must be remembered, was far from remaining pure, have been found isolated on the outskirts and crowded in the centre. Without apparent connection with the previous civilizations, the nearest of which are almost completely unknown to us (we have not one late Bronze Age station in Spain), this culture came in at a time which may be placed, in virtue of the daggers with bronze antennæ, between 600 and 500 B.C.

North of the Pyrenees we have attributed it hypothetically to the Celts. South of the Pyrenees we have positive reasons for doing so.

II

THE ANCIENT HISTORIANS

North of Italy and the Adriatic, where the Celts had advanced in the sixth century, the Greeks did not come into direct contact with them. The result is that their advance

---

[1] Estacio da Veiga, **DXXIV**, iv, xxxiii, 268 ; V. Correia, *Uma Conferencia sobre a necropole de Alcacer do Sal*, repr. from **XXXIII**, 1925.

[2] Bosch Gimpera, **DXVIII**, p. 189.

[3] Cartailhac, **DVII**, p. 246, figs. 358–60 ; Déchelette, ii, 2, p. 686 (Cividade Velha de Santa Luzia) ; Bosch Gimpera, **CCCCXCIX**, pp. 40 ff. ; Mendez Correa, **DXIII**, passim.

[4] Cordova Museum. Bosch Gimpera, op. cit., p. 51.

[5] Siret, **DXXIII** ; H. Sandars, " The Weapons of the Iberians," in **XVIII**, 1913, pp. 205 ff.

[6] Bosch Gimpera, op. cit., p. 14 ; **XV**, 1920, vi, p. 590.

went unrecorded in classical literature (except in Livy, who may have had other sources), ånd therefore we have not been able to argue anything from this absence of evidence in the ancient authors.

In Spain Greek mariners were doing trade before the sixth century,[1] and we have an uninterrupted series of testimonies about the Peninsula and its people, some furnished by sure witnesses, namely writers who had travelled and seen what they described with their own eyes. Now among the inhabitants of the country they mention the Celts fairly early, and after them the Celtiberians.

The first [2] to speak of the Celts in Spain is Herodotos.[3] " The Danube," he says, " starts from the country of the Celts and the city of Pyrene. It flows through Europe, which it divides down the middle. The Celts are outside the Pillars of Heracles and march with the Cynesii, who are the western-most people of Europe." Herodotos's geography, so far as the interior of Europe is concerned, is vague ; but it is definite in respect of the coasts. He belonged to a people of sailors, which would naturally have nautical information, and his geographical sources must have been of the *periplus* class, which is very well represented in Greek literature. The Cynesii were a Ligurian people, whom Polybios calls Κόνιοι. Their cities were Conistorgis, the site of which is not known, and Conimbriga, which was well to the north ; both were in the south-western end of the Peninsula, between the Guadiana and Cape St. Vincent.[4] Aristotle, in his *Meteorologica*, faithfully records the information supplied by Herodotos [5] ; he speaks, if not of the city, of the mountain of Pyrene, *in the Celtic country*, from which, he says, both the Danube and the Tartessus rise.

About this Tartessus, that is the Guadalquivir, and its valley, which was a sort of Eldorado to the ancient mariner,

---

[1] The voyage of Colæos of Samos, about 660 : Hdt., iv, 152 ; d'Arbois, **CCCI**, ii, p. 306 ; Schulten, **DXX**, p. 25. Tradition of the voyages of Heracles : Pherecydes of Samos (ca. 480 B.C.), p. 33 ; Sil. Ital., iii, 357 ; Philipon, **DXV**, p. 33.

[2] Unless we are to see a distortion of the name of the Celts in that of the Γλῆτες, mentioned with the Cynetes and Tartessians by Herodoros of Heracleia (ca. 500 B.C.), frag. 30 ; A. Blasquez, in **XXXIV**, 1915, lxvi, p. 164. Strabo, iii, 4, 19, gives Ἰγλῆτες ; Philipon **DXV**, p. 132.

[3] ii, 33.

[4] Schulten, **DXIX**, p. 91.

[5] i, 13, 19.

Herodotos gives a detail which has not received the attention which it deserves. It is the name of the King of Tartessus, Arganthonios,[1] who was on the throne when the Phocæans were making their first attempts at colonization, round about the time of the foundation of Marseilles. Herodotos says that Arganthonios gave them money to build the wall behind which Phocæa for some time defied the Persians of Cyrus. Tartessus was famed for its silver mines ; Arganthonios is the Silver King. If his name were Iberian, like the name of Tartessus itself, there would be a very great argument, though perhaps an only one, for classifying the Iberians as Indo-Europeans. But it is based on the Celtic form of the word for silver—*arganto*.[2] Either there were Celts at Tartessus, or the Phocæan legend of the Silver King contains an admixture of Celtic elements. The Celts of the Alcores were not far away, and there is no reason why a Celtic chief should not have become king of the Iberian state of Tartessus, perhaps by marriage, or even that he should not have made a name for himself in the world.

Arganthonios was dead when the Phocæans founded Alalia in Corsica in 564. He was a semi-legendary person, and had been given a reputation for proverbial longevity. Herodotus says that he reigned eighty years and lived a hundred and twenty ; later they gave him a hundred and fifty or three hundred. In any case, we must suppose that he reigned roughly about 600 B.C., and place the arrival of the Celts in Bætica as far back as that. The tombs of the Alcores are older than the cemeteries of Castile, and contain objects earlier than the Certosa brooches.

About 350 Ephoros, in his history of the world, described the extent of the Celtic domain, which reached as far as

---

[1] Hubert, in **CXL**, 1927, pp. 78 ff. ; Hdt., i, 163.

[2] According to Schulten (op. cit., p. 61), the name is Ligurian. But the Ligurians probably had another name for silver, from the same root as the English word. The name of Piz Silvretta, near Klosters, in Grisons, a region of Ligurian place-names, bears witness to it. Also, the Ligurian place-names of the south of Spain, among which are a Mons Argentarius (Avien., *Ora Marit.*, 291) and an Ἀργυροῦν ὄρος (Strabo, iii, 148), include a Mons Silurus (Avien., 433), which seems to form a pendant to them, to say nothing of the people of the Silures. The Celtic etymology of Arganthonios presents two difficulties : (1) the writing of the dental in the stem ; but the Negau inscription shows that in the sixth century the Brythonic *t* was pronounced in such a way that it could be expressed by a letter bordering on θ ; (2) there was, in Bithynia, an Arganthonion, first mentioned by Apollonios of Rhodes (i, 1176). Cf. Philipon, **DXVI**, 55, 65.

Cadiz.[1] At the end of the century Aristotle gave the name of "Celtic" to the whole mountain mass of the Peninsula.[2] Some years later Pytheas made his voyage, the account of which was largely used by Timæos and Eratosthenes. Timæos speaks of the rivers which flow into the Atlantic as going through the mountains of the Celtic country.[3] Eratosthenes was censured by Strabo because he said that the western coasts of the peninsula belonged to the Celts.[4] But with Timæos and Eratosthenes, the Celtiberians seem to have made their first appearance in literature. Celtic expansion in Spain had reached its maximum. Henceforward we shall only see it recede.

About the time of Herodotos, the author of the *periplus* which Avienus used in his *Ora Maritima* gave the names of the Celtic peoples which had settled close to the Portuguese coast. "North of the Cynetes," he says [5] :—

Cempsi atque Saefes arduos colles habent
Ophiussae in agro, propter hos pernix Ligus
Draganumque proles sub nivoso maxime
Septentrione conlocaverant larem.

The country was called Ophiussa. These people who had squeezed themselves in between the Ligurians and the Cynetes, pushing back the former to the north into the Pyrenees and beyond, are probably the Celts of Herodotos.[6] The Cempsi must have bordered not only on the country of the Cynetes, but inland on the northern frontier of the kingdom of Tartessus. The Saefes must have been a continuation of them northwards.

In the east the same author tells us for the first time of another Celtic people. He has just spoken of the River Tyrius, now the Turia, and adds : "But as the country lies further from the sea it stretches out in ridges covered with

---

[1] In Strabo, ii, 19 ; Schulten, op. cit., p. 93.
[2] *De Animalium Generibus*, 38.
[3] Schulten, op. cit., p. 96.
[4] Strabo, ii, 4, 4.
[5] 195 ff. ; Schulten, **DXVII**, p. 80 ; id., **DXIX**, p. 89.
[6] Bosch Gimpera, **CCCCXCIX**, p. 5. For a contrary view, see Philipon, op. cit., p. 71. The name of the Cempsi, which is also mentioned by Dionysios Periegetes (338), may be connected with the Celto-Ligurian root of the name of the Cevennes, *cemm*. The Cempsi had come down further south and occupied the island of Cartare, not far from Cadiz (Avien., 255).

undergrowth. There the Berybraces, a rude and savage people, used to wander among their great herds of cattle. Living on a hard fare of milk and fatty cheese, they showed a spirit like that of wild beasts." [1] The Berybraces, elsewhere called Bebryces, are much better known than the two other peoples. They are definitely described as Celts by the *perigetes* Scymnos of Chios, who summarized the geography of Ephoros.[2] We have no difficulty in associating their name with a family of Celtic words—Bebrinium, Bebriacum, Bebronne, Bibrax, Bibrori (in Brittany)—which contain the name of the beaver, *bebros*.[3] Writers whose evidence, it is true, is not of much value for these distant times, Dion Cassius,[4] Silius Italicus,[5] and Tzetzes,[6] place the Bebryces at various points along the coast.

Whereas the Marseilles geographer used by Avienus shows the interior of the Peninsula as being in the possession of three great Celtic tribes, he mentions no one in the Pyrenean isthmus except the Dragani, who were Ligurians. Here he apparently contradicts the archæological data. We must presume from what he says either that the Celts only occupied limited districts between the central plateau and the Pyrenees, or that their settlements there did not last as long as those in the south and on the coast. There is nothing against this in the archæological finds.

Avienus's three tribes vanished from history after the time of Ephoros. Later writers mention only a very few names of Celtic peoples outside the Celtiberian group. The Berones,[7] in the upper valley of the Ebro, are described as Celts. Their neighbours, the Autrigones,[8] may be Celts, too.

---

[1] 483 ff. :—

> At qua recedit ab salo tellus procul,
> dumosa late terga regio porrigit ;
> Berybraces illic, gens agrestis et ferox,
> pecorum frequentis intererrabat greges.
> Hi lacte semet atque pingui caseo
> praedure alentes, proferebant spiritum
> vicem ad ferarum.

[2] In *F.H.G.*, 199 ; Avien., 483–9 ; Schulten, **DXIX**, p. 35.

[3] Jullian, **CCCXLVII**, i, p. 259. Philipon (op. cit., xiii) makes them an Iberian people.

[4] Frag. 53.

[5] 3, 442.

[6] In Lycophron, 1305 ; Schulten, op. cit., pp. 91 ff.

[7] Strabo, 3, 4, 5. Cf. Scholia on Lucan (Usener's ed.), iv, 10 ; Isid., *Orig.*, ix, 2, 114. " Gallohispani," St. Jerome, *Comm. on Isaiah*, xviii, 66, 9.

[8] The towns of Uxama Barca and Deobriga are in their country.

So may the Turmogidi,[1] on the other side of the watershed between the basins of the Ebro and Douro. I should say the same of the Nemetati,[2] whom Ptolemy mentions on the right

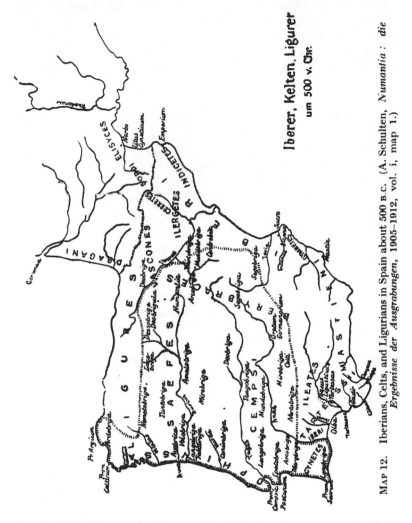

MAP 12. Iberians, Celts, and Ligurians in Spain about 500 B.C. (A. Schulten, *Numantia : die Ergebnisse der Ausgrabungen*, 1905–1912, vol. i, map 1.)

bank of the Douro in the north of Lusitania ; we see in their name a Celtic word, *nemeton*. Further north were the Artabri, whose name, formed on the model of that of the Cantabri,

---

[1] With the town of Deobrigula.
[2] Ptol., ii, 6, 40.

also appears as Arotrebæ, which may be Celt [1] ; they had three towns with Celtic names—Ardobriga, Acobriga, and Brigantium, not to mention the Promontorium Celticum (Cape Finisterre) in their territory. South of the Artabri, the Bracari,[2] with their town of Caladunum, appear to be Celts. These last two peoples are, however, included among the Lusitanians,[3] like the Callæci [4] (who gave their name to Galicia), whose name is made to cover the same territory and probably the same peoples. We do not know whether the Celtic tribes had their territory to themselves, or shared it with people belonging to Iberian or Basque tribes. Nor do we know the date at which these peoples began to settle in the districts in which they are reported, nor whether they were fractions of the great groups of the sixth century or had stepped into their place.

Apart from the Celtiberians, the Celts of Spain are also designated by names which look like generic names—Celti or Celtici, Κελτοί or Κελτικοί. The writers tell us of a group of Celtici or Celti in the south, between Bætica and the Tagus,[5] and of another in Galicia about Cape Finisterre and astride the Tamara (the Tambre).[6] An intermediate group must have lived between the Tagus and Douro, where we later find a city near Salamanca named Celticoflavia. Κελτικοί seems to be a derivative name, perhaps Iberian, if it is not Greek and if it does not imply some delicate distinction, meaning, for example, people who were not quite Celts.[7] In any case, this racial name provided the Celts of Spain with a large number of proper names—Celtigun, Celtillus, Celtius, Celtus, Celtitanus.[8]

---

[1] Pliny, iv, 3, 119 ; Mela, iii, 13. Cf. Irish *Artaige* (M. E. Dobbs, in **LXXX**, 1916, p. 168).

[2] *Braca.* Cf. Holder, **CCVII**, s.v.

[3] Strabo, iii, 147, 151, 154 (Celtiberians).

[4] Sil. Ital., iii, 344 ff. ; Norden, **CCCXIV**, p. 145 ; Hübner, in Pauly and Wissowa, **CCCLXVIII**, s.v. ; Isid., *Orig.*, ii, 2, 110 (similarities between the Callæci and the Gauls).

[5] Schulten, op. cit., p. 109. Their territory approached the right bank of the Bætis. Pliny, iii, 11, *oppida Hispalensis conventus* : *Celti, Axati,* etc. ; iii, 13 ; *Ant. Itin.*, 414, 5 ; Ravennas, 44, 315, 2.

[6] Celtici Nerii, Præstamarici, Superstamarici ; Mela, ii, 2 ; Pliny, iv, 3 ; Jullian, op. cit., i, p. 307.

[7] Pliny, iii, 13 : *Celticos a Celtiberis ex Lusitania advenisse manifestum est sacris, lingua, oppidorum vocabulis, quae cognominibus in Bætica distinguuntur.*

[8] Schulten, op. cit., p. 107 ; Fidel Fita, in **XXXIV**, 1916, lxix, p. 114 (inscriptions of Peñaflor).

Does this mean that the Celts of Spain and, by extension, those of the first migrations were Celts as opposed to the Gauls ? No doubt there were slight differences of vocabulary and pronunciation between the Celts of Spain and the Gauls of Gaul. We have a great number of Celtic names from Spain. There are none ending in -*marus* among them. I know of only one instance of a name in -*rix* (Thiureigs). On the other hand, the names Boutius, Cloutius, and Mælo are found there. Ambactus appears in the form Ambatus, and Camulus in the form Camalus.[1] But these differences are not to be compared to those separating Goidelic from Brythonic.

III

THE TERRITORY OCCUPIED BY THE CELTS

The Celtic place-names of the Peninsula enable us to determine fairly accurately, if not the whole extent of the territory occupied by the Celts, at least that of the country in which they were established long enough to leave place-names. The most interesting are the names of towns. Among these there is a series which seems to go back to the first Celtic immigration, namely those in -*briga*, such as Segobriga (Segorbe) and Laccobriga (Lagos).[2] This ending appears so often in Spain that it has been regarded as Iberian.[3] This is quite wrong. Names in -*briga* are found in regions in which the Iberians certainly never lived—Admagetobriga in the Franche-Comté, Artobriga in Bavaria, etc.[4] It is the Gaulish equivalent of German *burg*.[5] The name of the goddess Brigid comes from the same stem, with the vowel *i*. There is no doubt, therefore, that the word is Celtic.[6] It is true that it is found attached to names, the first part of which is not or does

---

[1] Schulten, op. cit., p. 31, n. 5.
[2] D'Arbois, **CCXCIX**, 98 ; Schulten, op. cit., pp. 23, 110 ; Schumacher, **CCCCIX**, 122 ; according to whom it applies to river-crossings.
[3] Philipon, **DXVI**, p. 158 ; id., **CCCLXIX**, p. 217 : Names ending in -*briga* were formed by the Latins from race-names in -*q*, based on town-names in -*bri* (e.g. Segobriges ; Hübner, *Monumenta Linguæ Ibericæ*, Berlin, 1883, pt. i, Nummi, No. 89).
[4] D'Arbois, op. cit., p. 98.
[5] In Irish, *bre*, gen. *breg*, means "hill". In Welsh, *bre*, plur. *breon* ; Penbre. *Brig* meant "end".
[6] Jullian (in **CXXXIV**, 1906, p. 47) has tried, on not much ground, to make it a Ligurian word.

not seem to be Celtic—Uollobriga, Langobriga, Talabriga, Conimbriga, Cottaiobriga, etc.[1] Some, too, are Latin names in a Gaulish dress—Augustobriga, Cæsarobriga, Juliobriga, Flaviobriga.[2] But there are enough wholly Celtic names to make it unnecessary to look for the origin of the first part in another language. There are, for instance, Eburobriga,[3] Nertobriga,[4] Medubriga,[5] Nemetobriga,[6] Deobriga, etc.[7] All the same, only six names in *-briga* are known in Gaul and Germany, whereas there are thirty-five of them in the Peninsula.[8] On the whole they are more numerous in the west and centre than in the south and east.[9] They are lacking in Catalonia, in the provinces of Valencia, Alicante, and Murcia, and in the governments of Granada and Seville. There are thirteen in the province of Corunna, four in the Douro, and three in Portuguese Estremadura.

There are other Celtic names, distributed in the same manner, which corroborate the Celtic nature of those ending in *-briga*—Brigantium, Trigundum, Novium, Deva, Uxuma, Ugultiniacum, Ebora, Eburobritium,[10] Ocelodurum.

The limit of the Celtic settlements [11] can be traced by Deobriga among the Autrigones, in the valley of the Ebro, and Nertobriga, in the valley of the Jalón; on the east, going through Contrebia on the Jiloca, by Segobriga, the town with a Celtic name which on this side is nearest the coast; and on the Andalusian side by Mirobriga and Nertobriga in the Sierra Morena.

North of the Ebro, in Aragon, the River Gallicus and the

---

[1] D'Arbois, op. cit., p. 99.
[2] Ibid., p. 108.
[3] Irish *ibar* " yew ". Dottin, **CXCVI**, p. 255.
[4] Irish *neart*, Welsh *nerth* " strength ". Ibid., p. 275.
[5] Irish *mid* " mead " ; Welsh *medd.* Ibid., p. 271.
[6] Irish *nemed* " sanctuary ". Ibid., p. 224.
[7] *Devo-* : Irish *dia*, gen. *dié* " god ". We might add Segobriga, which Philipon makes an Iberian name and Schulten a Ligurian one (**DXIX**, p. 68). It is true that *sego* comes into many Ligurian place-names (Segusio, (?) Susa ; Segobrigii, above, p. 237), but it perhaps comes into more Celtic names (Segodunum, Rodez and Würzburg ; Segedunum in Britain ; Segura, Bressuire). Irish *seg* " strength ".
[8] D'Arbois (op. cit., p. 98) adds fourteen names in *-obre*, which he derives from ancient names in *-briga*—Canzobre, Cillobre (p. 103). The derivation is doubtful. Names in *-briga* produced names in *-brega*, and those in *-obre* may have come from town-names in *-bris*. Philipon, *Peuples*, p. 216.
[9] Schulten, op. cit., p. 110.
[10] *Eburo-* is likewise Ligurian. D'Arbois, **CCCI**, ii, 199.
[11] Schulten, op. cit., p. 106.

towns of Forum Gallorum and Gallica Flavia seem to belong to a later stratum of Celtic names.[1] Further west the region covered by Celtic names reaches the coast in two rivers called Deva, one among the Carietes and the other among the Cantabri. The Celts, who did not drive out the previous occupants of the Pyrenees, certainly mixed with them.[2] In the east, between the Celts and the coast, there was a tract of Iberian settlements into which they certainly penetrated, but without apparently making a serious breach in them. In the south were the Tartessians. The west coast, on the other hand, is dotted with Celtic names along its whole length, and the Celtic towns are on the shore.

If we were to make up a map from these names it would not quite correspond to the archæological map. It would leave outside the Celtic area the cremation-cemeteries of the provinces of Gerona and Barcelona on the one hand[3] and, on the other, the Alcores district with its cremation-tumuli. From this I conclude that in both cases the archæological finds represent settlements which did not last long. Catalonia and Bætica were the chief territories of the Iberians and Tartessians. That small bands of Celts should have passed through the one and insinuated themselves into the other, or even established themselves there, is of little consequence ; either they were absorbed or they have slipped through the meshes of the net of history.

This map based on names seems to indicate the route of the Celtic invasion.[4] The main route, in any case, seems to have been by the western passes of the Pyrenees, the famous road of Roncesvalles. From there it must have run to the valley of the Ebro by Suessatium[5] among the Varduli, a town with a Celtic name recalling that of the Suessiones, and Deobriga, to ascend the plateau by the Pancorbo gorge. Beyond, it followed the valleys of the Pisuerga and Douro. From the plateau they must have spread over the rest of the Peninsula. I am quite prepared to believe that smaller bands entered by the eastern passes of the Pyrenees ; but I am

[1] See the following volume in this series.
[2] Schulten, op. cit., p. 23, n. 5 : Celtic personal names.
[3] Bosch Gimpera, " La Necrópolis de Perelada," in **XV,** vi, 1915–1920, pp. 590 ff.
[4] Schulten, op. cit., p. 106.
[5] D'Arbois, **CCXLVIII** (Droit), p. 41.

not at all inclined to think, as some have suggested, that the Celts came by sea and worked up the great rivers of the west.[1]

Like the Celts of Aquitaine, they must have come from a great distance. It is not certain that the name of Suessatium, with its resemblance to that of the Suessiones, dates from the earliest Celtic settlements.[2]   But that of Brigantium,[3] the Celtic town which stood on the site of Corunna, among the Cantabri, probably belongs to the oldest stratum of Celtic names in Spain.   Now this is significant.   It is the name of Bregenz on the Lake of Constance, and it is the name of the Brigantes who must have come to England from the same region.

The place-names also give an important piece of information about the character of the Celtic settlements. Whereas in Gaul there are plenty of names in -*magus* and -*ialum*,[4] common nouns meaning " plain " and " field " which designate settlements in the plains, probably agricultural, the abundance of names in -*briga*, indicating settlements on hills and fortified hills, is very significant.   These names tell of insecurity, a state of war or danger of war, and we can imagine the Celts of Spain who had conquered only the least attractive parts of the country, scattered in the midst of Ligurian tribes, driven off, broken up, but still formidable and keeping watch on the Iberian or Tartessian states whose military power is always represented as considerable in the ancient writers.   That power held the fertile valleys of the south and east, which the Celts were powerless to seize from it.   The rapid advance of the Celts in such a huge country was able to set up a chain of posts all over it, but could hardly establish a continuous mass of population.

The historians [5] represent the Celts of the Spanish plateau as leading a hard and penurious life as very savage herdsmen. The mountaineers, the herdsmen and peasants of the *meseta*,

---

[1] Philipon, **DXVI**, p. 140 ; id., **CCCLXIX**, p. 190 ; Hirt, **CCCXXXVIII**, i, p. 168.

[2] See the following volume in this series.

[3] D'Arbois, **CCXCIX**, 121.

[4] Ibid., 90 : -*magos*, Irish *mag*, Welsh *ma* " plain " ; -*ialon*, Welsh *ial* " open space ".   Cf. Dottin, op. cit., s.v.

[5] See the passage of Avienus about the Berybraces above, p. 290 ; Schulten, op. cit., p. 106.

still live fairly roughly. But by their side live a middle class of townsfolk and an aristocracy.

Now the Celts had dealings with Tartessus. It was through Tartessus that the gold, copper, and tin of the Celtic country were exported in the time of Ephoros.[1] They were, therefore, linked up with the general economic life of the world, and they profited by it. The Celts were never, in any country, people to resist civilizing influences from outside. As a fact, the Celts of Spain have left evidence of the great extent to which they borrowed from others. Those who buried their dead in the tumuli of the Alcores were well supplied with Carthaginian articles of bronze and ivory.[2] Those of Aguilar de Anguita and other places in Castile and Portugal bought Iberian and Greek pottery.[3] They adopted part of the armament of the Iberians—their round shields, the iron portions of which are found in their tombs, their body-armour,[4] composed of two round plates held on by braces, which the Iberians had copied from the Italians, the bits of their horses, and even the horse-shoe,[5] which appears here for the first time in the Celtic world.

But the things taken from foreign cultures become scarcer as one approaches the Garonne, and the sepultures of Aquitaine, taken as a whole, if compared with contemporary tombs of the Rhine valley and Southern Germany, give an impression of being poor, particularly in articles of luxury of Greek manufacture.

Altogether, then, there are very extensive but not at all populous settlements of pastoral and warlike peoples, which very rapidly spread across the plateaus and made their way to the sea down the great rivers of the Atlantic side—the Douro, Tagus, and Guadiana. They easily conquered the first Ligurian occupants of the country. But they stopped at the edge of the fertile valleys and coasts already occupied by the Tartessians and Iberians. These last give the impression of being the powerful peoples of the Peninsula, and the story of the Celts will be chiefly subordinate to theirs.

[1] Ibid., p. 92.
[2] Bonsor, in **CXXXIX**, 1899, 2, pp. 251, 280, 288.
[3] Déchelette, ii, 2, p. 692 ; Bosch Gimpera, **CCCCXCIX**, pp. 38 ff.
[4] Déchelette, p. 688 ; cf. p. 692, n. 1.
[5] Ibid., p. 690.

IV

THE SURROUNDING OF THE CELTIC SETTLEMENTS. THE IBERIAN INVASION OF LANGUEDOC AND AQUITAINE

Some decades after the Celtic invasion the Iberians of the Ebro valley gained ground to the north at the expense of the Ligurians.[1] They probably organized military expeditions against the Ligurians and waged a war of destruction on them. But they followed up these ravages by extending their settlements. It is possible that the whole series of Iberian states was involved in this movement, or that it was produced by pressure, of which we know little at present, from the south.[2]

At the time of Hecatæos of Miletos the region of Narbonne, Béziers, and Montpellier was held by the Ligurians.[3] There one Ligurian people, the Elisyces, formed a state which was known far and wide, almost as well as Tartessus. In the days of the Homeric poems it stood for the wonderful West, the happy, distant land to which the dead retired.[4] When the Carthaginians fell on Gelon of Syracuse in 480, when he was about to go to the help of the Greeks against the Persian invaders, and were defeated at Himera, there were Elisyces serving in their fleet as mercenaries, with Ligurians, Sardinians, and Corsicans.[5]

At the time when the Marseilles *periplus* used by Avienus was written, the glory of the Elisyces was only a memory. "The nation of the Elisyces," Avienus writes,[6] "first occupied these parts, and Narbo was the chief head of its haughty realm." He bears witness to the destruction wrought by the Iberians on their way. "Ancient tradition tells that Bezera (Béziers) stood there,[7] but now the Heledus (the Lys) and the Orobus (the Orb) flow through empty fields and piles of ruins which speak of the prosperity which is gone."[8] At that time, according to the same author, the Iberian

---

[1] Schulten, op. cit., pp. 81 ff. ; Jullian, **CCCXLVII**, i, p. 265.
[2] R. Lantier, in **LI**, xxvi, p. 18.
[3] Hecat., frag. 19.
[4] Müllenhoff, **CCCLXII**, i, pp. 63 ff.
[5] Hdt., vii, 165.
[6] *Ora Marit.*, 586.
[7] Philipon, **CCCLXIX**, p. 155. The Tartessian name of Béziers seems to indicate an earlier advance of the peoples established in the south of Spain (ibid., p. 303).
[8] 591–4.

frontier reached the Hérault (Oranus) and the lake of Thau (Taurus palus).[1] Later it extended as far as the Rhone.[2]

It is possible that the Iberians went up the Rhone valley. A great part of ancient ethnology has come down to us in the form of fables and myths through the epic and lyric poets and the polygraphers. The author of a Περὶ Ποταμῶν ascribed to Plutarch speaks of one Κελτίβηρος, brother of Arar, who seems to be a river which flows into the Saône.[3] Here we perhaps have a recollection of those ancient campaigns of the Iberian bands. One may, too, wonder whether the advance of the Iberians in the fifth century was not preceded by extensive movement in both directions on the Ibero-Ligurian borders.

On the other side the Iberians established themselves in force between the Pyrenees and the Garonne. Eliberre (Auch), Hungunverro,[4] between Toulouse and Auch, and Calagurris,[5] between Toulouse and Saint-Bertrand, were Iberian towns, as were Elusa (Eauze), Iluro (Oloron), Tolosa (Toulouse), and Carcaso (Carcassonne).[6] To these we must add Burdigala [7] (Bordeaux) and perhaps Corbilo [8] (Nantes). The foundation of these cities shows that the Iberians left other things than ruins in their track. They left remains of their civilization, and in particular their pottery,[9] which is

---

[1] 612–614, 628–630. The Ceretes of Cerdagne and the *litus Cyneticum* extend beyond the Pyrenees (ibid., 550–2, 566).

[2] Scylax, 2. Cf. Strabo, iii, 4, 19 (166) ; Pliny, xxxvii, 32 ; Scymnos of Chios, 206–8.

[3] Pseudo-Plut., 6 ; Schulten, op. cit., p. 22.

[4] *Jerusalem Itinerary*, 550, 10.

[5] *Antonine Itinerary*, p. 457.

[6] D'Arbois, op. cit., p. 91 ; Strabo, iv, 1, 1.

[7] Jullian, op. cit., i, p. 264, n. 4.

[8] Schulten, op. cit., pp. 82–3.

[9] Déchelette, in **CXXXIX**, 1908, 2, pp. 400 ff. ; id., *Man.*, ii, 3, pp. 1492 ff. ; Joulin, in **CXXXIX**, 1920, 2, pp. 296 ff. ; P. Thiers, *Recherches sur les Ibères du Roussillon*, repr. from **XL** ; H. Rouzaud, *Notes et observations sur le pays narbonnais*, repr. from **XL**, vii ; id., " L'Oppidum pré-romain d'Ensérune " in **XL**, 1923 ; E. Pottier, " Les Fouilles de Montlaurès," in **LVIII**, 1909, pp. 981 ff. ; P. Thiers, " Fouilles de Castel-Roussillon," in **XXXVIII**, 1910, p. 149 ; E. Pottier, *Les Fouilles d'Ensérune* ; A. Mouret, " Note archéologique sur la céramique d'Ensérune," in **CCCXIII** ; G. Vasseur, " Découverte de poteries peintes à décoration polychrome dans les environs de Marseille," in **LVIII**, 1905, pp. 383 ff. ; id., " La Poterie ibérique pseudo-mycénienne aux environs d'Arles," in **XLIV**, 1907, p. 54. Although there are geometric vases of the fourth century among this pottery, it does not all date from the Iberian occupation ; imported vessels may have been added to it. Besides, it lasted longer than the Iberian occupation, and seems to be the prototype of the painted ware of Montans (La Tène III).

well known from the exploration of Montlaurès, Ensérune, Castel-Roussillon, and le Baou-Roux. It has been found at Marseilles and in the environs of Arles. Sculptured monuments, such as the Grézan statue [1] with the Iberian belt and the bust from Substantion (Sextantio),[2] which wears the same hood as the Grézan statue, tell the same story even more definitely.

The establishment of the Iberians in Aquitaine in the fifth century had one consequence of great importance to the Celts of that region and those of Spain. They were cut off for a long period from the main Celtic body. They no longer received anything from it, and lived on the old stock of Celtic culture which they had brought with them. This is the reason of their local peculiarities. For two or three hundred years there can have been very little direct communication between the Celts of Spain and those of Gaul and Britain, except by sea. There was some, but it has left no visible trace save in the west, besides some indirect traces on the southern edge of the Peninsula, where a few gold or bronze torques and a few brooches of La Tène I have been found, which are absent everywhere else.[3]

The Iberians seem to have held their ground in the Pyrenean country west of the Garonne. But in Languedoc they retreated after less than a hundred years. The *Periplus* of Scylax, attributed to an admiral of Darius but really written about 350 B.C., gives a very different picture of the region from that of Avienus. It places the limit of the Iberians near Emporion, south of the Pyrenees. Between Emporion and the Rhone the Iberians and Ligurians are mixed together—Λίγυες καὶ ῎Ιβηρες μίγαδες.[4] So the Ligurians had returned as the conquerors had retreated, and the latter had come to terms with them or were holding themselves on the defensive.

---

[1] Espérandieu, **CCCXXV**, i, 427.
[2] Bonnet, in **XC**, 1924, p. 14. We should also add the two busts found at St.-Chaptes, which have the same hood (Espérandieu, op. cit., No. 7614).
[3] Bosch Gimpera, **CCCCXCIX**, p. 41 ; F. Macineira, in **XCVII**, 1923, p. 80 (Gallic gold torque) ; Mariano Sanjuan Moreno, in **XXXIV**, 1916, lxvii, p. 181 (brooches of La Tène I at Castellar de Santisteban, Jaen). Cf. Lantier, **DXI**, pp. 109 ff.
[4] Scylax, 3, D, 17. Cf. Pseudo-Scymnos, 199 ff. He places the Ligurians after the Bebryces, in the neighbourhood of Emporion (Ephoros, 357) ; Schulten, op. cit., 93.

This fact is important for us, for behind the Ligurians as they flowed back came another wave of Gauls, and the return of the Iberians into Spain had consequences on the Celtic settlements in the country which we must examine.

V

THE CELTS ON THE COAST OF PROVENCE

Two hundred years afterwards Timæos, writing about 260, included the Provençal coast of the Mediterranean in the Celtic world. In the *Marvels* attributed to Aristotle there is a passage, which probably comes from Timæos, describing the Heraclean road, that is the Corniche road which runs along the coast of Italy in the Celtic country and passes through the Celto-Ligurians to Iberia. " They say that from Italy into the Celtic country, among the Celto-Ligurians and the Iberians, there is a road which is called the Heraclean Road." [1] This is the oldest historical document which definitely mentions the Celtic country as coming down to the Mediterranean. It is to be supposed that the facts to which that was due, which are not mentioned before this date, happened at least a hundred years before, and are connected with the retreat of the Iberians, for which Scylax is the earliest evidence.

It is true that the Celts had come almost to the coast of Provence long before.[2] But evidence of a less conjectural kind than that with which we have been dealing hitherto is now furnished of their presence.

We read in Justin that about two hundred years after the foundation of Marseilles, that is about 400 B.C., the city was attacked by a coalition of peoples of the neighbourhood, which had taken for its leader a petty king named Catumandus.[3] You could hardly find a more thoroughly Gaulish name than that. Catumandus is He-who-directs-the-battle.[4] The coalition laid siege to the city, but its plans were

---

[1] Pseudo-Arist., 85. Hence the name of Gallicus Sinus given to the Gulf of Lions. Livy, xxvi, 19 ; Strabo, iv, 137 ; Ptol., ii, 10, 2 ; viii, 5, 2 ; d'Arbois, in **CXL**, 1983, p. 85.

[2] See above, pp. 251–2.

[3] Just., 44, 5 ; Schulten, op. cit., p. 93 ; Niese, in Pauly and Wissowa, **CCCLXVIII**, vii, p. 615.

[4] *Catu* : Irish *cath*, Welsh *cad* " battle " (Dottin, **CXCVI**, s.v.).

upset by some religious sign, so it abandoned the attack. The Marseilles people sent gifts of thanksgiving to the Temple of Delphi. On the return their messengers brought news of the capture of Rome by the Gauls. Therefore the incident occurred about 390.

The Celts had lived along the coast, associated or mingled with the Ligurians, since the end of the fifth century. I have said that the Carthaginians recruited mercenaries among the Elisycès on the coast of Provence in 480. Henceforward they would come there for Celtic or Gaulish mercenaries. In 263, when the Romans sent two legions into Sicily after concluding an agreement with Hieron of Syracuse, the Carthaginians sent there an army of Iberian, Ligurian, and Celtic mercenaries.[1] The last-named were not Celts of Spain, for at this time, as we shall see, these would have been not Celts but Celtiberians. They were Celts of Gaul. This recruiting must have started a long time before, for these are probably the men to whom reference is made in a curious speech which Thucydides makes Alcibiades address to the Spartans. It is during the Sicilian war, in 415. Alcibiades has been banished and turns traitor ; he proposes to go and enlist an army of Iberians and other very special barbarians who have appeared in that quarter : καὶ ἄλλους τῶν ἐκεῖ ὁμολογουμένως νῦν βαρβάρων μαχιμωτάτους (" and others who are recognized to be the most warlike of the barbarians now there ").[2]

Having arrived on the Provençal coast in the last years of the fifth century, the Celts, who in this district never succeeded in completely absorbing the Ligurians, continued their advance in the direction of Languedoc.[3] The Iberians did not resist, and Polybios, an accurate and well-informed historian, wrote about 150 : " One meets nothing but Celts from Narbo and its neighbourhood to the Pyrenees." At all events, when Hannibal, sixty years before, in 218, passed through Roussillon and Languedoc on his way to the Alps, with an army largely composed of Celts, it seems that he met nothing but Gauls.

---

[1] Pol., i, 17, 4.
[2] Thuc., vi, 90, 3.
[3] Joulin, in **CXXXIX**, 1923, 2, p. 197. La Tène tombs with red-figured Attic pottery at Toulouse, Ensérune, Mataro, and San Feliú de Guixols.

BIBLIOGRAPHY

I. SOURCES

Greek and Latin authors are indicated by the usual abbreviations. *F.H.G.* stands for Carolus Müller, *Fragmenta Historicorum Græcorum,* in the Collection Didot.

[Certain English editions have been added in square brackets, but the footnotes do not refer to the pages of these editions unless it is so stated.—Trs.]

II. INSCRIPTIONS

Corpus Inscriptionum Latinarum, consilio et auctoritate Academiæ Regiæ Borussicæ, Berlin, 1863, etc. . **I**

Ephemeris Epigraphica . . . . . **II**

Allmer (A.), *Inscriptions antiques de Vienne,* Vienne, 1875–8 . . . . **III**

Dittenberger (G.), *Sylloge Inscriptionum Græcarum,* 2nd ed., Leipzig, 1898 ; 3rd ed., 1915–1923 . **IV**

Durrbach (F.), *Choix d'inscriptions de Délos,* Paris, 1921 . . . . **V**

Rhys (Sir John), *The Celtic Inscriptions of Gaul and Italy,* London, 1910 . . . . . . **VI**

—— *Gleanings in the Italian Field of Celtic Epigraphy,* repr. from **CXXI**, London, 1915 . . . . **VII**

—— *Notes on the Coligny Calendar,* London, 1910 . **VIII**

III. PERIODICALS

Abhandlungen der königlichen preussischen Akademie der Wissenschaften, phil. hist. Klasse, Berlin . **IX**

Abhandlungen der naturhistorischen Gesellschaft zu Nürnberg, Nuremberg . . . . . **X**

Annales de la Faculté des sciences de Marseille . . **XI**

Annales de la Société Éduenne, Autun . . . **XII**

Année sociologique, Paris . . . . . **XIII**

Anuari de l'Institut d'Estudis catalans, Barcelona . **XIV**

Anthropologie, Paris . . . . . . **XV**

Antiquaries' Journal, London . . . . . **XVI**

Anzeiger für schweizerische Altertumskunde (Indicateur d'antiquités suisses), Zurich . . . . **XVII**

Archæologia, or miscellaneous tracts relating to antiquity, published by the Society of Antiquaries of London, London . . . . . . **XVIII**

Archæologia Cambrensis, Cambridge . . . . **XIX**

Archaeologischer Anzeiger, Berlin . . . . **XX**

Archaelogiai értesitö, Budapest . . . . **XXI**

Archeologo portugues, Lisbon . . . . **XXII**

304 BIBLIOGRAPHY

Mitteilungen der Anthropologischen Gesellschaft, Zurich CI
Mitteilungen des deutschen archäologischen Instituts, Athenische Abteilung, Athens CII
—— —— Römische Abteilung, Rome . . . CIII
Mitteilungen der prähistorischen Commission der kais. Akademie der Wissenschaften, Vienna . . CIV
Mitteilungen (wissenschaftliche) aus Bosnien und Herzegowina, Vienna CV
Monumenti antichi pubblicati per cura della R. Academia dei Lincei, Milan CVI
Monuments Piot, Paris CVII
Musée Belge, Liége and Paris CVIII
Musée Neuchâtelois, Neuchâtel CIX
Nassauische Annalen CX
New Ireland Review, Dublin CXI
Notizie degli scavi di antichità, Rome . . . CXII
Nouvelles Archives des missions scientifiques, Paris . CXIII
Orientalische Literaturzeitung, Berlin . . . CXIV
Památky archœologické, Prague CXV
Philologica, Journal of Comparative Philology, London CXVI
Portugalia, Oporto (1899–1908) CXVII
Prähistorische Zeitschrift, Berlin CXVIII
Pro Alesia, Paris CXIX
Pro Nervia, Bavay CXX
Proceedings of the British Academy, London . . CXXI
Proceedings of the Royal Irish Academy, Dublin . CXXII
Proceedings of the Society of Antiquaries of London . CXXIII
Proceedings of the Society of Antiquaries of Scotland, Edinburgh CXXIV
Rassegna delle scienze geologiche, Rome . . . CXXV
Reports of the Research Committee of the Society of Antiquaries of London CXXVI
Report of . . . the British Association, London . CXXVII
Rendiconti della R. Accademia dei Lincei, classe di scienze morali, storiche e filologiche, Rome . CXXVIII
Reports of the Smithsonian Institute, Washington . CXXIX
Revue d'anthropologie, Paris CXXX
Revue de l'Instruction publique en Belgique, Bruges . CXXXI
Revue de Nîmes CXXXII
Revue de phonétique, Paris CXXXIII
Revue des Études anciennes, Bordeaux . . . CXXXIV
Revue des Études grecques, Paris CXXXV
Revue des questions scientifiques, Paris . . . CXXXVI
Revue du Mois, Paris CXXXVII
Revue anthropologique, Paris CXXXVIII
Revue archéologique, Paris CXXXIX
Revue celtique, Paris CXL
Revue historique, Paris CXLI
Revue numismatique, Paris CXLII
Revue préhistorique. Annales de palethnologie, Paris CXLIII
Rheinisches Museum für Philologie, Frankfort on Main CXLIV
Rivista archeologica della provincia di Como . . CXLV
Rhodania, Vienne CXLVI
Scottish Review, Edinburgh CXLVII

Sitzungsberichte der koenig. preussischen Akademie der
    Wissenschaften, Berlin CXLVIII
Sitzungsberichte der kais. Akademie der Wissenschaften
    zu Wien, philos. hist. Klasse, Vienna . . . CXLIX
Société de statistique, d'histoire et d'archéologie de
    Marseille et de la Provence. Volume du
    Centenaire CL
Sonderhefte des österr. arch. Institut, Vienna . . CLI
Symbolæ Osloenses, Oslo CLII
Syria, Paris CLIII
Transactions of the Honourable Society of
    Cymmrodorion CLIV
Travaux de la section numismatique et archéologique
    du musée de Koloszvar CLV
Trabalhos da Sociedade portugueza de Antropologia e
    Etnologia, Oporto CLVI
Trierer Jahresberichte, Treves CLVII
Verhandlungen der Berliner Gesellschaft für Anthro-
    pologie, Ethnologie und Urgeschichte, Berlin . CLVIII
Veröffentlichungen des oberhessischen Museums und der
    galischen Sammlungen zu Giessen, Abteilung für
    Vorgeschichte CLIX
Westdeutsche Zeitschrift für Geschichte und Kunst,
    Bonn CLX
Wiener Studien, Vienna CLXI
Indogermanisches Jahrbuch CLXII
Wochenschrift für klassische Philologie, Berlin . . CLXIII
Wörter und Sachen CLXIV
Würtembergische Vierteljahrsschriften für Landes-
    geschichte, Stuttgart CLXV
Zeitschrift der deutsch. Morgenländischen Gesellschaft,
    Leipzig CLXVI
Zeitschrift der Savigny-Stiftung für Rechtsgeschichte,
    Berlin CLXVII
Zeitschrift für deutsche Altertumskunde . . CLXVIII
Zeitschrift für Ethnologie, Berlin CLXIX
Zeitschrift für romanische Philologie, Halle . . CLXX
Zeitschrift für celtische Philologie CLXXI
Zeitschrift für Sozialwissenschaft CLXXII
Zeitschrift für vergleichende Literaturgeschichte, Berlin CLXXIII
Zeitschrift für vergleichende Sprachforschung, auf dem
    Gebiete der indogermanischen Sprachen, Berlin . CLXXIV

IV. MISCELLANIES

Festgabe für Hugo Blümner, Zurich, 1914 . . . CLXXV
Festschrift W. Stokes, Leipzig, 1900 . . . CLXXVI
Festschrift zur Feier des fünfundsiebzigjährigen
    Bestehens des röm.-germ. Centralmuseums zu
    Mainz, 1902 CLXXVII
Heilbronner Festschrift CLXXVIII
Mélanges Ch. Bémont, Paris, 1913 CLXXIX
Mélanges R. Cagnat, Paris, 1912 CLXXX
Mélanges L. Havet, Paris, 1909 CLXXXI

Essays and Studies presented to William Ridgeway,
 Cambridge, 1913 . . . . . . **CLXXXII**
Mélanges de Saussure, Paris, 1908 . . . . **CLXXXIII**
Mélanges Vendryès, Paris, 1925 . . . **CLXXXIV**
Opuscula archaeologica Oscari Montelio dedicata,
 Stockholm, 1913 . . . . . . **CLXXXV**
Recueil d'études égyptologiques dédiées à la mémoire
 de J.-F. Champollion, Paris, 1922 . . . **CLXXXVI**
Recueil Kondakow, Prague, 1926 . . . . **CLXXXVI**

V. LANGUAGE

ARBOIS DE JUBAINVILLE (H. d'), *Éléments de la
 grammaire celtique*, Paris, 1903 . . . . **CLXXXVIII**
MACBAIN (Alexander), *An Etymological Dictionary of
 the Gaelic Language*, 2nd ed., Inverness, 1911 . **CLXXXIX, CXC**
BERNEKER (E.), *Slavisches etymologisches Wörterbuch*,
 Heidelberg, 1908–1913 . . . . . **CXC**
BUDINSZKY (A.), *Die Ausbreitung der lateinischen
 Sprache*, Berlin, 1881 . . . . . **CXCII**
CLINTON (O. H. Fynes), *The Welsh Vocabulary of the
 Bangor District*, Oxford, 1913 . . . . **CXCIII**
Corpus Glossariorum Latinorum, Leipzig, 1888–1901 . **CXCIV**
CRAMER, *Rheinische Ortsnamen*, Düsseldorf, 1901 . **CXCV**
DOTTIN (Georges), *La Langue gauloise*, Paris, 1920 . **CXCVI**
—— *Manuel d'irlandais moyen*, vol. i (grammar),
 Paris, 1913 . . . . **CXCVII**
ERNAULT (E.), *Glossaire moyen-breton*, Paris, 1895–6 . **CXCVIII**
FINCK (F. N.), *Die Araner Mundart*, Marburg, 1899 . **CXCIX**
FISCHER (F. T. T. A.), *Die Lehnwörter des Altwest-
 nordischen* (Palaestra, lxxxv), Berlin, 1909 . . **CC**
FRASER (John), *History and Etymology*, Oxford, 1923 . **CCI**
GILES (Peter), *A Short Manual of Comparative
 Philology*, London, 1901 . . . . . **CCII**
GILLIES (H. C.), *Elements of Gaelic Grammar, based on
 the work of the Rev. Alexander Stewart*, London,
 1902 . . . . **CCIII**
GINNEKEN (van), *Principes de linguistique psychologique*,
 Paris, etc., 1907 . . . . . . **CCIV**
HENEBRY (Richard), *Contribution to the Phonology of
 Desi-Irish*, Greifswald, 1901 . . . . **CCV**
HERMET (Abbé F.), *Les Grafittes de la Graufesenque*,
 Rodez, 1923 . . . . **CCVI**
HOLDER (A. T.), *Alt-celtischer Sprachschatz*, 3 vols.,
 Leipzig, 1896–1913 . . . . . . **CCVII**
JONES (Sir John Morris), *A Welsh Grammar, historical
 and comparative*, Oxford, 1913 . . . . **CCVIII**
KEIL (Heinrich), *Grammatici Latini*, Leipzig, 1857–80 . **CCIX**
KLUGE (F.), *Etymologisches Wörterbuch der deutschen
 Sprache*, 6th ed., Strasburg, 1899 [*An Etymological
 Dictionary of the German Language*, London, 1891] **CCX**
—— *Vorgeschichte der altgermanischen Dialekte*, in
 H. PAUL, *Grundriss der germanischen Philologie*,
 vol. i, 1901 . . . . **CCXI**

LONGNON (A.), *Noms de lieux anciens de la France*,
Paris, 1926 . . . . . **CCXII**
LOTH (J.), *Chrestomathie bretonne*, Paris, 1890 . . **CCXIII**
—— *Vocabulaire vieux-breton* (Bibl. É.H.É., vi), Paris,
1884 . . . . **CCXIV**
MACALISTER (Robert A. Stewart), *Studies in Irish
Epigraphy*, 3 vols., London, 1897–1907 . . **CCXV**
MEILLET (A.), *Les Dialectes indo-européens*, Paris, 1922 **CCXVI**
—— *Introduction à l'étude comparative des langues
indo-européennes*, 3rd ed., Paris, 1912 . . . **CCXVII**
—— and COHEN (M.), *Les Langues du monde*, Paris,
1924 . . . . **CCXVIII**
MOLLOY (John H.), *A Grammar of the Irish Language*,
Dublin, 1867 . . . . **CCXIX**
MORRIS (Meredith), *A Glossary of the Demetian Dialect*,
Tonypandy, 1910 . . . . . . **CCXX**
MOULTON (James H.), *Two Lectures on the Science of
Language*, Cambridge, 1903 . . . . **CCXXI**
MEYER (W.), *Fragmenta Burana*, Berlin, 1901 . . **CCXXII**
NICHOLSON (Edward W. Byron), *Keltic Researches:
studies in the history and distribution of the ancient
Goidelic language and peoples*, London, 1904 . . **CCXXIII**
—— *Sequanian: first steps in the investigation of a
newly discovered ancient European language*,
London, 1898 . . . . **CCXXIV**
O'DONOVAN (John), *A Grammar of the Irish Language*,
Dublin, 1845 . . . . **CCXXV**
O'NOLAN (Rev. Gerald), *Studies in Modern Irish*,
Dublin, 1919 . . . . **CCXXVI**
PEDERSEN (Holger), *Vergleichende Grammatik der
keltischen Sprachen*, Göttingen, 1909–13 . . **CCXXVII**
QUIGGIN (Edmund C.), *A Dialect of Donegal*, Cam-
bridge, 1906 . . . . **CCXXVIII**
REID (Duncan), *A Course of Gaelic Grammar*, Glasgow,
1902 [3rd ed., 1908] . . . . . . **CCXXIX**
RHYS (Sir John), *Celtæ and Galli*, London, 1905 . **CCXXX**
ROWLAND (T.), *A Grammar of the Welsh Language*
Wrexham, n.d., 4th ed. . . . . **CCXXXI**
[For **CCXXXII**, see below, STOKES, **CCXXXVI**]
SOMMERFELT (A.), *Dē en Italo-celtique: son rôle dans
l'évolution morphologique des langues italo-celtiques*,
Oslo, 1920 . . . . **CCXXXIII**
—— *The Dialect of Torr, Co. Donegal*, Oslo, 1922 . **CCXXXIV**
STOKES (Whitley) and STRACHAN (J.), *Thesaurus
Palæohibernicus*, 2 vols., Cambridge, 1901–3 . **CCXXXV**
—— *Three Irish Glossaries*, London, 1862 . . **CCXXXVI**
—— *Urkeltischer Sprachschatz*, trans. BEZZENBERGER,
Göttingen, 1894 [pt. iii of A. FICK, *Wörterbuch der
indogermanischen Grundsprache*, 4th ed., 1890–1909) **CCXXXVII**
Beiträge zur Kunde der indogermanischen Sprachen,
Göttingen, 1877–1900 . . . . . **CCXXXVIII**
[For **CCXXXIX**, see above, STOKES, **CCXXXVII**]
THURNEYSEN (Rudolf), *Keltoromanisches*, Halle, 1884 . **CCXL**
VALLÉE (F.), *La Langue bretonne et le français*, 4th ed.,
Saint-Brieuc, 1916 . . . . . . **CCXLI**

VENDRYÈS (Joseph), *Grammaire du vieil irlandais*, Paris,
1908 . . . .   **CCXLII**
WALDE (A.), *Lateinisches etymologisches Wörterbuch*,
2nd ed., Heidelberg, 1910 . . . .   **CCXLIII**
—— *Über älteste sprachliche Beziehungen zwischen
Kelten und Italikern*, Innsbruck, 1917 . .   **CCXLIV**
WINDISCH (E.), in GROEBER, *Grundriss der romanischen
Philologie*, 2nd ed., Strasburg, 1905, pp. 390–4 .   **CCXLV**
ZIMMER (H.), *Keltische Beiträge, Studien*, in **CLXXIV**,
1888 . . . .   **CCXLVI**

VI. LITERATURE

Ancient Laws of Ireland, 6 vols., Dublin, 1865–79 .   **CCXLVII**
ARBOIS DE JUBAINVILLE (H. d'), *Cours de littérature
celtique*, 12 vols., Paris, 1883–1902 . . .   **CCXLVIII**
—— *Essai d'un catalogue de la littérature épique de
l'Irlande*, Paris, 1883. . . . . .   **CCXLIX**
—— *Le cycle mythologique irlandais et la mythologie
celtique*, Paris, 1884 [*The Irish Mythological Cycle
and Celtic Mythology*, Dublin, 1903] . . .   **CCL**
ARNOLD (Matthew), *The Study of Celtic Literature*,
London, 1891 [new ed., 1910] . . . .   **CCLI**
BEST (R. I.), *Bibliography of Irish Philology and
Literature*, Dublin, 1913 . . . . .   **CCLII**
CAMPBELL (John F.), *Leabhar na Feinne*, London, 1872   **CCLIII**
—— *Popular Tales of the West Highlands*, Edinburgh,
1890 . . . .   **CCLIV**
CURTIN (Jeremiah), *Hero-tales of Ireland*, London, 1894   **CCLV**
Domesday Book . . . .   **CCLVI**
CROKER (Thomas Crofton), *Fairy Legends and Traditions
of the South of Ireland*, London, 1882 . . .   **CCLVII**
FARADAY (Winifred), *The Cattle Raid of Cuailnge*,
London, 1901 . . . .   **CCLVIII**
GREGORY (Isabella A.), Lady Gregory, *Cuchulain of
Muirthemne*, London, 1902 . . . .   **CCLIX**
GUEST (Lady Charlotte), *The Mabinogion* . . .   **CCLX**
GWYNN (Edward), *The Metrical Dindsenchas* (Todd
Lectures, viii, ix, x), 3 vols., Dublin, 1908–13 .   **CCLXI**
HULL (Eleanor), *A Text-book of Irish Literature*, 2 pts.,
Dublin, 1906 . . . .   **CCLXII**
—— *The Cuchullin Saga in Irish Literature*, London,
1898 . . . .   **CCLXIII**
HYDE (Douglas), *A Literary History of Ireland*, London,
1899 . . . .   **CCLXIV**
Irish Texts Society, *Publications*, London, 1899, etc. .   **CCLXV**
JOYCE (P. W.), *The Origin and History of Irish Names
of Places*, 2 ser., Dublin, 1869–75 . . .   **CCLXVI**
—— *Old Celtic Romances*, London, 1879 [2nd ed., 1894]   **CCLXVII**
MACALISTER (Robert A. Stewart) and MACNEILL (John),
ed., *Leabhar Gabhála. The Book of Conquests of
Ireland*, 1917 . . . .   **CCLXVIII**
Lives of Saints, from the Book of Lismore, ed. W. STOKES,
Oxford, 1890 . . . .   **CCLXIX**

LOTH (J.), *Les Mabinogion*, 2 vols., Paris, 1913 . . **CCLXX**

MARTIN (Martin), *A Description of the Islands of Scotland*, London, 1703 . . . . . **CCLXXI**

MEYER (Kuno), *Fianaigecht*, Dublin, 1910 . . . **CCLXXII**

—— *Totenklage um König Niall Noigiallach*, in **CLXXVI** **CCLXXIII**

—— and NUTT (Alfred), *The Voyage of Bran*, 2 vols., London, 1895–7 . . . . **CCLXXIV**

NUTT (Alfred), *Celtic and Medieval Romance*, London, 1899 . . . . **CCLXXV**

—— *Cuchulain, the Irish Achilles*, London, 1900 . **CCLXXVI**

—— *Legends of the Holy Grail*, London, 1902 . . **CCLXXVII**

O'CURRY (Eugene), *Lectures on the Manuscript Materials of Ancient Irish History*, 8 vols., Dublin, 1861 . **CCLXXVIII**

O'GRADY (Standish), *Silva Gadelica*. 2 vols., London, 1892 . . . . **CCLXXIX**

RENAN (Ernest), *La Poésie des races celtiques*, Paris [*The Poetry of the Celtic Races*, London, 1896] . **CCLXXX**

RHYS (Sir John), *Studies in the Arthurian Legend*, Oxford and New York, 1891 . . . . **CCLXXXI**

—— *Lectures on the Origin and Growth of Religion as illustrated by Celtic Heathendom* (Hibbert Lectures), London, 1888 . . . . **CCLXXXII**

—— *The Mabinogion*, London, 1901 . . . **CCLXXXIII**

—— and EVANS (J. G.), ed., *Mabinogion*, Oxford, 1887 . . . . **CCLXXXIV**

Sanas Cormaic, ed. K. MEYER, Halle, 1912 . . **CCLXXXV**

SCHIRMER (G.), *Zur Brendanus-Legende*, Leipzig, 1888 . **CCLXXXVI**

SKENE (William F.), *Four Ancient Books of Wales*, 2 vols., Edinburgh, 1868 . . . . . **CCLXXXVII**

STOKES (Whitley), *Three Middle Irish Homilies*, Calcutta, 1877 . . . . **CCLXXXVIII**

THURNEYSEN (Rudolf), *Die irische Helden- und Königssage bis zum siebzehnten Jahrhundert*, Halle, 1921 . . . . **CCLXXXIX**

—— *Sagen aus dem Alten Irland*, Berlin, 1901 . . **CCXC**

Todd Lectures, Dublin, 1885–1924 . . . . **CCXCI**

Transactions of the Ossianic Society, Dublin, 1855–61 . **CCXCII**

Waifs and Strays of Celtic Tradition, Argyllshire series, 3 vols., London, edited by Lord Archibald CAMPBELL and others . . . . . **CCXCII**

WESTON (Jessie L.), *King Arthur and his Knights*, London, 1899 . . . . **CCXCIV**

WINDISCH (E.), *Irische Texte*, Leipzig, 1880 . . **CCXCV**

—— *Die altirischen Heldensage, Táin Bo Cuailnge, nach dem Buch von Leinster*, Leipzig, 1905 . . **CCXCVI**

VII. GENERAL WORKS

ÅBERG (Nils), *Das nordische Kulturgebiet in Mitteleuropa während der jüngeren Steinzeit*, 2 vols., Upsala, 1918 **CCXCVII**

—— ALLEN (John Romilly), *Celtic Art in Pagan and Christian Times*, 2nd ed., London, 1912 . . **CCXCVIII**

ARBOIS DE JUBAINVILLE (H. d'), *Les Celtes depuis les temps les plus reculés jusqu'en l'an 100 avant notre ère*, Paris, 1904. . . . . . . **CCXCIX**

ARBOIS DE JUBAINVILLE (H. d'), *Les Druides et les dieux celtiques à forme d'animaux*, Paris, 1906 . . **CCC**
—— *Les Premiers Habitants de l'Europe*, 2nd ed., 2 vols., Paris, 1889–94 . . . . . **CCCI**
ARMSTRONG (E. C. R.), *Guide to the Collection of Irish Antiquities. Catalogue of Irish Gold Ornaments in the Collection of the Royal Irish Academy*, Dublin, 1920 . . . . **CCCII**
BERTRAND (A.), *Archéologie celtique et gauloise*, Paris, 1876 . . . . **CCCIII**
BIENKOWSKI (P.), *Les Celts dans les arts mineurs gréco-romains*, Cracow, 1928 . . . . . **CCCIV**
BIENKOWSKI (P. R. von), *Die Darstellungen der Gallier in der hellenischen Kunst*, Vienna, 1908 . . **CCCV**
BLANCHET (A.), *Traité des monnaies gauloises*, Paris, 1905 . . . . **CCCVI**
BOAS, *The Social Organization and the Secret Societies of the Kwakiutl Indians*, Washington, n.d. . . **CCCVII**
BUSHE-FOX (J. P.), *Excavations at Hengistbury Head*, in **CXXVI** 1915, ... **CCCVIII**
CASTILLO YURRITA (A. del), *La Cultura del vaso campaniforme*, Barcelona, 1928 . . . . **CCCIX**
CAVAIGNAC (E.), *Histoire du Monde*, Paris . . **CCCX**
CHAPOT (V.), *Le Monde romain*, Paris, 1927 [*The Roman World*, in this series, London and New York, 1928] . . . . **CCCXI**
COOK (A. B.), *The European Sky-god*, repr. from **LXIV**, 1904 . . . . **CCCXII**
Corpus Vasorum Antiquorum . . . . . **CCCXIII**
MACCULLOCH (Rev. John A.), *The Religion of the Ancient Celts*, Edinburgh, 1911 . . . . **CCCXIV**
DAREMBERG and SAGLIO, *Dictionnaire des antiquités grecques et romaines*, Paris, 1877–1919 . . **CCCXV**
DAVY (G.), *La foi jurée*, Paris, 1922 . . . **CCCXVI**
DÉCHELETTE (J.), *La Collection Millon. Antiquités préhistoriques et gallo-romaines*, Paris, 1913 . . **CCCXVII**
—— *Manuel d'archéologie préhistorique, celtique, et gallo-romaine*, 4 vols., Paris, 1908–14 . . **CCCXVIII**
DELATTE (A.), *Études sur la littérature pythagoricienne*, Bibl. É.H.É., Paris, 1915 . . . . . **CCCXIX**
DENIKER (J.), *Les Races et les peuples de la terre*, Paris, 1900 [*The Races of Man*, London, 1900] . . **CCCXX**
DOTTIN (G.), *Les Anciens Peuples de l'Europe*, Paris, 1916 . . . . **CCCXXI**
—— *Manuel pour servir à l'étude de l'antiquité celtique*, 2nd ed., Paris, 1915 . . . . . **CCCXXII**
—— *La Religion des Celtes*, Paris, 1904 . . . **CCCXXIII**
EBERT (M.), *Reallexikon der Vorgeschichte*, 15 vols., Berlin, 1924–32 . . . . . . **CCCXXIV**
ESPÉRANDIEU (E.), *Recueil général des bas-reliefs de la Gaule*, Paris, 1907–30 . . . . . **CCCXXV**
FEIST (S.), *Kultur, Ausbreitung, und Herkunft der Indo-germanen*, Berlin, 1913 . . . . . **CCCXXVI**
FELICE (P. de), *L'Autre Monde: mythes et légendes. Le purgatoire de Saint Patrice*, Paris, 1906 . . **CCCXXVII**

FLEURE (Herbert J.), *The Races of England and Wales*, London, 1923 CCCXXVIII

FÖHR (Julius von), *Hügelgräber auf der Schwäbischen Alb*, ed. L. MAYER, Stuttgart, 1892 . . . CCCXXIX

FORRER (R.), *Reallexikon der prähistorischen, klassischen, und frühchristlichen Altertümer*, Berlin, 1907 . CCCXXX

FOUGÈRES (G.), GROUSSET (R.), JOUGUET (P.), and LESQUIER (J.), *Les Premières Civilisations*, vol. i of *Peuples et civilisations*, Paris, 1926 . . . CCCXXXI

FRAZER (Sir James G.), *Les Origines magiques de la royauté*, Paris, 1920 [*Lectures on the Early History of the Kingship*, London, 1905] CCCXXXII

—— *Le Totémisme*, Paris, 1898 [*Totemism*, Edinburgh, 1887] CCCXXXIII

FUSTEL DE COULANGES (N.-D.), *Histoire des institutions politiques de l'ancienne France*, 2nd ed., 5 vols., Paris, 1900–7 CCCXXXIV

GÖTZE (Alfred), *Führer auf die Steinsburg bei Römhild*, in **CXVIII**, 1921–2 CCCXXXV

HASTINGS (James), *Encyclopædia of Religion and Ethics*, Edinburgh, 1908–18 CCCXXXVI

HIRSCHFELD (H. O.), *Timagenes und die gallische Wandersage* (*Kleine Schriften*, Berlin, 1913) . . CCCXXXVII

HIRT (H. A.), *Die Indogermanen, ihre Verbreitung, ihre Urheimat, und ihre Kultur*, 2 vols., Strasburg, 1905–7 CCCXXXVIII

HÖRNES (Moriz), Yr., *Urgeschichte der bildenden Kunst*, ed. O. MENGHIN, 3rd ed., Vienna, 1925 . . CCCXXXIX

HOLLEAUX (M.), *Rome, la Grèce et les monarchies hellénistiques au IIIe siècle avant J.-C.*, Paris, 1921 CCCXL

HOMO (Léon), *L'Italie primitive et les débuts de l'impérialisme romain*, Paris, 1925 [*Primitive Italy*, in this series, London and New York, 1927] . CCCXLI

HOOPS (J.), ed., *Reallexikon der germanischen Altertumskunde*, Strasburg, 1911–12 . . . CCCXLII

HUBERT (Henri), *Le Culte des héros et ses conditions sociales*, Paris, n.d. CCCXLIII

—— *Divinités gauloises. Succelus et Nantosuelta, Epona, dieux de l'autre monde*, Mâcon, 1925 . . CCCXLIV

JARDÉ (A.), *La Formation du peuple grec*, Paris, 1923 [*The Formation of the Greek People*, in this series, London and New York, 1926] CCCXLV

JULLIAN (Camille), *De la Gaule à la France*, Paris, 1922 CCCXLVI

—— *Histoire de la Gaule*, 3rd ed., Paris, 1920, etc. . CCCXLVII

KAUFMANN (F.), *Deutsche Altertumskunde*, 2 vols., Munich, 1913–23 CCCXLVIII

KEANE (Augustus H.), *Man, Past and Present*, Cambridge, 1899 [revised ed., 1920] . . . CCCXLIX

KEMBLE (John M.), *Horae Ferales ; or, Studies in the Archæology of the Northern Nations*, London, 1863 CCCL

LEUZE (O.), *Die römische Jahrzahlung*, 1909 . . CCCLI

MAINE (Sir Henry J. Sumner), *Lectures on the Early History of Institutions*, 8 vols., London, 1875 CCCLII

MEITZEN, *Siedelung und Agrarwesen der Westgermanen und Ostgermanen*, Berlin, 1895 CCCLIII

MEYER (Éduard), *Geschichte des Altertums*, 1st and 3rd eds., Stuttgart, 1893–1913 CCCLIV
—— *Histoire de l'Antiquité*, vol. i, *Introduction à l'étude des Sociétés anciennes*, Paris, 1912 CCCLV
MEYER (Kuno), *Miscellanea Hibernica*, Urbana, 1916 . CCCLVI
MONTELIUS (O.), *Die älteren Kulturperioden in Orient und Europa*. i. *Die Methode*, Stockholm, 1913 . CCCLVII
MOMMSEN (Theodor), *Monumenta Germaniæ historica*, Berlin CCCLVIII
—— *Histoire romaine*, translation, 8 vols., Paris, 1863–72 [English translation, London and New York, 1911] CCCLIX
MORET (A.) and DAVY (G.), *Des clans aux empires*, Paris, 1923 [*From Tribe to Empire*, in this series, London and New York, 1926] CCCLX
MUCH (A.), *Kunsthistorischer Atlas*, Vienna, 1889 . CCCLXI
MÜLLENHOFF (K. V.), *Deutsche Altertumskunde*, 2nd ed., Berlin, 1890, etc. CCCLXII
MUNRO (Robert), *Les Stations lacustres de l'Europe aux âges de la Pierre et du Bronze*, Paris, 1907 [*The Lake Dwellings of Europe*, London, 1890] . . CCCLXIII
NIEDERLÉ (Lubor), *Manuel de l'antiquité slave*, 2 vols., Paris, 1923–6 CCCLXIV
NIESE (B.), *Geschichte der griechischen und makedonischen Staaten*, 2 vols., Gotha, 1893–1908 . . . CCCLXV
PARKYN (E. A.), *An Introduction to the Study of Pre-historic Art*, London, 1915 CCCLXVI
PAUL (H.), *Grundriss der germanischen Philologie*, 3 vols., 2nd ed., Strasburg, 1901, etc. . . . CCCLXVII
PAULY and WISSOWA, *Real-Encyclopädie der klass. Altertumswissenschaft*, Stuttgart, 1894, etc. . . CCCLXVIII
PHILIPON (E.), *Les Peuples primitifs de l'Europe méridionale*, Paris, 1925 CCCLXIX
RANKE (J.), *Der Mensch*, 2 vols., 2nd ed., Leipzig, 1890 CCCLXX
RIDGEWAY (Sir William), *The Origin of Tragedy*, Cambridge, 1910 CCCLXXI
REINACH (Salomon), *Description raisonnée du Musée des Antiquités nationales*. ii. *Bronzes figurés*, Paris, 1895 CCCLXXII
—— *Catalogue illustré du Musée des Antiquités nationales au Château de Saint-Germain-en-Laye*, vol. i, 2nd ed., Paris, 1926 ; vol. ii, 1924 . . CCCLXXIII
—— *Cultes, mythes et religions*, 4 vols., Paris, 1905–12 [*Cults, Myths, and Religions*, London, 1912] . CCCLXXIV
—— *Les Gaulois dans l'art antique et le sarcophage de la vigne Ammendola*, Paris, 1889 . . . CCCLXXV
—— *Répertoire de peintures grecques et romaines*, Paris, 1922 CCCLXXVI
—— *Répertoire de la statuaire grecque et romaine*, 7 vols., Paris, 1897, etc. CCCLXXVII
RIPLEY (William Z.), *The Races of Europe*, London, 1900 CCCLXXVIII
ROGET DE BELLOGUET (D. F. L.), *Baron, Ethnogénie gauloise*, 2nd ed., 4 pts., Paris, 1872 . . . CCCLXXIX
ROSCHER (W. H.), *Ausführliches Lexikon der griechischen und römischen Mythologie*, Leipzig, 1884, etc. . CCCLXXX

BIBLIOGRAPHY

315

SCHRADER, *Die Indogermanen*, 1911 . . . . **CCCLXXXI**
—— *Reallexikon der indogermanischen Altertumskunde*,
2nd ed., Berlin, 1917–28 . . . . . **CCCLXXXII**
SCHUCHARDT (C.), *Alt-Europa*, Strasburg and Berlin,
1919 . . . . **CCCLXXXIII**
SMITH (Reginald A.), *Guide to Early Iron Age
Antiquities* (British Museum), 2nd ed., London, 1925 **CCCLXXXIV**
SMITH (William Robertson), *Kinship and Marriage in
Early Arabia*, Cambridge, 1885 [New ed., London,
1903] . . . . **CCCLXXXV**
—— *Lectures on the Religion of the Semites*, Edinburgh,
1889 [3rd ed., London, 1927] . . . . **CCCLXXXVa**
TAYLOR (Isaac), [*The Origin of the Aryans*, London,
1890] *L'Origine des Aryens*, Paris, 1895 . . **CCCLXXXVI**
THIERRY (Amédée), *Histoire des Gaulois*, 10th ed.,
Paris, 1877 . . . . **CCCLXXXVII**
TOUTAIN (J.), *Les Cultes païens dans l'Empire romain*,
3 vols., Paris, 1907–20 . . . . **CCCLXXXVIII**
VERWORN (M.), *Keltische Kunst*, Berlin, 1919 . . **CCCLXXXIX**
VINOGRADOFF (Sir Paul), *Historical Jurisprudence*,
Oxford, 1020 . . . . **CCCXC**

VIII. GERMANY

BEHRENS (G.), *Bronzezeit Süddeutschlands* (*Katalog d.
röm.-germ. Central-Museums*, 6), Mainz, 1916 . **CCCXCI**
GÖTZE, HÖFER, and ZSCHIESCHE, *Die vor- und früh-
geschichtliche Altertümer Thuringens*, Würzburg,
1909 . . . . **CCCXCII**
GROSS (V.), *La Tène. Un oppidum helvète*, Paris, 1886 **CCCXCIII**
GRUPP (G.), *Kultur der alten Kelten und Germanen*,
Munich, 1905 . . . . **CCCXCIV**
KOSSINNA (G.), *Die deutsche Vorgeschichte* (Mannus-
Bibliothek, 9), 2nd ed., Berlin, 1925 . . . **CCCXCV**
—— *Ursprung und Verbreitung der Germanen in vor-
und frühgeschichtlicher Zeit* (Mannus-Bibliothek, 6),
Leipzig, 1926 . . . . **CCCXCVI**
KRAUSE (W.), *Die keltische Urbevölkerung Deutschlands*,
Leipzig, 1906 . . . . **CCCXCVII**
KROPP (P.), *La-Tènezeitliche Funde an der keltisch-
germanischen Völkergrenze zwischen Saale und
Weisser Elster* (Mannus-Bibliothek, 5), Würzburg,
1911 . . . . **CCCXCVIII**
LINDENSCHMIT (L.), *Die Altertümer unserer heidnischen
Vorzeit*, Mainz, 1858–1911 . . . . . **CCCXCIX**
MONTELIUS (O.), *Chronologie der ältesten Bronzezeit in
Nord-Deutschland und Skandinavien*, Brunswick,
1900 . . . . **CCCC**
Nationalmuseet : Bogspændefund fra de Seneste, Copen-
hagen, 1925 . . . . **CCCCI**
NAUE (J.), *Die Bronzezeit in Oberbayern*, Munich, 1894 **CCCCII**
—— *Die Hügelgräber zwischen Ammer- und Staffelsee*,
Stuttgart, 1887 . . . . . . **CCCCIII**
NORDEN (E.), *Die germanische Urgeschichte in Tacitus
Germania*, Berlin, 1922 . . . . **CCCCIV**

NORDEN (A.), *Kivike graven och andra fornminnen i Kivikstrakten*, Stockholm, 1926   CCCCV

REINECKE (P.), *Zur Kenntniss der La Tène Denkmäler der Zone nordwärts der Alpen*, in *Festschrift des röm.-germ. Central-museums zu Mainz*, Mainz, 1902   CCCCVI

SCHAEFFER (F. A.), *Les Tertres funéraires préhistoriques dans la forêt de Haguenau*, 2 vols., Hagenau, 1926–30   CCCCVII

SCHUMACHER (N.), *Materialen zur Besiedelungs-Geschichte Deutschlands (Katalog des röm.-germ. Centralmuseums*, 5), Mainz, 1918 . . .   CCCCVIII

—— *Siedelungs- und Kulturgeschichte der Rheinlande.* i. *Die vorrömische Zeit*, Mainz, 1922 . . .   CCCCIX

—— *Verzeichniss der Abgüsse und wichtigere Photographien mit Gallier Darstellungen*, Mainz, 1911 .   CCCCX

WAGNER (E.), *Hügelgräber und Urnenfriedhöfe in Baden*, Carlsruhe, 1895   CCCCXI

IX. BRITISH ISLES

ABERCROMBY (Hon. John), *A Study of the Bronze Age Pottery of Great Britain and Ireland and its Associated Grave-Goods*, Oxford, 1912 . . .   CCCCXII

ANDERSON (Alan Orr), *Early Sources of Scottish History*, A.D. 500 to 1286, 2 vols., Edinburgh, 1922 . .   CCCCXIII

ANDERSON (Joseph), *Scotland in Pagan Times*, 2 vols., Edinburgh, 1886   CCCCXIV

ARMSTRONG (L. A.), *Archæological Notes from Ireland*, 1909–1910   CCCCXV

BRUTON, *The Caratacus Stone on Exmoor* . . .   CCCCXVI

BULLEID (Arthur) and GRAY (H. St. G.), *The Glastonbury Lake Village*, 2 vols., Taunton, 1911–17 .   CCCCXVII

COFFEY (George), *The Bronze Age in Ireland*, Dublin, 1913   CCCCXVIII

COLLINGE, *Roman York*, Oxford, 1927 . . .   CCCCXIX

COLLINGWOOD (R.), *Roman Britain*, London, 1923 .   CCCCXX

CONRADY (Alexander), *Geschichte der Clanverfassung in dem schottischen Hochlande*, Leipzig, 1898 . .   CCCCXXI

O'CURRY (Eugene), *On the Manners and Customs of the Ancient Irish*, 3 vols., London, 1873 . . .   CCCCXXII

CZARNOWSKI (S.), *Saint Patrick et le culte des héros en Irlande*, Paris, 1919   CCCCXXIII

EVANS (John), *Ancient Stone Implements*, London, 1897   CCCCXXIV

—— *Ancient Bronze Implements*, London, 1898 . .   CCCCXXV

FARAL (Edmond), *La Légende arthurienne*, 3 vols., Paris, 1929   CCCCXXVI

FURNEAUX and ANDERSON, ed., TACITUS, *Agricola*, Oxford, 1923   CCCCXXVII

GOUGAUD (L.), *Les Chrétientés celtiques*, Paris, 1911 [*Christianity in Celtic Lands*, London, 1932] .   CCCCXXVIII

GREENWELL (William) *British Barrows*, Oxford, 1877 .   CCCCXXIX

GUEST (Edwin), *Origines Celticæ*, London, 1883 .   CCCCXXX

HAVERFIELD (Francis J.), *The Roman Occupation of Britain*, revised by Sir George MACDONALD, Oxford, 1924   CCCCXXXI

HENDERSON (George), *Survivals in Belief among the Celts*, Glasgow, 1911 CCCCXXXII

HOLMES (T. Rice), *Ancient Britain and the Invasions of Julius Cæsar*, Oxford, 1907 CCCCXXXIII

JOYCE (P. W.), *A Social History of Ancient Ireland*, 2 vols., London, 1903 CCCCXXXIV

KEATING (Geoffrey), *The History of Ireland*, New York, 1866 [London, 1902–14] CCCCXXXV

KEITH (Sir Arthur), *The Antiquity of Man*, London, 1915 [new ed., 1925] CCCCXXXVI

LETHABY, *Roman London*, London, 1924 . . . CCCCXXXVII

LLOYD (John E.), *A History of Wales*, London, 1911 . CCCCXXXVIII

MACALISTER (Robert A. S.), *Ireland in Pre-Celtic Times*, Dublin and London, 1921 . . . CCCCXXXIX

MACDONALD (Sir George), " The Agricolan Occupation of North Britain " in **LXXIX**, ix (1919) . . CCCCXL

MacNEILL (Eoin), *Phases of Irish History*, Dublin, 1919 CCCCXLI

MILLER (S. N.), *The Roman Fort at Balmuildy on the Antonine Wall*, Glasgow, 1922 CCCCXLII

WHITE (Newport J. D.), *St. Patrick, his Writings and Life*, London, 1920 CCCCXLIII

MONTGOMERY (William E.), *The History of Land Tenure In Ireland*, Cambridge, 1889 . . . CCCCXLIV

O'DONOVAN, *The Tribes and Customs of Hy Many*, Dublin, 1843 CCCCXLV

PARKYN (E. A.), *An Introduction to the Study of Prehistoric Art*, London, 1915 CCCCXLVI

PEAKE (Harold), *The Bronze Age and the Celtic World*, London, 1922 CCCCXLVII

POKORNY (J.), *The Origin of Druidism (Ann. Report of Smithsonian Institute*, 1911) . . . CCCCXLVIII

RHYS (Sir John), *Lectures on Welsh Philology*, 2nd ed., London, 1879 CCCCXLIX

—— *Celtic Folk-Lore*, 2 vols., Oxford, 1901 . . CCCCL

—— *Early Britain, Celtic Britain*, 3rd ed., London, 1904 CCCCLI

—— and JONES (David Brynnor), *The Welsh People*, 4th ed., London, 1906 CCCCLII

LEROUX (H.), *L'Armée romaine de Bretagne*, Paris, 1911 CCCCLIII

SAGOT (François), *La Bretagne romaine*, Paris, 1911 . CCCCLIV

SKENE (William F.), *Celtic Scotland*, 3 vols., Edinburgh, 1876–80 CCCCLV

—— *Chronicles of the Picts, Chronicles of the Scots, etc.*, Edinburgh, 1867 CCCCLVI

—— *The Highlanders of Scotland*, 2 vols., Edinburgh, 1836 [new ed., 1902] CCCCLVII

SPENSER (Edmund), *View of the State of Ireland*, Dublin, 1713 CCCCLVIII

SQUIRE (Charles), *The Mythology of the British Islands*, London, 1905 [new ed., 1910] . . . CCCCLIX

TAYLOR (M. V.), *The Roman Villa at North Leigh*, Oxford, 1923 CCCCLX

THOMPSON (A. Hamilton), *Military Architecture in England during the Middle Ages*, Oxford, 1913 . CCCCLXI

X.   GAUL

BEAUPRÉ (J.), *Les Études préhistoriques en Lorraine de* 1889 *à* 1902, Nancy, 1902   .   .   .   .   **CCCCLXII**

BÉNARD LEPONTOIS, *Le Finistère préhistorique*, Paris, 1929   .   .   .   .   **CCCCLXIII**

BLANCHET (A.), *Les Enceintes romaines de la Gaule*, Paris, 1907   .   .   .   .   .   .   **CCCCLXIV**

—— *Les Souterrains-refuges de la France*, Paris, 1927   **CCCCLXV**

BLEICHER (G.) and BEAUPRÉ (J.), *Guide pour les recherches archéologiques . . . dans l'Est de la France*, Nancy, 1896   .   .   .   .   **CCCCLXVI**

BLOCH (G.), *La Gaule romaine* (E. LAVISSE, *Histoire de France*, vol. i, 2), Paris, 1901   .   .   .   **CCCCLXVII**

BONSTETTEN (G. de), Baron, *Notice sur des armes et chariots de guerre découverts à Tiefenau, près de Berne, en* 1851, Lausanne, 1852   .   .   **CCCCLXVIII**

BULLIOT (J. G.), *Mémoire sur l'émaillerie gauloise à l'oppidum du Mont-Beuvray*, Paris, 1872   .   .   **CCCCLXIX**

CHATELLIER (P. du), *Les Époques préhistorique et gauloise dans le Finistère*, Rennes and Quimper, 2nd ed., 1907   .   .   .   .   **CCCCLXX**

—— *La Poterie aux époques préhistorique et gauloise en Armorique*, Paris, 1897   .   .   .   .   **CCCCLXXI**

DÉCHELETTE (J.), *Les Fouilles du Mont-Beuvray de* 1897 *a* 1901, Paris, 1904   .   .   .   .   **CCCCLXXII**

—— *Les Vases céramiques ornés de la Gaule romaine*, 2 vols., Paris, 1904   .   .   .   .   **CCCCLXXIII**

DESJARDINS (E.), *Géographie historique et administrative de la Gaule romaine*, 4 vols., Paris, 1876–93 .   .   **CCCCLXXIV**

FUSTEL DE COULANGES (Numa D.), *La Gaule romaine*, Paris, 1891   .   .   .   .   .   .   **CCCCLXXV**

GERIN-RICARD (H. de), *Le Sanctuaire pré-romain de Roquepertune*, Marseilles, 1928   .   .   .   **CCCCLXXVI**

GOURY (G.), *Les Étapes de l'Humanité*, 2 vols., Nancy, 1911   .   .   .   .   **CCCCLXXVII**

GRENIER (A.), *Les Gaulois*, Paris, 1924   .   .   **CCCCLXXVIII**

ISCHER (T.), *Die Pfahlbauten des Bielersees*, Biel, 1928   **CCCCLXXIX**

LOTH (J.), *L'Émigration bretonne en Armorique du V*ᵉ *au VII*ᵉ *siècle*, Paris, 1883   .   .   .   .   **CCCCLXXX**

LOT (F.), *Mélanges d'histoire bretonne*, Paris, 1907   .   **CCCCLXXXI**

MARTEAUX and LEROUX, *Les Fins d'Annecy*, Annecy, 1913   .   .   .   .   **CCCCLXXXII**

MOREAU (F.), *Collection Caranda aux époques préhistorique, gauloise, romaine, et franque*, St. Quentin, 1877, 1881, 1887   .   .   .   .   .   **CCCCLXXXIII**

MOREL (L.), *La Champagne souterraine*, Rheims, 1898   **CCCCLXXXIV**

NICAISE (A.), *L'Époque gauloise dans le Département de la Marne*, Paris, 1866   .   .   .   .   **CCCCLXXXV**

PEYNAU (B.), *Découvertes archéologiques dans le Pays de Buch*, Bordeaux, 1926   .   .   .   .   **CCCCLXXXVI**

PHILIPPE (Abbé), *Cinq ans de fouilles au Fort-Harrouard*, Rouen, 1927   .   .   .   .   .   .   **CCCCLXXXVII**

POTHIER (General), *Les Tombes du Plateau de Ger*, Paris, 1900   .   .   .   .   **CCCCLXXXVIII**

VESLY (L. de), *Les Fana*, Rouen, 1910 . . . **CCCCLXXXIX**
VIOLLIER (D.), *Essai sur les fibules de l'âge du fer trouvées en Suisse. Essai de typologie et de chronologie*, Zurich, 1907 . . . . . **CCCCXC**
—— *Le Cimetière gallo-helvète d'Andelfingen*, Zurich, 1912 . . . . **CCCCXCI**
—— *Essai sur les rites funéraires en Suisse des origines à la conquête romaine* (*Bibl. de l'Éc. des H.-Études, sciences relig.*, vol. xxiv, 1), Paris, 1911 . . **CCCCXCII**
—— *Les Civilisations primitives de la Suisse. Sépultures du IIe âge du fer sur le plateau suisse*, Geneva, 1916 . . . . **CCCCXCIII**
VOUGA (P.), *La Tène*, Leipzig, 1923 . . . **CCCCXCIV**

XI. SPAIN AND PORTUGAL

ÅBERG (N.), *La Civilisation énéolithique dans la péninsule ibérique*, Upsala, 1921 . . . . . **CCCCXCV**
BONSOR (G.), *Les Colonies agricoles préromaines dans la vallée du Bétis*, Paris, 1899 . . . . **CCCCXCVI**
—— and THOUVENOT, *Nécropole ibérique de Setefilla*, Paris and Bordeaux, 1929 . . . **CCCCXCVII**
BOSCH-GIMPERA (P.), *La Arqueologia pre-romana hispanica*, Barcelona, 1920 . . . **CCCCXCVIII**
—— *Los Celtas y la civilización celtica en la peninsula iberica*, Madrid, 1923 . . . . . **CCCCXCIX**
—— *Els Celtes y la cultura de la primera edat del ferro a Catalunya*, Barcelona, 1924 . . . . **D**
—— *La Ceramica iberica*, Madrid, 1915 . . . **DI**
—— *Ensayo de una reconstruccion de la etnologia prehistorica de la peninsula iberica*, Santander, 1923 **DII**
—— *El problema etnologico vasco y la arqueologia*, St. Sebastian, 1923 . . . . . . **DIII**
—— *La Prehistoria de los Iberos y la etnologia vasca*, Santander, 1926 . . . . . **DIV**
—— *Prehistoria catalana*, Barcelona, 1919 . . **DV**
BOUDARD (P. A.), *Essai sur la numismatique ibérienne*, Paris, 1859 . . . . . . **DVI**
CARTAILHAC (E.), *Les Âges préhistoriques de l'Espagne et du Portugal*, Paris, 1886 . . . . **DVII**
CERRALBO (Marquis de), *El Alto Jalon*, Madrid, 1909 . **DVIII**
DÉCHELETTE (J.), *Essai sur la chronologie préhistorique de la péninsule ibérique*, Paris, 1909 . . **DIX**
Fontes Hispaniæ antiquæ. Avieni Ora Maritima, ed. A. SCHULTEN and P. BOSCH, Barcelona and Berlin, 1922 . . . . **DX**
LANTIER (R.), *El Santuario iberico de Castellar de Santisteban*, Madrid, 1917 . . . . **DXI**
LEITE DE VASCONCELLOS (J.), *Religiões da Lusitania*, 4 vols., Lisbon, 1904, etc. . . . **DXII**
MENDEZ-CORREA (A. A.), *Os Povos primitivos da Lusitania*, Oporto, 1924 . . . . **DXIII**
PARIS (P.), *Essai sur l'art et l'industrie de l'Espagne primitive*, 2 vols., Paris, 1902–04 . . . **DXIV**

PERICOT (L.), *La Prehistoria de la peninsula iberica*,
Barcelona, 1923 . . . . . .   DXV
PHILIPON (E.), *Les Ibères*, Paris, 1909 . . .   DXVI
SCHULTEN (A.), *Hispania*, Barcelona, 1920 . .   DXVII
—— *Numantia : eine topographisch-historische Unter-
suchung (Abhandl. d. Göttinger Ges. d. Wiss.*, 1905)   DXVIII
—— *Numantia.* i. *Die Keltiberer und ihre Kriege mit
Rom*, Munich, 1914 . . . . .   DXIX
—— *Tartessos*, Hamburg, 1922 . . . .   DXX
SIRET (H.) and (L.), *Les Premiers Âges du Métal dans le
sud-est de l'Espagne*, Antwerp, 1887 . . .   DXXI
SIRET (L.), *Questions de chronologie et d'ethnographie
ibérique*, Paris, 1913 . . . . .   DXXII
—— *Villaricos y Herrerias*, Madrid, 1908 . .   DXXIII
VEGA (Estacio da), *Antiguedades monumentaes do
Algarve*, 4 vols., Lisbon, 1886–91 . . .   DXXIV

XII. ITALY

BRIZIO (E.), *Il Sepolcreto gallico di Montefortino*, Rome,
1901 . . . .   DXXV
CASTELFRANCO (P.), *Cimeli del museo Ponti nell' Isola
Virginia (Lago di Varese)*, Milan, 1913 . .   DXXVI
DUHN (F. von), *Italische Gräberkunde*, Heidelberg, 1924   DXXVII
DUCATI (P.), *Storia di Bologna.* i. *I Tempi antichi*,
Bologna, 1928 . . . .   DXXVIII
GRENIER (A.), *Bologne villanovienne et étrusque*, Paris,
1912 . . . .   DXXIX
ISSEL (A.), *Liguria preistorica*, Genoa, 1908 . .   DXXX
MAGNI (A.), *Le Necropoli ligure-gallice di Pianezzo nel
canton Ticino*, Milan, 1907 . . . .   DXXXI
MARCHESETTI (C.), *La Necropoli di S. Lucia presso
Tolmino*, Trieste, 1886 . . . . .   DXXXII
MILANI, *Studi e materiali di archeologia e numismatica*.   DXXXIII
MONTELIUS (O.), *La Civilisation primitive en Italie
depuis l'introduction des métaux.* i. *Italie sep-
tentrionale*, Stockholm, 1904 . . . .   DXXXIV
—— —— ii. *Italie centrale*, 1910 . . . .   DXXXV
MODESTOW (B.), *Introduction à l'histoire romaine*, Paris,
1907 . . . .   DXXXVI
NISSEN (H.), *Italische Landeskunde*, Berlin, 1902 .   DXXXVII
PAULY (C.), *Altitalische Forschungen*, 3 vols., Leipzig,
1885–91 . . . .   DXXXVIII
PEET (T. E.), *The Stone and Bronze Ages in Italy and
Sicily*, Oxford, 1909 . . . . .   DXXXIX
SERGI (G.), *Arii e Italici*, Turin, 1898 . . .   DXL
ULRICH, *Graberfeld Bellinzona* . . . .   DXLI

XIII. DANUBIAN CELTS

BERTRAND (A.) and REINACH (S.), *Les Celtes dans
les vallées du Pô et du Danube*, Paris, 1894 . .   DXLII
FORRER (R.), *Keltische Numismatik der Rhein- und
Donaulande*, Strasburg, 1908 . . . .   DXLIII

JOUGUET (P.), *L'Impérialisme macédonien et l'hellénisation de l'Orient*, Paris, 1926, [*Macédonian Imperialism*, in this series, London and New York, 1928] . . . .   DXLIV
MEHLIS, *Raetia* . . . .   DXLV
ODOBESCO (A.), *Le Trésor de Petrossa*, Paris, 1889 .   DXLVI
PARVAN (Vasile), *Dacia*, Cambridge, 1928 . . .   DXLVII
—— *Getica*, Bukarest, 1926 . . . . .   DXLVIII
PIČ, *Le Hradischt de Stradonitz en Bohême*, Leipzig, 1906 . . . .   DXLIX
RADIMSKY (W.), *Nekropola na Jezerinama u Pritoci cid Bisca*, repr. from *Glasnik Zemaljskog museja u Bosni i Hercegovini*, Sarajevo, v, 1893 . .   DL
REINACH (T.), *Mithridate Eupator, roi de Pont*, Paris, 1890 . . . .   DLI
RICHLY (H.), *Bronzezeit in Böhmen*, Vienna, 1891 .   DLII
RIDGEWAY (Sir William), *Early Age of Greece*, Cambridge, 1901 . . . . . .   DLIII
STAEHELIN (P.), *Geschichte der kleinasiatischen Galater*, Leipzig, 1907 . . . .   DLIV
STOCKY (A.), *La Bohême à l'âge de la pierre*, Prague, 1924   DLV

INDEX

NOTE.—References are given to figures and notes, but only where there is no reference for the subject to the text of the same page.